THE WYATTS
AN ARCHITECTURAL DYNASTY

Frontispiece Belvoir Castle, Leicestershire, ceiling of the Elizabeth Saloon, by Matthew Cotes
Wyatt, 1824–5,

THE WYATTS

AN ARCHITECTURAL DYNASTY

by John Martin Robinson

with a Foreword by Woodrow Wyatt

OXFORD UNIVERSITY PRESS
1979

Oxford University Press, Walton Street, Oxford OX2 6DP

OXFORD LONDON GLASGOW NEW YORK
TORONTO MELBOURNE WELLINGTON CAPE TOWN
IBADAN NAIROBI DAR ES SALAAM LUSAKA
KUALA LUMPUR SINGAPORE JAKARTA HONG KONG TOKYO
DELHI BOMBAY CALCUTTA MADRAS KARACHI

Published in the United States by
Oxford University Press, New York

British Library Cataloguing in Publication Data
Robinson, John Martin
The Wyatts, an architectural dynasty.
1. Wyatt family   2. Architects—England
I. Title
720'.92'2 NA997.W/   79-40412
ISBN 0-19-817340-7

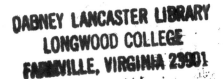
Typesetting and binding by The Pitman Press, Bath
Printed in Great Britain by The Garden House Press Ltd, London

FOREWORD

by Woodrow Wyatt

When I was a child there was much talk in the family about our being descended from Sir Thomas Wyatt, the poet, and his son Sir Thomas Wyatt the Younger who led an unsuccessful rebellion against Queen Mary. So convincing was the propaganda, particularly from a dearly loved old aunt, that for many years I believed it. Was not our Coat of Arms, properly registered and granted to John and James Wyatt in April 1780 by the College of Arms, the same? True, there was the little matter of our having a different motto but that was easily glossed over. Pictures of both the Thomas Wyatts hung in the hall and with such a distinguished poet for an ancestor I was prompted to think how agreeable it would be to have a literary career.

There was occasional mention of James Wyatt and some of Thomas Henry Wyatt, but the other architects, and the inventors, manufacturers, sculptors, artists in the family, were never spoken of. In esteem they were far below a courtier of Henry VIII once in difficulties because he was attracted by Anne Boleyn before she met the King.

As I grew more interested in the architects I looked closer at our connection with Sir Thomas. There is none, or if there is it can only be a distant cousinage originating long before Sir Thomas and any record of it is lost. Even the most desperate genealogical attempt to establish a descent from either Sir Thomas relies on someone having been married, with progeny, at the age of four or thereabouts.

When Sir Thomas Wyatt, the poet, was born in Kent in about 1503 the Wyatts who are my family must already have been long established, perhaps for centuries, many miles away in the little village of Weeford in Staffordshire. Solid freehold farmers, nearly gentry but not quite, theirs were prominent names on the first page of the Parish Register when it began in 1562. My direct ancestor, Humphrey Wyatt, born in 1540, and his parents were certainly long settled there.

It was Victorian affectation and snobbery which prompted the worship of non-existent ancestors at the expense of our taking a proper pride in our real ones. These were too much connected with trade as timber merchants, builders, craftsmen, cement manufacturers, inventors to please the Victorian ego. It was an attitude increasingly common in the nineteenth century and one which accelerated the decline of Britain by attaching social inferiority to commerce and to those who created wealth in the tough world of factories and hard bargaining. Yet the family to which we truly belonged was one of the most remarkable ever to flourish in England.

For nearly 150 years, after Benjamin Wyatt and his sons expanded from farming and timber into building in the 1750s, in England they dominated architecture, the highest form of art. Twenty-eight Wyatts were architects, all of skill and mostly of distinction. From Swinfen Hall in 1755 to Knightsbridge Barracks in 1877, recently and foolishly demolished, they built everywhere for kings, governments, institutions, and the very rich. Few important constructions were contemplated without asking for a design or advice from a Wyatt.

Frequently cousins married each other. I have counted twenty-one marriages between cousins and there may be more. The family was cohesive and its members helped each other. John Wyatt, born in 1735, an eminent surgeon and a Fellow of the Royal Society, helped his younger brother James with valuable introductions when he came to London. Samuel Wyatt, born in 1737, when he built Shugborough, got the slate to face it with from the quarry established by his younger brother Benjamin who was land-agent at Penrhyn.

Twelve Wyatts who were not architects were land-agents. My grandfather, great-grandfather, and great-great-grandfather were land-agents to the Ansons (Lichfields) whose descendant, Lord Lichfield, was responsible for the photographs in this book. A great-great-great-great-grandfather of mine (through cousins intermarrying) was land-agent to the Uxbridges (Angleseys). It is likely that through this connection James Wyatt came to build Plas Newydd for Lord Anglesey.

Whenever they could they put work in each other's way. The architects used Wyatt's cement and a special thin copper roofing developed by Charles Wyatt, son of John Wyatt, the inventor. Edward Wyatt, the carver, whose work is frequently mistaken for that of Grinling Gibbons, was given much to do by his architect cousins. Matthew Cotes Wyatt, the sculptor and painter, was employed by his father James and other Wyatt architects at Windsor Castle, Belvoir Castle, and elsewhere. The ten sculptors, painters, and carvers in the family, when not helped directly by the architects, were helped by their fame.

The Wyatts were amazingly prolific. Sometimes their brilliance was almost casual. Charles Wyatt, born in 1758, happened to be a captain in the Engineers in India when Lord Wellesley, the Governor-General, decided that the British capital, Calcutta, needed a palatial Government House. Charles ran it up for him and it remains the finest eighteenth-century building in India. Charles then lost interest in architecture and returned to England to do nothing save amuse himself as a Member of Parliament. Benjamin Wyatt of Penrhyn, though not a professional architect, whenever he needed a harbour, or an inn, or a farm building just designed and built it himself.

The Wyatts were thoroughly enmeshed in industry and willing to try anything which might make a profit. William Wyatt, born in 1734, developed his uncle Job's (born 1719) device for making the first machine-produced screws in the world. John Wyatt, born 1701, invented mechanical spinning twenty-five years before Arkwright. He also invented the level weighing-machine which, with modifications, is still used by British Rail. He invented ball-bearings, a machine for making buttons, and anything else which caught his interest. He would have died rich had he not been an appallingly bad business man.

Wyatts were concerned with building canals in the Midlands and across England. They were close to Matthew Boulton who manufactured anything from decorative objects and coinage Mints to steam-engines (with James Watt). John Wyatt III travelled for him in 1799 to St. Petersburg to deal with the problems of Catherine the Great's Mint.

Wyatt activities criss-crossed England simultaneously with the rising momentum of the Industrial Revolution. They were very much a part of it, assisting and profiting from it. It was appropriate that the 1851 Great Exhibition, the high point of the Industrial Revolution, should have had as its Secretary Sir Matthew Digby Wyatt (1820–77). As well as organizing the Exhibition he constructed the Crystal Palace from Paxton's designs – a task Paxton was not capable of.

My favourite is James Wyatt (1746–1813). He drank excessively. His financial affairs were in fearful disorder. He maddened his customers by long and inexcusable delays and then charmed them back to good humour when at last he arrived to attend to their work. He never gave up chasing pretty women and when he was killed in a road accident it was characteristic that a servant girl in his household should be pregnant by him.

Throughout his life he was talked and written about from the moment when, at the age of twenty-three, he started to build the marvellous Pantheon, later sadly destroyed by fire. Though disorganized he was not lazy. He travelled endlessly and his output was prodigious in the many styles of which he was a complete and original master. He had a singularly active and creative mind and in the middle of one project would be tempted to work on a new one if it excited him. It was his bad luck that most of his major buildings in London have been destroyed, but one cannot travel far in the countryside or to the towns in England without going near one.

The ease and speed with which James secured and executed great commissions, the passion with which he was pursued by the leading figures of the day (including Catherine the Great who wanted him to be her architect) led to understandable envy among his rivals. His unconventional habits distressed the Victorians and he suffered from many small-minded detractors after and during his life. Until recently even the Dean and Chapter of Salisbury Cathedral, which James made into one of the four or five most beautiful cathedrals in Europe, designated him as 'Wyatt the Destroyer', though without his magnificent reconstruction less than half the tourists now pouring into Salisbury Cathedral would bother to visit it. His skill as an architect has frequently been denigrated because his success came from his being the most fashionable architect of the period. But to be the most fashionable architect when the English taste in architecture and kindred matters was at a superb peak never surpassed before or since would seem more praise than criticism. His artistic judgement was amazingly comprehensive and sure. Not even the use of his influence to hold up the election of Turner as a full member of the Royal Academy marred it. It was not Turner's pictures he objected to but his scruffy appearance and dress. Turner could not have resented this much as he continued to paint pictures of James Wyatt's buildings – a practice he had begun in 1792 when he was seventeen with 'The Pantheon the Morning after the Fire'.

Perhaps Samuel Wyatt (1737–1807) and Lewis Wyatt (1777–1853) were the two other architects who came nearest to James Wyatt in skill. That is discussed by Dr. Robinson later in this book.

Jeffry Wyatt (Sir Jeffry Wyatville) seems to me to have had more compe-tence than genius, though I always experience a little thrill of pleasure as I see the silhouette of Windsor Castle against the sky from the M4 motorway. Maybe that comes more from knowing that all that is visible from the motorway is his work rather than from appreciation of architecture – just as my enjoyment is heightened, or my boredom diminished, at a function at Lancaster House by knowing that Benjamin Dean Wyatt designed the interior and exterior.

Jeffry Wyatt, too, had his detractors always ready with an inaccurate sneer. One which has stuck to him is that, suffering from *folie de grandeur*, he asked George IV's permission to change his name to Wyatville. In fact it was the King who asked him to change it because he wanted it to be understood that the Wyatt who reconstructed Windsor was different from the other Wyatt architects.

But whichever Wyatt is preferred as the best of the architects it is astonishing how many of them were so extraordinarily gifted and that their talents were not confined to architecture but extended to painting, sculpture, and carving. It is impossible to study my family and retain a belief that environment is more important than heredity. Several Wyatts, even when they had not intended to become architects, could, by calling on their inherited family gifts, rapidly turn themselves, whether for a long or a short time, into architects of the highest class.

That our family has, unfortunately, lost its talent for architecture and the visual arts is further proof that heredity is more important than environment. The environment has been there all right but the genes failed to reproduce the talent. The last architect who built anything really worth looking at was my cousin Matthew (the son of Thomas Henry) who died in 1892. He was more than usually eccentric for a Wyatt, apart from dying of drink. In his will he left instructions designed to prevent beneficiaries from engaging in horse-racing, though they were encouraged to hunt, and to restrict the number and length of visits his detested brother-in-law might make to his house.

In this century there has been little from my family to excite the eye or the mind. My uncle Horace wrote a best seller in the First World War, *Malice in Kulturland*. My cousin R.E.S.Wyatt, who captained England and played in many test matches, scored more runs in first-class cricket as an amateur than any other cricketer save W.G.Grace. His achievements have but a tenuous connection with the visual arts.

So the inherited genius has died or is dormant. It marched with the rise of Britain as the world's leading industrial and political power. It sank with Britain's decline. Perhaps in future generations there may be, through some well-balanced marriage, a throwback to the past. It is a pity we do not take as much care as race-horse breeders in choosing partners from whom issue is intended.

I asked Dr. John Martin Robinson to undertake this work on my family not merely out of family pride but because I thought there was some social and historical importance in seeing them as a whole. Books and commentaries have been written about several of them separately. They have never before been fitted into the background of England as a precise group who knew what they were about and who had a beginning, a middle, and, alas, an end.

Dr. Robinson is a young historian with a splendid eye for architecture, an understanding of the world's behaviour past and present, and a remarkable knowledge of detail. As the chief guide at Shugborough pointed to a side table saying 'That is Chippendale' his quiet voice politely but firmly announced 'I'm afraid it's not, it's by Samuel Wyatt'. When the Duchess of Beaufort at Badminton ascribed carvings to Grinling Gibbons the voice was heard again. 'I'm afraid they're not. They're by Edward Wyatt.'

Owners of the numerous houses I have visited with him have learned much from Dr. Robinson not only of the Wyatts who worked on them but of other

artists, architects, and carvers whose names were forgotten or not appropriately credited. His work has been well supported by Lord Lichfield's sensitive
appreciation of the illustrations required.

CONTENTS

ACKNOWLEDGEMENTS

In many ways this book is a joint effort. Without the help of friends I would not have trespassed so recklessly into fields of art history about which I am not qualified to write. I am particularly grateful to three people: Mr. Woodrow Wyatt, for his generous backing and for writing the foreword, Mr. Howard Colvin, for his scholarly guidance, advice, and example, and Mr. Roger Ellis for carefully reading my text and making many helpful suggestions and improvements.

I should also like to thank Lord Lichfield, Sir Geoffrey Shakerley, and Mrs. Caroline Hickie for organizing the photographs, Mrs. Ruth MacFarlan and Miss Camilla Straghan for typing my manuscript, and a large number of people for help, encouragement, hospitality, useful information, or permission to quote from documents: including the archivists at various public record offices and libraries as well as many private individuals, especially Mr. Nigel Forbes-Adam; Nancy, Lady Bagot; Mrs. Isabel Barnes; the Marquess of Bath; the Duchess of Beaufort; Mr. Felix Bedford; Mr. P. A. Bezodis; Mr. Peter Bicknell; Mr. Lindsay Boynton; Sir Evelyn Delves Broughton; Mr. John Kenworthy-Browne; Mr. Geoffrey Budenburg; the Earl Cadogan; the Viscount Camrose; Mr. Timothy Clifford; Major S. F. B. Codrington; Mr. John Cornforth; Dr. J. M. Crook; Mrs. Janet Don; Mr. Timothy Eckersley; Sir John Every; Dr. Frances Fergusson; Mr. Constantine FitzGibbon; Mr. Brinsley Ford; the Lord Forester; Dr. Terry Friedman; Mrs. Ruth Gates; Mr. Douglas Hague; Mr. John Hardy; Mr. John Harris; Mr. Leslie Harris; the Lord Harris; the Earl of Harrowby; Dr. and Mrs. W. O. Hassall; Major Robert Hereford; Revd. W. R. Hesketh; Mr. Myles Thoroton Hildyard; Mr. Arnold Hyde; the late Col. Claude Lancaster; Dr. Derek Linstrum; Mr. James Miller; Dr. B. W. Paine; Mr. Robert Parsons; Mr. Herbert Pitchford; Mr. Homan Potterton; the Lord Raglan; Mr. Peter Reid; the Viscount Ridley; Mr. Neil Rimington; Hon. Mrs. Jane Roberts; the late Mr. W. Robbins; the Duke of Rutland; Mr. Andrew Saint; the late Viscount Scarsdale; Mr. Colin Sheaf; Professor A. W. Skempton; Mr. David and Lady Caroline Somerset; Mr. Gavin Stamp; Mr. Timothy Stevens; Mr. Gervase Jackson-Stops; Miss Dorothy Stroud; Sir John Summerson; Miss Eleanor Hamilton Thompson; Mrs. V. Tunnicliffe; Mrs. Rosemary Warburton; Sir Arnold Weinstock; the Duke of Wellington; and Sir Randle

Baker-Wilbraham.

It is probably necessary to say a few words about the treatment of the subject. I have tried to give some impression of the work of all the Wyatts because I think they are more important as a dynasty than as individuals. On the other hand, I have decided not to devote too much of the book to the famous Wyatts such as James and Sir Jeffry Wyatville. This was partly because it seemed more worth while to resurrect the lesser-known members of the family, particularly Samuel and Lewis, both of whom are much underrated. Besides this there is already an excellent biography of Jeffry Wyatville by Dr. Derek Linstrum and a detailed architectural monograph on James Wyatt is currently being prepared by Dr. Frances Fergusson. There was therefore no point in repeating at length what is contained there.

My treatment was also dictated to a certain extent by the survival of source material. For instance, while a great number of Matthew Cotes Wyatt's personal papers have survived, all of Lewis Wyatt's have been lost. This explains why I have given more personal details about Matthew Cotes Wyatt than about Lewis Wyatt.

There are four principal public collections of Wyatt papers: the Wyatt MSS. in the Victoria & Albert Museum Print Room, the Wyatt MSS. in the RIBA Drawings Collection, the Wyatt papers in the Egerton MSS. in the British Museum, and the Wyatt MSS. in the Birmingham Reference Library. There are also drawings, correspondence, and building accounts for individual buildings in the Public Record Office and in the County Record Offices, though a number still remain in the places with which they are connected.

The largest proportion of Wyatt papers survive in the hands of descendants. The most important groups are the Wyatville and Thomas Henry Wyatt papers in the possession of Mrs. Janet Don, the John Wyatt III papers belonging to Miss Hamilton Thompson, the family notes and genealogical material in the collection of Captain John Wyatt, the Edward Wyatt sketch-book and other papers belonging to Mrs. Vera Tunnicliffe, the Sir Matthew Digby Wyatt–Edward Lear correspondence owned by Dr. B. W. Paine, and Matthew Cotes Wyatt's diary in the possession of Mr. Geoffrey Budenberg. More details about these and other lesser sources can be found in the footnotes and in the catalogues at the end of the book. In the footnotes, unless otherwise stated, place of publication is London.

John Martin Robinson, December 1976

LIST OF ILLUSTRATIONS

Chapter III

Chapter IV

ABBREVIATIONS

AH	*Architectural History*
AJ	*Art Journal*
Anon.	Anonymous
APSD	Wyatt Papworth (ed.), *Architectural Publication Society Dictionary* (1852–92)
AR	*Architectural Review*
AU	*Art Union*
BL	British Library (manuscripts)
BM	British Museum (prints and drawings)
BN	*Building News*
BoE	Nikolaus Pevsner, *Buildings of England*
Br.	*The Builder*
BR	British Rail
BRL	Birmingham Reference Library
C.Life	*Country Life*
Coll.	In the collection of
Colvin	H.M.Colvin, *Biographical Dictionary of English Architects 1660–1840* (1954)
Dec.	Decorated
Eccl.	*The Ecclesiologist*
EE	Early English
Farington	Joseph Farington Diary (MS.), Royal Library, Windsor
Gent's Mag.	*The Gentleman's Magazine*
Gunnis	R. Gunnis, *Dictionary of British Sculptors 1600–1851* (1951)
ILN	*Illustrated London News*
King's Works	H.M.Colvin (ed.), *History of the King's Works*, vi (1973)

LS	*London Survey*
Metropolitan	Metropolitan Museum of Art, New York
n.d.	No date known
Neale	J.P.Neale, *Views of Seats*
NMR	*National Monuments Record*
NPG	National Portrait Gallery
Ormerod	George Ormerod, *History of Cheshire* (2nd Edn., 1882)
Perp.	Perpendicular
PRO	Public Record Office
RA	Royal Academy
RCHM	*Royal Commission on Historical Monuments*
RIBAD	Royal Institute of British Architects, Drawings
R.O.	Record Office
Roy.Arch.	Royal Archives, Windsor Castle. Quoted by Gracious Permission of Her Majesty the Queen
R.S.A.	Royal Society of Arts
S.L.	Salt Library, Stafford
T.H.	Trinity House
T.L.S.	*Times Literary Supplement*
V & A	Victoria and Albert Museum
VCH	*Victoria County History*

1. The Pantheon, London. Designed by James Wyatt and built by Samuel Wyatt, 1769–72.
Painting attributed to William Hodges and Johann Zoffany.

CHAPTER I

The Rise of the Wyatts

In January 1772 the new Pantheon in Oxford Street was completed to the designs of young Mr. James Wyatt and opened its doors to London society as 'a winter Ranelagh'. The description was Horace Walpole's; he was quite overcome by its splendour. He thought it 'the most beautiful edifice in England' and the resurrection of 'Balbec in all its glory'. Walpole was then working on a biography of the Tudor poet, Sir Thomas Wyatt. It occurred to him that the brilliant young architect of the Pantheon might be a descendant – such talent, he supposed, could not have sprung from nowhere.

On 26 July 1772 he wrote accordingly

I beg your pardon for asking you perhaps an impertinent question. It is whether you are descended from Sir Thomas Wyatt who lived in the reign of Henry 8th? I am employed in collecting material for his life and very solicitory to find out some of his family . . . You have so much Genius and Merit yourself, sir, that it can be of no consequence to you whether you are related to that family or not. No man with such talents as yours wants to be distinguished by the Lustre of others. My curiosity you see is founded solely on my own business and I trust you will excuse me making the application to you – nor was I sorry to take an opportunity of telling you how extremely I admire your taste.

This flattering communication arrived while James Wyatt was in Staffordshire attending his father's funeral at Weeford near Lichfield. On his return to London at the beginning of August he replied in a style that was not to be outdone by Walpole in courtesy:

The loss of the best of Fathers, an account of whose death I received on Tuesday last prevented my answering your very obliging and polite letter as soon as I wished.

I cannot but regret the want of materials to furnish me with the means of giving you that Intelligence you seek, for my pursuits having been of a different nature the knowledge I have of my family is derived from oral traditions only, and goes no further back than my Great Grandfather, who, as I have been told was a farmer in Staffordshire, where I myself was born, whether therefore we are descendants of Sir Thomas Wyatt or not is a subject I am not in the least acquainted with or be assured Sir the honour of having contributed the least matter for the industry of your pen could have been exceeded by nothing but your approbation of the works of

    Sir

        your most obedient humble servant

           James Wyatt.[1]

[1] B. L., Egerton MS. 3515.

By perusing the Weeford parish registers it is possible to trace back the Wyatt family history a further three generations beyond James Wyatt's great-grandfather to Humphrey Wyatt (1540–1610) and an elder brother, Robert Wyatt (d.1608). The fifth entry in the parish register records the baptism of Robert's son Thomas on 29 July 1562. Beyond that date there is no documentary evidence but there seems no reason to doubt that the Wyatts had been settled at Weeford for several centuries.

They were a family of yeoman farmers. It is probable that the sixteenth-century farmhouse at Thickbroom where James Wyatt's grandparents lived had been in the Wyatt's possession since it was built. It is called Thickbroom Hall in the 1562 parish register and the Wyatts as its owners occupied one of the two front pews in the parish church, which suggests that originally the house was more distinguished than it appears today.

Weeford is situated in a valley south of Watling Street in good farming country. William Pitt in his *Topographical History of Staffordshire* tells us that there is 'a beautiful tract of narrow but rich meadows on the banks of the brook in the vicinity of this village [Weeford] bounded by low and fertile eminences'. This was the pleasant but unspectacular background to the rise of the Wyatts and not the feudal battlements of Allington Castle in Kent as some Victorian members of the family would have liked to believe.

The myth that the Wyatts of Weeford were descended from Sir Thomas Wyatt of Allington Castle gained ground only in the mid-nineteenth century. Thomas Henry Wyatt, in particular, used to boast that both Sir Thomas Wyatts were his ancestors and hung portraits of Tudor Wyatts in his dining-room. Recently, however, when the portrait of Sir Thomas Wyatt which belonged to him was taken for inspection to the National Portrait Gallery it was declared to be a nineteenth-century fake. This neatly sums up the legend. The claim of descent from Sir Thomas Wyatt tells us more about nineteenth-century romanticism and snobbery than about the earlier history of the family.

The rise of the Wyatts is a fascinating story. It is also typical of the emergence of many English families who after centuries of obscurity suddenly emerged into prominence in the eighteenth and nineteenth centuries as a result of the development of England's industry and trade and the expansion of her empire.

It is a story that illustrates the classic three-stage progression which is such a feature of the English social system. From being originally farmers in a remote part of the country, in the late eighteenth and early nineteenth centuries they made their fame and fortune as inventors, industrialists, artists, and architects. Finally in the mid-nineteenth century they passed into the ranks of the landed gentry, marrying into such established families as the Hilliers of Wiltshire, the d'Estcourts of Gloucestershire, and the Nicholls of

2. Weeford, St. Mary's Church. John Wyatt I is buried under the table tomb on the right. The church was designed by James Wyatt and built by Benjamin Wyatt of Sutton Coldfield, 1803.

3. Weeford, Thickbroom. Drawn by Henry Wyatt.

Monmouthshire. Sir (Matthew) Digby Wyatt died at Dimlands Castle in Glamorganshire in 1877 and Thomas Henry Wyatt was lord of the manor of Weston Patrick in Hampshire when he died in 1880.

In 1742 John Wyatt I of Thickbroom in Weeford died and was buried in the graveyard there. His grave, shared by his wife Jane, is marked by a slate slab inscribed with the following epitaph composed, no doubt, by his third son Samuel who considered himself to have a talent for verse:

> Their tender and parental care was to their children known
> How good their other virtues were who knows but God alone,
> Envy if thou hast ought to say that may their name debase
> Suspend it till the judgement day, they'll meet thee face to face.

John and Jane left eight sons: John II (the Inventor), William I (agent to Lord Uxbridge), Samuel I (stay-maker in London), Edward I, Joseph, Benjamin I (builder and architect), James, and Job. Of these, John II, William I, Edward I, and Benjamin I were to father long lines of inventors, land-agents, sculptors, and architects. Collectively they formed a dynasty which is unique in English history for its close association with the development of art and architecture over some two centuries, during which England was at the height of her power and influence. The buildings, sculpture, and paintings of the Wyatts can be found in St. Petersburg, Naples, Rome, Florence, Lisbon, Poland, Canada, Burma, India, and Malta as well as Great Britain and Ireland. In large parts of England and Wales there is hardly a town, a country house, or a church that cannot show some work by one or other of the Wyatts. In Monmouthshire, Wiltshire, Staffordshire, and Cheshire it is almost exceptional to come across a building of any importance which has absolutely no connection with any of the Wyatts.

Altogether between 1746 and 1946 the family produced no fewer than twenty-eight architects, five sculptors and carvers, five painters, a President of the Royal Academy, and a President of the Royal Institute of British Architects. There were also twelve land-agents and the substantial quota of generals, lawyers, clergymen, and surgeons to be expected of any Victorian upper-middle-class family. The Wyatts are therefore the pre-eminent English example of an architectural dynasty and no other family, not the Hardwicks, Cundys, nor even the Scotts, can compare with them.

The extent to which talent is hereditary is debatable. The Wyatts, however, would seem to furnish a very strong argument that it is. They frequently intermarried, and on many occasions first cousins married each other, which helped to keep the genius in the family. Several who eventually became architects first tried their hands at something else. Both Lewis Wyatt and Jeffry Wyatville started their careers by running away to sea. Benjamin Dean

Wyatt spent several unhappy years in India. Thomas Henry Wyatt began life as a business man before choosing architecture. They were irresistibly drawn towards bricks and mortar, almost against their conscious inclinations.

The first member of the family of more than local note was John Wyatt II who is appropriately known to posterity as 'John the Inventor'. He was born at Weeford in 1700 and attended Lichfield School before settling in his native village as a master carpenter. An oak gate-leg table made by him when a young man still survives in the possession of a descendant, Miss Hamilton Thompson. He did not remain a simple carpenter for long. His knowledge of mathematics and mechanics and his prolific inventiveness were quite exceptional. In the City Library at Birmingham are preserved two large volumes filled with his notes and sketches which give a clear indication of his interests and extraordinary ingenuity.

He soon became well known locally as an 'ingenious and expert workman' and began to experiment with machines for doing tasks hitherto executed manually. His first major experiment of this type, begun when he was thirty, was to invent a machine to cut files.

To cut a file by hand was an extremely laborious business, as anything between 21 and 216 cuts per inch might be needed, so the advantage of a machine that could do this is obvious. After two years of experimenting Wyatt had produced a workable machine but needed capital in order to exploit its potential. He therefore sold the machine to a Birmingham gunsmith, Richard Heeley. Unfortunately, Heeley's financial affairs became distressed; he was unable to pay Wyatt and the machine reverted to its inventor. John II was consistently unfortunate in his business associates and it was at this stage that he fell in with the worst of them, Lewis Paul.

Lewis Paul was the son of a Huguenot *émigré*. His father had made a fortune in London as a druggist but Paul dissipated most of his inheritance. With the remnant he went into the slightly macabre business of manufacturing shrouds, making use of a machine he had invented for stamping crape. John II met him on a visit to London in September 1732 and succumbed to his charm and plausible manner. Despite this superficial attractiveness Paul was extravagant, pretentious, untrustworthy, and incapable of concentrating on anything for more than short periods of time. All of which made him totally unsuitable as a business partner for an unworldly inventor. John II asked Paul to co-operate with him in the development of the file machine and Paul agreed but soon lost interest and reconveyed the invention to the inventor who by now had himself lost interest and had begun to develop another idea instead.[2]

In the 1730s the machinery for weaving cloth had been developed further

[2] Anon., *John Wyatt, Master Carpenter and Inventor* (1885), 5–10.

than that for spinning, thus creating a shortage of yarn and imbalance in the textile industry. John II saw that this need could be met by spinning yarn mechanically with two rollers moving at different speeds. He set to work to devise a machine to do this. He first referred to it in a letter of 1733 in which he stated that he intended to live near Birmingham as he had 'a gymcrack there of some consequence'. He shut himself up in a room at Sutton Coldfield working in solitude on his new machine 'all the time in a pleasing but trembling suspense'. There he spun the first thread of cotton yarn ever produced by mechanical means.[3]

He soon reached the stage where money was needed to develop his invention further. Once again he turned to Paul with whom he entered into an agreement on 7 April 1735. Wyatt's family were horrified to hear that he was associating once again with Paul. They had no illusions about the dubious character of the man to whom they referred disparagingly as 'Monsieur' Samuel Wyatt I, John II's younger brother, warned him that Paul was 'a slippery character' and a 'common sharper' and that he had 'been in most prisons in London'. Worse still, in Samuel's eyes, his mother had been a servant – a housekeeper, in fact. This damning report did not deter John II and he pressed on with his partnership.[4]

Paul agreed to accept the machine when it was completed, in return for an initial payment and a guarantee to finance the work necessary. A year later a serious quarrel occurred between the partners. The exact cause of it is unknown. There was a general shortage of money which seems to have exacerbated tempers and led to destructive recriminations. On 22 September 1736 John II wrote to Paul 'I understand from brother Sam that I am by your artful harangue made ye chief author of all your misfortunes.'[5] Paul seems to have been offended by the aspersions on his character and was sulking as a result. In April 1736 Paul wrote disagreeably about the spinning-machine to John II: 'I know your grand secret and will use you as I please.' In 1737 William Wyatt I wrote to John II grumbling about £20 that 'Monsieur' owed him and adding, 'I think it very hard, people should live at the rate they do and not regard their friends to whom their Grandeur is in measure owing.'[6]

Only John Wyatt himself seems to have come through this crisis without saying unforgivable and unforgettable things. He possessed a pleasingly placid character free from bitterness and affectation. In 1737 he reassured Paul, 'Did you know how much I have been advocate for you in your absence against most of those that know us both and found occasion to talk of you.'[7]

---

[3] Ibid.
[4] BRL, John Wyatt MSS. 93189–90.
[5] Ibid.
[6] Ibid.

John II's loyalty to his friend helped to dispel Paul's sulks and hostility. The quarrel was made up. Paul's letters to Wyatt were again addressed to 'friend John'. Work on the machine went ahead in the face of all difficulties. John II was undaunted. Paul was convinced that it was likely to be successful in the long run. He left London and came to live in Birmingham. For four years he paid John II a weekly wage to devote his time entirely to work on the machine. Even so John II was extremely short of money and was forced to pawn most of his clothes to support his wife. His one suit became so ragged that he was ashamed to be seen abroad in it. In 1738 Mr. Warren, a Birmingham bookseller, in whose house Dr. Johnson lodged for six months, put up more money and the model was finished in that year.[8]

No sooner had John II finished one invention than he started work on another. Often he was working on several projects at once. At this time he turned his mind to developing the possibilities of suspension bridges. He wrote an 'Essay on Bridges with one Arch' and prepared a model for the new Westminster Bridge according to his ideas, much to the astonishment of his family. In 1737 William I wrote facetiously to him 'I have never heared of arches being hung in the air nor can I form any idea of such unless you will carry them so near the moon as they may be equally attracted by her and the earth.'[9]

John II produced different versions of his proposal and made a model to demonstrate it which he submitted to the Westminster Bridge Committee in association with another of his disastrous partners, William Bartlett.

Unfortunately, Wyatt's model for a timber suspension bridge with a span of 400 feet was not completed in time. The committee had already decided on a traditional stone arched bridge when it was finally submitted. The model was returned to Bartlett and was lost when shortly afterwards he died in Scotland, so that this imaginative venture ended on the sad note that marked many of John II's schemes. His brother Samuel I was forced to advertise for information about the whereabouts of the model, but whether it was ever found is not known.[10]

Meanwhile work on the spinning-machine was still progressing. In 1738 Paul took out a patent which embodied for the first time the important principle incorporated in John II's invention, namely spinning by rollers revolving at different velocities. A company was formed to exploit the invention at a cotton mill in Upper Priory, Birmingham. Two hanks of cotton produced there are still preserved in the museum at Birmingham with a note in Wyatt's own hand testifying that they were spun in about 1744. The motive

---

[8] *John Wyatt*, 13 and 14.
[9] BRL, John Wyatt MSS. 93189–90.
[10] Ibid.

power was 'two or more asses walking round an axis'. The concern languished, however, partly because of defects in the machinery and heavy costs, partly because of Paul's inefficiency. For while John II was in London Paul forgot to feed the asses and let them die.

John II was imprisoned for debt in 1740. He was again in the Fleet Prison for debt the following year and by 1744 Paul is reported to have owed him £850 and the spinning business had failed utterly. The mill at Upper Priory together with its machinery was sold to the proprietor of the *Gentleman's Magazine*, but he also failed to exploit its potential. John Barton, a friend of John II, wrote to him 'all the world is sorry for you and thinks the worse of Paul than ever'.[11] In 1747 John II was again in debtors' prison. While there he occupied himself by contriving various devices to make the warders' lives easier and the building more secure.

The failure of the spinning speculation did not deter John II unduly. In the course of the following ten years he devised schemes for piped water supplies, a 'hydraulic bucket', and ball-bearings, or, as he called them, 'friction rollers'. He constructed a double-headed lathe for making buttons out of bone pearl which was still used in the late nineteenth-century. He invented and made two fire-engines for Birmingham Corporation at a price of £26 and £43. 7s. respectively. The volume of his notes and sketches in the Birmingham Library shows an amazing array of interests. One page is covered with designs for a gun harpoon, an ice saw, and a variety of ingenious hooks. On others are road surveys and notes on bridges. There is an essay on mechanical spinning and complicated notes on water-mills, water-wheels, canals, and hydrostatics made at various dates between 1740 and 1758.[12]

His principal invention of these years and his most successful enterprise was the compound lever weighing-machine for assessing the contents of loaded carts, an improved version of which is still in use at railway stations today. The purpose of this was to stop short measures of hay or coal (a prevalent means of fraud) by enabling the buyer to test his purchase on the town's public weighing-machine. John II never patented this invention which was a serious financial error.

His first weighing-machine was set up at Snow Hill in Birmingham. Another was erected in Liverpool in 1744 and one in Abbey Foregate at Shrewsbury in 1745. After the failure of his other schemes this one was comparatively successful and soon became well known. In 1752 he received a letter from the Town Clerk of Chester asking for one and another from the Chamberlain of Hereford in 1754. He also supplied machines to Gloucester and Lichfield. A model of the latter is in the Science Museum. Despite all these

---

[11] BRL, John Wyatt MSS. 93189–90, John Barton to John Wyatt II, 18 Apr. 1743.
[12] Ibid., John Wyatt MSS. 93189–90, vol. ii.

orders he did not make a great deal of money from the invention because after his initial payment for the machine he received no further return or royalties. The town corporations who bought the machine enjoyed the profit. For instance in Shrewsbury the charge was 6*d*. per waggon and 4*d*. per cart.[13] Even a percentage of this on his various machines would have provided John II with a comfortable income for the rest of his life but with his customary lack of aptitude for business he had failed to secure it. So by the late 1750s he was again in dire financial straits. Such payments as the £21 from the Corporation of Bristol for a model of a drawbridge hardly covered his working expenses.

His family urged him to take employment at Soho under his friend and neighbour Matthew Boulton. This he finally agreed to do. On 9 February 1760 he wrote to Boulton a letter showing his deprecating self-awareness:

I am on the brink of Ruin, even this day may complete the Business except I can be assisted by my friends with about £20 to buy iron, pay men, support credit etc. etc. Such a sum may keep me in status quo for some time but am afraid would scarce enable me to go through the summer without loss. Methinks I could wish Mr. Beech and Mr. Garbett to know as much as this without giving any further at present.

I am sorry to give you this trouble but if I attempt to speak to this purpose the subject chokes me.

I am father to a young family in an age too old for general approbation yet would I fain leave them out of the power of ill will to reproach them with their father was a poor whimsical old fool etc, etc, or the widow deserves no better for yoking with such a scatterbrain, old enough for her father.

I am attempting the general state of affairs and if annihilation must be, am afraid shall prove insolvent.[14]

John II had married twice. His first marriage produced no children but by his second wife, Marabella Craven, he had two sons and four daughters. Boulton responded generously and offered him a post in his employment. John II spent his last years as a foreman at Soho while still devoting some of his time to working out new ideas and inventions. The two sons, John III and Charles I, were also given places as apprentices in the Soho Works.

John II died in 1766 and was buried in the graveyard of St. Philip's Church, now the Cathedral, in Birmingham. Three years later Richard Arkwright took out his patent for a perfected form of spinning-jenny which he was able to exploit successfully. As a result he became very rich and was knighted. Had John Wyatt been less unworldly a similar prosperity would have been his.

Both John II's sons were also inventors but failed to give their father's work the publicity it deserved. Charles I, the eldest son, born in 1750, regrettably treated his benefactor, Matthew Boulton, with unbecoming ingratitude. After his apprenticeship at Soho was completed Boulton employed Charles as a clerk

---

[13] *John Wyatt*, 27.
[14] BRL, Tew MSS., John Wyatt II to Matthew Boulton, 9 Feb. 1760.

and treated him with 'extraordinary indulgence and generosity'.[15] Charles, however, fell in love with his cousin Jane ('Jenny') Wyatt, sister of the architect James. In order to marry her he decided he needed a larger salary than Boulton could pay so he went to London to seek his fortune. In October 1771 he wrote disingenuously to Boulton: 'My services or abilities could not merit such a salary from you as would settle me in marriage so soon as I could wish . . . this induced me to apply to my cousin Jim Wyatt who recommended in very advantageous colours, painting ornaments for rooms . . . to talk of quitting your service after I have received such benefits from it seems indeed to carry an air of ingratitude – yet what must I do?'[16]

He was torn between love for his cousin and loyalty to his benefactor. In fact the idea of becoming an architectural painter did not come to anything and this whole misjudged episode was probably inspired by James Wyatt's spectacular London success as architect of the Pantheon. Boulton replied to Charles's letter coolly but with an echo of kindness. 'When I took you [as] an apprentice my view in your favour extended further than expiration of your indenture but those views cannot avail anything now. You have long withdrawn yourself from under my wing, you have launched out your plans of Life and there remains nothing now to be done but to pursue that plan with vigour. It is not in a way that I can serve you or I should be inclinable to do it.'[17]

Boulton was hurt by Charles's desertion. He had seen their relationship more as one of father and son than master and employee.

Charles, however, failed to find satisfactory employment in London and eventually returned to Soho like the Prodigal Son. Boulton gave him a post in a new branch of the business at a salary of £100 a year. Charles was thus able to marry his cousin Jenny at Weeford on a warm August day in 1773.[18] Four years later Charles left Boulton's employment and moved to London for the second time. This time the break was final. In March 1777 he wrote to Boulton from London attempting to explain his precipitate departure but to no avail.

Boulton was doubly annoyed and upset by the manner of this second desertion. Nevertheless, he behaved towards Charles with forbearance and generosity. Charles owed him £400 and if Boulton had pressed for payment he could have ruined him. He did not do so for the sake of Charles's wife and children. Jenny's eldest brother, William II, who also owed Boulton money, tried to smooth things over: 'I canot help wishing for the sake of my sister and the family that you will moderate your resentment and be assured no part of his conduct was ever encouraged by her.' Later he added: 'My unthinking

---

[15] Ibid., Charles Wyatt I to Matthew Boulton, Oct. 1771
[16] Ibid.
[17] Ibid., Matthew Boulton to Charles Wyatt I, Oct. 1771.
[18] Weeford Parish Register, 17 Aug. 1773.

brother-in-law Charles has behaved with such ingratitude towards you that I do not know how to offer any apology.' He went on to say that he hoped that Boulton would once again give him a 'trial in your manufactury'. In September William II wrote again about Charles's behaviour. 'What Charles is about I know not but I fear building castles in the air . . . I cannot help being a little anxious and wishing to see him under the direction of somebody with more judgement than he seems to be master of himself.'[19] Boulton was willing to moderate his resentment but he was not willing to have Charles back in his employment under any circumstances. Again and again he had overlooked his conduct and every time he had been treated ungratefully. Charles, he decided, could now make his way unaided.

Charles did in fact thrive on his own account. In 1789 he was back in Birmingham manufacturing metal goods independently. He took out several patents including one for the manufacture of tinned copper sheeting for use as a roof material. He supplied this in large quantities in 1803 to the Office of Works for the Lazaretto, a quarantine hospital, at Chetney Hill in Kent designed by his cousin and brother-in-law James Wyatt.[20] In the 1790s he moved once again to London and lived until 1802 in New Bridge Street and after that at Bedford Row.

From 1796 till the end of his life he was involved in the manufacture of cement. He was an original partner in the firm of Parker, Wyatt & Co., makers of Roman cement, sometimes called Parker's or Wyatt's cement. It was patented in 1796 by James Parker of Northfleet who got the material for it from the Isle of Sheppey. 'It possessed the peculiar property of hardening under water'. Accordingly it was used extensively in hydraulic work as well as for conventional stuccoing. It was employed on a considerable scale by Charles's architect cousins, particularly James, Samuel, Lewis, and Jeffry, and they helped make it fashionable. Though in fairness it must be added that its success was also due to its superiority over earlier patent stuccoes and cements. Because of its specific water-proof qualities Samuel Wyatt used it for lighthouses, including that at Dungeness in 1801 and at Needles in 1806. James used it so widely, particularly in his Gothic work, that his enemies thought he must have some financial interest in it; and John Carter denounced his 'Cement Influenza' in the *Gentleman's Magazine*.

It was not entirely satisfactory as a building material. It was expensive and had an unpleasant pink tinge; nor was it easily capable of being transported long distances. For instance, the cement supplied to Lord Bagot for gothicizing Blithfield was found to be unusable on arrival and had to be thrown away. This

[19] BRL, Tew MSS., William Wyatt II to Matthew Boulton, 22 Sept. 1777.
[20] *King's Works*, 447–9.

4. Model of Weighbridge at
Lichfield. Invented by John Wyatt
II.

5. John Wyatt III. Drawn by Sir
George Hayter.

almost caused a lawsuit between Charles Wyatt and Lord Bagot.[21]

Despite these drawbacks the cement was greatly used and Charles was able to make a comfortable profit out of its manufacture. Even Matthew Boulton sufficiently overcame his annoyance with the producer to use it to stucco his office wing at Soho in 1798.[22] After his death at the age of sixty-nine the business was carried on by his eldest son James.

A catalogue published in 1841 shows that by that time the firm had branched out into the sale of marble and artificial stone garden ornaments including statues, urns, and fountains as well as tessellated pavements, Roman tiles, and scagliola columns and pedestals. The factory at that time was established in Holland Street near the south end of Blackfriars Bridge.[23]

In the 1840s John Marriott Blashfield, a former employee, part-purchased the company for £10,000. He continued to manufacture artificial stone garden ornaments under his own name. Today Blashfield is chiefly remembered as the speculative builder who went bankrupt over the development of Kensington Palace Gardens.[24]

John Wyatt III, the younger son of John the Inventor, was born in 1752. He too became an apprentice at Soho and was treated as a son by Matthew Boulton. Unlike Charles he behaved with gratitude and was a dependable employee. After a time as a clerk, in February 1776 he was appointed as Boulton's agent in London to deal with the fashionable end of the metalware trade: silver, ormolu, dress-swords, buckles, buttons, and jewellery. This was then known as the 'toy' trade. John III's job was to show potential customers objects and designs and to retail their orders to Soho. He was paid a 10 per cent commission on anything he sold.[25]

At first he had no premises of his own but waited on potential customers. He found that this was bad for business because when he called on people, whether gentry or shopkeepers, they were often out or were too busy, too haughty or too undecided to place definite orders for goods. He advised Boulton to build a show-room or 'Theka' in London where his goods could be permanently on display and all those interested could place their orders: 'Almost every person I have been with is desirous to know where your curious productions are to be seen and would gladly call anywhere for that purpose . . . Sam Wyatt has three spots in which he could build you a room – in Oxford Street at his own house. In Bond Street and in Gerrard Street.'[26] Nothing came of this proposal, partly because of the cost and partly because Boulton was afraid of the plagiarism

[21] Staffs. RO, Bagot MSS.
[22] BRL, Tew MSS., Samuel Wyatt to Matthew Boulton, 10 July 1798.
[23] Wyatt, Parker & Co., *A Catalogue of Statues, Furniture, Vases etc.* (1841).
[24] *L.S.* xxxvii (1973), 156, 158 n.
[25] N. Goodison, *Ormolu: The Work of Matthew Boulton* (1974), 87.
[26] BRL, Tew MSS., John Wyatt III to Matthew Boulton, 27 Feb. 1776.

that might be incurred by the permanent display of his designs in a shop.

John III himself rented lodgings in a house in Henrietta Street, Covent Garden. From there he successfully conducted the London end of the 'toy' trade for two years until 1778 when he was replaced by John Stuart.[27]

John III's job in London included ordering specialist objects for use at Soho, such as plaster of Paris for making moulds, and scientific instruments. In 1776 Boulton asked him to buy for the March meeting of the Lunar Society from 'Mr. Parker's' in Fleet Street 'one of his glass aparatus for impregnating water with fixable air which Dr. North invented'.[28] John III also negotiated with the artists and architects employed by Boulton for his designs, including James Wyatt and Angelica Kauffmann.

The least attractive side of the job was dealing with the more difficult of Boulton's fashionable customers, some of whom were almost impossible to please. One of the worst was Lady Morton, for whom Boulton was making silver to James Wyatt's design. On 8 March 1776 John III wrote to Boulton: 'Lady Morton is so damned tedious, whimsical and ill natured that I despair almost of getting her to determine upon anything.' Elsewhere, however, he advised Boulton that though her order was not worth the trouble they ought to persevere with it as 'it would be impolitick to offend her if it can be avoided'.[29]

As well as representing him in London between 1776 and 1778, John III later also travelled to the Continent on Boulton's behalf. In 1784 he went to Paris.[30] His great journey, however, was to St. Petersburg in the winter of 1799 and 1800. His letters to his wife during this period survive and give a vivid picture of the discomfort and tediousness of long-distance travel at the time.

He left England in October and sailed to Hamburg whence he travelled to St. Petersburg overland via Berlin, Danzig, Königsberg, and Riga. Leaving Hamburg on 25 October he reached Berlin on the twenty-eighth, 'having been just three nights and days on the road, a distance only of about 165 English miles – the roads are certainly the worst I ever saw, but the horses and harness even much worse than the roads. If I had time to enjoy it however this city would make amends for the roughness of the roads to it – for the width of the streets and the handsome appearance of the houses, hotels and palaces is beyond anything I have ever seen.'

He asked at this stage whether his cousin Samuel Wyatt, who was then designing and building houses in London and the country for Lord Grenville, could obtain from Lord Grenville a letter of introduction to 'our ambassador at Petersburg' as 'I cannot be too strongly recommended there'.

[27] Goodison, 95.
[28] BRL, Tew MSS., Matthew Boulton to John Wyatt III, 24 Feb. 1776.
[29] Ibid., John Wyatt III to Matthew Boulton, 8 Mar. 1776.
[30] Coll. Miss E. Hamilton Thompson, Letters addressed to his wife from John III in Paris.

Though able to speak French he found that this was not of much use. 'I find the want of the German language a most serious evil. Contrary to all information previous to my leaving London I have found but one innkeeper on the road from Hamburg that could speak a word of French and I find it quite as bad in that respect from here forward. I hope my dear boys will see by the difficulties which this deficiency in language occasions to me, the necessity of their applying themselves to learn French without which I should appear like a block to all about me'.

He went on to describe some of the more amazing sights he had encountered on the way including 'an elegant handsome Princess' who mounted a horse like a man. 'She raised her foot to the stirrup and threw over the other leg with as much ease and as little concern as one of our grooms and through the habit petticoat which was open before like the English Joseph's discovered a fine stout leg and knee etc. – in Pantaloons of silk knit.'

On another occasion he described how he had slept in the carriage rather than the inn where about fifteen or twenty people of both sexes were all sleeping together in one room 'about half the size of our back parlour and most abundantly perfumed, besides the sweet efluvia of the ladies' breaths with the fumes of stinking oil emitted from the frying pans employed in preparing their delicious ragout of sour cabbage etc.' He was offered some of this but was 'a little *particular* and declined – the different groups were nearly in a state of nature'.

He reached Riga on 17 November, the roads between Danzig, Königsberg, and Riga being even more appalling than those between Hamburg and Berlin. He related that 'generally speaking they are up to the axle tree in stiff mud and *agreeably* interspersed with deep holes half filled with huge stones and stumps of trees – you will imagine therefore our bones and skins are not a little bruised and that we should enjoy even a slumber on *Still* boards – for their beds are little better – bad however as they are we should be glad to indulge ourselves on them, but were we to do so frequently we should never get to the end of our journey'. Another source of unpleasantness was, of course, the cold and the fact that sixteen hours of the day were in total darkness which made it impossible to see the landscape which he was so painfully traversing.

Further irritation was caused by the delays involved in the frequent examination of passports, 'which delays on this account since our arrival on Russian ground have been incessant and exceedingly troublesome – for though they had been scrupulously examined at the frontier Barrier we were detained again and again at different towns'. After a month's travel from Hamburg he finally reached St. Petersburg on 26 November.

The letters do not make clear the exact nature of his business but it was probably connected with the construction of the new Royal Mint in the Peter and Paul Fortress for which Matthew Boulton had provided the coining machinery. It seems that there had been a quarrel with a 'Mr. H' which had led to a lawsuit.

John III had been furnished with powers of attorney and had gone to St. Petersburg to treat with the recalcitrant 'Mr. H' who could perhaps have been William Hollins of Birmingham. Traditionally William Hollins is reputed to have designed the Mint at St. Petersburg. In fact the building itself was designed by a Russian architect, Voronikhin, but Hollins may have been responsible for supervising the installation of Boulton's machinery inside.

Whatever the exact nature of this mysterious business Wyatt seems to have settled it satisfactorily during his one and a half months' stay in St. Petersburg. In January he set off for home again, arriving in Hamburg around 14 February, but he had to wait there for a further two weeks until a boat was ready to sail to England.

As well as his official business he seems to have taken the opportunity to study the buildings on the way. He wrote that he had found 'prodigious entertainment in taking plans of German and Russian houses'. He told Charles, who was then manufacturing his patent cement, 'the whole city of Petersburg is stuccoed', as were all the towns in Germany and Russia, 'much of it being very bad'. It seems unlikely, however, that Charles ever contemplated exporting his own superior product to make up for this deficiency. John III also noted that the houses in Petersburg had roofs covered 'with plate iron in the manner of copper' which would also have been of interest to Charles.[31]

At some time unknown, probably in the 1790s, John III ceased to work full time for Matthew Boulton and set himself up as a bookseller and publisher in London. His chief venture in this field was the founding of the *Repertory of Arts and Manufactures*, a volume published annually between 1794 and 1825. This included specifications of new inventions, the transactions of learned societies, translations of foreign works, and miscellaneous communications to the editor. It was intended to publicize new ideas, machines, and techniques and to make them more widely available in a cheap and popular form. The first volume in 1794 included patents for dyeing handkerchiefs, a hat-making machine, James Watt's copywriting machine, John Wilkinson's patent for making cast iron, Joseph Bramah's for a 'water cock upon a new construction', as well as observations on pruning orchards and descriptions of a new method of tanning, the Chinese method of making large sheets of paper, directions for curing 'the disorder of sheep called scab', an account of the method of making Stilton cheese, and a treatise on saltpetre. Altogether the first volume included 63 essays on a wide variety of subjects with 25 engraved plates. The *Repertory*

---

[31] Ibid., Letters from John Wyatt III to his family from Germany and Russia.

of Arts had a considerable success and sold well. It was the ancestor of all popular scientific journals. The articles are interesting and well written.

John III was assisted in its production by his second son, Walter Henry (Harry) Wyatt, who was an inventor in his own right. He patented a new method for separating silver from copper. He also published in 1826 a *Compendium of the Law of Patents.* The elder son, John Francis (Frank), also patented a new type of brick in 1814.[32] At least as a young man Frank was interested in architecture as many of the references of buildings in his father's letters from St. Petersburg were specifically directed at him. He did not, however, adopt the Noble Art as his career.

John III's daughter Cordelia married her first cousin John Wyatt (Jack) Dobbs of Ramsdell Hall near Stoke-on-Trent, the second son of Thomas Dobbs the canal engineer and inventor of Albion Metal who owned a printing business in London. Harry Wyatt seems to have been employed here by his brother-in-law for a time though later he kept his own bookshop in Picket Street, near Temple Bar, until his death in 1849.

Harry and Frank Wyatt remained on intimate terms with Jack and Cordelia Dobbs throughout their lives, frequently staying at each other's houses, and a great deal of the correspondence between them has survived.[33]

To return from John II's grandchildren to his younger brother Job is to be confronted with yet another Wyatt inventor. Job, who owned a water-mill for grinding corn at Tatenhill near Burton-on-Trent, conceived the idea of converting it into a screw factory. He applied himself to devising the necessary machinery. He may have been helped by John II, some of whose drawings show an interest in the same problem. Job patented his invention in 1760 under the title: 'a certain method of cutting screws of iron commonly called wood screws in a better manner than had been heretofore practised'.[34]

The process involved three separate machine operations. The first to file flat the head of the screw; the second to cut the nick in the head of the screw; and the third, and most complex, to cut the thread of the screw. The patent is particularly notable as being 'the earliest recorded instance of the application of machine tools to interchangeable manufacture'.[35]

Job died before he was able to exploit his patent and the mill at Tatenhill became the property of his brother, Benjamin I, founder of the Wyatt building business. On Benjamin I's death in 1772 the mill passed to his eldest son, William II, who in 1776 carried Job's scheme into effect by converting the mill into a screw factory at a cost of £1,100.

[32] Patent No. 3683.
[33] Coll. Miss E. Hamilton Thompson, Letters between Harry and Frank Wyatt and Jack and Cordelia Dobbs.
[34] Patent No. 751.
[35] H. W. Dickinson, 'Origin and Manufacture of Wood Screws', *Newcomen Society,* xxii (1946), 80–1.

The mill was not a financial success, however and William II lost interest in it. In 1777 he wrote to Matthew Boulton telling him that he intended to sell the screw mill and business as 'my plan of life seems to bend itself another way'.[36]

The mill was bought by Shorthouse, Wood & Co. for £250 which represented a substantial loss to William Wyatt. The new owners were able to improve the machinery and as a result contrived to produce 700 gross of screws a week and to employ thirty people. It continued in profitable use well into the nineteenth century.[37]

The 'other way' in which William II's plan of life seemed to bend itself was architecture. In order to understand why, it is necessary to look at the career of his father, Benjamin Wyatt I, who was born in 1709, the sixth son of John Wyatt I of Thickbroom. Benjamin Wyatt I began life as a farmer at Black-brook, Weeford. The house, which must have been new when he moved there, still survives. It is a comfortable red-brick early Georgian building, five bays wide, and is typical of the more substantial midlands farmhouses of the period.

From farming Benjamin I branched out into timber-selling. It was a shrewd move as he was in the midst of heavily wooded Staffordshire countryside. While selling timber to other builders it struck him that it would be much more profitable if, as well as providing the timber, he did the building work himself. Once he had started to act as a builder it was only a short step under the conditions of the time to designing structures and to becoming an architect as well.

The building business was run as a family firm. Most of the surviving drawings and accounts are signed 'Benj. Wyatt & Sons'. His eldest, third, fourth, fifth, and sixth sons were brought up to help with the business. Samuel was trained as a carpenter and Joseph as a mason. Benjamin II was used as a draughtsman. James, the most talented of the brothers, was able to travel to Italy to study the monuments of antiquity and the Renaissance at first hand. William II, as the eldest son, was employed by his father as the architect to the family and most of the buildings of this period associated with the Wyatts, where documentation survives, can be shown to have been designed by him.

Benjamin I made a comfortable living out of his business and was able to amass property which on his death in 1772 was valued at more than £5,670. It included freehold premises in Burton worth £1,000; leasehold premises in Burton worth £760; freehold property at Barton-under-Needwood worth £150; the mill, house, and land at Tatenhill worth £1,000; the farm at Blackbrook worth £960; a third share in several freehold and 'burgage' houses in Lichfield worth £350 and a share of sundry other freeholds and leaseholds at Burton worth £1,450.[38]

---

[36] BRL, Tew MSS., William Wyatt II to Matthew Boulton, 1777.   [37] Dickinson, 81.
[38] BRL, Tew MSS., William Wyatt II to Matthew Boulton, 9 Mar. 1773.

I   Swinfen Hall, Staffordshire *facing p.18*

The Wyatts are first encountered as established architects and builders in the 1750s. Between 1755 and 1759 they were employed by Sir John Every to rebuild Egginton Hall in Derbyshire. Both Samuel Wyatt and William Wyatt II were paid for work on their father's behalf.[39] In the same years Benj. Wyatt & Sons also built Swinfen Hall, just outside Weeford, for Samuel Swinfen.[40]

Both Egginton and Swinfen were large red-brick houses with heavy stone dressings and roof balustrades more in the provincial architectural tradition associated with Smith of Warwick than the austere neo-classical style which the Wyatts made their own from 1769 onwards. Such an old-fashioned semi-baroque style is just what one would expect from a provincial builder turned architect in the mid-eighteenth century.

The 1760s were the important years in the development of the building firm. A combination of luck, shrewd business acumen, and the patronage of various local grandees enabled the Wyatts to break out from their provincial background on to the national stage. Most important was the help and encouragement of the Wyatt's old friend Matthew Boulton and the help of two local landowners – Sir William Bagot of Blithfield and Lord Scarsdale of Kedleston.

Matthew Boulton was particularly concerned to raise the standard of workmanship and design in Birmingham. He cultivated the new-classical taste and aimed at satisfying the fashionable market with his ormolu and silver. He collected books and prints of the best antique sources as models for his designs. He also travelled to France. On his first visit in 1766 he was greatly impressed by the architecture and decorative objects which he saw in Paris. He imparted his enthusiasms to the Wyatts and used his local influence to get them architectural commissions.[41]

He asked Benj. Wyatt & Sons to design the factory and house at Soho when his original architect T. Lightoler proved unsatisfactory. The front range, nineteen bays wide, was designed by William II in 1765. He was helped with the drawings by his eighteen-year-old brother, Benjamin II. When finished in 1766 the new factory was the largest in Europe. It was a plain brick building with a clock cupola, looking like a stable block.[42]

To an extent Soho replaced Lichfield as the social and intellectual centre of that part of the Midlands. It became the regular meeting-place of the Lunar Society, a show-place and a centre of hospitality visited from all parts of England as well as from abroad. It was the first Wyatt building to be seen by a large public: Boulton himself referred to his house as 'l'hôtel de l'amitié sur Handsworth Heath'. Contemporaries were greatly struck by the transformation of a 'barren heath' into a 'populous village or town' where 600 people were

[39] Egginton, Every MSS., Account Books 1753–83.
[40] Lichfield Joint R.O., Swinfen MSS.
[41] BRL, Tew MSS., William Wyatt II to Matthew Boulton, 22 Jan. 1766.
[42] Ibid., 16 Sept. 1763; 22 Jan. 1766.

6. Weeford,
Blackbrook Farm. The
home of Benjamin
Wyatt I.

7. Swinfen Hall,
Staffordshire.
Entrance-Hall.

8. Egginton Hall,
Derbyshire. Benj.
Wyatt & Sons, c. 1758.
Demolished.

employed. One visitor was moved to exclaim in verse:

Soho! Where Genius and the Arts Preside,
Europa's wonder and Britannia's pride.[43]

Through Boulton the Wyatts got the commission for the new General Infirmary in Stafford. The Infirmary, a typical Midlands enterprise of the period, was founded in 1765 and Matthew Boulton was appointed one of the trustees. In 1766 William II asked him 'When you can spare half an hour it will be obliging to bestow it in giving me your thoughts in regard to the infirmary and if you can encourage me I will be preparing designs to lay before your committee.' Benj. Wyatt & Sons were officially appointed in 1769 and the new building, 'a plain and useful design', was finished in 1772.[44]

The experience gained from the Stafford Infirmary enabled the Wyatts to set themselves up as experts on hospital design, a family reputation which Thomas Henry Wyatt was to sustain through most of the nineteenth century. In 1767, for instance, four different sets of plans submitted for the Leicester Royal Infirmary were sent to Benjamin I for his opinion. As a result of his criticism he was himself appointed architect and the new Leicester Infirmary was begun to the design of Benj. Wyatt & Sons in 1773.[45]

Boulton remained a constant patron. He helped Samuel to gain many commissions in the Birmingham area, such as the new façade of the Theatre Royal in 1777 and Heathfield House for James Watt in 1787. He employed James to design silver for him. When James and Samuel Wyatt established themselves in the 1770s they were able to repay Boulton by recommending his manufactures to their clients.

Boulton's support for Benj. Wyatt & Sons included financial help at a critical moment in 1772, a year of general credit collapse in England. Many of the Midlands industrialists were bankrupted. It was a difficult time for Boulton, but he pulled through with the help of a loan of £3,000 from the banker Thomas Day. Several of Wyatts' clients, including Lord Donegal and Lord Uxbridge, were unable to pay for building work and timber. William II had to borrow £200 from the hard-pressed Matthew Boulton to meet his own commitments. Boulton's generosity on this occasion enabled Benj. Wyatt & Sons to survive.[46]

Another significant influence on the careers of the Wyatts was the patronage of the Bagots of Blithfield. The connection began through timber and led to

[43] W. Pitt, *Topographical History of Staffordshire* (1817), 157–8; quoted in H. W. Dickinson, *James Watt* (Cambridge, 1936), 48.
[44] BRL, Tew MSS., William Wyatt II to Matthew Boulton, 26 Jan. 1766; Staffs. R.O., D685/11/1, Minute Book of Stafford Infirmary; D685/12/1, Annual Reports of Stafford Infirmary.
[45] Leicester R.O., LM 13D54/12/7–10, Benj. Wyatt & Sons' plans for Leicester Royal Infirmary.
[46] BRL, Tew MSS., William Wyatt II to Matthew Boulton, 12 May 1772; 25 Feb. 1773; Matthew Boulton to William Wyatt II, 12 Sept. 1772.

9. Soho Works, Handsworth, Staffordshire. Designed by William Wyatt and built by Benj. Wyatt & Sons for Matthew Boulton, 1765. Demolished.

10. Stafford Infirmary. Designed by William Wyatt and built by Benj. Wyatt & Sons, 1769–72.

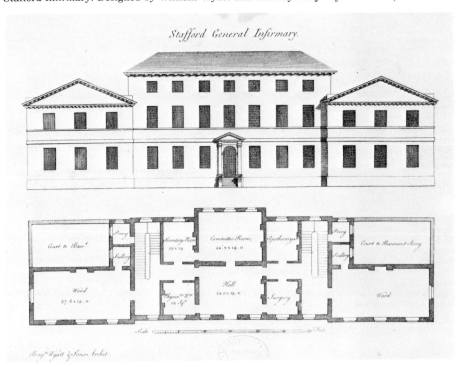

architecture. The Bagot estate was renowned for fine oaks and Benjamin I bought trees from Sir William Bagot. On visits to Blithfield he was no doubt accompanied by one or other of his sons. Sir William was struck by their unusual talents, especially those of James, the sixth son.

In 1762 Sir William's younger brother Richard went to Venice as secretary to the ambassador Lord Northampton. He took James Wyatt with him to study painting, architecture, and music. James stayed in Italy for six years, returning to England in about 1768. It was as a result of this that he acquired the accomplishments and polish which fitted him to become the most fashionable architect of the late eighteenth century.

Sir William Bagot also employed the Wyatts as builders. In 1769 Samuel and Joseph built an orangery to 'Athenian' Stuart's design at Blithfield Hall. This led to Samuel's involvement in the design of the house. Stuart had made plans for rebuilding part of the ancient quadrangular structure but Sir William found them too ambitious and turned to Samuel Wyatt for less extensive alterations. Samuel made various drawings and a large new drawing-room and new family rooms were built to his design in 1769. He was paid £21 for his plans.[47]

Like Boulton, the Bagots continued to support the Wyatts. Sir William's youngest brother, Lewis Bagot, when Dean of Christ Church, Oxford, appointed James to design the new Canterbury Quadrangle. This introduction to the university was to bring James many commissions from other colleges.

Later, when he became Bishop of St. Asaph, Lewis Bagot employed Samuel Wyatt to design a new episcopal palace. Richard Bagot (who later adopted his wife's name of Howard) also asked Samuel to execute Bonomi's design for Ashtead Park (Surrey) and to design the stables there.[48]

The patronage of Matthew Boulton and the Bagots widened the knowledge and improved the taste of the Wyatts. It introduced them to the fashionable world and brought them many commissions. Though less direct in its impact, the influence of Nathaniel Curzon, first Lord Scarsdale, was equally important. The great neo-classical palace which he built at Kedleston between *c.*1757 and 1766 had more effect on the evolution of the Wyatt style than any other building.

After comissioning designs from Matthew Brettingham, James Paine, and 'Athenian' Stuart, Lord Scarsdale entrusted the completion of his house to the most original architect in England, Robert Adam. Samuel Wyatt had worked as a carpenter at Kedleston since May 1760. Adam, after his appointment as architect, instituted considerable changes in the organization of work. 'We

[47] Staffs. R.O., Bagot MSS., D1721/3/215, Building Accounts 1769–70.
[48] Oxford, Christ Church MSS., XXXIII A1, B3, Canterbury Accounts 1772–91, 1783–4; F. E. Paget, *Some Records of the Ashtead Estate* (1873).

have had the greatest revolutions at Sir Nat's that you ever heard of. Mr. Swann the Great is dismissed and Mr. Wyatt the carpenter now fills his place, which is I think mostly brought about by me', he wrote to his brother.[49]

At the age of twenty-three Samuel Wyatt became clerk of works at Kedleston with total control of building, landscaping, and arranging the collection. He also had the chance to design small objects such as pedestals for statues and minor farm buildings. His job was essentially that of an architectural go-between. He executed Adam's plans and relayed Lord Scarsdale's opinions to the architect in London.

Samuel's experience at Kedleston amounted to an architectural training. He had the opportunity to develop his talent as a draughtsman and to make use of Lord Scarsdale's library which included all the standard books on architecture and art. His contact with Adam also led him to subscribe to the *Ruins at Spalato* which was published in 1764.

He lived continuously at Kedleston until 1768 when he returned to Weeford which was his Midlands base until 1774. While at Kedleston he married on 7 January 1765 Ann Sherwin, the daughter of one of Lord Scarsdale's tenant farmers.[50]

In about 1769 James Wyatt also arrived back in Weeford. After his return from Italy he had stayed for a time in London with John IV, the second of the Wyatt brothers. John IV was a distinguished surgeon and a Fellow of the Royal Society. His portrait hangs in the Middlesex Hospital where he worked for thirty-two years. He had a house in Newport Street which was used as a London base by Samuel and William, as well as James Wyatt.

The exchange of ideas after the reunion of the brothers led to the creation of the Wyatt style as expressed in the famous Pantheon project in London, in the new organ and Town Hall at Burton, and in a series of country houses including Beaudesert, Gunton, Hagley, and Heaton. James, Samuel, and William II worked closely together. James played the dominant role. He was the best draughtsman and had the most polished taste. He made the drawings and exhibited them at the Royal Academy. Samuel oversaw the practical work of building and William II ran the business side. At the Pantheon he was the treasurer.

Samuel must have shown James the new house at Kedleston and the drawings which Adam and Paine had produced for it. They made as great an impact on James as they had already on Samuel. All the buildings designed by them in the next decade are in a refined and less monumental version of Adam's style. For instance, 'An elevation for a great house in Sussex' made by

[49] John Fleming, *Robert Adam and his Circle* (1962), 258; Kedleston, Curzon MSS., Account Books and letters to and from Lord Scarsdale, Robert Adam, and Samuel Wyatt.
[50] Kedleston Parish Register, 7 Jan. 1765.

11. Unexecuted design for Gresley
Church, Derbyshire by Joseph Wyatt,
1785.

Elevation of the West End

12. Blithfield Hall, Staffordshire.
Unexecuted design for the Gallery by
Samuel Wyatt, 1769.

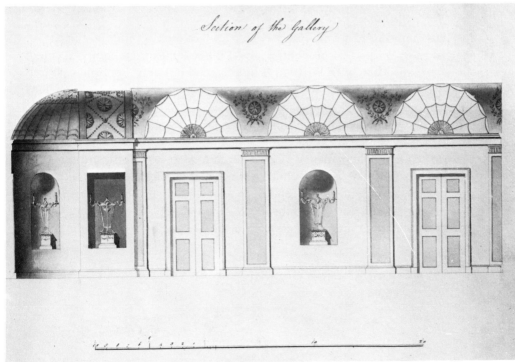

Section of the Gallery

James in 1771 is a close adaptation of the south front of Kedleston.[51] The rotunda of the Pantheon in Oxford Street owed as much to Adam's saloon at Kedleston as to its Roman namesake. Like all the major early Wyatt buildings it was executed by the same team of craftsmen as Kedleston, including Joseph Rose II the stuccoist, Biagio Rebecca the painter, Snetzler the organ-builder, and Domenic Bartoli the scagliola-maker.

Many of the owners of the early Wyatt houses were close relations of Lord Scarsdale's, including his brother Assheton Curzon at Hagley and his cousins Sir Thomas Egerton at Heaton and Sir Harbord Harbord at Gunton. All these were obviously commissions which followed from the Kedleston connection.

Yet at the same time as their joint work in Staffordshire and elsewhere between 1769 and 1774, the brothers were also developing independent architectural practices. James, besides working in England at Fawley Court and Aldwark, produced designs for a number of houses in Ireland. All but one of these were executed by local builders. James himself was in Ireland only once, for the building of Slane Castle in 1785.

Joseph, the fourth son of Benjamin I, set himself up as a stone-mason in Burton-on-Trent where he re-paved the market-place in 1772 and rebuilt the Trent bridge. He became road surveyor in that part of Staffordshire and in addition was responsible for building private drives in several country house parks, including Beaudesert for Lord Uxbridge.[52]

He made and sold chimney-pieces and objects such as urns in stone, alabaster, and marble and executed masonry for other architects. He also designed buildings on his own behalf and gained the reputation of being a 'clever but indolent architect'. He is now best remembered as the father of Sir Jeffry Wyatville.[53]

Joseph's main interest was church design though lack of funds on the part of the parishes he worked for prevented any of his schemes from being executed. In 1764 in association with William II he provided drawings for a new church at Lullington (Derbyshire). They are remarkably old-fashioned, with Gibbs surrounds and an obelisk-shaped spire.

In 1783 he was involved in a scheme for rebuilding the church at Breedon-on-the-Hill (Leicestershire) but again this came to nothing. Just before his death in 1785 he made plans for a new church at Gresley (Derbyshire) signed 'Jos Wyatt Burton'. These show that he was capable of producing on occasion designs that are not unworthy of his more talented brothers Samuel and James. If Gresley Church had been executed Joseph's reputation as an architect would stand much higher than it does today.[54]

[51] R.I.B.A..
[52] Staffs. R.O., Paget MS. D603/148, Estate Accounts.   [53] *APSD.*
[54] B.M., Church Briefs B xxiv. 4; Derbyshire. R.O., Joseph Wyatt's designs for Lullington and Gresley Churches.

Benjamin Wyatt I died in 1772.[55] The building and timber firm passed to William II. Under him the Staffordshire business flourished until his death in 1780. In 1774 James Wyatt married Rachel Lunn and moved to London. Samuel Wyatt also settled permanently in London at the same time. These moves and the establishment of independent households, drawing offices, and building yards were the end of the close association which had existed between them up to that time.

After 1774 there is no evidence of any formal professional association between James and Samuel. Both were able to manage on their own. In Samuel's case there was strong reason for wishing to do so. He was an astute business man, one of whose ambitions was to become rich. James, on the other hand, despite his brilliance as a designer was completely improvident and incapable of organizing his affairs. From now on their lives form two completely separate histories.

[55] Weeford Parish Register, 30 July 1772.

13. John Wyatt IV, the surgeon, by Robert Smirke, senior.

14. James Wyatt. Portrait medallion by Wedgwood.

CHAPTER II

Samuel Wyatt (1737–1807),

The Wonder-working Chip

Samuel's reputation has been overshadowed by that of the more brilliant James, though as an architect he was hardly less accomplished and was much more efficient as a business man. Samuel was nicknamed 'the Chip' because of his origins as a carpenter but contemporaries greatly admired the 'ingenious-ness' and 'elegant simplicity' of his designs.

The two brothers were very different. James was something of a Tory who worked for the fashionable world, the royal family, the Church, the university, the army, and the Government. Samuel was an architectural radical employed by the most progressive groups in late eighteenth-century England – the Foxite Whigs, including Coke of Norfolk, Lord Petre and Lord Anson, and the pioneer industrialists such as Thomas Williams and James Watt.

Samuel worked in a consistent neo-classical manner which was a develop-ment of the early Wyatt style but was more austere. He designed lighthouses, model farms, and moderate-sized country houses. He was an engineer and experimented in the use of new materials to a greater extent than any of his contemporaries, but, unlike James, he did not design movable furniture for his interiors; nor was he in the least interested in Gothic and made only five half-hearted Gothic designs in his whole career.

As has been seen already, Samuel worked closely with his brothers after leaving Kedleston up to 1774 when he settled permanently in London. In that year he leased a house and timber-yard from the Duke of Portland at 63 Berwick Street in a part of Soho inhabited by artists, sculptors, and architects.[1] Immediately his practice as a country house architect began to flourish. Till then it had consisted mainly of alterations and additions to existing buildings – a library at Dorfold Hall, a drawing-room at Berechurch Hall, and unexecuted schemes for enlarging Tatton Park.

In 1775 he was employed on a large Cheshire house, Bostock Hall, and in 1776 began work on two major buildings, Doddington Hall and Baron Hill, but Herstmonceux Place built in 1777 and Hooton Hall begun the following year are the first examples of his two personal types of country house. Herstmon-ceux has a main front with two domed bows to take advantage of the view. Like the elimination of the *piano nobile* and the lengthening of windows, which

---

[1] Nottingham Univ. Library, Portland MS. PW F9613, S. Wyatt to Duke of Portland, 13 Mar. 1774.

15. Samuel Wyatt, by L. F. Abbott, *c.* 1775.

16. Doddington Hall, Cheshire. Designed by Samuel Wyatt, 1776. The Coade plaques depict the signs of the zodiac. The earliest examples of the Wyatt version of the Venetian window.

17. Coton House, Warwickshire. Designed by Samuel Wyatt, *c.* 1785. His personal version of the Anglo-Palladian villa.

occurred at the same time, it was a response to the new sympathy for landscape. This is particularly obvious in a later house, Belmont, where the domes have little glazed gazebos on top like lighthouse lanterns. Samuel repeated the theme frequently, for instance at Penrhyn, Dropmore, and in an unadopted scheme for Digswell.

Hooton Hall was the earliest of his own versions of the anglo-Palladian villa. It had a central domed bow flanked by segmentally over-arched tripartite windows. At Hooton the staccato rococo characteristics, such as canted bow-windows, of the mid-century villas of Sir Robert Taylor and James Paine were replaced by a harmonious synthesis of cubes and semicircles. This was Samuel's favourite design and he used it on many different occasions, at Coton House, Delamere Lodge, Culford, Wrotham Rectory, Hurts Hall and Kinmel Park, as well as suggesting it for Heathfield House and Somerley Park.

Domed bows, looking like tea-canisters, are the most distinctive characteristics of his buildings. Other particular features are over-arched tripartite windows and the inclusion of an orangery in the main fabric of the house as at Tatton in 1785[2]. Both became common in the early nineteenth century, but in each case Samuel was the innovator. In 1776 at Doddington he was the first to use tripartite windows under a continuous lintel in place of the traditional Venetian window. Windows of this type were later known as 'Wyatt windows' particularly in Ireland where they were very popular.

Like James, Samuel was a master of interior decoration in the Adam manner. His work is even more delicate and attenuated than his brother's and makes Adam's seem almost gross by comparison. It is seen at its richest in the drawing-room at Lichfield House, the staircase dome at Culford, and the circular saloon at Doddington; at its most elegant in the Red Drawing-Room at Shugborough; at its simplest in the library at Belmont.

His buildings are particularly important for their plans, for he was among the most enterprising architects of his time in his handling of geometrical space. This can be seen at the beginning of his career in the oval library designed (but not executed) for Tatton in 1774 and the ingenious pair of hexagonal bedrooms over the saloon at Doddington. More complex are the plans for the Shire Hall in Stafford, with its arrangement of octagons and hexagons, and the internal layout of Sundridge Park. In the latter Samuel fitted rooms of all shapes round a circular staircase within Nash's and Repton's pre-existing shell.

His plans also show a trend towards greater flexibility. From the beginning he paid little attention to over-all symmetry. Office wings and orangeries were placed to one side of the main block. Many of his side elevations have

---

[2] The so-called 'Grand Design'. While work was in progress the orangery was converted into a wing of private rooms.

18. Belmont Park, Kent. Designed by Samuel Wyatt, 1782–92. Coade plaque depicting the house in a grove of palm trees.

19. Belmont Park, Kent, gazebos on top of the patent slated domes.

bow-windows randomly sited to suit the internal layout. The most curious case of asymmetry is Belmont where the side elevations differ in width and have different rhythms of window-bays.

Architecturally as interesting as Samuel's country houses were his subsidiary estate buildings. He was a leading designer of model farms and was employed by many of the great agricultural improvers including Coke of Norfolk for whom he designed over fifty buildings around Holkham. His farms reflect the great development in agriculture in late eighteenth-century England. They are also neo-classical designs of considerable interest showing the same love of geometry as his country houses. The plan of Demesne Farm at Doddington is composed of octagons and hexagons and may have been influenced by Adam's design for the home farm at Culzean Castle. Samuel's vanished layout of fourteen cottages at Longlands Village on the Holkham estate in the form of a faceted crescent was comparable with Michael Searle's Paragon at Blackheath. The semicircular poultry-yard at Winnington (now demolished) and the Octagon Cottage at Holkham were pieces of pure geometry comparable to the work of the French architect C. N. Ledoux. They are among the most original works of English neo-classical architects.

As well as designing farms and cottages at Holkham, Winnington, and Doddington he was responsible for the model estate buildings at Heaton, Thorndon, Sandon, Penrhyn, Somerley, Wimbledon Park, and Shugborough. Those which survive have carefully chosen primitive Roman detail – baseless Tuscan columns, overhanging eaves, Diocletian windows, and even, in the case of Kempstone Lodge farm on the Holkham estate, chimney-pots in the form of Roman altars.

Samuel's use of building materials, new constructional techniques, and patent devices was more progressive than that of any other eighteenth-century English architect. He was among the first users of Higgins's calcareous cement[3] and later made extensive use of Parker's (Wyatt's) cement. He used mathematical tiles, Coade Stone, copper sheeting for roofing, metal-composition astragals in his window-sashes. He himself invented an ingenious catch for sash-windows, a lantern for lighting staircase-halls, and the sympathetic hinge. The latter was a 'hey presto' device whereby both flaps of a double door open simultaneously. The only ones still in working order are at Doddington Hall.[4]

He was in the vanguard where the structural use of cast iron was concerned. The iron columns in the Winnington poultry-house (*c.*1782–5) were among the earliest known. The lantern of Dungeness lighthouse was built entirely of cast

[3] Bryan Higgins, *Calcareous Cement* (1780).
[4] Leeds, Archaeological Society Library, Payne Gallwey MSS., Sir Thomas Frankland's Notebook; Leeds City Library, Ramsden MSS., vol. 3B 142; *APSD*.

20. London, Lichfield House, 15 St. James's Square, Drawing-Room ceiling designed by Samuel Wyatt and executed by Joseph Rose II, 1782–94.

21. Belmont Park, Kent. Library. An example of Samuel Wyatt's style at its simple best.

iron. The staircase at Trinity House was supported on cast-iron cantilevers. His interest in iron culminated in his patent of 1800 for iron bridges and a system of fire-proof cast-iron construction for warehouses.

His use of slate was just as enterprising. His youngest brother, Benjamin II, was agent to Lord Penrhyn whose quarry monopolized late eighteenth-century Welsh slate production. Samuel helped his brother by encouraging clients to buy Penrhyn slate whenever possible. He became the leading purveyor of Welsh slate in London. He used it for shelves, cisterns, lavatory-seats, window-sills, and as a wall covering, as well as for roofing. Though never registered at the patent office he always called his slate facing 'patent slating'. It consisted of slate squares fixed flush to battens and sanded to represent smooth ashlar. The whole of the exterior at Shugborough was originally covered with it at great expense. Even the portico columns were clad in faceted strips of slate. At Penrhyn where everything, down to the mangers in the stables, was made of slate the total effect must have been a nightmare.

The year 1776, when his private architectural practice suddenly began to flourish, was also the time when his career as an official architect and builder began, with the grant of the principal carpentry contract at Somerset House from Sir William Chambers. Samuel's public career was more discreet than James's. He did not reach the highest positions nor did his conduct inspire so much controversy and vituperation. Nor did Samuel's public appointments result from James's influence as might be thought.

By the time James became Surveyor-General in 1796 Samuel had received three surveyorships, a clerkship of the works, and a host of carpentry contracts. Samuel only got one contract directly from James, that for carpentry at the Lazaretto at Chetney Hill in Kent. James allowed him to continue as carpenter for the Office of Works at Westminster and Somerset House after 1796 when, strictly, it was illegal for relations of the Surveyor-General to hold such posts. But Samuel's employment was of such long standing that this was understandable. By Wyatt standards it was hardly a flagrant act of nepotism. James's succession to the post of Surveyor-General was far from being to Samuel's advantage. As a result of the increasingly chaotic state of the Office of Works' finances he was not paid for any of his carpentry at Somerset House, Westminster, or Chetney Hill between 1796 and 1807, and at the time of his death he was owed £30,000 by the Office of Works.[5]

Samuel's official employments fall into two main groups, those which were primarily carpentry contracts and those which were architectural commissions. He got most of his carpentry contracts in the 1770s and 1780s beginning with that for Somerset House in 1776, followed in 1780 by that for the Victualling Office and to the Palace of Westminster under the Office of

[5] *King's Works,* 97, 98.

Works. The Westminster post involved, besides routine repairs, the preparations for state occasions, such as the adaptation of Westminster Hall for the
trial of Warren Hastings in 1788, or the transformation of Henry VII's Chapel
for the funeral of Princess Amelia in 1786.[6]

Carpentry for the Victualling Office was more worth while as his appointment came at an auspicious moment, during the American War of Independence, when the Victualling Office was in the process of enlarging its premises.
He was involved in the construction of large-scale timber storehouses in the
Yards at Weevil, near Portsmouth, and Deptford.

Some of the profit he made out of the Victualling Office was irregular. In
theory the Office's carpenter was not eligible for large new contracts. These
were supposed to be advertised and granted to whoever could execute the work
most cheaply. Samuel Wyatt applied for and obtained some in the name of his
employees. In 1787 a transaction of this kind was discovered by the Board and
he was discharged for his 'highly improper conduct' but was reinstated after
apologizing and promising to mend his ways.[7]

In both the Westminster and Victualling Office contracts Samuel Wyatt was
not paid a salary but received a commission of 5 per cent on all work executed.
He was also entitled to any old materials which were salvaged, and this was a
considerable source of income.

Samuel's fourth public carpentry contract came in 1781 and was for the
restoration of the Chapel at Greenwich Hospital under 'Athenian' Stuart. He
was employed there until 1788 and designed a new type of timber roof with
fewer trusses which was considered a model of its kind and was frequently
illustrated in handbooks of building methods.[8]

The last of Samuel Wyatt's official contracts in the 1780s was an order from
the Treasury for twelve 'moveable hospitals'. In December 1787 he wrote to
Matthew Boulton: 'I have received an order from the Treasury for twelve
moveable hospitals each 83 feet long and 20 feet wide . . . My plan is approved
and I propose to cover them with copper of $\frac{1}{2}$ lb. to the foot for which I shall want
24,000 ft. . . . These hospitals are so contrived as not to require artificers of any
kind to fix them up or take them down, not even a hammer will be necessary.'[9]
Samuel demonstrated this remarkably early example of large-scale prefabri-
cation at Somerset House, and it was described in the newspapers.

His Majesty . . . inspected the Military Hospital, which was erected for the purpose on
the Terrace [at Somerset House] on the front towards the Thames; and was graciously
pleased to express his admiration of the general construction.

[6] PRO, T52/64, ADM 111/83, Works 4/16, 5/75, Accounts 10.
[7] PRO, ADM 111/86, 87, 89, 96, 99, 109.
[8] PRO, ADM 65/106, 68/877–881; e.g. *APSD;* Peter Nicholson, *Architectural Dictionary* (1819); Joseph Gwilt,
Architectural Dictionary (1867).
[9] BRL, Tew MSS., Samuel Wyatt to Matthew Boulton, 10 Dec. 1787; Apr. 1788.

22. Shugborough,
Staffordshire, Red
Drawing-Room. Designed
by Samuel Wyatt, *c.* 1790.
The ceiling is by Joseph
Rose II and the
chimneypiece by Richard
Westmacott.

23. Shugborough,
Staffordshire,
Entrance-Hall. A perfect
neo-classical interior with
its circular plan and
'Delian' Doric columns.

24. Culford Hall, Suffolk.
Designed by Samuel
Wyatt, 1790–6. Detail of
plasterwork on the
staircase.

25. Holkham, Norfolk, Great Barn designed by Samuel Wyatt for 'Coke of Norfolk,' *c.* 1790. The finest of his model farm buildings.

26. Kempstone Lodge, Norfolk. Designed by Samuel Wyatt for 'Coke of Norfolk', 1788. The perfect example of his design for a large farm-house.

The Hospital is 84 feet by 22, the height at the side is 8 feet at the top 11; there are about 300 pieces, from 670 to 690 screws – there are on each side nine openings of about three feet and a half in length and two feet wide, which occasionally push up, and have the effect of a Venetian window, in order to admit the air. On each side are twenty windows, of one small pane of thick glass – the top beams go on hinges – the top is coppered.

The Inventor, Mr. Wyatt, is one of the proprietors of the Albion Mills. The Hospital may be removed in two waggons and the present one is intended for the West Indies (Barbadoes).

The Building was taken entirely to pieces in fourteen minutes, and put up again in forty, so that it was taken down and put up within sixteen minutes of an hour, though not without some danger to the persons employed, from their eagerness to perform with dispatch.[10]

Samuel adapted the design for the hospital from an idea in Dr. Brocklesby's *Economical and Medical Observations* (1764). The hospital created something of a stir. The French and Spanish ambassadors asked for copies of the designs to send home to their respective Courts.[11]

Samuel's important official architectural appointments all date from the early 1790s. Between 1792 and 1794 he became Clerk of Works to Chelsea Hospital, Surveyor to the Mint, Surveyor to Trinity House, and Surveyor to Ramsgate Harbour. He became Surveyor to Trinity House in February 1792. The post was important as their Surveyor was expected to have both architectural and engineering abilities.

The Corporation wanted to build a new headquarters and one of the factors governing their choice of a Surveyor was that he should be capable of designing it. Trinity House was also beginning to exercise much closer control over the construction of lighthouses and the old system of leasing out new lighthouses to private builders was soon to come to an end, creating more work for their Surveyor.

The expansion of London made the Corporation's estate at Southwark a potential area for planned urban development. In fact a project to develop the Southwark Estate did not come to anything in his time. Though in 1806 he designed one new street off Deptford Road nothing was achieved, and William Chadwick later developed the estate as Trinity and Merrick Squares in the 1820s.

Samuel's appointment as Surveyor to Trinity House was a result of the magnificent lighthouse at Dungeness (Kent) which he had designed for T.W. Coke of Holkham in 1791. It cost over £4,000 and was 86 feet high. The design was closely based on Smeaton's for Spurn Light. Dungeness incorporated an identical system of draught flues in the floor of the lantern.[12]

[10] *The World,* 12 Apr. 1788.
[11] Ibid., 18 Apr. 1788.
[12] Holkham, Coke MSS., Ralph Cauldwell's Accounts 1787–94; Audit Book 1795–1803.

Immediately after his appointment Samuel designed the new Trinity House on Tower Hill. Costing over £30,000, it was largely completed by May 1796, when the Corporation's annual Trinity Monday celebration and election of the Master took place there.[13] Trinity House is one of his finest works. The front, considerably revised and improved while work was in progress, is a well-integrated and excellently detailed design. It is the finest small façade of its date in London. The coade stone sculpture over the first-floor windows, executed by John Bacon and emblematic of 'the extensive commerce of Great Britain . . . the triumph of the British Marine . . . the wealth, and security, the prosperity and the glory of the Empire' is outstandingly good.

The interior was equally distinguished and, though destroyed in the Second World War, was accurately restored by Sir Albert Richardson in 1953 using Samuel's original drawings. The principal features were the semicircular staircase lit by a glazed clerestory reminiscent of a lighthouse lantern, and the Court Room with a ceiling painted by J. F. Rigaud to represent 'the security and prosperity of the British nation arising from the power of its Navy and the extent of its commerce'.[14]

The most obvious duty of the Surveyor to Trinity House was the design and repair of lighthouses. Maintaining lighthouses in weather-proof condition was a constant task because of their exposed sites. Samuel carried out repairs at Foulness, Needles, and Dungeness as well as rebuilding the upper part of the tower and designing a new lantern at Scilly St. Agnes.[15]

The first complete lighthouse built during his surveyorship was at Longships off Land's End, where there had long been a demand for a light. Trinity House waited before embarking on the project for a suitable lessee willing to build the lighthouse at his own expense in return for a long lease of the profits from lighthouse duties levied at the ports. This traditional policy, which saved the Corporation from a large capital outlay every time a new lighthouse was built, was increasingly criticized by radical opinion in the late eighteenth century and, as shown in the story of Longships, such delegation was not always successful. The lessee, Lieutenant Henry Smith, took six years to build the lighthouse and eventually went bankrupt.[16]

Nevertheless, the completed lighthouse was a success. It comprised a sturdy granite tower three storeys and 52 feet high. The diameter was 68 feet, greater than the height of the tower. Though the walls were simply tapered, not concave, they were dovetailed according to the principle devised by Smeaton

[13] T.H., Court Minutes, 2 Feb. 1792; 3 May 1792; Samuel Wyatt's Account Book 1793–6.
[14] George Richardson, *New Vitruvius Britannicus*, i (1802), 7.
[15] T.H., Cash Book, 8 Dec. 1792; Court Minutes, 6 Aug. 1795; By minutes, 25 July 1805; 13 Feb. 1806; 13 Mar. 1806.
[16] D. Alan Stevenson, *The World's Lighhouses before 1820* (1959), 65, 70; T.H., Court Minutes, 2 Aug, 4 Oct. 1792; 7 Mar., 1 Aug., 26 Sept., 3 Oct., 7 Nov. 1793; 4 Mar. 1794; 3 Dec. 1795.

27. Shugborough, Staffordshire, portico, 1790–5. The columns are built entirely of slate round a timber core.

28. London, Trinity House. Designed by Samuel Wyatt, 1792–7. Coade plaques by John Bacon.

29. Dungeness Lighthouse. Designed by Samuel Wyatt, 1792. Demolished.

30. Ramsgate Lighthouse. Designed by Samuel Wyatt, 1794. Demolished.

for Eddystone. The lantern had a double domed cap identical to that designed by Samuel at Scilly St. Agnes and the tower was lit by porthole windows like his lighthouse on Ramsgate pier.[17]

Samuel's last and most important lighthouse, Flamborough Head near Bridlington in Yorkshire, was built directly by Trinity House.[18] Royal assent for a new lighthouse was easily forthcoming, despite the opposition of Mr. Ogle Ogle, the eccentric proprietor of an existing ruined tower on the cliffs, which had been without a light for over a hundred years.[19] Samuel's preliminary design in 1806 placed the lightkeeper's house in a circular building round the base of the lighthouse. This was judged 'in some respects inconvenient' and Samuel revised the plan to provide a more conventional house adjoining. The tender was granted to a local builder, John Matson of Bridlington, who has been credited wrongly with the design as a result.

The lighthouse was speedily erected and took the form of a large unfluted Doric column 85 feet high, the capital being formed by the boldly moulded cornice supporting the gallery floor. From the interminable and hyperbolic speech given by Benjamin Milne (the local collecter of light duties) at the opening ceremony it is clear that the columnar effect was intentional.

Rome in the plenitude of power enriched with plunder of conquered provinces and elated with pride, erected stately pillars ornamented with exquisite sculpture to commemorate the achievements of her illustrious citizens; but those splendid embellishments were the ostentatious monuments of an unbounded ambition which grasped at universal dominion and in the career of victory extended a wide scene of ruin and desolation. Under the influence of a better principle and for purposes infinitely more useful this superb edifice for the exhibition of lights is erected.[20]

The month after becoming Surveyor to Trinity House, Samuel was appointed Clerk of Works to Chelsea Hospital on 5 March 1792.[21] This was the most attractive of his official posts, involving unexacting duties and carrying several pleasant perquisites. It was also a prestigious position occupied at that period by architects of the first rank; his predecessor was Robert Adam and his successor Sir John Soane.

On paper the duties of the Clerk of Works, as outlined by Sir Christopher Wren in 1692, were somewhat onerous, but by the late eighteenth century it had become traditional for a deputy and resident work-force to do all the routine maintenance. The Clerk of Works confined his attention to occasional matters of greater importance. Samuel was paid the original salary of £20 p.a. plus a special annual allowance of £200. He was given a house in the hospital

---

[17] W. Daniell, *Round the Coast of Britain,* i (1814), 6.
[18] Stevenson, 65.
[19] T.H., Court Minutes, 6 Feb. 1806; By-minutes, 10 Apr, 5 June, 12 June, 28 Aug. 1806.
[20] John Matson, *The Kidnapped Youth* (1842), 90–1.
[21] CGT Dean, *The Royal Hospital* (1950), 236.

precincts and a free issue of furniture, fuel, and light.[22] The Clerk of Works' house was a comfortable rambling structure of various dates tacked on to one end of Wren's stable block. Samuel, unlike most of his architectural contemporaries, did not have a villa outside London and it is probable that he viewed Chelsea, which was then still a detached village, as his country retreat.

No new buildings were erected at Chelsea to his design but he was responsible for various internal alterations and improvements including the installation of decent drains in place of the 'ill-constructed and extremely offensive' original cesspits. In 1805 he designed a block to house three hundred additional pensioners on the site of the Governor's Garden but it was not built.[23]

On 23 October 1793 Samuel was appointed to succeed John Vardy (Junior) as Surveyor to the Mint but was dismissed a year later for 'total neglect of the Dutys of your appointment'.[24] A compensation for this was the surveyorship to Ramsgate Harbour which he received in March 1794 as the successor to the great engineer John Smeaton. This was due to the influence of the Elder Brothers of Trinity House who were *ex officio* trustees of Ramsgate Harbour.

The harbour was already complete and Samuel's task was to design the buildings round it, including the Harbour-Master's House, the entrance gateways and flanking piazzas, storehouses, the Pier House for meetings of the trustees, and a lighthouse on the end of the pier, all without exception now destroyed. The post carried a salary of £200 p.a., the standard remuneration for surveyors to great public works in the eighteenth century. He also received extra gratuities from time to time, including a gift of 200 guineas from the trustees in October 1803.

As well as his executed buildings at the harbour he prepared designs for a new dry dock 125 feet long, workshops, and further storehouses. These had not been adopted at the time of his death and so were left for his successors, John Rennie and John Shaw, to execute at a later date.[25]

It was fortunate that these official posts had not fallen vacant in the 1780s for he would not have had much time to devote to them. Much of his effort in those years was devoted to one dominating interest, the Albion Mill. This was the first steam-powered flour mill and the most important industrial building of the day. It was Samuel's own conception. He bought the site, formed the mill company, and designed and built the mill. He managed it during its short-lived period of production, launching out into the coal and corn trades to supply it.[26]

[22] PRO, A03/ 1624, Chelsea Hospital Accounts 1794; Dean, 129.
[23] PRO, A03/628; Dean, 237–8, 255.
[24] PRO, Mint Record Book XIV, 236, 268.
[25] PRO, MT/22/32, 32, 34, Ramsgate Harbour Minutes; Ramsgate Public Library, S. Wyatt's designs for the Harbour; Sir John Rennie, *British & Foreign Harbours*, i (1854), 100.
[26] London Directories *c.*1783–1793, e.g. Lowndes and Kent, list Samuel Wyatt as a coal-merchant.

The project grew directly out of Samuel's friendship with Matthew Boulton and James Watt (Boulton's new partner). In 1781 Watt took out a patent for five different mechanisms for producing circular motion. This enabled the steam-engine to be harnessed for the first time to a mill for grinding corn. Samuel tried but was unable to interest such bodies as the Victualling Office in his friend's invention. So he decided to build his own mill in London as a pioneer demonstration. He intended to show that it could be both practicable and profitable. From the business point of view the venture was a failure but architecturally and technically it was a great success.

The machinery by James Watt and John Rennie has always been famous but Samuel's structure was also of special interest. It was the first building planned to contain rotative steam-engines and its construction was a considerable engineering achievement in itself. It was the largest example of an internal timber-framed building so far attempted and foreshadowed the concept of a building where the outer walls were merely protective cladding round an internal load-bearing structural framework.[27]

The mill was distinguished by foundations of considerable engineering interest in the form of a series of inverted brick tunnel vaults. The whole of the mill foundation formed a brick raft 160 by 120 feet whereby the weight of the building was evenly distributed over the whole site. This reduced downward pressure and danger of settling. The foundation raft was sunk about 9 feet. The depth of excavation created an upward pressure equal to about half the total weight of the building. The foundation was thus partially buoyant. It is the earliest example of a partially buoyant foundation raft such as was only to become common with the widespread use of concrete in the twentieth century.[28]

Construction began in 1783 and is better documented than any other of his buildings. Many of the letters have already been published.[29] The mill was situated at the south-east end of Blackfriars Bridge. The exterior was a more elegant version of the large classical warehouses of the period and gave no hint of the constructional ingenuities which it concealed. The total cost was £16,769 19s 7d. The mill was working by March 1786 when there was an official opening attended by, among others, Sir Joseph Banks, Henry Cavendish, Lord Penrhyn, and Josiah Wedgwood.[30]

Samuel Wyatt superintended the business side of the mill himself. James Watt wanted this done by a professional business man and had suggested a Mr.

---

[27] Erich Roll, *An Early Experiment in Industrial Organisation* (1930), 110.
[28] A.W. Skempton, 'The Albion Mill Foundations', *Geotechnique*, xxi (1971), 203–10.
[29] A.W. Skempton, 'Samuel Wyatt and the Albion Mill', *Architectural History*, xiv (1971), 53–73.
[30] BRL, Boulton & Watt Coll., Box 36; O. A. Westworth, 'The Albion Steam Flour Mill', *Economic History*, ii (1930), 33.

Jeffries of Kidderminster. Samuel, however, wanted to manage the mill just as he had built it and this was agreed. But there were endless difficulties. Sometimes Malcolm Logan, who maintained the engine, would turn up late 'drunk as any lord' and complain that 'the devil was in the engine'. Even more difficult to control was John Rennie, then working on the mill's second engine. Full of the arrogance of youth and genius he resented Samuel's protective fussing and meddling in matters which Rennie felt himself better qualified to deal with. In June 1786 he wrote to Watt complaining of 'Mr. Wyatt's strange overbearing disposition and his interference in matters he is by no means a judge of'. Fortunately, Watt was able to prevent Rennie's personal animosity from interfering with progress of the mill.[31]

Contrary to expectations the mill did not make a profit. The accounts usually showed a loss or at best broke even. Samuel remained unshakeably optimistic but Watt was more realistic. After inspecting the accounts for the last quarter of 1789 he wrote: 'let us always know the extent of our hopes and not wilfullfully deceive ourselves'. The preparations for war with Revolutionary France raised fresh hope of large orders from the Victualling Office. Watt hoped that it might prove possible to sell the mill itself to the Victualling Office, 'and thereby get ourselves all out of a concern which does not seem to promise much profit if we may judge from the past'.[32]

Deliverance of a more dreadful kind was at hand – in the early morning of 2 March 1791 the mill was totally gutted by fire. Only the Mill House escaped owing to the thickness of the walls. The fire was the most picturesque of the period. As such it was illustrated sixteen years later by Ackermann, who also supplied a gleeful description of the 'sad calamity':

'The flames burned out in so many different directions and with such incredible fury and intolerable heat that it was impossible to approach on any side till the roof and interior part of the building tumbling in completed the general conflagration in a column of fire so awfully grand as to illuminate for a while the whole horizon.'[33]

Poor Samuel was devastated by the catastrophe. The horror of the event was intensified by malicious gossip. Matthew Boulton complained to Samuel: 'I know not whether the catastrophe itself or the exaggerated paragraphs have given the most vexation.'[34] An anonymous attack in *Woodfalls' Journal* in June provoked them to reply:

The Albion Mill Company cannot think it necessary to answer anonymous writers who like assassins attack them from behind a *Bush* but when any person of respectability openly comes forward (as a man of probity always will do) they will then employ the

[31] BRL, Boulton & Watt Coll., Box 36, James Watt to Samuel Wyatt, 12 Dec. 1785; Tew MSS., Samuel Wyatt to Matthew Boulton, 1786; Boulton & Watt Coll., Box 36, John Rennie to James Watt, 28 June 1786.
[32] Boulton & Watt Coll., Box 36, James Watt to Samuel Wyatt, 3 Dec. 1789; 11 May, 22 Aug. 1790.
[33] R. Ackermann, *Microcosm of London,* ii (1808), 3643.
[34] BRL, Tew MSS., Matthew Boulton to Samuel Wyatt, 14 Mar. 1791.

II Doddington Hall, Cheshire, Saloon *facing p.*46

proper means to defend themselves. In the meantime they must consider those who so industriously labour to inflame the minds of the public against a fallen establishment as justly meriting to be ranked in the same class with the malicious incendiaries who set it on fire.[35]

The destruction of the mill was not the work of incendiaries but was caused by overheating of part of the engine. Fortunately, it was insured with various companies for a total of £41,000.[36] The tedious business of negotiating with them and deciding what to do with the burnt-out premises fell to Samuel. It occupied much of his time and gave rise indirectly to a number of engineering projects.

He decided to take advantage of the river-side site to convert the shell into a warehouse. Warehouse space was in short supply in the 1790s because it had not been extended since the sixteenth century as a result of the system of 'legal quays'. Designated in 1588 they restricted all the commerce of the city to a mere 1,400 lineal feet of quay on the north bank of the river west of the Tower. Such restrictions were ridiculous in the late eighteenth century but proposals to abolish them were strongly opposed by vested interests in the City.[37]

Samuel's first restoration plan was to convert the shell into a tobacco warehouse for the Government. This met with heavy opposition from the legal quays. Counter-petitions were immediately lodged with the Treasury by the Vinters Company, the Society of Tacklehouse Porters, the Ticket Porters, and the Fellowship of Carmen and Lightermen, all of whom 'being concerned in the trade of the free Quays of the City' regarded the scheme as materially prejudicial to their livelihood.[38]

As a result the Treasury prevaricated. A year and a half passed without any positive decision. Boulton complained: 'This is certainly a very disagreeable business to us all and therefore it is the most desirable it should be brought to a conclusion for 'tis better we should at once be shot with a cannon ball than be pricked to Death by Treasury pins and needles.'[39]

Samuel had the most to grumble about for it was he who had to answer the interminable quibbles and attend all the committee meetings as the matter shuttled backwards and forwards between the Treasury, the Customs, and the Tobacco Office. He gradually realized that the scheme was hopeless. In July 1795, however, a bill was passed for warehousing coffee. This offered a new opportunity for disposing of the site.[40]

In August Samuel offered the ruin to the Board of Excise with plans for restoring it as a coffee warehouse. As an optional extra (costing £4,000) he

[35] Ibid., Matthew Boulton to Samuel Wyatt, 27 June 1791.
[36] H. E. Raynes, *A History of British Insurance* (1964), 196–200.
[37] G. Broadbank *A History of the Port of London,* i (1921), 75.
[38] Guildhall Library, City Land Journal, 18 May 1792.
[39] BRL, Tew MSS., Matthew Boulton to Samuel Wyatt, 9 Nov. 1792.
[40] BRL, Boulton & Watt Coll., Box 36, Samuel Wyatt to Boulton & Watt, 11 July 1795.

proposed fire-proofing it by 'Iron plating the several floors, story posts etc.' This shows he was already experimenting with fire-proof construction.[41]

His calculations for the coffee warehouse were upset by developments in the Port of London. Following the outbreak of war in 1793 anxiety at the condition of the port had resolved itself into action in the form of meetings and pamphlets. This agitation was successful largely through the leadership of Samuel Vaughan, a Director of the Royal Exchange Assurance Company, and led to proposals for completely new docks and warehouses down-river to the east of the Tower. Such a scheme obviously reduced the value of sites up-river west of the obstructive old London Bridge.

Samuel decided that in the circumstances he ought to design new docks for the favoured site on the Isle of Dogs without any warehouses at all. Thus he entered the struggle over the future of the docks in the guise of civil engineer. He published a pamphlet, of which no copy survives, laying out his proposals. He expounded his views to anybody who would listen. Farington noted a typical instance; 'Dance and I called in to look at his designs for new docks and warehouses. Saml. Wyatt was there. He contends for the liberty of the wharfs for landing goods being allowed wherever a person possessing a certain portion of land on the banks of the River will them. This would extend the general convenience and greatly add to the respectable appearance of the banks of the river.'[42]

Early in 1796 a parliamentary committee was set up to report on the docks. Samuel submitted an ambitious plan for a complex of three parallel docks at the Isle of Dogs without any warehouses or even wharfs. He intended that ships in the docks should be loaded from lighters and all merchandise stored up-river in private warehouses. The only problem lay in assessing customs duty in a dock without a quay. Samuel and Matthew Boulton went to ingenious lengths to overcome the problem. They devised a 'floating wharf' equipped with a special weighing-machine constructed by Boulton at a cost of £50. It was based on those used on canals in the Midlands.[43]

The wharf was intended to draw up between the ship and waiting lighter so that all goods would be first transferred to it and 'each article . . . weighed or gauged and the duties immediately ascertained'. The goods would then be transferred to a lighter and ferried up-river. It was a practicable but inconvenient proposal. The Customs Commissioners considered that 'such a complete and wide departure from the ancient and approved mode of raising the revenue of customs is . . . inconsistent with and . . . over-turns the whole

---

[41] PRO, MR 98 and MPD124; BRL, Boulton & Watt Coll., Box 36, Samuel Wyatt to Matthew Boulton, 16 Nov. 1795.

[42] Broadbank, 76; BRL, Tew MSS., Matthew Boulton to Samuel Wyatt, 10 Sept. 1795; Farington, 21 Feb. 1796.

[43] Parliamentary Papers, Reports of House of Commons 1792–1802, XIV, 267–335; PRO, MPD40, S. Wyatt's plans for docks.

31. London, Albion Mill, on fire. Designed by Samuel Wyatt, 1784–6. Destroyed by fire 1791.

32. Tatton Park, Cheshire. Samuel Wyatt's design for completing the house in 1806. An example of his more monumental later style.

system of examination and control tried, established and sanctioned in this department'. So Samuel's scheme was not adopted.[44]

Having heard all the evidence Parliament resolved in 1799 to build new docks and warehouses at the Isle of Dogs. Sir John Call, one of the shareholders of the Albion Mill Company, passed on the bad news: 'Wet Docks at the Isle of Dogs are resolved on and it is reported that warehouses are also to be built there. Should such a plan take place the banks of the Thames especially above London Bridge will lose much of their value, so that our property seems on all occasions to experience depreciations.' Samuel's ingenious attempt to defend his financial interest in the banks of the Thames had failed.[45]

His design for London Docks had two engineering postscripts – his proposals for rebuilding London Bridge and a tunnel under the Thames at Gravesend. While investigating the condition of the port the parliamentary committee concluded that the medieval London Bridge was among the chief obstacles to shipping on the river. In 1800 it produced a third report advocating the rebuilding of the bridge upon 'improved principles'. The opinions of 'several eminent artists' including Telford, Mylne, Dance, and Samuel Wyatt were sought. Most of the proposals were for stone bridges except Telford's, Wilson's, and Wyatt's which were for iron bridges.[46]

Samuel submitted a 'very elegant painted model' for a bridge 'intirely constructed of cast iron except that he proposes to build the piers of granite and to fill up the superstructure with chalk in order to prevent any concussion from the passage of carriages'. The committee did not recommend any of the designs individually but contented itself with a generalized report on the merits of stone and iron bridges. Nothing came of this immediately and it was only in the 1820s that John Rennie designed the magnificent stone structure now in the Arizona Desert.[47]

Samuel's model for an iron bridge accorded with his patent of the previous month. This proposed that hollow iron tubes be fitted together without screws to form a ribbed framework. Iron plates were to cover this and support the road surfaces. Though ingenious this method of construction would have been too complex to carry out on a large scale. It was never put into practice.[48]

The attention drawn to the Thames east of the city by the dock proposals underlined the need for improved communication between the Kent and Essex banks of the river. Because of its width a tunnel seemed the only solution. Ralph Dodd, an obscure civil engineer from Newcastle, had advocated driving a tunnel under the river from Tilbury to Gravesend in 1798. He published a

[44] Parliamentary Papers, XIV, 442–50.
[45] BRL, Boulton & Watt Coll., Box 36, Sir John Call to Boulton & Watt, 20 June 1799.
[46] Parliamentary Papers, XIV, Report on London Bridge, 28 July 1800, 543–6.
[47] Ibid.
[48] John Wyatt, (ed.), *Repertory of Arts & Manufacturers*, xiv (1801), 145. Patent No. 2410.

pamphlet entitled *Reports etc. on the proposed dry tunnel at Gravesend* and organized public meetings. He quickly got influential backing including the support of the Board of Ordnance. In September a subscription list was opened and a committee selected from supporters of the scheme. It included Lord Petre and Claude Scott, both of whom were friends and patrons of Samuel Wyatt.

The new committee was not prepared to rely entirely on Dodd's expertise and asked Samuel Wyatt to survey the area and advise on the tunnel. He made several borings to ascertain the substrata and outlined his proposals in a letter to Matthew Boulton.

You have no doubt heard of a scheme projected by a Mr. Dodd for making a Tunnell from Gravesend in Kent to Tilbury Fort. Essex and Kentish Gentlemen who have subscribed £30,000 finding Mr. Dodd so trifling and unsteady in all his reports consulted me on the subject and I have submitted a plan to them which meets with general approbation. I recommend the sinking of large wells on each side of the river to the depth of 140 feet and about 10 feet from the bottom of these wells to drive a level or sough quite across the River which will serve as a drain for the water while the great Tunnell is carrying on by fixing a steam engine in each of these wells. At least this kind of trial will show the probability of carrying the great work into execution.[49]

Dodd resented Samuel's interference. His jealousy was one of the chief reasons for the failure of the project. At first there were considerable grounds for optimism. £30,000 had been subscribed, a site chosen and an Act of Parliament passed to incorporate a company to build the tunnel.[50]

The first experimental shaft was sunk under the direction of Samuel Wyatt, Colonel Twiss (a committee member), and Mr. Ludham (a mining expert from Northamptonshire). After 41 feet the shaft filled with water and Samuel claimed that a steam-engine was necessary to pump it dry. Ralph Dodd was now acting on the principle that if he were not to become redundant he must oppose all Samuel's proposals as a matter of course. He claimed that an ordinary horse-gin would be adequate. He was allowed to try and was proved wrong. A steam-engine was ordered from Boulton & Watt and arrived in mid-1802.

On 7 July John Rennie and William Jessop, two leading members of the engineering profession, inspected the well and supported Samuel's proposals. They advised sinking the well 145 feet to reach below the water-logged strata of chalk. This was never done. Gradually the whole scheme was abandoned. In October the engine-house was destroyed by fire. Between 1803 and 1810 when the project finally died every meeting was adjourned. The incomplete shaft alone had cost over £15,000.[51]

The final stage in the Albion Mill saga is also a story of failure and

[49] BRL, Tew MSS., Samuel Wyatt to Matthew Boulton, 13 Feb. 1799.
[50] Statute 39, Geo. III, *c*.73.
[51] R. P. Cruden, *History of Gravesend* (1843), 456–65.

disappointment. In 1800 the mill company was finally terminated. Boulton and Watt were each paid £1,666 to drop out and the shell was left in Samuel's sole possession. The affairs of the mill had almost reached their lowest point but Samuel's hopes for the future were still high. He had at last successfully devised a system of fire-proof iron construction after years of experiments. He patented it in 1800 and managed to interest an influential group in rebuilding the mill to this method. This group included the fifth Duke of Bedford, the third Earl of Egremont, Sir Frederick Eden, government officials, and city aldermen. It called itself the London Flour Company.

The project was fraught with difficulties. The company proved unexpectedly independent and at the first meeting and selection of directors in August 1800 Samuel and his associates were deliberately not elected. The board wanted 'no person among them who cannot act independently, among which they consider most of the proprietors of the late Albion Mill'. Despite this setback the scheme proceeded for a time. Samuel ordered four steam-engines from Boulton & Watt and made designs for rebuilding the mill. These are of the greatest importance. The internal structure was to be entirely of cast iron. The outer walls were to be non-load-bearing. The second Albion Mill would therefore have been the first building with an independent internal load-bearing structure. It was also the most advanced multi-storeyed iron structure so far devised. These revolutionary plans were never executed. On the death of the Duke of Bedford in 1802 the London Flour Company folded up.[52]

The street-front of the mill was converted into a row of houses and by 1811 the area behind was a timber-yard. John Rennie built a workshop on part of the site. Appropriately it was from here that he carried out his business as a mechanical engineer throughout his life. The site of the mill was finally obliterated by the Dover and Chatham Railway in the mid-nineteenth century.[53]

The Albion Mill included a house on the corner of Blackfriars Bridge with a splendid view of St. Paul's and the spires of the City. Samuel moved into it in 1798. Berwick Street was kept on as the office from where his business was run. His pupils lived there and exhibited designs at the Royal Academy from that address. They formed his drawing office under his chief clerk, John Harvey, who may have been a relation of the Wyatts. He came from Stafford and William Wyatt had married a Mary Harvey.

As well as his drawing office Samuel also had a permanent force of slaters and carpenters under a foreman, William Oldroyd. The total number of people employed by him was between twenty and thirty. At the time of the famous

---

[52] BRL, Boulton & Watt Coll., Box 36, Samuel Wyatt to Boulton & Watt, 20 Dec. 1799; John Rennie to Matthew Boulton, 2 Sept. 1800; A. W. Skempton, 'Samuel Wyatt & the Albion Mill', *Architectural History*, xiv (1971), 68.
[53] S. Smiles, *Lives of the Engineers*, ii (1862), 141.

Westminster election in 1796 he told Farington that he had formerly carried 30 votes 'and thought he could now carry 20'.[54]

In addition to his building yard in Berwick Street, between 1782 and 1794 he had another at St. Katherine's Docks. In them he kept stocks of timber and slate for his own use and to supply to others. His building business was the most profitable of his activities. An indication of its scale is that from 1796 to 1807 he was able to carry a debt of £30,000 owing to him for his carpentry at the Office of Works.[55]

In 1803 he gave up Berwick Street. It was converted into two dwellings. The building business was transferred to a new yard on the site of the Albion Mill. At the same time his architectural office was transferred to Surrey Street, off the Strand. This was more convenient for it was on the route between Chelsea and Blackfriars.

At the time of the move John Harvey was succeeded as chief clerk by Noah Siddons. Siddons was an old employee; originally a carpenter, he had proved a reliable draughtsman and business man. In 1783 he witnessed Samuel's will. John Harvey set up independently as an architect at 62 Berwick Street but his career was damaged by his inability to deal satisfactorily with the failing foundations of the Millbank Penitentiary in 1813.[56]

Though a distinguished architect Samuel never became a member of the Royal Academy. This was probably due to lack of interest. He found the company of engineers and scientists more congenial than that of his fellow architects and artists. Among his personal friends were only few artists but many industrialists and inventors, including Matthew Boulton, James Watt, Thomas Williams (the inventor of a new method of smelting copper), and Sir John Call (a military engineer). His scientific and engineering bent is suggested by the societies of which he was a member – the Smeatonian Society of Civil Engineers and the Royal Society of Arts. Though not a member, he frequently dined with the Lunar Society in Birmingham at Matthew Boulton's invitation.[57]

In 1780 Samuel's elder brother William II died, leaving a four-year-old daughter, Louisa Ann. Samuel, who was childless, adopted her and brought her up. Her name often appears in his letters to Boulton for Louisa was the same age as Boulton's daughter. They were friends and Louisa often stayed at Soho. In 1798 she married the Revd. Thomas Cobb of Lydd. He later became rector of Ightham and the couple settled in Kent. After Thomas Cobb's death Louisa remarried, Admiral Robert Lambert.[58]

[54] Farington, 27 May 1796.   [55] London Directories 1782–1794; *King's Works,* 97, 98.
[56] *L.S.* xxxi (1963), 233; PRO, Prof. 11. 1457. 162, Samuel Wyatt's Will; Colvin, 271.
[57] Minutes of the Smeatonian Society, 29 May 1781; Minutes of R.S.A., 9 Apr. 1788 (Ex info Professor A. W. Skempton.); BRL, Tew MSS., Matthew Boulton to Samuel Wyatt, 12 July 1791.
[58] Coll. Capt. John Wyatt, T. H. Wyatt II's Family Notes (MS.).

Samuel was a cheerful and optimistic man. Even the endless bureaucratic procrastination and continuous disappointments over the Albion Mill did not depress him unduly. His optimism and his unquestioning faith in the benefits of new techniques and materials seem naïve. He was, however, typical of his generation. Lord Penrhyn and Horace Walpole, for instance, hoped that the steam-engine would lead to the abolition of slavery in the West Indies. The bad side-effects on conditions of employment and on the environment of industrial development and scientific discovery were not to be apparent until much later.

Samuel was a loyal and jolly friend. He was on good terms with many of his architectural contemporaries. Humphrey Repton who quarrelled so furiously with John Nash was on the best of terms with Samuel Wyatt. In his 'Red Books' Repton always refers to him as 'my friend Mr. S. Wyatt'.

Samuel's relations with his clients were equally happy. Sir Thomas Broughton of Doddington, for instance, considered it 'one of the happiest circumstances' that he employed 'an architect who whilst he had paid every proper regard to elegance and embellishment has in no respect neglected the important considerations of solidarity, utility and convenience'. Samuel considered Thomas Coke of Holkham a great friend and thought highly of him. He was also on terms of intimacy with the Marquess Cornwallis for whom he designed Culford. This contrasts with James Wyatt who, though intimate with some of his clients, was on far from good professional terms with many of them.[59]

Samuel was a much more efficient architect and a more competent administrator than James. The best description of him at work is in a letter from the Revd. William Palgrave to William Weddell about Samuel's remodelling of 6 Upper Brook Street:

I stayed just a week in Town, with Mr. Auditor in Curzon Street, & took the opportunity of going with the *Chip* to see your rising glories in Brook Street. They are getting forward fast. The Cornice in the Drawing Room *comes out* most beautifully but the Trunk ceiling in the other room! Oh! no words can describe, no fancy paint the striking effect that will be produced from taste, beauty and elegance, so happily united to set the astonished World at gaze!

And then the *Chip,* the *wonder-working Chip* shewed me his *unfinished members* and design for filling up the niches on each side of the door. I must think his natural powers of genius and fancy seem to *dilate* and *enlarge* themselves with more freedom and energy under Mrs. Weddell's encouragement than under the cold hand of Lady Flemming. *Jack,* and the *Money Begum* must hide their diminished heads, nor their sattins, nor their Sandalwood, nor even the *Dowager Lady Aylsford,* will be able to support them.

You have seen, I conclude, the *Chip's* new invented design for lighting the staircase.

[59] Richardson, 18; Farington, 27 May 1796.

A fanciful *Machine* that pours forth such a blaze of glory, that the Sun in its Meridian splendor will shew to it but as a *rush light*.[60]

Samuel Wyatt was an astute business man. In the Hardwicke correspondence concerning 3 St. James's Square he is described as being 'as cunning as a fox'. He amassed a considerable fortune despite the failure of the Albion Mill project. Farington, in his diary, muddled him with the rich builder George Wyatt (no relation) whose fortune passed to Soane. To be rich was one of his ambitions; in 1785 he wrote to Boulton: 'It is not an easy matter to obtain reputation and get rich at the same time.'[61]

His health was good throughout his life and he was fully active until his death. The burning of the Albion Mill, however, was a great blow. Farington noted 'Samuel Wyatt is almost 59 years old [in fact he was 58]. He had remarkable strong eye-sight but never has been able to work without glasses since the time when the Albion Mills were burnt. The shock he felt at that time had so great an effect on his nerves.' The destruction of the mill affected him as would the death of a friend or near relation. It was a month before he could bring himself to reply to Boulton's first letter of sympathy. Then he wrote: 'Owing to the great variety of objects that occupy my mind every day I am probably diverted from reflecting so much upon the chaos of our poor mill which alas is no more – yet I cannot help declaring that at Times I am ready to sink with the loss of it.' Towards the end of his life he was troubled on occasion by gout. In April 1805, for instance, he excused himself for not visiting Boulton and Watt on the grounds that he was suffering from a 'fit of gout'.[62]

The years between 1800 and 1807 saw no relaxation in his activity. There was even a change in his architectural style after 1800. His buildings (particularly Tatton, Hackwood, and Digswell), became plainer and more monumental, foreshadowing the rather anonymous grandeur of the work of his nephew Jeffry Wyatville. He continued designing until his death and he left a number of works incomplete such as the Headmaster's House at Rugby School, and Tatton, Hackwood, and Panshanger among his country houses.

He literally died in his boots. Farington describes the sad event: 'Samuel Wyatt, brother to James Wyatt, was very well on Saturday last and with his workmen in his state yard. On Sunday he was to have gone out of Town to the Honble Mr. Cowper's [Digswell, Hertfordshire] for whom he was building. He was pulling on his boots when he was suddenly struck with an apoplexy and died that evening.' He was buried in the graveyard of the Royal Hospital at Chelsea.[63]

[60] Leeds City Library, Ramsden MSS., vol. 3b 142, Revd. William Palgrave to Wm. Weddell, 8 Nov. 1789 (ex info Mr. P. A. Bezodis).
[61] Farington, 10 Oct. 1794; BRL, Boulton & Watt Coll., Box 36, Samuel Wyatt to Matthew Boulton, 1785.
[62] Farington, 28 July 1795; BRL, Tew MSS., Samuel Wyatt to Matthew Boulton, 19 Apr. 1791; 27 Apr. 1805.
[63] Farington, 13 Feb. 1807.

CHAPTER III

James Wyatt (1746–1813)

Wyatt, the Destroyer

James Wyatt's sudden fame at the age of twenty-six quickly brought him other commissions. Praise for the Pantheon was unanimous but the work that followed was subject to violently varying opinions. Some of those who were against it were doubtless irritated by his easy and early success. Horace Walpole remained enthusiastic, describing later buildings as 'the invention of a genius' and 'the most perfect thing I ever saw'. But there were others, including the bitter antiquarian John Carter, whose denigration is responsible for the legend of 'Wyatt, the Destroyer'. A. W. Pugin, writing after James Wyatt's death, put the extreme case against him: 'This monster of architectural depravity – this pest of cathedral architecture. Horror! Dismay! The villain Wyatt had been here, the west front was his. Need I say more? No! All that is vile, cunning and rascally is included in the term Wyatt.'

It is almost impossible to find a balanced view even among modern writers. Eastlake in his history of the Gothic revival is the fairest but he too fell far short of full appreciation.

No English architect has perhaps been so much overrated by his friends or so unfairly abused by his enemies ... neither his admirers nor his maligners have done him thorough justice. Raised by private interest and the caprice of public taste to be the fashionable architect of his day – loaded with commissions from every quarter ... it is no wonder that this highly favoured and fortunate gentleman not only believed himself to be a great architect, but induced the world to think so too.[1]

In Italy the fourteen-year-old James Wyatt studied architecture with enterprising thoroughness. He drew crowds of admiring Italians in St. Peter's and the Pantheon by the daring with which he made measured drawings of both those buildings lying on his back on a ladder slung horizontally under the dome with nothing to catch him if he fell.

In Rome he was attracted more by the remains of antiquity than the great sixteenth- and seventeenth-century buildings. He later told Farington that he thought St. Peter's 'bad architecture – it is divided into little parts. It is the size which makes it striking. – There is no good modern architecture in Rome – the best specimens are by Raphael. – That of Michael Angelo is very bad.' He was impressed, however, by the buildings of Palladio.[2] This anti-baroque taste is

[1] J. M. Crook (ed.), *Eastlake's Gothic Revival* (1970), 93.
[2] Farington, 7 Nov. 1797.

33. James Wyatt. Attributed to Matthew Cotes Wyatt.

typical of his generation. The Adam brothers were equally disparaging about 'modern' Italian architecture and even included the generally admired works of Palladio in their dismissal of all they saw.

In Venice James studied under Antonio Visentini, the artist and friend of Consul Smith. He made remarkable progress, especially in architectural painting, and his works were even claimed to rival those of Pannini. 'His talents in architecture, painting and music were so equally developed that it was only his preference for the first which decided his career', wrote an obituarist.[3]

Curiously, none of his Pannini-like paintings has survived though he is known to have kept pictures by his painting-master, Visentini.[4] While staying at Smith's house in Venice he was introduced to Richard Dalton, Librarian to George III, who was negotiating the purchase of Smith's collection for the King. Dalton and Wyatt remained lifelong friends. It was almost certainly as a result of this friendship that James was introduced later to the royal family, an event which was to have so much influence, both for good and bad, on his career.

The Pantheon started a craze for James similar to that stimulated now by a new pop group. The startled Peter Pindar commented:

> I know the foolish kingdom all runs riot,
> Calling Aloud for Wyat, Wyat, Wyat,
> Who on their good opinion hourly gains,
> But where lies Wyat's merit? . . . Where his praise?
> Abroad the roving man spent half his days,
> Contemplating of Rome the great remains.

This enthusiasm continued for a number of years during which the Pantheon was the building most admired by the fashionable world. But by the time of its destruction by fire on 14 January 1792 the novelty had worn off.

As a place of public entertainment the Pantheon placed its architect before the whole of fashionable London. No other young English architect has had such good fortune with one of his first buildings. But as so often in this interlocking family, James's success would not have been possible without the practical experience of his two elder brothers. In 1770, on the strength of the design for the Pantheon which was exhibited in that year, James was elected an associate of the Royal Academy at the astonishingly early age of twenty-four (he became a fully fledged Academician in 1785).

Among his admirers were the Dukes of Northumberland and Richmond and it may be that the unexecuted design for a house in Sussex in the R.I.B.A. Drawings Collection was produced for the latter. In the possession of the Duke

---

[3] *The Monthly Mag.*, Sept. 1813; *Gent's Mag.* (1813), ii, 296–7.
[4] Farington, 8 July 1798.

III   Brocklesby, Lincolnshire, Mausoleum *facing p.*58

of Northumberland are various unrealized drawings by James for stucco decoration in the loggia at Syon which date from this time. Probably they were commissioned in order to have specimens of the architect's skill and to encourage him, rather than with any serious intention of carrying into effect the work concerned.

Another of James's admirers was the Russian ambassador. He was empowered by Catherine the Great to offer James any salary he asked if he would go to St. Petersburg to be her architect.[5] The fear that he might never be allowed out of Russia again deterred him and Charles Cameron became Catherine's architect instead. The very threat of losing James, however, was enough to cause several English noblemen to club together to pay him a retaining fee of £1,200 to act as their architectural adviser.

James instantly supplanted Robert Adam as the most fashionable architect of the day. Adam deeply resented this easy success, particularly as he had had to work so hard at establishing himself in London ten years before. Adam was paranoiac not only about the success of James but of all the Wyatts from the moment they emerged as major architects. When the Pantheon was under construction he thought that Samuel Wyatt was becoming too grand to speak to him.[6] This was entirely imaginary. What particularly angered Adam was the feeling that the Wyatts' success was partly due to their knowledge of his designs for Kedleston. He continually accused them of plagiarism. Horace Walpole interpreted the foreword of Adam's *Works in Architecture* (which came out in 1773) as a veiled attack on the Wyatts but added that James Wyatt used the antique with more taste than Adam in any case.[7] Adam went so far as to tell George III that James Wyatt had been his clerk and had stolen his drawings in order to use the ideas in his own work. This was not quite true. It was Samuel, not James, who had been clerk of works at Kedleston and it was his acquaintance with Adam's designs for that house which may well have stimulated the early Wyatt style. Perhaps Adam would not have been so eager to contrive the downfall of 'Mr. Swann the Great' if he had been able to foresee the eventual outcome. In any case Adam's insinuations had very little effect upon the triumphal progress of James Wyatt's early career.

From the start James was subjected, on the one hand, to the boundlessly enthusiastic admiration of the fashionable world and, on the other, to the jealous sniping of slighted rivals. This dichotomy persisted throughout his life, culminating in the virulent personal attacks of John Carter. Carter wrote no fewer than 212 letters to the *Gentleman's Magazine* denouncing Wyatt and his works. These in turn were to contribute to Pugin's view of 'Wyatt, the

[5] T. F. Hunt, *Archittetura Campestre* (1827), xiii–xvi.
[6] Kedleston, Curzon MSS., R. Adam to Lord Scarsdale, 7 and 27 Dec. 1769.
[7] H. Walpole to Revd. William Mason, 29 July 1773, J. Mitford (ed.), *Correspondence of Horace Walpole and the Revd. W. Mason*, 2 vols., 1851).

Destroyer' which has lasted to the present.

One of the reasons for the lack of balance in popular judgement of James Wyatt is that, with the exception of Horace Walpole, those of his contemporaries who admired him were not such articulate writers as those who denigrated him. This has affected our view of his character and achievement. It is the picturesque denunciations of disappointed clients, such as Beckford, or jealous rivals, like Carter, which stuck.

Modern writers have criticized James mainly for lack of consistency in his architecture. 'The Wyatt *œuvre* is a puzzle and leaves one asking what was the real, the personal Wyatt? Was there in this various variable conscienceless artist any such thing?'[8] In fact his genius as a designer lies in the opposite qualities, in the range and variety of his work. He was the first great English architect who thought that all styles were more or less equally valid. His choice was associational and depended on the setting and function of a particular building. In his eclecticism James was no less sophisticated than the architect who believes in the absolute 'truth' of one established style. Variety is no less honourable as an artistic ideal than uniformity. His eclecticism foreshadowed nineteenth- and twentieth-century attitudes. That is what makes him historically so important. He was not, however, entirely alone in the late eighteenth century; the architecture of his friend S. P. Cockerell, for instance, was equally varied.

James Wyatt's eclecticism is less superficial than is generally believed. He was inspired by more than a wish to keep abreast of fashion. 'Grecian must be Grecian – but fancies – such as Gothic, Moorish, Chinese Etc. might be imitated – some of them [are] capable of being reduced to rules.'[9] That he considered styles other than classical capable of being reduced to rules shows that he took them seriously. Another sign that his eclecticism was sincere is that his own house had interiors in various styles.

When he was asked to erect a column to the memory of the Chief Justice, Sir Edward Coke, at Stoke Poges he suggested that it should be 'agreeable to the Architecture of that day – something like the designs of Inigo Jones before he went to Italy – a mixture of Gothic and Roman manners'.[10] This was a remarkably early argument for reviving Jacobean architecture. The client, however, was not convinced and the monument as built was a simple Doric column.

The tower he designed on Broadway Hill for Lord Coventry is neo-Norman, or, as he called it, 'Saxon'. Some of the interiors remodelled at Windsor continued the baroque style of the Caroline originals with painted ceilings and 'Grinling Gibbons' carvings. Though he used 'the antique' with more taste

[8] John Summerson, 'James Wyatt', *New Statesman* (29 July 1950), 128.
[9] Farington, 24 Mar. 1798.
[10] Ibid., 8 Dec. 1798.

34. Broadway Tower,
Worcestershire. Designed by James
Wyatt 1794 in the 'Saxon' style.

35. Dodington Hall,
Gloucestershire. Designed by
James Wyatt, 1798–1813.
Staircase. An example of his Roman
style.

36. Doddington, Gloucestershire, Bath Lodge. A design influenced by C. N. Ledoux.

37. Sheffield Park, Sussex, Staircase. an early example of Wyatt Gothic.

than Adam himself this was only one facet of his classical work. As well as the pretty Adamesque style of his early buildings and many of his interiors, there is the academic neo-classicism, inspired by Sir William Chambers, of his noblest work such as the mausoleums at Cobham and Brocklesby; the heavy Roman style of the Downing College design, Liverpool Town Hall, and Dodington; the neo-Greek of Sandhurst and Stoke Park. He was also aware of the work of his Continental contemporaries. The Bath Lodge at Dodington, for instance was influenced by a design of Ledoux. The vast octagonal scheme for enlarging Goodwood was not far removed from the megalomania of the French neo-classicists.

His remark that 'there had been no regular architecture since Sir William Chambers – that when he came from Italy he found public taste corrupted by the Adams and he was obliged to comply with it' is often quoted as being architectural hypocrisy.[11] It could mean no more than that he thought the Adam style had been used too widely. It was good enough for drawing-rooms, which is where he chiefly used it, but other styles were better for exteriors. Like many generalized statements it was not entirely true. The Adam brothers had not inhibited him much. He worked in various styles, gothic as well as classical, from the start. The Great Hall at Beaudesert was gothic as early as 1772 – it had a quadripartite plaster vault and ogee-arched doorways.

Accomplished though his classical works were, Gothic was his favourite style. 'His genius revived in this country the long forgotten beauties of Gothic Architecture . . . Pre-eminently and indeed without a rival did he, and for the longest period of his professional life, indulge in this his favourite order.'[12] He played a significant role in the history of the Gothic revival in England. He came mid-way between the rococo freedom of buildings like Strawberry Hill and the more archæological correctness of the nineteenth century.

James Wyatt's Gothic work was distinguished for two particular qualities – its detail and its massing. The detail of his mature Gothic work was remarkably accurate and was usually adapted from well-known ecclesiastical sources, as can be seen clearly at Ashridge. His Gothic compositions showed a flair for the arrangement of asymmetrical parts to form a picturesque whole. 'His strength was very great in that most architectural of processes the composition of masses, in which he may be considered almost a second Vanbrugh.'[13]

The supreme example of picturesque asymmetrical composition was Fonthill Abbey. It is sometimes considered a sublime freak unequalled in James's work. This is not so. Lee Priory had the same octagonal core, derived from Batalha in

[11] Ibid., 4 Jan. 1804.
[12] *Gent's Mag.* (1813), ii, 297.
[13] H. Goodhart-Rendel, quoted in Crook (ed.), 52.

38. Ashridge, Hertfordshire. Designed by James Wyatt, 1808–13. Fan vault over the Great Staircase. Plasterwork by Francis Bernasconi.

39. Ashridge, Hertfordshire, Chapel. Designed by James Wyatt. Completed by Jeffry Wyatville. Stalls carved by Edward Wyatt.

Portugal, and radiating wings. Fonthill merely developed the Lee Priory concept to its ultimate possibilities and beyond. Sheffield Park, one of the earliest Gothic houses, dating from 1776, had been partly asymmetrical though the detail was still rococo, particularly the exceptionally pretty staircase.

When well sited, as at Belvoir, James's castellated and Gothic houses are spectacular. Architecturally among the most interesting of them were Norris Castle (1799) and Pennsylvania Castle (1800) which demonstrate his flair for asymmetrical massing without relying on historicist detailing. Not all his Gothic work was so successful. His additions to Wilton, for instance, however good in themselves, showed too much enthusiasm for its history as a medieval abbey and too little concern for its importance as the *locus classicus* of English Renaissance architecture. His remodelling of the House of Lords at a cost of over £200,000 was disastrous. The brick and stucco battlements, cast-iron window-frames, and lath and plaster oriels pleased nobody. John Carter called it an 'august pile of brickbats and stucco'. George Dance II thought it displayed 'beastly . . . bad taste'. Others said it looked like a cotton mill or a gentlemen's lavatory.[14]

The cathedral restorations were more controversial still. Even if some of the vandalism attributed to him was perpetrated by other hands it cannot be denied that he was responsible for many 'improvements' which show a lack of feeling for the historical integrity of a building. However spectacular his proposals for adding a spire to Durham Cathedral or for re-using Bishop Neville's reredos as a rood-screen to support the organ, they were indefensible historically and it is fortunate that they were not executed.

It is impossible to agree that his scheme for enlarging the quadrangle at Magdalen College, Oxford would have been 'perfectly consonant with the Hall Chapel and Tower . . . [and] have a good effect'.[15] The destruction of the medieval wall-paintings in St. Stephen's Chapel at Westminster in order to accommodate a few extra benches for Irish Members of Parliament is unforgivable.

On the other hand, his restoration of Henry VII's Chapel, begun in 1809, was exemplary in its careful reproduction of old masonry detail but much of the credit for that is due to Gayfere, the mason. Nevertheless, it is a milestone in the development of modern restoration techniques. His tidying-up at Salisbury was largely responsible for the perfectly unified effect of that building both inside and out. Prince Pückler-Muskau was typical of the majority view when he wrote enthusiastically about James's work at Salisbury.

[14] *King's Works,* 514–9.
[15] Oxford, Magdalen College MSS., James Wyatt to Dr. Routh, Apr. 1795.

The exterior is peculiarly distinguished by an air of newness and neatness, and by the perfection of its details. For this it is indebted to two grand repairs which in the course of time it has undergone; the first under the superintendance of Sir Christopher Wren; the second of Mr. Wyatt ... It stands like a model, perfectly free and isolated on a smooth-shaven plain of short turf ... The interior of this magnificent temple is in the highest degree inspiring, and has been improved by Wyatt's genius. It was an admirable idea to remove the most remarkable old monuments from the walls and obscure corners and to place them in the space between the great double avenues of pillars ... Nothing can have a finer effect than these rows of Gothic sarcophagi.[16]

Despite his large number of public commissions James was pre-eminently a country house architect. He was not greatly interested in London houses and after 1780 designed few there. But for over forty years he directed the lion's share of country house work in England. His houses vary greatly from the major mansions such as Heaton, Heveningham, and Dodington to minor additions, entrance-lodges, and interior decoration as at Blagdon.

As well as the well-known great houses he designed an infinite number of smaller houses in different styles. They range from the crisply classical Aston Hall (Shropshire) to the toy-fort Gothic of Lasborough Park (Gloucestershire). On the whole his classical houses are of two principal types: the self-contained cube or rectangle of villa form such as Bowden and an adaptation of the Palladian plan for a great house with a central block and flanking wings as at Heaton, Castle Coole, and Roundway Park.

The criticism of contemporaries was aimed more at James's character than his work. It was generally agreed that he had four major professional faults: lack of business acumen; an incapacity for consistent application; chronic unpunctuality; and complete irresponsibility. This combination would have been disastrous even if he had been merely a private architect but he was also the holder of the most important public architectural posts in the country.

In 1776 he succeeded Henry Keene as Surveyor to the Fabric of Westminster Abbey. In 1782 he became Architect to the Board of Ordnance. In 1796 he was appointed Surveyor-General and Comptroller of the Office of Works in succession to Sir William Chambers. He was also Deputy Surveyor of the Office of Woods and Forests, Surveyor to Somerset House, and Honorary Architect to the Middlesex Hospital.[17]

To have coped with these as well as his vast architectural practice would have required an administrative genius with an unusual capacity for delegation. James, however, hardly bothered at all about his official functions. The results were often a calamity, particularly in the Office of Works. In fairness to James it must be said that he did not seek any of these posts. Unlike his sons he never needed to intrigue for positions. The post of Surveyor-General was

---

[16] Prince Pückler-Muskau, *Tours in England* (4 vols., 1832), ii. 226–7.
[17] Westminster Abbey MSS.; *King's Works,* 47; Middlesex Hospital MSS., Minute Book.

40. Pennsylvania Castle, Dorset. Designed by James Wyatt, 1800. An asymmetrical Gothic composition.

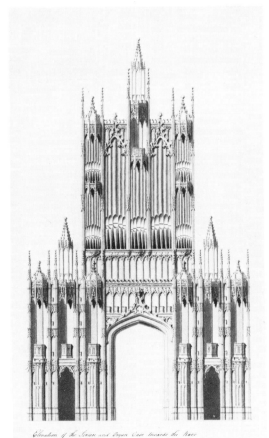

Elevation of the Screen and Organ Case towards the Nave
Durham Cathedral

41. Durham Cathedral. Unexecuted design by James Wyatt for a new organ-case and rood screen to be constructed out of the Neville reredos.

42. Heaton Hall, Lancashire,
Cupola Room. Designed by
James Wyatt, 1772.
Decorated by Biagio Rebecca.

43. Heaton Hall, Lancashire,
ceiling of the Cupola Room.

offered to him by the King partly because he did not ask for it, partly as a recompense for the time and trouble taken over Frogmore, and partly because the King considered him to be 'the first Architect of the Kingdom' – and therefore the most proper person for the position.[18]

The historian of the Office of Works has written that James's appointment as Surveyor-General 'inaugurated a period of extravagance and confusion . . . His absenteeism began as occasional and ended up as habitual desertion'.[19] Between 1796 and 1806 he attended only 303 out of 558 meetings of the administrative board of the Office of Works. In 1807 he was absent for fifty successive weeks and from 1808 to 1810 he attended only 38 out of 183 meetings. He occupied his room at Whitehall so infrequently that one of his clerks told John Bacon that a cleaning woman ran a girls' school there, hastily disbanding her class on the rare occasions when the Surveyor came in.[20] James never gave reasons for missing meetings or for his unpunctuality. Business was performed intermittently when he was in London. Otherwise vague instructions were sent from wherever he happened to be working at the time. After 1800 he was most likely to be found at Windsor directing the Gothic reconstruction of the State Apartments for George III, so soon to be magnificently obliterated by Wyatville.

Nor when he was absent did he always bother to read letters sent on to him begging for directions or drawings. C. R. Cockerell describes how he 'would stay six weeks [at Dodington] contriving his drawings, his letters remaining unopened. When recommended to do so, would say, no they can wait.' On one occasion in 1807 the Works minutes break off when James was asked to return some important official letters. They arrived after his death seven years later. At Kensington Palace the Duke of Kent's apartments 'crumbled away with dry rot' waiting for James to write the necessary report on their condition and specify what work was needed to put them in order.[21]

Perhaps the main casualty of James's neglect was the financial accounts. In a time of soaring expenditure, caused by both the extravagance of George III and rising building costs in wartime, the accounts needed regular checking and tight control. This they never received. James's prolonged absences threw the whole system into confusion. Many employees did as they pleased – one went on holiday to the seaside and stayed away for three years. Unpaid bills piled up on all sides. When James did oversee the accounts it was in the most perfunctory manner and he once certified a bill that contained an error of £2,000 in the tradesman's favour. His estimates for work to be done were

---

[18] Farington, 7 June 1793.
[19] *King's Works*, 49, 50.
[20] John Bacon (Junior), Reminiscences (MS.). Copy in the possession of Mr. Timothy Clifford.
[21] John Harris, 'Cockerell's Iconographica Domestica', *AH* 14 (1971); *King's Works*, 50.

equally slapdash. That for the restoration of the Banqueting House, for instance, was exceeded by 250 per cent.[22]

James's attitude to the accounts which were his responsibility is indicated in a letter of 2 December 1804 showing favour to his son Matthew Cotes Wyatt: 'Copy the enclosed and send to Mr. Craig. Write to Mr. Crocker and say that I told you he was to put you down for an advance of your painting £250 – the same as Mr. Rigaud. Do this immediately as I believe the Windsor accounts will be brought into the office on Friday next. P.S. I beg you will not think of going to town in your Buggy but take a post chaise.'[23]

Another example of James's haphazard working methods is in a letter to Matthew Cotes Wyatt at Windsor from Fonthill on 10 October 1806:

I have had a letter from Barker who I find is at Windsor and in want of a Frogmore measuring which is in one of the Drawers but whether in the mahogany table drawer or in the upper drawer of the Commode which stands in the large room over the gateway I cannot tell but your key unlocks the commode, the other is *quite* a common lock. I am pretty sure you will find it in one of these drawers, but if not it must be in one of the Deal Tables, it is a green covered book to the best of my recollection.[24]

It is not known whether Matthew Cotes's random ransacking of his father's office produced the necessary document.

James Wyatt held the office of Surveyor-General for seventeen years, of which the final decade was a 'period of uninterrupted investigation and recrimination'. Serious inquiries began in 1806. James had received large sums of money from the Treasury which were unaccounted for. On the other hand, complaints from dissatisfied tradesmen were 'numerous and urgent'. His brother Samuel alone was owed £30,000 by 1807.

James's sudden death in 1813 left affairs in a state of chaos. The Office of Works was more heavily in debt than ever before and a parliamentary inquiry was initiated to disentangle the mess. The evidence this assembled led to the reform and reorganization of the office and abolition of the post of Surveyor-General in 1815. It was a convincing indictment of James's tenure of office. Jeffry Wyatville was not exaggerating when he remarked that his 'uncle's neglect had destroyed the office of works as it was'.[25]

The conduct of his private architectural practice followed a similar course. Total disaster here, too, was only averted by the valiant efforts of his sons Benjamin Dean, Charles Burton, Matthew Cotes, and Philip, and his two nephews Jeffry and Lewis. They all worked for him at different times, in addition to his several architectural pupils and his drawing office staff of four clerks under the indispensable Joseph Dixon. Dixon had been with James

---

[22] A. H. Gomme, 'By Royal Command', *T.L.S,* (26 Sept. 1975), 1109.
[23] B. L., Egerton MS. 3515.
[24] Ibid.
[25] *King's Works,* 77–100; Farington, 2 Nov. 1812.

44. Heveningham Hall, Suffolk.
Designed by James Wyatt, *c.* 1780–4.
Orangery.

45. Heveningham Hall, Suffolk,
Entrance-Hall.

46. Heveningham Hall,
Suffolk, Dining-Room.

47. Bowden Park,
Wiltshire,
Drawing-Room.

since the days of the Pantheon and acted as his principal draughtsman.

James's professional practice was enormous, the largest of any eighteenth-century architect. His total architectural output amounts to upwards of two hundred items and he travelled 4,000 miles a year on business.[26] Architectural activity on this scale would have been too much for a man far more capable of organizing his affairs than James. His poor organization caused endless maddening delays and a serious lack of supervision of his various building schemes. The central tower of Fonthill eventually collapsed because the inverted arches specified to support it were left out by the builder. A lot of the medieval stained glass at Salisbury Cathedral was thrown away accidentally as rubbish by the workmen. At Wilton all the woodwork in the new cloisters was found to be infected with dry rot; the chimneys caught fire the first time they were used; the new roof leaked and had to be almost entirely rebuilt.

It was not that James was intentionally negligent or idle but, like many artists, he worked with intermittent bursts of enthusiasm and inspiration. He spent too much time on buildings he was excited by to the detriment of the rest of his architectural practice. He continually allowed himself to be enticed into designing new schemes though unable to control the amount of work he had in hand already. This was a permanent anxiety to his sons who were desperately trying to prevent ruin. This comes out in a reply of 1806 written to Matthew Cotes after the latter had remonstrated with his father over the excessive time he had spent at Ragley:

It is perfectly true that all the concern I had at Ragley was undertaken and begun for the express accommodation of His Majesty and His Family whom Lord Hertford at the time the works were begun and for a considerable time afterwards had some reason to expect he should have been honoured with their Majesty's Company. These works were so extensive and the completion of them so necessary to the comfort of the House that, had they not been put into the state I left them by a very extraordinary exertion, the Marquis's family alone could not have inhabited the house. Of course much less would it have been in a state to receive his Royal visitor, but I had no concern in any decoration of Ragley or anything out of my own immediate line of my profession nor had I need, for that kept me very arduously employed the whole time I was there . . . I assure you I would not upon any account have entered into any new project.[27]

The instances of disappointment and anger caused to private individuals by James's methods are legion. Even at the beginning of his career he found it impossible to be punctual. A letter from Lord Ducie to William Weddell in 1776 sets the tone for the complaints which followed: 'Since our arrival we have been daily, nay hourly expecting Mr. Wyatt, but no such person [h]as yet arrived, and if he does not present himself soon, I very much doubt, whether he will gain admittance, as I cannot think, his Abilitys will sufficiently atone for his Impertinence.'[28]

[26] Farington, 20 July 1796.   [27] B.L., Egerton MS. 3515.
[28] Leeds City Library, Ramsden MSS., Lord Ducie to William Weddell, 6 Nov. 1776.

The rage of two men in particular, Lord Pembroke and William Beckford, still burns fierce across the centuries. In 1809 Farington reported that 'after Wyatt's conduct in neglecting Lord Pembroke's alterations at Wilton . . . Lord Pembroke had given him up, his patience having been exhausted'.[29] The events leading up to this breach can be reconstructed from James Wyatt's surviving replies to what were obviously furious letters from Lord Pembroke.

From 1801 to 1805 James did not visit the works at Wilton once. On 13 July 1805 he wrote,

with respect to myself My Lord, I have nothing more to offer in apology, than what I believe you are aquainted with; my confinement to a particular part of my Duty has obliged me in many instances to neglect others and I am sorry, and extremely sorry, that your Lordship is amongst that number, but if you can forgive this neglect, I will in future take care that you shall have no additional cause of complaint and I will endeavour in the course of the next fortnight to visit Wilton, if that is likely to be convenient to your Lordship.

He did not go and this invoked another angry letter from Lord Pembroke to which James replied on 4 August 1805.

I am sorry it has not been in my power to be at Wilton, within the time mentioned in your Lordship's letter . . . I am sorry you should discredit what I have offered to you in some measure as an apology as I can again in truth assert it to be the case and that I cannot admit of your Lordship's charge of neglect for five years . . . you say you have enquired and find that others in my profession, even the most remiss of them attend their works about once in a month or five weeks; I have never heared yet of such attendance . . . but even this I will engage to do if your Lordship is persuaded by the enquiries you have made that a building cannot be carried on properly without [it] – I have conducted some of the largest in this kingdom without that process and flatter myself that I can do so still, but as I am satisfied that for the last twelve or eighteen months I have not given you that attention you might expect from me I shall readily submit to your wishes in future.

James seems to have kept his word and frequently stopped at Wilton on his way to Fonthill during the following two or three years. Good relations were restored and all was quiet for the time being but then James relapsed into his old ways. This and the obvious inadequacies of the work when completed elicited from Lord Pembroke in May 1809 a final explosive letter which severed relations for ever, despite a reply from James which ran to nine sides and is his longest surviving letter:

The letter which I had the Honour to receive from your Lordship on 17th inst has equally hurt and surprised me – I could not have conceived it possible that you should have entertained the sentiments and opinions stated in that letter relative to the works at Wilton House, because I had flattered myself (and I am sure not without reason) that your Lordship as well as many of your Friends were not only highly pleased with all

[29] Farington, 22 May 1809.

48. Wilton House, Wiltshire. James Wyatt's
Gothic Entrance Front, since replaced. An
unfortunate attempt to transform the most
important seventeenth-century classical house
into a medieval abbey.

49. James Wyatt. Drawn by George Dance II.

50. Fonthill Abbey, Wiltshire. Design by James Wyatt for William Beckford, 1796–1812. Spire not executed.

51. Fonthill Abbey, Wiltshire. As executed.

that has been done there, but have frequently join'd your Lordship in expressing to a degree of astonishment their surprise at the improvements which have been made at Wilton under my direction.

The difference between us appears to be too great to admit of an easy adjustment without the intervention of some other competent person or persons who might judge fairly between us.

An interesting aspect of this correspondence is the seemingly genuine surprise with which James reacted to Lord Pembroke's outbursts and refusal to pay for the work which had dragged on for ten years.[30]

Of all James's architectural quarrels perhaps that over Fonthill Abbey is the most notorious. Between 1796 and 1813 he was almost continuously employed on the construction of that fantastic Gothic extravaganza for the homosexual recluse William Beckford. Beckford's enthusiasm for the work rapidly turned sour as James's initial energy disappeared and he proved to be elusive at the critical moments of decision-making. The combination of Beckford's impetuosity and James's absenteeism brought about the first collapse of the great tower in 1800.

Relations between the two men fluctuated violently, as is reflected in Beckford's letters. Up to 1807 all went more or less well. Beckford wrote in that year: 'The Tower and Great Octagon are being finished . . . we enjoy the spaciousness and great architectural effect of an edifice which without exaggeration does honour to the great artist who has executed it; Wyatt merits and I am sure will receive the highest praise.'

This mood was not to last for long. On 23 September Beckford complained:

It is wretched weather with fog everywhere and in this lovely sky there are no cherubim to be seen except the dwarf, the Ghoul and pale Ambrose. I can hear nothing except Mr. Wyatt lamenting like a Prime Minister at the Court of the most watery and pissful Tertian Fever. He is of a healthy cadaverousness and stinks as only those beneath ground do . . . I am condemned by cruel destiny to run a hospital and to hear nothing but the maladies of that . . . Bagasse Wyatt – how much better it would be to have some sweet invalid to dose with cordials.

If for James to turn up and then be ill was bad enough, not to come at all was worse. In 1808 Beckford was driven to distraction by 'this twisting and turning between Hanworth and Windsor'. On 29 June he ordered Gregory to 'tell Wyatt that unless he wants to irritate and torment me to death he must come. The confusion into which everything will be thrown and the impossibility of finishing anything . . . if he doesn't come at once, is not to be borne.'

Relations grew worse in the years that followed. By 1811 Beckford's patience, never very strong, had vanished. 'Where infamous Beast, where are you? What putrid inn, what stinking tavern or pox-ridden brothel hides your

---

[30] Wilton, Pembroke MSS., Correspondence between James Wyatt and Lord Pembroke 1801–9.

hoary and gluttonous limbs . . . One can't trust the infamous Bagasse in the slightest thing. Every day brings new proofs of his negligent apathy. Just imagine the pinnacles have to be fixed in the the following divine manner with wooden spars! . . . when I saw this horror I thought I would faint'.

In 1812 it was at first the same: 'From the infamous Swine *nothing!* . . . The heat and these eternal ridiculous tormentings by Bagasse will make me go mad and throw up all the works. I swear that if he does not leave with you I will have everything stopped and go on a journey God knows where. This utter indifference to all that concerns me and his own honour, these repeated and renewed proofs are too much for me . . . If he goes to Bilgewater [the Earl of Bridgewater at Ashridge] first I'll not receive him here.'

James came and stayed for two weeks. Instantly Beckford's tone changed. 'Up to now there is no sign of the disappearance of Bagasse. He works with a brio, a zeal, an energy, a faith that would move the largest mountain in the Alps . . . My angelic Bagasse has not yet breathed the slightest word or hint of departure. He is all ardour and zeal as never before . . . I do not believe that my Angelica [the capricious heroine of Ariosto's *Orlando Furioso*] has any more thought of going than I of abandoning the hope of rousing the Beloved Sleeper of Hounslow [a gipsy youth in whom Beckford was interested].'[31]

The way in which Beckford's feelings were transformed when James finally arrived and spent a fortnight working at Fonthill (while presumably the Earl of Bridgewater awaited him at Ashridge) is one of the most amazing aspects of James's relations with his clients. As the Bishop of Durham remarked, 'you forgave Wyatt his disappointing you when he appeared'. He had enormous personal charm. John Bacon elaborates on this. When James did finally visit a client, 'he had such a peculiar talent in making everyone feel that he was so entirely absorbed in the wishes of his employer that his want of respect in not coming was soon forgotten'.[32] It should also be remembered that the eighteenth century was willing to overlook shortcomings when allied to genius or even talent. Architects, in particular, enjoyed great consideration and independence and felt they had no need to flatter the great. James Wyatt's French contemporary Claude Nicholas Ledoux, for instance, when invited by the Landgrave of Hesse-Kassel to design a palace for him, wrote back, 'your excellency is not rich enough to have an architect like me'.[33]

James possessed the 'breeding and parts' necessary for his role as a fashionable architect. Contemporaries remarked upon his 'mild and gentlemanly manners'.[34] These were probably as much reponsible as his genius for

[31] Boyd Alexander, *Life at Fonthill* (1957), 41, 44, 67, 71, 73, 74, 75, 104, 131, 132, 97, 129.
[32] John Bacon (Junior), Reminiscences.
[33] Quoted in Michael Gallet, *Paris Domestic Architecture of the 18th Century* (1972), 25.
[34] *European Mag.* (Oct. 1813), 64, 275.

52. Oxford, Radcliffe Observatory. Designed by James Wyatt, 1776–94. Architecturally the finest observatory in Europe.

his success and made bearable his outstanding professional faults. Moreover, he had an exceptionally amiable character, and was 'one of the best-tempered men living'.[35]

James's relations with his clients went beyond those usually found between architects and their patrons and he became intimate with many of them. As a social companion he was much more agreeable than as a business associate. He was an easy and undemanding guest. Porden recorded that 'in private society his conversation consists chiefly of jokes and light matter'.[36]

In later life this changed and he became noted for falling asleep at table or at meetings and dozing throughout proceedings. He also became increasingly a glutton and a heavy drinker. Once after leaving Beckford at Fonthill Abbey he spent three days at old Fonthill House drinking with Foxhall, the carpenter.[37] He doubtless found the latter's society a necessary and refreshingly earthy contrast to the artificiality and superficiality of life with the affected, change-able, and self-indulgent Beckford. On another occasion in 1813 Beckford recorded with heavy irony that 'My Bagasse shows a moderation at table worthy of a Carthusian Monk, and a shameful flush that is the colour of port-wine with a bush.'

Time decayed rather than handsomely weathered the brilliant youth of the 1770s with his fashionable clothes and dress sword which on one occasion he lent to Matthew Boulton, but only for a week as he could not be parted with it for longer. 'This is a bad time of year to strip one long of such a piece of necessary ornament, I shall lay by my Chappeau Bras and paper my Gold Buttons till I have news of my Sword again. You now know, the consequence of depriving me of it for long.'[38]

James's sporadic method of working was a symptom of artistic temperament rather than of laziness. His interest in practical affairs and money-making was small but his interest in architecture and design was a passion. This is why he never turned down new commissions though there was no chance of giving them satisfactory attention. Also why he spent weeks at a time on one particular design when more important business called for him elsewhere. He loved solving difficult architectural problems. C. R. Cockerell recorded that

Wyatt liked to meet with those difficulties and accidents from which agreeable circumstances of effect might be derived . . . Would make any number of drawings and destroy them for others with pleasure. If with advantage to the work, would knock down whole ceilings if not pleasing to him, without remorse. Always doubtful and uncertain of himself – would sit whole evenings wrapped in consideration of his plans.[39]

This is a very different picture from the popular one of James devoid of artistic

---

[35] Farington, 2 Nov. 1812.
[36] Ibid., 9 June 1806.
[37] Ibid., 29 Mar, 1804.
[38] Coll. Miss E. Hamilton Thompson, James Wyatt to John Wyatt III, 20 Nov. 1776.
[39] Harris, 14.

IV   Bowden Park, Wiltshire *facing p.*80

conscience dashing off drawings with infinite ease and facility. He took endless trouble over his designs, occasionally even leaving the dinner-table to go back to his drawing-board.

If he had been willing to churn out competent drawings in a business-like manner he would have satisfied his customers, made a fortune, and left a lot of very boring buildings. Instead he created a series of architectural works which include the most staggering gothic house ever built, two or three of the most beautiful neo-classical houses in England, architecturally the finest observatory in Europe, and after Hawksmoor's at Castle Howard, the two most perfect mausoleums of the eighteenth century.

James Wyatt trod the opposite path to his nephew Jeffry Wyatville who did produce competent drawings, boring buildings, satisfied clients, and a fortune. Naturally pedestrian, Jeffry thought his uncle a singular man:

He will often employ himself upon trifling professional matters which others could do while business of importance is waiting for him. When a [new] commission . . . is proposed . . . he will eagerly attend to it till he has got all the instructions necessary for the commencement of the work, but he then becomes indifferent to it and he has lost many commissions by such neglect . . . at times he will, when at the house of an employer, work very hard in making designs and will frequently leave the company and bottle after dinner to go to his clerk. Such is the irregularity of his habits.[40]

James would work incessantly at projects which filled him with enthusiasm, such as Ashridge or Dodington. 'That', said Jeffry, 'is just what he should not have done . . . there were other works standing still, which, if he divided his time properly would not have been the case'.[41]

These bursts of creative enthusiasm and inspiration were broken by relapses, which became more frequent as he grew older. He would drink for days or disappear to bed with whoever had taken his fancy. Beckford's nickname for him, 'Bagasse', is best translated by the American slang 'whore hopper'. Dr. Thorpe, a friend of James, observed that his love of women led him away from his other pursuits and at the time of his death one of his servants was pregnant by him and within three weeks of her confinement.[42]

The most time-consuming of James's works and most deleterious in their effect on his general architectural practice were those for the royal family. Again and again when work elsewhere was halted for want of proper directions or working drawings James was to be found at Windsor. As already noted, his connection with the royal family probably arose from his friendship with Richard Dalton, the King's librarian who was able to present him to the King. Certainly after the opening of the Pantheon George III had noted James with favour. His first royal work was the design of a 'petit Trianon' for Queen

[40] Farington, 16 Oct. 1806.
[41] Ibid., 2 Nov. 1812.
[42] Ibid., 17 May 1818.

Charlotte at Frogmore. This small estate adjoining Windsor Castle was bought by the King in 1790. At first the Queen was chiefly concerned with landscaping the grounds and James was asked to design various minor garden structures including a Gothic Ruin.

Work began on the main house in 1792. James produced many designs for it, some of them Gothic. As executed, the original house was enlarged by the addition of an extra storey, and by flanking pavilions connected by a colonnade along the whole length of the west front. The interior was arranged to contain the Queen's collections of china, plants, lacquer, and flower pieces painted by Mary Moser, as depicted in Pyne's charming aquatints of the royal residences. Faced in gleaming white stucco Frogmore is the most attractive residence owned by the royal family. James did not receive any '[financial] compensation for the trouble and loss of time which he had suffered in the attendance of the Queen and Princess [Elizabeth] building Frogmore etc. . . . Indeed Wyatt told a person that the expenses and great loss of time in attending upon the Royal Family had been the ruin of him.' George III was aware of this and it was by way of recompense that he appointed him Surveyor-General.[43]

Despite the debilitating effect of these royal commissions on his architectural practice James obviously got great pleasure from the favoured position he enjoyed at Windsor, and the intimacy he had with the King, Queen, and Princesses. 'Wyatt considers the Queen a very warm friend of his . . . [and] is always treated with great respect at Windsor'.[44] When Frogmore was completed the transformation of Windsor Castle itself was entrusted to him. Before long he was living at the castle in the apartments once occupied by Christopher Wren and dining at the Equerries' table with the Lord Chamberlain.

A letter from Princess Elizabeth to James survives written on pretty neo-classical paper; 'Princess Elizabeth thinks it right to inform Mr. Wyatt that the King named him as wishing to see him two or three times yesterday saying he had some money matters to settle . . . The Queen thinks the most agreeable time for His Majesty to see Mr. Wyatt will be at Windsor – either Saturday or Sunday.'[45]

By an odd chance the tone but not the actual words of a conversation between George III and James Wyatt has been preserved in John Galt's novel *Sir Andrew Wylie*. Galt bases an encounter between his Scottish hero and the King on a conversation he had overheard between James Wyatt and George III on a visit to Windsor Castle. Galt and his friends had climbed into the scaffolding of the new Great Staircase to inspect the work when the King and the architect came in.

[43] Ibid., 11 Dec. 1806.   [44] Ibid.
[45] B. L., Egerton MS. 3515.

53. Frogmore House, Windsor. Designed by James Wyatt for Queen Charlotte, 1792–5.

54. Belvoir Castle, Leicestershire, detail of bedroom frieze designed by James Wyatt.

The King observed us, particularly myself who was so conspicuous, and lingered with Mr. Wyatt until he had satisfied his curiosity by looking at us; speaking all the time . . . and looking about as he was speaking. It was evident that he spoke more at random than seriously addressed the architect, being occupied in noticing us. Something in his manner drew my attention and from that interview which lasted probably several minutes, I caught a durable remembrance of his peculiarities – I can see him still.[46]

The conversation that Galt constructed on the basis of this encounter runs as follows:

Before he had advanced many paces the old gentleman [the King] turned round . . . 'Strange man – don't know him – don't know him' . . . 'Gude-day Sir' said Wylie as he approached . . . 'Scotchman eh!' said the old gentleman; 'fine morning, fine morning Sir – weather warmer than with you? What part of Scotland do you come from? How do you like Windsor? Come to see the King eh?' and loudly made the echoes ring with his laughter.[47]

A result of the royal favour enjoyed by James was that the opposition to Benjamin West's ruling clique in the Royal Academy chose James Wyatt as their leader. In November 1805 following internal political manœuvring Benjamin West was forced to retire and James was elected as President in his place. He was the Academy's first architect President.

James's presidency was a failure. Instead of resuscitating the Council and starting a rotating presidency, as his supporters wanted, he slept in committee, mumbled his speeches, and failed to turn up for meetings.[48] At the Royal Academy Birthday Dinner in 1806 sitting next to the Prince of Wales, he was a 'sad president and gave the toasts in so low a voice that he could scarcely be heard'. Matthew Cotes's remark, 'Why should not my father be President? A President has nothing to do', obviously sums up the family view of the situation.[49] After only a year James resigned and West was re-elected. All he had achieved was to make as many enemies in the Academy as he had already made in the Society of Antiquaries from which he had been blackballed in September 1797 as the 'Destroyer' of Durham, Hereford, Lichfield, and Salisbury Cathedrals.

This resulted from the machinations of John Carter and Sir Henry Englefield who managed to enlist the support of the Duke of Norfolk. George III jokingly referred to it as a popish plot. Despite this initial set-back James was elected to the Society in December 1797 much to Carter's chagrin.

On the whole James preferred the company of the aristocracy and the royal family to that of his fellow artists. Indeed his devotion to the royal family was such that he acquired a country property at Hanworth in order to be near the

[46] John Galt, *Sir Andrew Wylie* (1841), 463 (ex info Mr. H. M. Colvin).
[47] Ibid. 332.
[48] Farington, 23 Apr. 1806.
[49] Ibid., 3 May 1806; 21 Dec. 1804.

Court. He never missed the King's birthday and his distracted patrons knew that they could always track him down at Windsor on that occasion. He was fond of repeating remarks made to him by the King and was proud of presents from the royal family, the gold pocket-watch from George III (perhaps a tactful hint concerning his unpunctuality) and the silver teapot and ink-well from Queen Charlotte and Princess Elizabeth.

A less attractive facet of this snobbery was a contempt for his fellow artists. Hoppner argued against his candidature for the presidency of the Royal Academy on the grounds that 'a man who speaks as he does against artists, not only those in his own department, but in every other, is a very unfit man to be placed at the head of such a society'. James voted against Turner being elected to the Royal Academy on the grounds of his slovenly appearance and habits.[50]

The last years of his life were overshadowed by the irretrievable muddle of his financial affairs. It is surprising that an architect with a practice on his scale should have died penniless, leaving his widow to beg for a small pension from the Government and his sons to struggle to establish themselves. Bartolini, 'a plaisterer', told Smirke in 1813 that 'Wyatt was in very distressed circumstances notwithstanding the vast opportunities afforded to him to make a fortune ... Bartolini said he himself was a creditor for £3,000 and that he knew that Wyatt's house in Foley Place was mortgaged to the utmost. He said Wyatt owed his draughtsman, Dixon, £900.' Dr. Thorpe told Farington the same story; James's irregularity and 'habitual neglect' and 'general bad management' lost him a fortune.[51]

Yet from the beginning of his career everything James touched had turned to gold. The Pantheon, in which he had a substantial number of shares, was a great financial success. He charged five guineas a day whenever he visited a building, in some cases staying for two, three, or even six weeks, drawing that fee all the time. On 4,000 miles travel a year he charged 2s. 6d. mile. He had numerous official salaries: £510 from the Office of Works, £280 from the Board of Ordnance, and £200 p.a. each from Somerset House, Westminster Abbey, and the Department of Woods and Forests, as well as £50 p.a. from the Duke of Devonshire, as Surveyor to Devonshire House from 1776 to 1790.[52] On top he charged 5 per cent on the total estimated cost of his buildings. This alone should have been a substantial source of income. He was engaged on all the largest building projects of his time and the cost of some of them was vertiginous. Fonthill Abbey cost £270,000, George III's works at Windsor £300,000, the Lazaretto at Chetney Hill for the Office of Works £170,000, Kew Palace for George III £500,000. He also had his own building business and did

[50] Ibid., 26 Dec. 1806.
[51] Ibid., 18 Sept. 1813; 17 May 1818.
[52] Staffs. R. O., Trentham MSS., Stafford House Law Suit, Evidence of Henry Harrison; Farington, 20 July 1796; Chatsworth Household Account Books 1770–1790.

a lot of the contracting himself.

His style of living was not particularly lavish. His house in Queen Anne Street was of considerable architectural distinction but was not very large. His country place at Hanworth, a property of 90 acres, was more a *ferme ornée* than a seat. The two houses combined could only muster a total of fifty windows. The scale of his household was not enormous. Altogether in his two houses he had six male servants, one carriage, three horses for riding and two in husbandry.[53] His drinking and other pastimes cannot have been all that expensive.

How then was it possible for him to die in penury? The answer is that in many cases he never received his attendance fees, his travel expenses, or his 5 per cent commission. His patrons were quite as dilatory in payment as Wyatt was in performance, and he never dunned then. He lost £2,000 or £3,000 a year 'from mere neglect in respect of order in his accounts'.[54] He had a gentlemanly distaste for demanding payment even when hard-pressed. Towards the end of his life his sons were forced to go behind his back and write to his clients asking for the money they owed. A typical example is Benjamin Dean Wyatt writing to Lord Pembroke in 1809:

If your Lordship will have the goodness to order the payment of our Father's account (of which I enclose an abstract) you will confer a most important obligation on him.
I beg leave to assure your Lordship that much of my Father's present embarrassment arises from the reluctance which he has always felt to press any of his employers for money and most especially those in whose honour and friendly disposition towards him he has the same reliance which he has on those of your Lordship. My father's delicacy . . . is extreme and would rather prompt him to hazard any degree of embarrassment than admit of his taking such steps as those which I am now taking.[55]

The result of this exteme delicacy was that on his death in 1813 James Wyatt was owed more than £20,000. Among the debtors were the Corporation of Liverpool £6,500, Christopher Codrington £1,200, the Duke of Portland £3,500, Lord Carrington £400, William Beckford £1,000, Lord Chesterfield £500, the Department of Woods and Forests (residue of salaries) £1,000, Downing College, Cambridge £500, the Military Commissioners £1,000, Lord Pembroke £1,000, the Duke of Rutland £600, and various other sums totalling a further £5,000.[56]

In addition to these debts Wyatt's financial position was weakened in other ways. Throughout his surveyorship of the Office of Works he was paid only half of his salary annually. The other half was meant to be made up but never was. Nor did he benefit from the total cost of his various building projects as he drew

[53] RIBAD, Wyatt MSS., Solicitor for Taxes to B. D. Wyatt, 25 Oct. 1813.
[54] Farington, 26 Dec. 1806.
[55] Wilton House, Pembroke MSS., B. D. Wyatt to Lord Pembroke, 13 Apr. 1809.
[56] Edinburgh Univ. Library, La II 426/529, Lists of James Wyatt's creditors (ex info Mr. H. M. Colvin).

his commission on the original estimate, not on the final cost, In his own words: 'When business is done the other way it is a great temptation to architects to increase expense for the sake of percentage.' An example of his failure to benefit from the total cost of a building is Henham Hall in Suffolk which he designed for Lord Rous (later first Earl of Stradbroke). This house cost £20,000 to build but James's estimate was only £12,000. His percentage was calculated on that.[57] The cost of most of his buildings exceeded their original estimates by at least double, and he lost a considerable amount of money as a result.

His muddled finances do not seem to have disturbed James's easygoing temperament. His sons strugged valiantly to stave off his bankruptcy but the main worry must have fallen on his wife Rachel. It was she who was left poor in the end. She seems to have had a miserable life lacking a strong enough character to stand up to the world. She allowed herself to be crushed by fate. She always had head-aches and vapours, stopping the carriage at the village of Kensington on the way down from Queen Anne Street to Hanworth in order to buy hartshorn and smelling salts. Farington records that she was so affected by the death of her only daughter Jane that she did not enter the drawing-room for five years afterwards.[58] When her sons Benjamin Dean and Charles left for India she made dreadful, hysterical scenes. On Charles's departure from Portsmouth in April 1798 Matthew Cotes records how he was kept awake half the night before by 'the half uttered sentences of my weeping mother who was then in the next room bathing Charles with her tears'. After Charles had left for his ship she sent a message after him beseeching him to come back.[59]

Despite the threat of impending financial ruin and the wretchedness of his wife, James Wyatt's home life was in many ways idyllic. The Queen Anne Street house, which he had designed himself in the full flood of his youthful enthusiasm, was the most attractive of its size in London. It would have been impossible to remain depressed in a house with so beautiful a staircase. In spite of Rachel Wyatt, who hated them, there were two dogs, and Charles's pointer puppy as well as Matthew Cotes's tame squirrels and a blackbird in a wicker cage.

At Hanworth he could enjoy the delights of country life. Bathing and fishing for perch and pike in the river. Games of quoits after dinner. Picnics of boiled eggs, biscuits, and oranges. Haymaking in June and July with the farmhands getting 'very merry' on forty jugs of beer a day. The servants getting tipsy on sherry to celebrate the King's birthday. A high spot was the annual village dance at Hanworth to mark the end of haymaking with the sons of the gentry

[57] Farington, 2 Nov. 1797.
[58] Ibid.
[59] Coll. Mr. Geoffrey Budenburg, M.C. Wyatt's Diary (MS.), 29 Apr. 1798.

and the farm labourers disguised as 'raffish clowns' and having a 'fine frolic'.[60]

The end of James's life was preceded by decline. By 1800 he was suffering from kidney trouble and possibly cirrhosis of the liver. In 1804 Lysons reported that James was paralytic and had his mouth drawn aside. In 1807 Farington noted that it was improbable that he would 'ever be restored to what he was before his last illness. . . The cause of his illness was as follows . . .' The rest of the page is blank and so it is left to the imagination to supply the cause.[61]

James once remarked to George Dance that he hoped for a sudden death. His wish was fulfilled. Farington, as so often, tells the story. On Saturday 4 September 1813 James

was on his way to London with Mr. Codrington, a gentleman of fortune in Wiltshire, in Mr. Codrington's carriage with four horses. While driving at a great rate a person on horseback met the carriage in a place where another carriage or cart stood, which made the passage between the carriages so narrow that the horse and his rider were thrown down and the wheels of Mr. Codrington's carriage passed over the rump of the horse [and] the carriage was overturned. Wyatt at the time was reading a newspaper and had his hat off. The top of his head struck with great violence the roof of the carriage and the concussion caused his instant death.[62]

The fatal accident took place near Marlborough in Wiltshire.

He died at an opportune moment. He had already been dismissed from his post as Deputy Surveyor to the Office of Woods, Forests, and Land Revenues and from the direction of works at the Royal Military College, Sandhurst. As Surveyor-General and Comptroller he could hardly have survived the reorganization of the office of Works which his neglect had provoked.

His funeral was in Westminster Abbey on 28 September. As Surveyor to the Fabric, he was buried in the south transept where a marble memorial tablet was erected with the following inscription:

Sacred to the Memory of James Wyatt Esqr.

Having devoted many years of his youth to the study of the pure models of antiquity abroad, was at the early age of twenty two transcendently distinguished in his profession as an architect in this country; and having sustained the dignity of that profession for forty five years during the principal part of which he held the offices of architect of this church and Surveyor-General of His Majesty's Works depart this life on the 4th day of September 1813.

He was a genius as an architect but the Prime Minister, Lord Liverpool, was right about his administration. 'Tho' he was in my judgement a man of the most considerable Talents as an architect, he was certainly one of the worse public servants I recollect in any office not, I am persuaded, from dishonesty or

[60] Ibid., 25 June 1798.
[61] Farington, 1 Dec. 1804; 20 Nov. 1807.
[62] Ibid., 3 July 1815; 17 May 1818.

want of zeal but from *carelessness* and from always claiming a great deal more business that he was capable of performing.'[63]

Beckford's remark on hearing of James's death was characteristically bitchy: 'Alas my poor Bagasse had already sunk from the plane of genius to the mire; for some years now he has only dabbled in mud.'[64]

[63] B. L., Add. MS. 38 568, Draft of letter from Lord Liverpool to Duke of Richmond, 8 Jan. 1814.
[64] Alexander, *Life at Fonthill,* 137, Beckford to Douglas, 23 Sept. 1813.

CHAPTER IV

The Struggle for the Succession

James Wyatt's death precipitated a scramble for his official posts among the next generation of the family. The heirs apparent included his eldest and youngest sons Benjamin Dean and Philip, his two nephews Jeffry (Wyatville) and Lewis William, and their cousins George I and Henry John. All of them had worked in James's office at different times and had been his architectural pupils.

Jeffry Wyatville wrote fifteen letters to different people asking for help in obtaining his late uncle's official posts. He did not succeed in this but did manage to get himself appointed to complete Ashridge for the Earl of Bridgewater in place of Benjamin Dean.[1]

Philip raced in the middle of the night to Ragley, where the Prince Regent was staying. He burst into the royal bedchamber at 3 a.m. to announce the 'melancholy' news of his father's death. The Regent was much affected, even shedding tears. The messenger then proceeded with his 'real business', namely 'to solicit the Regent to bestow upon him such of the advantages possessed by his late father as His Royal Highness might think proper'. The Regent promised nothing but merely 'returned a civil answer in a general way'.[2] Philip returned disappointed to London.

Benjamin Dean enlisted the help of various influential men, including Samuel Whitbread and the Dukes of Richmond and Wellington. He wanted to be Surveyor-General like his father before him. The Prime Minister explained why this was impossible in a letter to the Duke of Richmond.

Thank you for your letter recommending Mr. Benjamin Wyatt for one of the architectural appointments ... I am sorry that the arrangements which have been made preclude me from the possibility of complying with your request. The Prince Regent is naturally desirous of employing his own architect Mr. Nash upon what immediately concerns himself and it has been settled to add Mr. Soane and Mr. Smirke as two of the architects of the most established character in the country. I believe from all I have heard that Mr. B. Wyatt is a very able man but he is new in the profession and certainly he has no precedence on the ground of the claims of his Father, for ... he was certainly one of the worst public servants I recollect in any office.[3]

---

[1] Jeffry did not change his name to Wyatville until 1824 but for the sake of clarity he will be referred to as Wyatville throughout.
[2] Farington, 18 Sept. 1813.
[3] BL, Add. MS. 38.568, fo. 224, Lord Liverpool to Duke of Richmond (draft), 8 Jan. 1814.

Benjamin Wyatt, Esq.

*Engraved by T. Blood for the European Magazine
from an Original Painting by S. Drummond, A.R.A.*

London, Published by J. Asperne, Cornhill, Nov.¹ 1812

55. Benjamin Dean Wyatt, 1812. Engraved by J. Blood after S. Drummond.

Both Benjamin Dean and Philip thought themselves their father's true architectural heir: Benjamin Dean because he was the eldest son, and Philip because he had been brought up as his father's assistant. After the preliminary struggle they realized that nothing was to be gained from independent rivalry. Therefore, with their mother's encouragement, they swallowed their differences and Benjamin Dean drafted a letter to the Prince Regent on behalf of the whole family. He asked for a pension for his mother and 'posts and encouragement' for himself and his three brothers.[4]

Rachel Wyatt was given a small government pension of £130 p.a. for the rest of her life and Benjamin Dean received the surveyorship to Westminster Abbey.[5] That was all. Philip got nothing. The post of Surveyor-General was abolished as one of the reforms provoked by James Wyatt's neglect of the Office of Works. So nobody got the job in the end. Instead Soane, Nash, and Smirke, the distinguished leaders of the profession, were appointed architectural advisers to the Office.[6]

The careers of the nephews, Jeffry and Lewis, were not greatly affected by their uncle's death. Jeffry was already a successful architect in his own right. He was also a prosperous builder. An official position would have been welcome recognition but it was not necessary for survival. Lewis had money of his own and was also an architect of distinction. Though he is now almost forgotten, he was among the more interesting architects of his generation. With James and Samuel he is one of the three great architects produced by the family. He and Jeffry will be discussed in more detail in the next chapter.

The cousins George I and Henry John were also established architects. George had several country houses to his credit. Born in 1782, he was the youngest son of Charles I, the maker of Wyatt cement. He was a pupil of James Wyatt from 1798 to 1800. He then set up independently in Albany where he stayed till 1812. His office was taken over in 1813 by Lewis who was his brother-in-law as well as cousin.

In 1806 George designed a Doric portico for the entrance-front of Culford Hall (Suffolk) where another cousin, Henry Wyatt, was agent to Marquess Cornwallis.[7] He also rebuilt Brome Hall for Lord Cornwallis incorporating panelling from the old house in the new dining-room. Work was still in progress in 1815.[8]

Later he remodelled Howick Hall in Northumberland for Earl Grey. He moved the entrance round to the north front and built a new hall with Roman Doric columns. He also designed Twizell House in the same county for Sir

---

[4] BL, Add. MS. 38.256, fos. 14–16.
[5] BL, Add. MS. 38.260, Rachel Wyatt to Lord Liverpool, 7 Dec. 1814 and draft reply.
[6] *King's Works*, 101.
[7] Coll. Lord Cadogan, Design for entrance-front of Culford, s. 'George Wyatt Dec. 1806'.
[8] Ipswich Public Library, Fitch Coll., Hartismere Vol., Letters from George Wyatt about Brome.

P. J. Selby in 1811. Between 1809 and 1812 he transformed a red-brick Queen
Anne house at Rowton in Shropshire into a convincingly Gothic castle for
Colonel R. Lyster. A toll-house by him on the Bath road, just outside Devizes, is
in the same Gothic style as Rowton and has been saved from demolition partly
by the intervention of Mr. Woodrow Wyatt.

George gave up architecture early in life. Between 1815 and his death in
1856 he enjoyed a long retirement living off a share in the proceeds of his
father's cement business. Nevertheless, his work between 1806 and 1815
shows that he was a competent master of both the neo-classical and the Gothic
styles. If he had continued in his career he would have been a successful rival
to his cousins.[9]

Henry John Wyatt is a more shadowy figure than George. He was the third
son of Edward Wyatt II, the carver and frame-maker (see p. 157). He was born in
1789 and in 1806 became a pupil of James Wyatt. He stayed in James's office
until 1811 and received a thorough architectural training. In 1809 at the age of
twenty he was admitted to the Royal Academy Schools and won the silver
medal in the same year for the best drawing of the Admiralty screen.

He first exhibited at the Royal Academy in 1806, sending in a design for the
entrance to a park. In the following years he exhibited designs for a villa, a
public bath, an exchange, and a national cenotaph. His earliest executed
building was St. Mary's Church at Hammersmith which was built between
1812 and 1813 (demolished 1944). In 1823 he designed a farmhouse at
Barcombe in Sussex which was built. He also built some houses in Great
George Street, Westminster, but they do not survive. He died in 1862.[10]

In 1813 Benjamin Dean and Philip, together with their brothers Charles
Burton and Matthew Cotes (who were not architects), were left destitute and
without employment. How had this happened? Why had James Wyatt with his
'numerous opulent connections, friends and relations' failed to establish his
sons in lucrative careers? The answer is that he had, but they had not taken
advantage of their opportunities. 'James Wyatt's sons have been very improvident. The eldest, had he remained at Calcutta, would have been appointed by
Marquess Wellesley, Secretary to the Governor-General, a place of £10,000 p.a.
He complained of ill health but it was said to be only a Home fever – a desire to
go home.'[11]

Benjamin Dean was educated at Westminster and Christ Church, Oxford
where he got into debt to the tune of £200 and came down early without a
degree. He was originally intended for the law but James, through the
influence of the Queen, was able to get him a job in India.[12] This was the great

[9] *APSD*; RA Catalogue; Colvin, 721.
[10] *APSD*; RA Catalogue; Colvin, 722; Coll. Mrs. Tunnicliffe, Will of Edward Wyatt II.
[11] Farington, 10 Oct. 1806.
[12] Ibid., 1 Dec. 1796.

56. Culford Hall, Suffolk. Design by George Wyatt for adding a portico, 1806. The main part of the house was designed by Samuel Wyatt, 1790–6.

57. Government House, Calcutta. Designed by Charles Wyatt II, 1798–1803. Aquatint by James Fraser.

opportunity young men longed for in the late eighteenth century. It offered the chance to make a fortune relatively quickly and to retire early to a pleasant country property in England.

In 1797 Benjamin Dean was given an appointment in the Secrets' Department of the East India Company's office in Calcutta. He described his work, in a letter to Matthew Cotes, as affording 'the fullest scope for the aquirement of general information on the actual and probable state of political affairs in India'.

He spent most of his day at Government House deciphering incoming letters and putting into cipher those going out. Normally he went to the office at 9.30 a.m. and stayed till 5 or 6 p.m., but when there was a lot of work he would stay till midnight with only a two-hour break for dinner. His initial enthusiasm soon flagged and he got 'heartily tired of the vile drudgery to which I am intensely confined'. Only the prospects of promotion and his respect for Lord Wellesley kept him at it. He told his friend Ozias Humphrey that Wellesley was 'particularly fitted for his situation' by reason of his fine character and intellect.

After two years he hoped to get the head assistantship in the office with a salary of £800 p.a. and after a further two years a registership in one of the law courts worth £1,200 p.a. He thought it possible to save a 'modest competency' of around £30,000 to £40,000 which would enable him 'to live genteelly' on his retirement to England. This would need 'diligent application to business and frugal economy', neither of which were his strong points.

He concluded sadly that 'those *Golden Tales* you hear in England (about India) are all an illusion which serve mightily well to please the imagination but in reality do not exist'.[13] Nevertheless, he stayed in India for six years. In 1798 he was joined by Charles Burton who had just left Eton. The arrival of his brother made him less lonely and homesick.[14]

Benjamin Dean's cousin Charles II was also in Calcutta He was an officer in the Bengal Engineers. Born in 1758, Charles II was the son of William II, James Wyatt's eldest brother (who had designed Soho Works for Matthew Boulton). Charles II entered the army as a cadet in 1780 and set sail for India on the *Mount Stuart* on 27 June in the same year. His voyage was not without excitement. The ship was captured by the combined fleets of France and Spain on 9 August and was returned to England. He set out for the second time a year later and eventually arrived in India in 1782.

In 1800 he was promoted to captain and made Commander of Police. Like many military engineers in subject countries he was used as an architect by the Government. In June 1803 he was appointed Superintendent of

[13] RIBAD, Wyatt MSS, B.D.Wyatt to M.C.Wyatt, 20 Sept. 1798; 16 Nov. 1798; RA Library, HU/5/72–3, B.D.Wyatt to O.Humphrey, 6 May 1799.
[14] Coll. G.Budenberg, M.C.Wyatt's Diary. This includes a description of Charles's departure from Portsmouth.

Public Works and a member of the committee to report on the Calcutta improvements. Among other things this made him responsible for the roads in the province.[15] His great opportunity came in 1798 when the Marquess Wellesley arrived in Calcutta as Governor-General. Wellesley was inspired by the vision of a unified British Empire in India. He saw Calcutta as the capital and seat of supreme authority, but considered the existing government buildings unworthy. From the moment he arrived, Wellesley determined to build a new residence. Without bothering to consult the directors of the East India Company he set to work on his own authority. The Company's architect, Edward Tiretta, and Charles Wyatt II were both asked for designs and those of Charles were chosen, probably because they were the grandest.

His plan was striking. It comprised a central block linked to four corner pavilions by sweeping quadrant wings. There was a domed bow on the garden front and a huge portico approached by a straight flight of steps on the entrance front. The basic layout was obviously derived from Kedleston, and both Paine's and Adam's designs were sources.

Charles knew Kedleston personally; it had been built under the direction of his uncle Samuel. He probably owned the printed designs: James Paine's *Plans, Elevations and Sections of Noblemen and Gentlemen's Houses* published in 1783 and Robert Adam's *Works in Architecture* which came out in 1773. The entrance-gate based on Adam's screen at Syon is obviously derived from the *Works*.

The foundation-stone of the new house was laid in 1799 and it was completed by January 1803. The cost was tremendous and caused a quarrel between Wellesley and the East India Company. It was one reason for his eventual recall. Farington as usual can be relied on to provide some details. 'Marquess Wellesley built a palace at Calcutta which cost the East India Company £180,000 and he wrote home for furniture to an equal amount of expense.'[16]

Lord Valentia defended the building and its cost.

The new Government House erected by Lord Wellesley [is] a noble structure . . . not unworthy of its destination. The sums expended upon it have been considered as extravagant by those who carry European ideas and European economy into Asia, but they ought to remember that India is a country of splendour, of extravagance and of outward appearances; that the head of a mighty Empire ought to conform himself to the prejudices of the country he rules over; and that the British in particular ought to emulate the splendid works of the Princes of the House of Timour.[17]

Government House in Calcutta was the first and undoubtedly the finest Wyatt building in India. The Indian buildings of Sir (Matthew) Digby Wyatt

---

[15] India Office Library, List of the Officers of the Bengal Army 1758–1834, pp. 533–4.
[16] Farington, 25 Sept. 1820.
[17] Quoted in S. Nilsson, *European Architecture in India* (1968), 101.

built in the last years of the East India Company before the mutiny are not of the same interest. Government House survives unchanged. By reason of its vast scale and stuccoed façades it looks more like a Russian neo-classical palace than an English house. It would not be out of place in St. Petersburg. In its heyday in the nineteenth century it had a staff of 600 servants.

As well as designing Government House Charles II was responsible for some less important buildings. In 1800 he supervised the repair and alteration of Lord Wellesley's country residence at Barrackpore. He may also have designed the temporary decorations for the opening ceremonies of Government House. These included obelisks and Temples of Valour and Peace.[18]

Charles II had a successful career in India and was able to amass a respectable fortune. Five years after his arrival, in 1787, he married Charlotte Drake (widow of Captain Greentree) and she may have brought him some of her own money. He retired in October 1806 to a country villa near London called Ealing Grove in an area where Sir John Soane also had a small country property. On James Wyatt's death he bought James's London house in Queen Anne Street, by then known as Langham Place.

He was rich enough on his retirement to take part in politics and spent a great deal on contested elections. A Tory, he supported Perceval, the Prime Minister. He was M.P. for Sudbury for two successive parliaments from 1812 to 1818 but did not stand again and died a year later in 1819.[19]

Neither Charles II's success nor the certain prospect of advancement was enough to make Benjamin Dean persevere in the Indian Civil Service. Early in 1803 he came back to England armed with a vague but effective doctor's certificate. After a period as an assistant in his father's office he became private secretary to Sir Arthur Wellesley, Lord Wellesley's younger brother, and accompanied him to Ireland in 1807. They stayed in Dublin till 1809 when Wellesley left for the Peninsular War and a future which was to bring him fame, fortune, and the dukedom of Wellington.

Benjamin Dean returned once more to his father's office. He is typical of several members of the family who eventually became architects after first trying other jobs without much enjoyment or success. His architectural career did not run as smoothly as hoped. It led to a second quarrel with his father. The previous one, concerning his debts at Oxford, had blown over when he paid them out of his Indian salary instead of buying a new carriage.[20]

Benjamin Dean had a disagreeable and unstable character. He spent much of his life quarrelling with other people, family, friends, and clients. Beckford christened him 'His Bitterness Benjamin' because of his general grumpiness and bad temper.

---

[18] Ibid. 123, 133.   [19] Coll. Capt. John Wyatt, T.H. Wyatt's Family Notes (MS).
[20] RIBAD, Wyatt MSS, B.D. Wyatt to M.C. Wyatt, 28 Sept. 1798.

The great architectural opportunity of the moment was the Drury Lane Theatre. Henry Holland's theatre was destroyed by fire in 1809, as Adam's had been before it. James Wyatt hoped that Philip would get the chance to rebuild it. Benjamin Dean was determined to win the commission and devoted himself to a study of theatres.

In May 1811 a competition was opened by the committee for rebuilding the theatre under the chairmanship of Samuel Whitbread. Benjamin Dean's design was chosen as the best, largely because Whitbread preferred it. James Wyatt was furious at his eldest son for entering the competition against his wishes and ruining 'poor little Philip's' chances. In consequence James forbade him ever to enter his house again. This quarrel was never patched up.[21]

George Wyatt I also made a design for the theatre and was deeply disappointed when this was passed over in favour of Benjamin Dean's. In 1812 George published his design under the title *A Compendious Description of a Design for . . . erecting a Third Theatre in the Metropolis*. The newspapers alleged that Benjamin Dean had cribbed his theatre from George's. Benjamin denied the 'unfounded and scandalous insinuation' at some length in the 1813 edition of his own book *Design for the Theatre now building in Drury Lane*. He wrote that his object was 'to unite a due attention to the profits of the theatre with adequate provision in every respect for the accommodation of the public'. He took great pains to overcome the more obvious defects of other London theatres. The form of the auditorium, for instance, was settled after experiments in acoustics carried out on the lines suggested by George Saunders in his *Treatise on Theatres* (1790).

He gave special attention to the problem of access so that in case of another fire the theatre could be emptied quickly. For this reason the principal staircases were duplicated symmetrically. Another fire precaution was the installation of an 'ingenious' water-sprinkling apparatus devised by Colonel Congreve.[21a]

He exercised particular care over the problem of 'decorum among the several orders and classes of the visitants to the Theatre'. His aim was to protect the respectable classes from contact with the lower orders. The communications were arranged so that the former were not 'obliged to pass through Lobbies, Rooms and Avenues crowded with the most disreputable Members of the Community and subject to scenes of the most disgusting indecency'.

His plans were modified and the exterior simplified to keep the cost within the £150,000 budgeted. The interior nevertheless forms a series of finely related spaces culminating in the domed rotunda, between the twin staircases, on the *piano nobile*. It is grandly Roman with Corinthian columns, derived

[21] Farington, 2 Nov. 1812.
[21a] *Gent's Mag.* (1812), ii. 312.

58. Drury Lane Theatre. Designed by Benjamin Dean Wyatt, 1812. Rotunda.

from the Temple of Jupiter Stator, supporting a Pantheon-style dome.

The lavish use of rich materials and strong colours is a hallmark of his style. The auditorium was crimson and gold, adorned with bronze and verde antico marble. The columns of the staircases and rotunda resembled Egyptian porphyry and their capitals were gilded. The auditorium has been remodelled on several occasions but the staircases and public rooms survive as the outstanding monument in England of Georgian theatre design in the grand manner, despite their present decoration.

The new theatre was widely admired. Crabb Robinson recorded in his diary for 30 November 1812 that he 'went to Drury Lane to see the house not the performance. It is indeed a magnificent object.'[22] An aide at Carlton House wrote to Samuel Whitbread: 'The Prince Regent very emphatically commanded me to express on the subject of H.R.H.'s Box at Drury Lane Theatre that it was in point of comfort, taste, convenience and access more perfect than anything he could have expected or even pretended to wish for and that he was charmed with the beauty and elegance of the whole theatre'.[23]

This gratifying praise was passed on to Benjamin Dean Wyatt. It must have given him high hopes for the future. These were not fulfilled. He never become an object of royal patronage. His early promise was belied by his subsequent career and he was to die poor despite a small number of brilliant commissions.

Meanwhile Charles Burton, after a spell in India, had moved to Canada, where he was appointed Surveyor of the Crown Lands. He had not been in Canada long when 'an unfortunate collision' occurred with Colonel Gore, the Governor of the province. Gore suspected him of misusing his office to his own financial advantage and published his suspicions in a pamphlet. Charles Burton sued him for libel, gained a favourable verdict, and was awarded £5,000 in damages.[24] This led to a full investigation into the administration of the colony and the intervention of the Secretary of State and the Lord Commissioners of the Treasury. Charles Burton was able to explain 'everything, which could be deemed charges against him but in the interest of good government it was considered advisable for him not to resume his situation in Canada.'[25] That was the end of his career in the colonies. On his return to England in 1809 he helped his father. Following James's death he again found himself without employment or income.

Despite his four years in James's office he did not persist with architecture. Instead he entered the wine trade and is last heard of in 1822 on his way to France to buy stock. Presumably he earned his living as a wine merchant for the rest of his life.[26]

[22] Quoted in *LS* xxxv (1970), 61.
[23] V & A, 86.22170, Wyatt MSS, J. McMahon to Samuel Whitbread, 10 Nov. 1812.
[24] Farington, 24 May 1814.   [25] BL, Add. MS. 38.256, fo. 16.
[26] RIBAD, Wyatt MSS., Charles III to M.C. Wyatt, 15 Apr. 1822.

Philip William, James Wyatt's youngest son, pursued the most unprofitable career of all up to 1813; nor did it improve much afterwards. He was the least successful of the Wyatt architects. His failure was not due to lack of talent, nor lack of patrons, nor absence of personal charm. He had all those. His executed works are of high quality. His patrons included the most powerful group of architectural enthusiasts and critics in post-Waterloo England – the fifth Duchess of Rutland and her friends. His personality was so engaging that Beckford dubbed him 'Sweetness' in contrast to bitter Benjamin Dean. Like his father, he was easygoing and good-tempered.[27]

His failure was due partly to bad luck and partly to weaknesses of character. He inherited all his father's failings to a greater degree. He was unpunctual, inconsistent, untrustworthy, extravagant, and improvident. He was involved as defendant in a divorce case which damaged both his pocket and his reputation before his career had properly begun.

Despite repeated efforts to establish himself independently as an architect he spent most of his life as an assistant to others. Until 1813 he was with his father and later with his brother Benjamin Dean. They never entered into a formal partnership because Benjamin Dean considered such an arrangement 'too precarious'. But they shared the same office and Benjamin Dean paid Philip an allowance. Philip's role was that of subservient assistant. He did not, however, do very much and the arrangement was more an act of kindness on Benjamin Dean's part than anything more productive. Despite his grumpiness and quarrelsome nature Benjamin Dean was genuinely fond of Philip and willing to help him; but Philip was to treat his generousity with scant gratitude in the end.

Whereas his three elder brothers went to Westminster or Eton, his mother could not bear to have Philip sent away so he was schooled at home by a private tutor, the Revd. John Owen of Fulham.[28] As the baby of the family he was the favourite of his parents and was spoilt as a result. From the first he was destined to be his father's assistant 'to relieve his labours' in old age.

Philip was the only one of James's sons educated purposely for the architectural profession. He accompanied his father on perambulations of the country during which his presentable appearance drew the favourable attention of clients, including William Beckford and the Duchess of Rutland. It was not long, however, before he began to cause anxiety by his general fecklessness. A worried letter survives from his mother in which she encourages him to persevere in becoming an architect:

Your father is at present at Wilton and I am sure if you will but soothe him and exert those abilities I know you possess you will be able to do what you want with him and for

---

[27] Ibid., B.D. Wyatt to M.C. Wyatt, 28 Sept. 1798.
[28] BL, Add. MS., 38.256, fo. 16.

yourself also – pray my *Dearest Creature* set a *resolution* at once to be a man of *some consequence*, you must be aware that Architecture is the profession of a Gentleman and that none is more *Lucrative* when it is *properly attended to* – and you would come into it with greater advantages than anyone would. I wish you were with your father at Wilton and that you would go with him everywhere. The Duchess of Rutland has been enquiring for you and hopes to see you at Belvoir when your father goes there.[29]

A particular cause for concern was Philip's liaison with the wife of Hugh Doherty, an officer in the 25th Light Dragoons. Hugh Doherty was a typical friend of Philip's, a hard drinker and something of a ruffian. Philip often stayed with the Doherties at Laurel Lodge, their house in Hampshire, and became very fond of Hugh's wife, Ann.

In May 1806 Hugh Doherty was imprisoned for debt and Philip accompanied Ann to her parents' house. She never returned to Laurel Lodge. Philip told her father that her husband ill-treated her. He took her into his own protection and it was not long before they were living in 'open, avowed, undisguised, unconcealed, profligate adultery'. They took lodgings, first in Nottingham Street then in Devonshire Place under the assumed named of Mr. and Mrs. Daniel. At Philip's instigation Ann Doherty instituted a suit in the Ecclesiastical Court to dissolve her marriage and in 1809 she and Philip went to Gretna Green and bigamously contracted some form of Scottish civil marriage.

Their establishment was comfortable with servants. Fresh fruit and vegetables were sent up from the country by her parents. James Wyatt dined with them every Sunday when he was in London. They lived happily together until Hugh Doherty came out of prison in October 1810. He immediately began legal proceedings against Philip for 'criminal conversation' with his wife and claimed damages of £20,000. The case came up in the Court of the King's Bench on 23 February 1811 before the Chief Justice, Lord Ellenborough, and a special jury. Philip pleaded not guilty but the evidence against him was conclusive, not least that of an apothecary who had brought him medicine one evening in 1810 and had found him in bed with Mrs. Doherty. The verdict was found for the plaintiff and Philip was forced to pay damages of £1,000.[30] This was a large sum for an unemployed young man to find. Presumably it was paid by his father on the condition that he mended his ways and put some effort into becoming an architect.

The chance to save his career by winning the competition to rebuild the Drury Lane Theatre was lost, despite his father's help with his model and drawings. Though his design was placed second it was greatly admired nevertheless both by the Prince Regent and the committee:

---

[29] BL, Egerton MS. 3515, Rachel Wyatt to Philip, 18 Oct. 1808.
[30] BL, Printed Report of the Cause between Hugh Doherty Esq. plaintiff and Philip William Wyatt Esq. defendant, 23 Feb. 1811.

V   London, Apsley House, Waterloo Gallery *facing p.*102

The model and designs of Mr. Philip Wyatt appear to the sub-committee to be deserving of high commendation. The model itself of Mr. Philip Wyatt appears to the committee to surpass in execution anything that has ever been produced of the same nature and the elegance, richness and architectural knowledge shown in the whole design as well as the judicious distribution of many of its parts to claim warm applause.

The committee have found it difficult to make a selection in a contest of so much genius and in determining upon one they deeply regret the necessity of rejecting either of the other two designs, that of Mr. Wilkins or that of Philip Wyatt, but they congratulate the country on the exhibition of such powers and they cannot help remarking upon the distinguished rank held in this competition by the two sons of Mr. James Wyatt, himself confessedly pre-eminent in the profession of architecture.[31]

Philip, having failed to establish himself on his own, was left as his father's assistant. This state of affairs was terminated by James's death. Bereft of employment and a home he was forced to live with his mother in her lodgings at 6 Lindsey Row, Chelsea. He was 'dependent for his support on . . . [her] bounty as few private works during this period enabled him to add by his labours to the scanty means of his parent'.[32]

In 1813 he was engaged to supervise the restoration of the parish church at Great Yarmouth. This commission was probably an indirect result of his father's work at the naval arsenal at Yarmouth in 1806. In 1814 he exhibited a design for a staircase at the Royal Academy, his only submission to that body. In 1815 he co-operated with his brother, Matthew Cotes, in the latter's unexecuted proposal for a monument to commemorate Waterloo. None of these brought in any money.

It was about this time that he fell in with another disreputable associate, a rich young man who took him to Paris and employed him as an artistic and architectural adviser. The incident is best described in Beckford's words:

Yesterday the Calf ushered into my room when I least expected it, Sweetness in person – more hirsute, bearded and baboon-like than the fantastic faces one can see on coconuts; very amiable, very thin, pretty poor I don't doubt, but bursting with sublime plans. He has been in Paris and goes back there the day after tomorrow under the orders of a new *Fortunate Youth* worth £800,000 who bears the illustrious name of Ball, or something of the kind, the heir and bastard of a Lady Hughes, widow of an admiral (despoiler of the Indies) of that name. This Philipine gem has bought treasures of the most capital Buhl, ebony carvings after your own heart and heaven knows what marvels; and there still remains many a mine of sublime things and artistic marvels to be bought in Paris. He is making a pied-à-terre for the said Fortunate One (who'll be twenty-one in a month or two) in Brook Street for the modest price of £4,000; meanwhile it is proposed to aquire all the land in Berkeley Square a front 169 feet beginning from Thomas's Hotel as a site for a house.

The ostensible object of his call was first to ask for news of the Chevalier Franchi and then for my protection with the Duke of Hamilton. On both matters I answered with

[31] V & A, 86 22170, Wyatt MSS., cutting from the *Morning Chronicle*, 19 Oct. 1811.
[32] BL, Add. MS. 38.265, Philip Wyatt to H.R.H. Prince Regent, 1817.

59. The Waterloo Palace.
Unexecuted design by Benjamin
Dean Wyatt.

60. The Waterloo Palace.
Unexecuted design for the
Entrance-Hall by Benjamin Dean
Wyatt.

equal benignity, for the rogue really is a person of taste and is always as alive as quicksilver. I regret not being still young and roguish enough to profit by the Fortunate Youth in every respect – in front and behind, above and below.

Not a word was breathed about the Abbey, the deceased Bagasse, the quarrel with his infernal brother Benjamin etc. Making a most dandified bow and asking if I had any orders for Paris (I said 'no', with a suave expression) he decamped.[33]

Edward Ball Hughes (1798–1863), nicknamed the 'Golden Ball' because of his fortune, was among the great gamblers and dandies of the day. He soon dissipated his inheritance. In 1823 he married a Spanish dancer and subsequently disappeared to France where he died in obscurity and poverty. Nothing came of the Berkeley Square palace.

In 1813 Benjamin Dean's prospects seemed the best of all the brothers. Within twelve months the most important opportunity of the period fell to him. This was a palace for his former employer who returned to England in 1814 as Duke of Wellington. Like Marlborough a century earlier, the Duke was offered a country seat as a gift from the grateful nation. Wellington asked Benjamin Dean to find an estate and design the new house which, like Blenheim, was to be a memorial of British gratitude towards one of the 'greatest and most successful of heroes'. Benjamin worked on the palace for six years, producing five different sets of highly finished drawings. In the end none was adopted. The great project turned out to be a waste of time. Wellington was too busy to bother about architecture and in any case hated extravagant expense. He made do with the existing unpretentious house at Stratfield Saye.[34] The nearest Benjamin Dean got to designing a Waterloo Palace was the remodelling of Apsley House and the cost of that alone caused an acrimonious quarrel between him and the Duke.

Wellington bought Apsley House from his brother, Lord Wellesley, in 1816 for £40,000. It was a sign he had finally won the steeplechase between the Wellesley brothers. In 1822 the Duke decided to enlarge it and allowed himself to be persuaded by his friend Mrs. Arbuthnot and Benjamin Dean into a thorough remodelling. The main alteration was the addition of the Waterloo Gallery on the west side and the cladding of the exterior in Bath stone.

While work was in progress the building was found to be seriously dilapidated. Putting these defects right, together with the lavish interior decoration, added greatly to the expense. Benjamin Dean's original estimate was consequently exceeded. Mrs. Arbuthnot, who was largely responsible for the extravagance of the scheme, joined the Duke in self-righteous indignation:

The Duke came here last night and annoyed me dreadfully by telling me that he had received the bills of his house and that Mr. Wyatt had just exceeded his estimate *three times over* and had made the sum so enormous that he did not know how to pay it and

---

[33] Alexander, *Life at Fonthill*, 295–6, 10 Mar. 1819.
[34] RIBAD, Benjamin Dean Wyatt's designs for Waterloo Palace.

had seriously been thinking of selling the house. I never saw him so vexed or so annoyed. He said the shame and ridicule of being so cheated and imposed upon and having been led on to an expenditure which must ruin his family made him quite miserable, that he cd. not bear the sight of the house and really did not know what to do. It was with some difficulty I got him to tell me what it had cost and only under a promise I would not tell it to anyone. [£43,657. 18*s*. 6*d*.] I told him I thought it the most preposterous cheat I ever heared of and I asked him what Mr. Wyatt said for himself. He told me he had abused him furiously and told him it shd be the last conversation he wd ever have with him, that he had known him for 40 years, knew all his circumstances and with his eyes open he had ruined him . . . I tried to comfort him as well as I cd and said that, if the work was fairly measured and valued, he wd know at least that he had his money's worth; and that tho' it was certainly most provoking, still the house is beautiful and as it will hold his pictures and all his fine things he must consider it as his Waterloo House and use part of that money.[35]

Wellington's annoyance did not last and in 1838 he employed Benjamin Dean to improve Stratfield Saye by adding a porch and a conservatory. As he grew older the Duke became more and more dependent on Benjamin Dean in all architectural matters and even sought his advice on such trivia as cleaning chimneys and trimming hedges. Nearly 400 letters survive from Benjamin to the Duke in the muniment room at Stratfield Saye and are evidence of a remarkable professional relationship. The Duke's letters to Benjamin Dean also survive in a private collection.

By the 1830s much of the promise of Benjamin Dean's earlier career had come to nothing. His attempt to establish a country house practice like his father's failed. He was not able even to retain his father's unfinished buildings. At Ashridge, for instance, though he designed some Gothic furniture and the staircase-balustrade in 1813 and 1814 he was not kept on by the Earl of Bridgewater. The completion of the house was entrusted instead to Jeffry Wyatville. At Fonthill he also failed to secure the commission for finishing the abbey. Beckford disliked him and in any case was unable to continue with building because of lack of money. All Benjamin Dean did there was to design a Gothic gateway which was not executed.

Altogether his attempts to design country houses are a dispiriting spectacle. Apart from the failure of the Waterloo Palace, his designs for other houses, including the remodelling of Charlecote, the rebuilding of Westport, and the extension of Clumber, were not adopted. He was, however, employed to do some minor internal work at Clumber and his design for a library at Westport was executed but has since been demolished.

If the Duke of Wellington failed to be the Maecenas whom Benjamin Dean hoped for, the Duchess of Rutland was a good substitute. His success in London was also some compensation for the failure of his country house practice. The

[35] J. Bamford and Duke of Wellington (eds.), *The Journal of Mrs. Arbuthnot* (1950), 355–6.

fifth Duchess of Rutland was an enthusiastic architectural amateur. She landscaped the park at Belvoir and designed the home farm there. She painted landscapes in the manner of Claude and her architectural drawings were considered worthy of a professional. 'She was the builder of the castle and Belvoir is indebted to her for all its beauty and decorations. She certainly was a woman of genius and talent mixed up with a great deal of vanity and folly.'[36]

When the castle, designed originally by James Wyatt, was partially destroyed by fire in 1816 the Duchess asked Matthew Cotes, Benjamin Dean, and Philip to recreate the interior, though the Revd. Sir John Thoroton restored the exterior. Benjamin Dean (with Philip's assistance) designed the new State Dining-Room and the Picture Gallery in the grandiose Roman style which he had hoped to use for the Waterloo Palace.

The Duchess was delighted and adopted the Wyatt brothers as her favourite architects. She involved them in abortive schemes for improving London and recommended them to her friends. More important was the effect on their taste, for she was an enthusiast for French decoration and furniture. On a visit to Paris in 1814 she had bought tapestries and furniture for Belvoir, and she wanted her principal drawing-room decorated in the French style. Matthew Cotes Wyatt designed it in 1824, making use of genuine Louis XV *boiseries*, pier glass frames, and other carvings combined in a decorative ensemble of great richness. The carpet was specially woven for the room at Tournai in Belgium and Matthew Cotes painted the ceiling in the manner of Verrio with mythological scenes. The carvings were bought in Paris as a job lot for 1,450 guineas by Matthew Cotes and the rest of the work was made up to match either on site or in London. Altogether 115 craftsmen were employed in the embellishment of the room.[38] The Elizabeth Saloon at Belvoir is the earliest example of what was called the Louis-Quatorze style and is a dazzling display of Matthew Cotes's brilliance as a theatrical designer.

The Wyatts had all visited France more than once – Matthew Cotes in 1814, 1824, and 1830; Benjamin Dean in 1814, 1815, and 1817; Philip in 1814 and on two occasions in 1819. Both Matthew Cotes and Philip were involved at different times in buying French furniture and carvings for English customers. This interest in French decoration was encouraged by the Duchess. Some rooms designed in 1826 by Benjamin Dean and Philip for her friend the Duke of York were also Louis-Quatorze but were not executed.[39]

The new style first made its appearance in London in 1827 at Crockford's Club in St. James's designed by Benjamin Dean Wyatt. It was an immediate success and Louis-Quatorze was in the long run to become the normal

[36] *Journal of Mrs. Arbuthnot*, 230.
[38] Belvoir, Rutland MSS., 2.20.3, Letters between Duke of Rutland and M.C.Wyatt, 1825.
[39] Royal Library, Windsor, 18971–8, Benjamin Dean Wyatt drawings for York House 1825.

61. London, Crockford's
Club, St. James's Street
(now the Jamaican High
Commission), Staircase.
Designed by Benjamin
Dean Wyatt, 1827. The
earliest example in
London of the
Louis-Quatorze style.

62. London, Crockford's
Club, St. James's Street,
Staircase ceiling.

decoration for London drawing-rooms. Benjamin Dean was immediately asked to create suites of rooms with French decoration in a number of aristocratic town houses: Apsley House for the Duke of Wellington (1828), Londonderry House for the Marquess of Londonderry (1828), 6 Carlton House Terrace for the Marquess of Tavistock (1831), and Stafford House for the Duke of Sutherland (1833–7).

The Louis-Quatorze revival marked a revolution in Benjamin Dean's architectural style. He was considered its originator and the only architect able to create the *tout ensemble*. He had a special flair for decoration and this is where his importance as an architect lies. His exteriors are mere platitudes but his interiors are always excellently planned and richly decorated.

The revival coincided with the influx into this country of large quantities of fine French furniture and objects. This was caused by the Revolutionary Government's systematic dispersal of the contents of the French royal palaces for political reasons. Fashionable English collectors, headed by the Prince Regent, competed with each other to obtain the best examples at bargain prices. Naturally the possessors of such opulent pieces wanted to house them appropriately. Benjamin Dean's interiors were the perfect setting. His secret was to use Jackson's putty for the decoration rather than real wood carving or antique work. This was much quicker and cheaper and once it was gilded nobody could tell the difference.

The Louis-Quatorze style was inspired largely by Versailles. The Corinthian columns and balustrades of the staircase at York (later Stafford) House and Crockford's Club were both derived from the chapel there. Many other details, doors, chimney-pieces, and stucco look more Louis XV than Louis-Quatorze. Such decoration was, however, intended to be evocative rather than accurate. Its purpose was to create an ambiance of *ancien régime* splendour such as could not be afforded by 'persons of small fortune'. This intention is admirably summarized in a mid-nineteenth-century description of Crockford's:

The suite of apartments upstairs may vie in magnificence, taste and splendour with any others in Europe. . . . Many of our readers are no doubt acquainted with the principal leading palatial mansions in this metropolis. The most conspicuous of them, with regard to their luxuriant splendour and truly aristocratic grandezza, were called into existence at the period of George IV and his royal brothers; . . . one all surpassing in splendour [is] the Club-House erected with astounding liberality in St. James Street . . . the style of the decoration has been more-or-less, in its architectural details, strictly copied from the best specimens of Versailles . . . and other numerous examples of the periods of 'Louis Quatorze' and 'Louis Quinze' . . . When on former occasions, a humble individual of the people obtained the privilege of entering the Higher Regions of Aristocracy, the surrounding atmosphere of these stately edifices seemed to exercise an awe-stricken influence over his mind, in beholding a grandeur he had never before witnessed.[40]

[40] *The Royal Hotel Guide to London* (1853–4), 9 (ex info Mr. Christopher Monkhouse).

Such rooms were perfectly expressive of the mood of the English aristocracy in the halcyon years following Waterloo. England had survived Continental war and revolution. She had emerged victorious from the long struggle against Napoleon. The landed classes had preserved their power and privileges intact and were richer than ever before. Industry, banking, urban development, canals, and coal had swelled their incomes and augmented their rent-rolls. Between 1790 and 1815 there was an agricultural boom as the country strove to remain self-sufficient. Rents reached an unprecedentedly high level and landowners consolidated their estates to achieve maximum efficiency.

The period between 1800 and 1832 was an Indian summer of the territorial aristocracy. Pride in family with all its accompanying snobbery matched newly inflated incomes. Names were medievalized and long pedigrees fabricated, going back to the Norman Conquest or even Charlemagne. Extinct medieval titles and privileges were called out of abeyance. The sixth Duke of Bedford even claimed the right to issue all the marriage licences on his Bedfordshire estates as successor to the Abbot of Woburn.

Many estates were virtually independent principalities with their own customs, courts, rituals, and even time. Households were maintained with ever-increasing lavishness. Greville recorded on a visit to Chatsworth that there were 150 servants in the house. At Ashridge 500 men were employed, including one whose sole job was to inspect the park fences. At Belvoir the Duke of Rutland had his own regimental band which roused his guests every morning with strains of martial music.

This is the world revealed in the diaries of Charles Greville, Thomas Creevey, Mrs. Arbuthnot, and the sixth Duke of Devonshire; in the letters of Princess Lieven and Prince Pückler-Muskau; and re-created in such novels as Disraeli's *Coningsby* and Thackeray's *Vanity Fair*. This magnificence had as much relevance in early nineteenth-century industrial England as the Court of Louis XIV had in seventeenth-century mercantile Europe. It is ironically appropriate, therefore, that the one should have modelled itself on the other.

Prince Pückler-Muskau describes the England of his day with the superficial insight of a foreigner, unaware of the strength of the Whig tradition and the survival power of the English upper classes. He was struck by the haughtiness, magnificence, and riches of the aristocracy but wrongly saw it as doomed. 'England is now in a similar state to that of France thirty years before the Revolution.' He was intelligent enough, however, to notice that though 'everything is in the highest degree ultra-aristocratic' neither money nor rank were the ultimate gods of society but fashion, and fashion was Louis-Quatorze. 'On the whole fashionable Englishmen . . . betray the most intense desire to rival the dissolute frivolity and jactance of the old Court of France.'[41] As they

[41] Prince Pückler-Muskau, *Tours in England*, 9, 370, 2, 6.

owned most of the furniture of the 'old Court of France' and had Benjamin
Dean Wyatt to re-create Versailles in London, they were able to do this
convincingly.

The Regency aristocracy as a whole represented the last class of European
art patrons in the Renaissance princely tradition. Such enthusiasms as the
Duke of Devonshire's for sculpture and the Duchess of Rutland's for architecture enriched this country immeasurably. The Wyatts of the early nineteenth
century, whether architects, painters, or sculptors, were among the main
recipients of a lavish patronage. Their works survive as the most complete
monument to this society and its tastes, to the optimistic years of victory and
the fragile glories of the Regency and reign of George IV.

In London the most evocative survival of the age is Stafford House (now
Lancaster House). It took twenty years to complete and is Benjamin Dean's
masterpiece. The scale and decorative richness of the interiors are overwhelming. It started as York House and he received the commission through the
intervention of the Duchess of Rutland on his behalf. In about 1820 the Duke of
York started to build a new house to the design of Robert Smirke. The Duchess
of Rutland disapproved and encouraged Benjamin Dean to produce alternative
proposals under her personal supervision.

She was a close friend of the Duke of York and had no difficulty in getting
him to accept Benjamin Dean's plans. Smirke was mortified. He wrote to the
Architect's Club complaining of Benjamin Dean's conduct as unprofessional.
The secretary wrote to Benjamin in December 1825 demanding an explanation
of his conduct. In a typical outburst of fury Benjamin resigned from the Club
and threatened to publish a full account of the affair in the newspapers. This
would have dragged in a number of 'persons of high rank', but, fortunately, he
did not carry out this threat.[42]

The foundation-stone was laid on 17 June 1825 and the shell rose rapidly
during the following months. The Duchess maintained a close interest in its
progress. Models of the proposed elevations were submitted for her approval.[43]
Then disaster. The Duchess of Rutland died suddenly of appendicitis. She was
buried near Belvoir in the style in which she had lived. The funeral procession
accompanied by the tolling of many bells took three hours to wind its way from
the castle to Bottesford Church. A long line of servants and tenants dressed in
black escorted the Duchess's empty carriage and her favourite white horse led
by a groom. Finally came the hearse itself flanked by four pages with
silver-tipped staves. In front of it walked the house steward solemnly bearing
her coronet on a purple velvet cushion.[44]

[42] H. M. Colvin, 'The Architects of Stafford House', *AH* i (1958), 17–30.
[43] Belvoir Castle, Rutland MSS., Letters from B. D. Wyatt to 5th Duchess of Rutland.
[44] The Revd. Irvin Eller, *History of Belvoir Castle* (1841), 136.

63. London, Lancaster House
(originally York House), Staircase.
Designed by Benjamin Dean Wyatt,
c. 1827–33. Water-colour, 1850.

64. London, Lancaster House,
Green Drawing-Room, *c.* 1833.

She was not to rest at Bottesford for long. The disconsolate Duke decided to build a mausoleum on the hill next to the castle in a grove of venerable yew-trees. Benjamin Dean Wyatt was chosen as the architect. He was assisted by Philip, and Matthew Cotes Wyatt carved the monument to the Duchess. The Wyatts' first proposal was for a Greek temple but the Norman style was adopted as preferable for its association of antiquity. The mausoleum was intended to look like an ancient family chantry recently restored and brought back into use to serve as the Duchess' funerary chapel.

The brothers took a great deal of trouble over the Belvoir mausoleum. It was to contain the patroness they revered. Plaster models of all the carved stonework were provided to guide the masons. The ironwork of the entrance-doors was carefully copied from that of Sempringham Church in Lincoln-shire.[45]

The foundation-stone was laid on 1 March 1826 by the Duke of York with a golden trowel.[46] The architects attended the ceremony. As they stood there amongst the purple velvet, the mud, and the leafless trees on a windy hilltop in Leicestershire they could not foresee that within a year the Duke of York would have followed his closest friend to the grave. This gave them the opportunity to design another monument – the Duke of York's Column in Waterloo Place.

The Duke of York died in January 1827, leaving an unfinished palace, an unpaid architect, and debts amounting to £200,000. The uncertainty over the future of York House was resolved in December 1827 when it was sold unfinished to the Marquess of Stafford, one of the richest men in England, for £70,000. The Marquess re-engaged Benjamin Dean and Philip as his architects. When he died (as Duke of Sutherland) in 1833 the second Duke again employed Benjamin Dean to add an extra storey for his servants and to decorate the state rooms in the Louis-Quatorze style. There was one mortifying condition. Benjamin Dean's drawings were to be executed under the supervision of another architect – Sir Robert Smirke.

It is not clear why the Duke called in Smirke. It was a tactless move. Benjamin Dean believed that the Duke 'thought that he might be the gainer by the two architects being a check upon each other'. So they were, but not in the sense the Duke hoped. Their mutual dislike was scarcely calculated to forward the work. There was constant misunderstanding. An acrimonious correspondence between the Duke and Benjamin Dean culminated in the most spectacular dispute of his quarrelsome career.

He was seventy years old and poor. His temper, never very good, burst out with the pent-up irritation of years. He had had 'ample evidence of the extreme

---

[45] Belvoir Castle, Rutland MSS., Letters from B. D. Wyatt to Duke of Rutland 1827–9.
[46] Eller, 352.

65. London, Lancaster House, Gallery, *c.* 1833

degree of pretension to taste on the part of both the Duke and the Duchess with very little sound knowledge, taste or judgment on such subjects'. He had enjoyed 'no sinecure in attending to all their notions and at the same time protecting the design against great absurdities'. He submitted a bill for his services over the preceding five years amounting to the large sum of £1,772. 14s. 11d.

He claimed that the Louis-Quatorze style with its complex ornament involved extra work because the drawings had to be more accurate and inventive than with other styles. The Duchess's changes of mind and interference involved him in great additional labour. His assistant, William Payne, claimed that the drawings for Stafford House were three times the number needed for a similar amount of work at Windsor.

In 1838 the Duke of Sutherland, on the advice of his agent, James Loch, refused to pay and employed Charles Barry as his architect instead. Benjamin Dean took out a writ against the Duke in the Court of Common Pleas for £1,772. The case was slow but much of the evidence was gratifying. Witness after witness came forward to testify that Benjamin Dean was the best designer of the Louis-Quatorze style. He had been responsible for introducing it to London. Thomas Hopper told the court that Benjamin was a 'superior architect'. Stafford House was described as the 'most brilliant house of the day'.[47] Even bitter Benjamin must have been mollified by such a chorus of praise. It was the high point of his career. To crown all the Court found in his favour and the Duke had to pay his fees. It was a triumph for the disillusioned old architect. It was also the end of his professional career. He did not design anything further and died in about 1850 in Camden Town. He left all his possessions including his gold watch by Rundell & Bridge to his loyal housekeeper, Martha Turner, who had been with him for many years.[48]

A victim of the Stafford House quarrel was Philip. In 1833 he had finally broken away from Benjamin Dean and tried to get the Duke of Sutherland to take him on as sole architect. Philip's patron, Sir Frederick Trench, had pressed his case with the Duke but to no avail. The Duke kept Benjamin Dean and turned down Philip's offer. It was the end of the association between the two brothers. Philip was left hopeless and penniless.

It is surprising that their association had lasted so long. Philip did not work very hard. At the Stafford House lawsuit Benjamin Dean claimed that Philip had not done any of the drawings for Apsley House, nor for Stafford House. If he had been able to work independently Philip would have left his brother earlier. Only his need for money had kept them together. There had been

---

[47] Staffs, R.O., Trentham MSS., Complete documentation of the lawsuit between Duke of Sutherland and B.D. Wyatt.
[48] P.R.O., Wills 882 – Benjamin Dean Wyatt.

intermittent quarrels before, but that over Stafford House was final. By any standards Philip had treated his brother and benefactor shabbily.

In the 1820s Philip's prospects had momentarily looked brighter. As well as helping Benjamin Dean with the Oriental Club, Crockford's Club, and Londonderry House he had done some work with Matthew Cotes including decoration worth £1,000 for Lord Blessington at 10 St. James's Square.[49] He also received two major independent jobs, Wynyard Park and Conishead Priory, and was closely involved in Sir Frederick Trench's and the Duchess of Rutland's schemes for metropolitan improvements.

In the years following Waterloo and throughout the reign of George IV a consistent effort was made to transform London into a great imperial capital, and to make it a worthy setting for the Government of the richest and most powerful nation in the world. As is well known, part of this was triumphantly carried into execution under the direction of John Nash with the creation of Regent's Park and Regent Street. Magnificent though that was, it was only the first phase and in the 1820s proposals were in hand for even grander improvements.

In 1824 a committee was set up including Sir Frederick Trench to promote a Thames embankment or quay between Charing Cross and Blackfriars in the form of a long arched viaduct supported on Doric columns. It was to be built of granite and adorned with statues and fountains. Beneath the supporting arches the existing wharfs were to be retained to preserve the commercial interests of the river bank.

In association with the quay various improvements of the adjoining streets were also proposed. These and the quay itself were designed by Philip for Sir Frederick Trench. His drawings were reputed to be 'very spirited and beautiful'. At the first meeting of the committee the Marquess of Londonderry (a friend of Trench's) recommended Philip as 'a professional friend' and said 'his plans and drawings for the proposed works did him great credit and marked his judgement and good taste'. As a result the scheme was unanimously adopted.

Public opinion in general, however, was hostile. The editor of *John Bull* on 24 July 1824 expressed surprise at the outcome of the meeting. He was under the impression that 'the original plan for the improvement of the Thames is actually and bona fide the design of Mr. Nash, it is a most extraordinary measure to call a meeting, at a time when Mr. Nash is absent from London to consider that plan and to mention the name of another gentleman whose only claim on public attention . . . is his name, as an architect likely to carry into execution the design'. He denounced the whole affair as a piece of 'private intriguing . . . to drag into notice obscure and incompetent artists'.

[49] BL, Egerton MS. 3515, M.C.Wyatt, 24 Feb. 1821.

66. Belvoir Castle, Dining-Room.
Designed by Benjamin Dean Wyatt,
c. 1816.

67. Belvoir Castle, Mausoleum.
Designed in the Norman style by
Benjamin Dean and Philip
Wyatt, c. 1830. The monument
to the fifth Duchess of Rutland is
by Matthew Cotes Wyatt.

68. Unexecuted design for monument to Duke of York by Benjamin Dean and Philip Wyatt, 1827.

69. Wynyard Park, Co. Durham. Designed by Philip Wyatt, 1822–8.

Fortunately for Philip this was false. On 1 August *John Bull* was forced to publish an apology together with a letter from Nash explaining that the quay was not his idea but Trench's. In 1826 a parliamentary bill to authorize the construction of the quay was defeated and there the matter rested through lack of money. It was only in 1864 that the Victoria Embankment was finally completed under the direction of Sir Joseph Bazalgette.[50]

Sir Frederick Trench and his associates, carried away by a heady enthusiasm for 'Improvement', were engrossed in ever more megalomaniac proposals for transforming the capital. He called these schemes, with studied understatement, 'Hints for further improvements'. The first of them involved gothicizing the river front of the old Houses of Parliament to Philip's design. Trench wrote that it need not be expensive. This caused a quarrel with Soane. He had been commissioned to design a front for the Law Courts adjoining Westminster Hall. When an estimate amounting to £9,000 was submitted, Trench, who was on the committee, produced an alternative scheme which he claimed was 'far more beautiful and extensive'. 'A distinguished artist' had said that the work could be done for half the sum mentioned by Soane. That artist was, of course, Philip Wyatt. Soane, always proud and sensitive, was hurt and angry. When Philip called the following day to explain that his estimate was 'merely an off-hand affair' for Trench, 'his intimate friend', Soane showed him the door.[51]

Other 'hints for improvement' included additions to the Adelphi to form a crescent, a new entrance to the Temple, a precinct for St. Paul's with a vista down to the river, and a new royal palace in Hyde Park with a forecourt 1,000 feet square. 'Of all the monarchs of Europe none is more miserably accommodated than the King of the most powerful and wealthy nation of the world.' Philip and Trench thought something more appropriate could be achieved for as *little* as £800,000. Of course the palace never had a chance of being carried into effect but it is an interesting reflection of the triumphalist euphoria which swept the country following Waterloo. Mrs. Arbuthnot's reaction was typical of the opposition:

We had Colonel Trench to shew us some plans he has for new buildings. He wants to have a palace in the park on what is called Buck Vine Hill and the execution of his plan would cause half Hyde Park to be occupied by buildings, courts and gardens. It is the worst plan of a house I ever saw and quite colossal, for he proposes a statue gallery 500 feet long, a drawing room 190 and the other rooms in proportion. It is the most ridiculous plan I ever saw for added to it is the idea of a street *200 feet wide* extending from the end of Hyde Park opposite the new palace to St. Paul's!! The king and Duke of York are madly eager for this plan; but the former says he supposes his damned ministers won't allow it . . . all the rest of us laughed at Col. Trench and his plans. We

[50] V & A, S1.G.9, S1.A.58; F. W. Trench, *Collection of Papers Relating to the Thames Quay* (1827).
[51] *Journal of Mrs. Arbuthnot*, 508.

70. Wynyard Park, Co.
Durham, Drawing-Room.

71. Conishead Priory,
Lancashire. Designed by
Philip Wyatt, 1821–36.

advised him to put his palace in Kensington Gardens and not to touch the 'lungs of the people of England' as the newspapers call the parks; and we reminded him that his new street would just go over Lady Jersey's house [38 Berkeley Square] who would make the town much too hot to hold him. He said she might go and live at her shop in Fleet Street [Child's Bank].[52]

Despite his over-all lack of success Philip was still fortunate enough to design two large country houses in the North of England, Wynyard Park and Conishead Priory. It is on these two building that his reputation as an architect rests. Both are splendid examples of their respective styles, Gothic and neo-classical. They are masterpieces.

Wynyard was the principal seat of the third Marquess and Marchioness of Londonderry who had an income in excess of £80,000 p.a. derived from collieries in Durham and estates in Ireland. The Marquess of Londonderry was a friend of Sir Frederick Trench and that explains how Philip got the commission.

It was a unique opportunity and he made the most of it. The house realizes many of Benjamin Dean's frustrated dreams for the Waterloo Palace. The entrance-front with an octostyle Corinthian portico is almost identical to the amended design for the Waterloo Palace. The plan with a central octagonal hall rising into a dome also exploits one of Benjamin Dean's cherished ideas for creating a grand effect by roofing over the centre of a building. At Wynyard the space is not a staircase but forms part of the Sculpture Gallery.

Work began in 1822 and was largely completed by 1828 at a cost of £102,097.12*s*.0*d*. Philip's commission came to £4,000. He was paid off in that year because, as Lord Londonderry told Sir Thomas Lawrence, his extreme inconsequence made him impossible to deal with.[53]

The house was fitted up in a rich cosmopolitan style. Even today when the rooms have lost most of their original furniture the effect is still magnificent. The Sculpture Gallery is surrounded by 48 pilasters of Jasper on plinths of Egyptian green marble. The door-cases are of Siena marble and the floor paved in white marble. The central octagon is 80 feet in diameter and 60 feet high.

The rooms along the south front – Boudoir, Library, Vestibule, Drawing-Room, and Ballroom – are decorated in the Louis-Quatorze style at its richest with gilded plasterwork, sheets of looking-glass, Boulle panels, and marble door-cases. Throughout the enfilade the floors are of mahogany inlaid with rosewood and satinwood. Together with Stafford House this is the most palatial interior created by the Wyatts in the early nineteenth century.

Wynyard perfectly evokes the characters of the third Marquess and Marchioness of Londonderry. Princess Lieven in a letter to Metternich compared

---

[52] Ibid. 336, 25 Oct. 1825.
[53] Durham R.O., Londonderry MSS., D/LO/E464, Accounts 1820–40; RA Library, LAW/5/262, Lord Londonderry to Sir T. Lawrence, 6 Aug. 1828.

the Marchioness to 'one of those effigies you see in Greek churches with no colour or shading but loaded with jewels'. She described the Marchioness's bedroom with mixed envy and shock. 'Above the bed is a coronet the size of the crown of the King of Würtemberg on the palace of Stuttgart – red velvet, ermine, everything that goes with it. From it hang heavy draperies held up at the four corners of the bed by four large gilt figures of Hercules, nude and fashioned *exactly like real men*.'[54]

The progress of Conishead was even more erratic than Wynyard. Begun in 1821 it was not completed till 1836. The style adopted is a free Perpendicular of collegiate and ecclesiastical derivation in the manner of James Wyatt. The composition is sweepingly asymmetrical and the whole forms an L-shaped pile. The entrance-front is specially successful with a central gatehouse flanked by turrets and spires. Many of the interiors are equally spectacular with attenuated plaster rib vaults. Together with Ashridge and Belvoir it is the best of the surviving Wyatt Gothic houses.

But Philip continually failed to produce drawings when they were needed or to supervise the work adequately. After repeated requests for estimates and plans the owner of Conishead, Colonel Braddyll's patience gave out in 1829, a year after the Marquess of Londonderry's, and he told Philip that his services were no longer required.[55] The priory was finished by other hands. When the bills arrived Colonel Braddyll found that the total cost was £140,000, a sum he could not possibly afford. He was forced to sell the entire estate, which had been the property of his family for centuries.

To complete a picture of cataclysmic ruin Wynyard was partially destroyed by fire in 1841. It was restored exactly using Philip's drawings, twenty volumes of which still survive among the Londonderry papers. The restoration cost a further £40,000 and was referred to by the Marquess in a letter to Matthew Cotes as 'your poor brother's resurrection'.[56]

'Poor little Philip' was committed to debtors' prison in 1833.[57] His bankruptcy involved Benjamin Dean as well. Philip had borrowed money until the interest on his debts greatly exceeded the original sum. Benjamin Dean unwisely stood surety for Philip. The result was calamitous. Benjamin Dean described his involvement to the Duke of Wellington:

I was induced by the urgent entreaties of a relation of mine and by an earnest desire on my part to serve him, to accept Bills for his accommodation and otherwise to make myself responsible for him to a very large amount; all of his liabilities have, from his entire failure in his engagements, lately fallen like a Thunder bolt upon me and my

[54] Brian Masters, *Wynyard Hall & the Londonderry Family* (privately printed 1973).
[55] Durham R.O., D/LO/C141 (18), Col. R.Gale Braddyll to Marquess of Londonderry, 5 Apr. 1829.
[56] Durham R.O., D/LO/E878, 882/9, Accounts for restoration 1841–5; V & A, Wyatt MS. 86.00.15, Marquess of Londonderry to M.C.W., 10 Oct. 1846.
[57] PRO, PriS 4/43/p.11.

affairs have in consequence been brought to a calamitous crisis ... I find myself without any alternative but to succumb to a commission of bankruptcy ... My situation is at present deplorable and the prospect attendant on beginning the World anew at the age of nearly 60, very disheartening.[58]

As a result Benjamin Dean had to give up his house in Foley Place and move to rented accommodation in Albany Street behind Regent's Park. The Duke of Wellington had recommended him to the trustees of Dover Harbour to design various improvements and new buildings but his bankruptcy forced the Duke to withdraw this recommendation. Benjamin Dean satisfied his creditors in March 1833 and was granted a certificate of discharge from bankruptcy but he remained poor. In his last years he had only the money won in the Stafford House lawsuit to live off.[59]

As for Philip, he died ruined three years later. His life had been a series of disastrous failures. If he looked back from his deathbed, the knowledge that two of his 'sublime plans' had got off the drawing-board must have been a small consolation even though in both cases he was sacked before the buildings were completed. But it is tragic that he was unable to make more of the 'taste and knowledge' so triumphantly expressed in the marble halls of Wynyard and the filigree turrets of Conishead.

[58] Stratfield Saye MSS., B.D. Wyatt to Duke of Wellington, 6 Feb. 1833.
[59] Ibid., B.D. Wyatt to Duke of Wellington, 21 Mar. 1833.

72. Sir Jeffry Wyatville, by Sir Thomas Laurence, 1828.

CHAPTER V

Sir Jeffry Wyatville (1766–1840) and Lewis Wyatt (1777–1853)

Compared to Benjamin Dean and Philip, Sir Jeffry Wyatville and Lewis Wyatt had successful careers. Of the two, Wyatville is the more famous. He was knighted, became a member of the Royal Academy, a Fellow of the Institute of British Architects, a Fellow of the Royal Society and of the Society of Antiquaries, and also received the Grand Cross of the Ernestine Order of Saxony. He made a fortune out of his profession and left his family over £70,000 when he died. He was almost exclusively a country house architect and was responsible for some of the most famous improvement schemes of the early nineteenth century, including the transformation of Windsor Castle and Chatsworth. In his speech at the presentation in 13 Lincoln's Inn Fields of a gold medal as a tribute of respect to Sir John Soane from the British Architects in 1835 Wyatville claimed that his 'rise in life . . . had been the effect' of his own endeavours; and that 'by a straightforward course' he had arrived at riches and 'eminence beyond expectation'.

Lewis Wyatt also designed country houses and, though not as prolific as Wyatville, was perhaps the better architect of the two. He was an architect-scholar with international tastes and connections. He too was a rich man but in his case a lot of the money was inherited. Lewis, far more than Jeffry, was James Wyatt's spiritual successor, extending his architectural career and achievement to the end of the Georgian era. In his country houses Lewis continued the brilliant eclecticism of his uncle. He carried on the family connection with the Office of Works, though in a less exalted capacity, as clerk of works in the Eastern Division and at Hampton Court. He also succeeded James as Surveyor to the Middlesex Hospital and the Ordnance Office. His architectural career, however, was prematurely cut short as a result of personal misfortune.

Jeffry Wyatville began by trying to run away to sea. He hoped to join Admiral Kempenfelt's flagship the *Royal George*, but failed and thereby escaped certain death at Spithead in 1782 when the ship sank with all its crew. The following year he went to London in search of another ship but was unsuccessful. The American War of Independence had just ended and the navy was more concerned with getting rid of extra men than with taking on new ones. Reluctantly he gave up his naval ambitions and turned to architecture instead.

He was the second son of Joseph Wyatt of Burton-on-Trent and is reputed to have had an unhappy childhood. His mother Myrtilla Wyatt died at his birth and he was brought up by his stepmother Mary Fortescue. He was the neglected child of a first marriage in contrast to the happy and indulgent upbringing of Benjamin Dean and Philip. This may partly explain the different outcome of their careers. Wyatville's youthful unhappiness was a spur to his ambition.

His father died in 1785, when he was eighteen. It was about then that he went into Samuel's office where he stayed for seven years. Under his uncle he gained 'considerable knowledge of the ordinary business of practical construction' and had 'opportunities of witnessing all the processes of designing, estimating and executing buildings of various kinds'.[1]

Around 1792 he transferred to his uncle James at Queen Anne Street and was inspired to emulate his achievement. 'When in my younger days I found there was a Surveyor-General of His Majesty's Works, and such a desirable thing as being a Royal Academician, I set out with a view to succeed to both if I could.'[2] Though he consciously modelled his career on that of James he disapproved of his uncle's erratic business methods and determined to avoid them. His own office and practice were methodically organized. He kept tight control over his buildings and visited them all two or three times a year. At the height of his career he employed ten clerks and gave his contractors 'precise drawings'. They were prepared in London and sent to the site by mail. The partially complete sets which survive show his care. Sometimes his presentation drawings were bound up in special albums for the owner's library, as at Chatsworth, Lilleshall, Woburn, and Wollaton. Similarly, the building accounts were copied into leather-bound volumes for the benefit of posterity.[3]

Wyatville set up his own building and architectural business in 1799 entering into partnership with John Armstrong. In 1802 he acquired a house at 39 Lower Brook Street which still survives and where he lived for the rest of his life. At the back he built a new wing with his drawing office on the ground floor and a gallery on the first floor for the reception of clients. At first he earned £500 a year from the building business but this soon doubled.[4] After Armstrong's death Wyatville carried on alone for another twenty years. In 1807 following the death of Samuel he took over most of his uncle's building business, including the Victualling Office carpentry contract and the Office of Works carpentry contract in Westminster.[5] Many of Samuel's builders also passed into his employment. William Jarrard, 'the blunt fellow' who had

[1] *Gent's Mag.* (May 1840), i. 545.
[2] Parliamentary Papers, Report of Select Committee on the Office of Works (1828), 99.
[3] D. Linstrum, *Sir Jeffry Wyatville* (Oxford, 1972), 19–27.
[4] Farington, 1 Aug. 1799.
[5] PRO, ADM 111/82, Victualling Office Mins., 10 Feb. 1807; Works 4/20, Mins., 20 Feb. 1807.

supervised Samuel's alterations to Soho House, became Jeffry's clerk of works at Dinton and Chatsworth. Jeffry was also, for a time, labourer in trust at Carlton House and held the carpentry contract under Nash at Brighton Pavilion.[6]

Much of his prosperity derived from his building business. In his alterations at Chesterfield House, for instance, he received £3,288.3s.6¼d. for carpentry compared to his architect's commission of £570.6s.2¾d. on the other tradesmen's bills.[7] It was only at the end of his career that he finally ended his association with the building trade and conformed to Victorian professional standards when in 1834 he was made an Honorary Fellow of the newly founded Institute of British Architects.

In his own career Wyatville had exemplified the changing attitude towards the architectural profession. Articled at first to an architect-builder-engineer, he had been trained in the eighteenth century tradition to learn the principles of surveying, measuring, costing and superintendance as well as the technique of draughtsmanship. From this comprehensive introduction to the whole field of building he had moved to the other avuncular sphere where he had acquired a degree of 'taste' and architectural scholarship, and been introduced to the world of the land-owning aristocracy and gentry. Like the profession as a whole he had attempted to combine all three activities in a single career. As early as 1799 he was claiming that 'the liberal profession of an architect' entitled him to the same consideration as a gentleman in independent circumstances, a status which could hardly be achieved without abandoning the traditional association with the practical side of building.[8]

In spite of his professional success and the honours which were showered upon him Wyatville retained his 'provincial character' to the end of his life. He lacked the urbane manners of his uncle James and his cousins Benjamin Dean, Philip, and Lewis. He remained unaffectedly jolly, good-humoured and plain-speaking. His manner matched his appearance, for contemporaries remarked on his 'low stature and inelegant personal form'. As an architect he was neither an intellectual nor a scholar. C. R. Cockerell noted disapprovingly that he was no gentleman and summed him up as 'vulgar-minded, good-natured and a great boaster'.[9]

The Duke of Devonshire was more charitable. After Wyatville's death in 1840 he wrote: 'My attachment to Sir Jeffry was most sincere, it was impossible to know him as I did and not to love him and his loss is one that cannot be repaired'. Elsewhere the Duke recalled him as a 'delightful man, good, simple, like a child, indefatigable, eager, patient, easy to deal with to the highest degree . . . He spoke the oddest dialect, if I may so call it, and at first I

[6] Roy. Arch. 33 963, 33 986, 33 334, Accounts for Brighton Pavilion.
[7] Guildhall Library, MS. 3070A, Chesterfield House Account Book 1813.
[8] Linstrum, 29. I am grateful to Dr. Derek Linstrum for permission to quote this passage.
[9] Coll. Mrs. Crichton, Plas Trefor, Anglesey, C. R. Cockerell, Diary (MS.).

feared that it would be a stumbling-block with Royalty, which however took to being amused and imitating it – perfectly, never ill-naturedly.'[10]

By a freak of survival an example of Royalty's imitation of Wyatville's accent is preserved in a letter from George IV to Sir William Knighton about some stained glass from Carlton House intended for Windsor: 'Wyatville hummed and hawed a good deal, however I brought him at last to say that he thought "He cud pleace soom of't to adwantage, though 'e 'ad not joust thin fix'd where."'[11] An example of Wyatville's accent was also recorded by the Duke of Devonshire: 'If you want an idea of the peculiarities you have only to be reminded of such words as these – "You enter the house (THEE OUSE) by the sub hall (SUBAWL)" and "The bastion is big enough for you to hoist (ICED) your tent there if you like (LAIKE)" . . . He was very popular with all the first artists and his brother academicians, and his manner was the same to all men whether comrades or "RYAL EYENESSES".'[12]

His popularity with fellow artists is born out by letters which survive from Sir Francis Chantrey who considered him a 'hearty, worthy and sincere friend'.[13] On the other hand, he was undoubtedly a snob. His country house practice made him 'architect to the whole peerage of England' and he carefully listed his patrons in descending order of rank on the back of his portrait by Henry Wyatt. An example of his deferential attitude to his noble employers is contained in the preface to the accounts for alterations at Chesterfield House in 1813:

My Lord,
   I beg humbley to acknowledge my sense of the honour conferred upon me by your Lordship in submitting the repairs of Chesterfield House to my care: the Bills for which are now in consequence of your desire collected into one Volume; and as this volume may possibly remain in your Lordship's Library for Ages, and become a matter of curiosity I have explained the manner in which the business was conducted.[14]

He was proud of his position as an officer in the Marylebone Volunteers. He became a lieutenant in 1798 and a captain in 1805. He carefully preserved everything to do with it, from notices of parades to plans of mess dinners. He was especially pleased that he was the only professional man in the Volunteers. He saw it as a mark of 'that respect which (history proves) has ever been paid in all ages and nations by the highest ranks and most enlightened men to the liberal profession of an architect'.[15]

---

[10] Coll. Mrs. Janet Don, Weston Patrick, Hants, 6th Duke of Devonshire to Mrs. Knapp, 19 Feb. 1840; 6th Duke of Devonshire, *Handbook to Chatsworth and Hardwick* (1845), 115.
[11] Roy.Arch. 51308.
[12] Duke of Devonshire, 115.
[13] Coll. Mrs. Janet Don, Francis Chantrey to Mrs. Knapp, 11 Mar. 1840.
[14] Guildhall Library, MS. 3070A, Chesterfield House Account Book 1813.
[15] Coll. Mrs. Janet Don.

Another sign of snobbery was his change of name to the grander-sounding Wyatville in 1824, but too much has been made of this by hostile critics. The suggestion came originally from George IV. In Wyatville's own words, 'the King had clearly favoured some distinction of a nature to set him above the large circle of Wyatts and himself suggested Wyatgate but the Knight expectant was better prepared "Might it not sound more befitting a Builder, please your Majesty, to terminate with 'ville'?"'[16]

Such medievalizing of surnames was common in the early nineteenth century. A Mr. Green became de Freville; a Mr. Wilkins, de Winton; a Mr. Morris, de Montmorency; and a Mr. Hunt, de Vere. Apart from a snobbish desire to seem more blue-blooded, it was also a sign of romantic yearning for 'olden time' when there was 'feasting in the hall and tilting in the courtyard, when the yule log crackled on the hearth and mummers beguiled the dullness of a winter's evening, when the bowling green was filled with lusty youths, and gentle dames sat spinning in their boudoirs, when the deep window recesses were filled with family groups, and gallant cavaliers rode out a-hawking'.[17]

Still Wyatville's naïve snobbery is small compared to the vanity of John Papworth who added Buonarotti to his name in 1815 because his friends though his talents and versatility worthy of Michelangelo.[18] Wyatville's hope of founding a new dynasty was disappointed. His only son George Geoffrey, who became an architect after leaving Westminster and Sidney Sussex College, Cambridge, died prematurely in 1833. Wyatville himself died in February 1840 and was buried in St. George's Chapel at Windsor.

His architectural career opened well with several country houses, including the remodelling of two major Elizabethan buildings, Longleat for the Marquess of Bath in 1800 and Wollaton for Lord Middleton in 1801. These established his reputation as an improver of old houses and for the rest of his life he was much in demand by those who wanted great cold barracks converted into comfortable modern residences.

At both Longleat and Wollaton work continued for many years and greatly increased their internal convenience. At Longleat a stable quadrangle and conservatory were added, successfully making the total layout a vast asymmetrical composition. However, Wyatville's hybrid 'Elizabethan' detailing in both houses is insipid, and it is regrettable that so much of the original decoration was sacrificed for it. It is easy to understand why it was found necessary to revamp the state rooms at Longleat in a full-blooded Venetian style later in the nineteenth century. Beckford's assessment of the improvements is just. 'Longleat is indeed as comfortable and as fine as a great house

---

[16] Annotated catalogues to RA Exhibitions, xxiii; quoted in Linstrum, 48.
[17] Crook (ed.), *Eastlake's Gothic Revival*.
[18] Colvin, 438.

can be without that touch of good taste, the lack of which one notices at every step. But there is a succession of apartments, some of them approaching the palatial – noble and spacious with commodious corridors and bedrooms in the best economical taste of the latest and most up-to-date furnished lodgings.'[19]

Some of Wyatville's completely new houses in the early part of his career show the same lack of creative spark. His Gothic houses in particular, Nonsuch, Rood Ashton, and Lypiatt, are dreary, though of some historical interest in their early use of Tudor details. The classical houses such as Denford, Stubton, and Woolley are better. They continue the style of Samuel Wyatt's latest, more monumental buildings. The best is Dinton, a sharply detailed neo-Greek house with a splendid central staircase-hall.

Historically the most important of Wyatville's early works is Endsleigh Cottage. It was built in 1810 for the sixth Duke of Bedford at a cost of £70,000. It is the first fully fledged *cottage ornée*. Magnificently sited in a Repton landscape and ingeniously planned, both for practical convenience and to take advantage of the views, it is a major monument of the Picturesque. But, as in so many of Wyatville's buildings, the total effect is ruined by harsh and heavy-handed detailing. The exterior is an undiscriminating mixture of Tudor, castellated, and rustic. The entrance-front is an inchoate mass which looks like a Victorian boarding-house on the banks of Windermere. The garden-front is more pleasingly irregular and successfully plays down the size of the building, but it is not light-hearted and pretty enough for a *cottage ornée*. The whole building is inferior to the similar work of Nash.

If these had been the only buildings designed by Wyatville he would be almost forgotten today. His best buildings date from the more mature phase of his career after 1815. While the trio of Tudor Gothic houses, Banner Cross, Lilleshall, and Golden Grove, together with the exteriors at Sidney Sussex College are no improvement on his earlier Gothic work, the enlargement of Ashridge between 1813 and 1822 was splendid and greatly enhanced the total appearance of the house.

Among his classical designs are some comparable with the work of his cousins. The dramatic two-storeyed vestibule at Bretton Hall is one of his best interiors. It has a true air of neo-classical megalomania and is one of his few exciting uses of space. The transformation of Henry Holland's Greenhouse at Woburn into a Sculpture Gallery produced an interior which is rich yet chaste. Before the recent removal of the sculpture, it was one of the finest neo-classical ensembles anywhere in Europe. Wyatville's Temple of the Graces, with yellow scagliola walls, a white and gold dome, and a floor of polished brass and marble is a superb climax, worthy of enshrining a masterpiece by Canova.

---

[19] Boyd Alexander, *Life at Fonthill*, 157.

73. Ashridge, Hertfordshire, Entrance Front, showing James Wyatt's central block and Wyatville's flanking ranges and entrance porch. Drawing by John Buckler, 1822.

74. Chatsworth, Derbyshire, north wing added by Wyatville and the sixth Duke of Devonshire, 1824–46.

Wyatville's greatest and best-known works were his alterations to Chats-worth and Windsor Castle. In both cases the spectacular results were as much due to others as to his own efforts and imagination. He was a competent but rather dull architect capable of designing well-planned, comfortable houses. Only when working for patrons with exceptionally strong tastes and ideas was he able to rise above the commonplace.

Between them Wyatville and the sixth Duke of Devonshire made Chats-worth the greatest country house in England, a pre-eminence which it has retained ever since. The over-all magnificence of its decoration, contents, setting, and upkeep make it difficult to judge Wyatville's achievement impar-tially. It is certainly the finest classical design with which he was associated. The restrained sumptuousness of the interiors and the daring and originality of the composition are unsurpassed. But these achievements are not his alone.

In my view almost everything which makes the neo-classical part of Chatsworth interesting is due to the sixth Duke of Devonshire himself. The new wing is an asymmetrical addition large enough in scale to change the effect of the house in its landscape. This idea was undoubtedly the Duke's: 'I admire an irregular room, if it is composed of regular parts and the same maxim is good for a house, and eminently so for Chatsworth.'[20]

In particular the Temple Attic which is the most prominent external feature and the key to the whole composition was the Duke's own invention. It was 'suggested . . . at Oxford by the tower of the Schools which forms part of the Bodleian. Sir Jeffry had not intended to build anything above the ballroom but readily adopted my plan'. The romantic classical ruins in the background of seventeenth-century paintings were also a source. Lady Wharncliffe, for instance, described the tower as 'the Poussin'.[21]

The antique marble columns used throughout the new rooms, the ormolu capitals of the Sculpture Gallery, the consoles based on some in the Vatican, the white scagliola walls of the Small Dining-Room (reminiscent of the Winter Palace), the Russian-style plate glass in the windows, and the inclusion of the Orangery all reflect the Duke's taste and international culture. The Duke supervised every detail of the arrangement and finishing of the interior as a setting for the collections which were his pride and joy. His enthusiasm for these rooms and their contents is best expressed in his own description of the Sculpture Gallery. 'The contents of this room afford me great satisfaction and pleasure and are among the excuses for an extravagance that I can neither deny or justify, nor (when I look at Endymion) repent.'[22]

The success of Wyatville's work at Windsor was due to the detailed guidance

[20] Duke of Devonshire, 80.
[21] Ibid, 117.
[22] Ibid. 88. Endymion is, of course, the statue by Canova.

75. Windsor Castle.
Remodelled by Wyatville,
1824–40.

76. Windsor Castle.
Design for a bedroom in
the south-east tower by
Wyatville.

77. Windsor Castle. Design
for the Crimson
Drawing-Room by Wyatville.

78. Windsor Castle. Design
for the Gothic Dining-Room
by Wyatville.

of Sir Charles Long, George IV's chief adviser on artistic matters. In 1824 Long suggested holding a limited competition between Nash, Soane, Smirke, and Wyatville for remodelling the castle. He drew up the programme for the restoration and sent it to Lord Liverpool before any architect had been chosen. He subsequently published his views anonymously:

I will state shortly and generally what has occurred to me upon the subject.

Approach
It is almost obvious that the principal Approach to the Castle should be by continuing the Line of the magnificent Avenue called the long Walk to the Court of the Castle itself. It would be desirable that the Court should be entered through a Gothic Arch; and the continuance of the same line would lead directly to the doors of Entrance to the State Apartments . . .

External Appearance
The Character of this Castle should be that of simplicity and grandeur, and as well from its History, as from the imposing style of Building belonging to that period, I should say the period of Edward the 3rd is that which should generally predominate, not however excluding the Edifices of earlier periods, where we find anything of grace or picturesque effect – Conway, Carnarvon, Harlech, Ragland, Bodiham, Haddon and many others, will furnish most useful Examples . . .

With respect to particular external Alterations, I will point out one or two which I think would be desirable. In an old Castle there should be some predominant feature, and the Keep seems to furnish such a feature in Windsor Castle. At present there are small Towers rising from the Castle as high as the principal Tower of the Keep. I would add to this tower 20 or 30 feet, carrying it up of the same dimensions as the present tower – a smaller Tower rising out of the present would destroy its dignity and grandeur. This elevated Tower seen from a distance would much improve the general effect of the whole Building. . . .

I would recommend also, both with a view to external appearance and internal Comfort, that there should be a Corridor in the interior Court on the South and East sides.[23]

Wyatville executed this programme down to the last detail. Thus the credit for much that is admirable in the transformation – the improvement of the total composition, the heightening of the silhouette, the addition of the Grand Corridor, the continuation of the Long Walk, and the formation of the George IV Gateway – is due to Long. On the other hand, the features which are so repellent on close inspection – the galleted black mortar, the harsh yellow masonry of the windows, and the clumsy machicolations – are Wyatville's responsibility.

As an architect, Wyatville was conscientious and capable but no more. Curiously the artistry which is lacking from so many of his executed buildings can be found in his drawings. He was a great draughtsman; one of the best of a

---

[23] BL, Add. MS. 38371, fos. 1–8 (ex info Mr. H. M. Colvin). The complete document has been published in *King's Works*, 381–3.

talented family. As a young man he produced freely drawn neo-classical visions in ink and wash of mausoleums, palaces, and ruins.[24] His finished architectural drawings are just as good in their different technique. Those for the private apartments at Windsor, most of which were recently acquired by the Royal Library, are minor works of art in themselves.

J. M. Gandy, the 'gifted architectural fantasist', was a pupil in James Wyatt's office at the same time as Wyatville and may have influenced him. Many of Wyatville's imaginary architectural scenes were exhibited at the Royal Academy – *Priam's Palace* in 1798, the *Palace of Alcinous* in 1799, *Ulysses Palace* in 1800, the *House of Fame* in 1804, and the *Burning of Troy* in 1806. The *Palace of Alcinous* took him a fortnight to do and was bought by Beckford for £50. These works were considered at the time to be 'poetic fancies . . . in which the arts of painting and architecture were happily combined'.[25]

Lewis Wyatt was born with all the advantages which Jeffry lacked. His background was successful and civilized. His childhood at Lime Grove on the beautiful Penrhyn estate in North Wales was a happy one. He was brought up as a gentleman. His family had a butler. Lewis chose architecture as a career because it interested him and not because he was dependent on a profession for his livelihood.

His father Benjamin Wyatt II was the younger brother of James and Samuel. Benjamin II was an architect, land surveyor, and estate agent. As a young man he made drawings for the family firm, for his uncle William (agent to Lord Uxbridge at Beaudesert), and for the road and enclosure commissioners in Staffordshire. The opening entry in his diary for June 1766 records that he had spent four days measuring for a new road through the Forest of Needwood from Yoxall to Draycott and another four days surveying the Sudbury–Ashbourne road 'in order to make plans to lay before the Commissioners of the different parts of the road where it required much alteration'.[26]

In 1772 Benjamin II married Sarah, daughter and co-heiress of William Ford, a brewer of Burton-on-Trent. Dr. Johnson's mother was also a Ford and Benjamin II and Sarah knew the great lexicographer. They regarded him as a cousin. An entry in Benjamin's diary for 8 February 1772 refers to Johnson: 'got into London about one – dined at ye Doctor's'.[27]

After James and Samuel settled permanently in the capital in 1774 Benjamin II continued to live at Blackbrook which became his property on William II's death. He sold it in 1798 to Matthew Hampshire, the publican at the Coach and Horses Inn next door.[28] While at Blackbrook he was agent to Sir

[24] BM, Print Room, 198·C15/65–206.
[25] H. Ashton (ed.), *Illustrations of Windsor Castle* (1841), i, ii; Farington, 1 Aug. 1799.
[26] Coll. Capt. John Wyatt, Diary of Benjamin Wyatt II (MS.), 12 June 1766.
[27] Ibid.
[28] Coll. Miss M. E. Greatorex, Indenture of sale, 1 Sept. 1798.

Robert Lawley, the largest landowner in Weeford. In 1785 he moved to North Wales following his appointment as agent to Lord Penrhyn. He owed this to the recommendation of Samuel Wyatt who was at that time rebuilding Penrhyn Castle.[29]

Lord Penrhyn was among the great improving landlords of the late eighteenth century. Like William Beckford he came from a family of wealthy sugar merchants. As well as Penrhyn he owned sugar plantations in the West Indies and land at Winnington in Cheshire where he developed salt works. When he inherited Penrhyn there was nothing but a ruined castle and barren mountain with a few small slate workings. Lord Penrhyn was a man of vision and his development of the estate was on an epic scale. It forms one of the great success stories of the time and brought him and his agent great riches. He developed the slate quarry into a national wonder comparable with Matthew Boulton's Soho. He built roads over the mountains; a town of model dwellings for his workers; a railway six miles long from the quarry to the coast and a harbour; while on the lower land round the castle a well-wooded agricultural landscape was created out of wilderness. In all these endeavours he was aided by Benjamin II.

The role of agent on a late eighteenth-century estate was close to that of a managing director in a large modern firm. Great estates were capitalist businesses. The owner put up the money for improvements and oversaw the general trend of development but all the detailed management was in the hands of the agent. The owner acted as chairman of the company and the agent as managing director. Agents of large estates were therefore important people. Altogether the Wyatts produced approximately twelve land-agents and some of the greatest estates in England were run by them for two or three generations, including Badminton, Beaudesert, Croxteth, Culford, and Shugbrough. Wherever there were Wyatt agents, other Wyatts were employed as architects and builders. When Harvey Wyatt was agent at Shugborough he even wrote some pamphlets on the Corn Laws and similar topics.

Benjamin II was unusual in the breadth of his activities. As well as planning the development of the estate and supervising its day-to-day running, he also designed many of the buildings himself. They included the inn and harbour office at Port Penrhyn; the park farm, dairy, poultry-yard, and marine bath at Penrhyn Castle; Lady Penrhyn's *cottage ornée* at Ogwen Bank; model cottages at the quarry; and the inn at Capel Curig.

His obituary in the *North Wales Gazette* praised these works as 'monuments of his well-cultivated taste'. Compared to the designs of Samuel and James they were amateurish. Nevertheless, they were admired by visitors who

---

[29] Coll. Capt. John Wyatt, T.H.Wyatt II's Family Notes.

79. Sheet of architectural drawings by Wyatville.

commented on their neatness and charm. The dairy, an 'ornamented lac-tarium', was 'the chastest specimen of elegant simplicity'; Ogwen Bank, 'a cottage in holiday clothes'; the Marine Bath, 'princely and unites magnificence with convenience'. Even the slate-workers' cottages were thought pretty and neat.[30] Many of the buildings were faced in slate. They were partly designed as advertisements for Penrhyn slate just as Ralph Allen's Prior Park demons-trated the virtues of Bath stone.

The greatest achievement of Lord Penrhyn and Benjamin II was the slate quarry itself, the source of money for all the other improvements. When Lord Penrhyn inherited there were various small workings on the mountainside producing about 1,000 tons of slate annually. He opened a new quarry and enlarged the labour-force to 600 men. Output trebled to 100 tons a day. By 1792, 12,000 tons of Penrhyn slate were being exported each year to London alone. As a result London was transformed from a city of red-tiled roofs to one of blue-grey slates.[31]

As scenery the quarry is truly sublime. There is a poignant contrast, particularly on a wet day, between the arcadian landscape round the castle and the grim grandeur of the quarry rising in terraces to 1,140 feet. It is the deepest slate working in the world. Prince Pückler-Muskau vividly described it in its heyday: 'Five or six high terraces of great extent rise one above another on the side of the mountain; along these swarm men, machines, trains of an hundred waggons attached together and rolling rapidly along the iron rail-ways, cranes drawing up heavy loads, water-courses etc. It took me a considerable time to give even a hasty glance at this busy and complicated scene.' The 'fearfully magnificent scene of operations' gave him the greatest thrill:

It was like a subterranean world! Above the blasted walls of slate, smooth as a mirror and several hundred feet high, scarcely enough of the blue heaven was visible to enable me to distinguish mid-day from twilight. The ground on which we stood was likewise blasted rock; just in the middle was a deep cleft six or eight feet wide. Some of the children of the workmen were amusing themselves in leaping across this chasm for a few pence.

The perpendicular sides were hung with men, who looked like dark birds, striking the rock with their long picks, and throwing down masses of slate which fell with a sharp and cluttering sound. But on a sudden the whole mountain seemed to totter, loud cries of warning re-echoed from various points, – the mine was sprung. A large mass of rock loosened itself slowly and majestically from above, fell down with a mighty plunge, and while dust and splinters darkened the air like smoke, the thunder rang around in wild echoes.

These operations, which are of almost daily necessity in one part or other of the

[30] R. Fenton, 'Tours in Wales 1804–13', *Archeologia Cambrensis*, 17 (1917), 210–13, 237–9.
[31] John Britton (ed.) *Beauties of England and Wales,* xvii (1812), 448–57; John Summerson, *Georgian London* (1945), 65.

quarry are so dangerous, that according to the statement of the overseer himself, they calculate on an average of an hundred and fifty men wounded and seven or eight killed in a year. An hospital exclusively devoted to the workmen on this property receives the wounded.[32]

Benjamin II presided over all this till his death in 1818. He was succeeded as agent at Penrhyn by his sixth son, James, who became Deputy Lieutenant of Carnarvonshire and a J.P. As well as managing Penrhyn he tried to develop his own quarry, the Croesor, near Portmadoc in the 1860s but was not successful. He lost thousands of pounds on the venture.[33] Edwin, the eldest son, took Holy Orders and became chapter clerk at St. Asaph's Cathedral. Arthur, the youngest, after five year's apprenticeship in the Middlesex Hospital rose to be a house surgeon there. His appointment to the hospital was no doubt influenced by the reputation of his uncle John who had been a surgeon there from 1765 to 1797.[34] After a spell in the hospital Arthur set up in private practice but failed. In 1822, through the influence of Sir Robert Preston, he joined the 57th Regiment of the Bengal Native Infantry as a surgeon. He died of fever aged twenty-eight at Kishoregunge in the Rungpore district of Bengal and was buried there. He is commemorated on the family monument in Llandegai churchyard where his epitaph introduces a whiff of eastern nostalgia and the romance of Empire to a remote corner of North Wales. The monument, which also commemorates Benjamin II and his wife, is most appropriately a slate pyramid.[35]

Lewis was the second son of Benjamin II. His thoughts did not immediately turn to architecture. Like Jeffry, he wanted to join the navy. In 1792, when he was fifteen and England was at war with Revolutionary France, he first went to sea but his naval career was shorter than intended. Lewis was injured in a fall from the foreyard and on his recovery did not return to his ship but entered his uncle Samuel's office to train as an architect instead.[36]

He stayed with Samuel Wyatt from 1795 to 1800 when, also like Jeffry, he transferred to James Wyatt's office for several years before beginning independent practice. He first exhibited at the Royal Academy in 1795. In 1797 and 1798 he showed drawings of buildings on the Penrhyn estate designed by his father and by Samuel Wyatt. They were part of a series he made for a pattern book of model estate buildings of a type then fashionable. It was published in 1800 under the title *A Collection of Architectural Designs Rural and Ornamental*.[37]

---

[32] Prince Pückler-Muskau, *Tours in England*, i. 46–9.
[33] Coll. Capt. John Wyatt, T. H. Wyatt II's Family Notes.
[34] E. Wilson, *The Middlesex Hospital* (1845), 225.
[35] Coll. Capt. John Wyatt, T. H. Wyatt II's Family Notes.
[36] Ibid.
[37] The only copy I have been able to discover is in the RIBA Library and it is incomplete.

80. Monument to Benjamin Wyatt II and his family in Llandegai Churchyard, Caernarvonshire. It is a pyramid of slate.

81. Downing College, Cambridge. Unexecuted design by Lewis Wyatt, 1805.

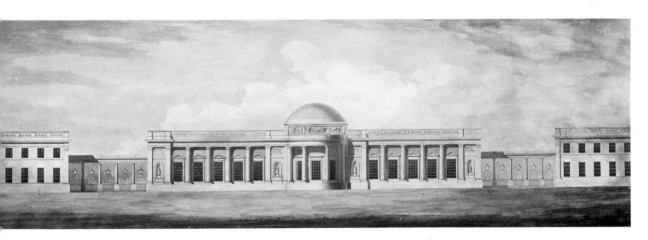

The help of James Wyatt was especially important in launching Lewis's career. When his parents visited London in June 1801 for a round of shopping, theatre, and opera his mother 'had a great deal of talk' with James about her son's future. Lewis owed his various public appointments to James. In 1800 he succeeded Jeffry Wyatville as labourer-in-trust at Carlton House. He treated the job as a sinecure and did not bother with the day-to-day administration which he left to an underling, William Lush. In 1812 he was criticized for this by the parliamentary commissioners. They disapprovingly reported that he 'follows private practice in the architectural line [and] has not given that attendance in his District and taken that account of the workmen employed on daywork or the materials used . . . which seem to be the proper duty of such an officer.' Nevertheless, he stayed till 1818 when he was promoted.[38]

He also assisted James at the Ordnance Office and for several years was Deputy Surveyor to the Ordnance. In 1818 he succeeded Edward Crocker as Clerk of Works for the Eastern Division of the Office of Works with responsibility for the Tower, the Mint, Somerset House, Greenwich, the Rolls House, and three prisons. In 1829, following the death of Thomas Hardwick, he transferred to Hampton Court, where as clerk of works he had a pleasant house within the palace precincts. His official employment finally ended in 1832 when the old Office of Works was amalgamated with the department of Woods, Forests, and Land Revenues. Many of the old officers were retired without pensions, including Lewis.[39]

In 1813 Lewis also succeeded James as Honorary Architect to the Middlesex Hospital. He held the post for sixteen years, resigning in 1829. During this period, like James before him, he supervised routine repairs but made no major alterations to James Paine's building. The Wyatts were architects to the hospital for about a century. Four of them in turn succeeded one another between 1791 and 1885 with only one break of ten years between Lewis and Thomas Henry. Lewis was also Surveyor to St. George's Hospital but resigned in 1827 when his design for a new building was passed over in favour of one by William Wilkins.[40]

Up till 1806 Lewis acted chiefly as James Wyatt's principal clerk though he made some designs on his own for houses, including Patshull and Wigginton Lodge in Staffordshire. They were executed by a cousin, another Wyatt architect, Benjamin Wyatt of Sutton Coldfield. He carried on the Wyatt building business in Staffordshire until the early nineteenth century. He built the Soho Foundry for Matthew Boulton, designed the Grandstand at Walsall Racecourse, and executed many of the designs made by his London cousins.

[38] Coll. Capt. John Wyatt, Journal of Sarah Wyatt, transcribed by T.H. Wyatt II, 1907 (MS.).
[39] *IVth Report of the Commission of Military Enquiry* (1806), 288; *King's Works*, 184.
[40] Middlesex Hospital MSS., Minute Books 1791–1885; *C.Life*, 11 Nov. 1976.

These included James Wyatt's for a new parish church at Weeford which was largely paid for by the Wyatt family. James was asked for drawings for Weeford Church in 1800. His first scheme was too ambitious and he promised to prepare a cheaper alternative. The revised drawings were held up by his usual dilatoriness. At that time Lewis was still working in James's office and Benjamin of Sutton Coldfield enlisted his help in getting the elusive drawings out of James. In April 1801 he wrote:

Dear Lewis,

   I am very much hurt and astonished at not having received the Plans for Weeford Church yet. I do beg you will lose no time in sending them off – the Gentlemen are become quite importunate to have the work begun and I can frame satisfactory excuses no longer.

Despite much 'abuse and raillery' the required drawings were not received in Weeford till the summer of 1803.[41]

In his early years Lewis spent much time making designs for ideal structures. On her visit to London in 1801, his mother described in her journal how he sat making drawings after dinner. Many were for the grandiose public buildings which excited the imagination of architectural students all over Europe at that time. In 1802, for instance, he exhibited a design for four national galleries at the Royal Academy.

In 1805 he made plans for Downing College, Cambridge but they were not accepted. James Wyatt had previously submitted a scheme for the College. The Master of Downing, Francis Annesley, rather surprisingly had sent James's heavy Roman designs to the then unknown Thomas Hope for his observations. Hope had written a pamphlet 'explaining at length how he alone in England was qualified to pronounce on architectural matters'. In his criticism of James's designs he maintained that Greek Doric was the only style worthy of serious imitation and hinted that the Cambridge architect, William Wilkins, was the man for the job. As a result James's designs were rejected.[42]

Usually even-tempered, James was, in this instance, provoked to fury and in retaliation insisted on Hope's name being struck off the list of guests invited to the annual Royal Academy dinner. The immediate consequence was that George Byfield was asked to submit an alternative design. William Wilkins, Francis Sandys, and Lewis Wyatt sent in designs on their own initiative. It has been suggested that those of Lewis were really an attempt by James to regain the commission. While Lewis was no doubt encouraged by his uncle, the drawings are definitely his own work and their French-influenced style is different from James Wyatt's. By 1806 the plans of Byfield and Sandys had

[41] S.L. M96, Wyatt MSS.; *VCH Staffs*. xvii (1976), 251.
[42] David Watkin, *Thomas Hope and the Neoclassical Ideal* (1968), 61–3, 130.

been rejected. Those of Lewis Wyatt and William Wilkins were submitted by the Court of Chancery to the 'superior judgment' of George Dance, S.P. Cockerell, and James Lewis, and William Wilkins's were chosen.[43]

If Lewis was disappointed by the eventual outcome of the Downing competition he soon found compensation in the expansion of his country house practice. In 1806 he was employed in the footsteps of James and Samuel Wyatt to design further improvements to Heaton Hall for the Earl of Wilton. He worked there for eighteen years and was responsible for the library, north front, chimney-stacks, orangery, and entrance-lodges.[44]

Lewis Wyatt made his name chiefly as a country house architect despite repeated efforts to win commissions for public buildings. His designs for the Houses of Parliament, St. George's Hospital, the National Gallery, the British Embassy in Paris, and the Royal Institution in Manchester all met the same fate as his Downing scheme and were passed over in favour of other architects. His country house practice, however, flourished and he rivalled his cousin Jeffry as an 'improver'.

In 1807 when Samuel Wyatt died Lewis completed Tatton and Hackwood. He was employed at both into the 1820s and they were major works. The rooms at Tatton are some of his best surviving interiors, though their rich colouring has been spoilt by squeamish modern taste. Those at Hackwood are among the earliest examples of Wren revival. Lewis succeeded Samuel as the principal country house architect in Cheshire and the surrounding area, working at Lyme, Rode, Oulton, Cranage, and Eaton-by-Congleton as well as Tatton.

In 1812 he began his masterpiece, Willey Park in Shropshire, for Lord Forester, the brother-in-law of the fifth Duke of Rutland. The designs were prepared in 1812 and 1813 and the house took ten years to complete. The exterior carries on and perfects James Wyatt's late classical style. The *porte-cochère* in the form of an octostyle Corinthian portico echoes Dodington while the side elevation has a domed bow ringed with giant columns as at Bowden. The principal interior is the great central hall which rises the full height of the house. It is a neo-classical masterpiece and is treated as an 'atrium' with a glazed lantern over the central open coffers of the wide spanned ceiling. On either side Corinthian columns of yellow scagliola support a gallery with a brass railing and bronze candelabra derived from Piranesi. The frieze with urns and griffins comes from Desgodetz.

In 1814 at the end of the war Lewis was able to visit France to study French architecture at first hand. This was the first of several visits to the Continent for 'professional improvement'. Napoleonic Paris made a deep impression and

---

[43] Ibid.; Lewis Wyatt's designs are preserved at Downing.
[44] Heaton Hall, Drawings by Lewis Wyatt on loan from Earl of Wilton; T. Clifford and I. Hall (eds.), *Heaton Hall Bicentenary Exhibition Catalogue* (1972).

82. Tatton Park. Cheshire.
Completed to the design of Lewis
Wyatt, *c.* 1807–25. Entrance-Hall.

83. Tatton Park, Cheshire. Library.
Water-colour by John Buckler.

84. Lyme Park, Cheshire, Dining-Room.
Designed by Lewis Wyatt, 1814–22. The
earliest surviving example of Wren
revival.

85. Stockport, St. Mary's Church. Designed by
Lewis Wyatt, 1813–17, in the Perpendicular
style. The nave looking west.

he returned to England bursting with plans for improving London. He wanted to make it a comparable neo-classical capital. In 1816 he published his views anonymously as a *Prospectus of a Design for Various Improvements in the Metropolis, principally about the Court.*

He wrote that 'London ought to possess in every possible circumstance an appearance proportionate to the power, the wealth, the population and the pride of the Empire, over which it may be said to predominate.' He wanted all the different parts moulded into 'one useful, commodious and splendid whole', as in Paris. Some of his proposals were so advanced that they were not adopted until the twentieth century. For instance, he suggested the designation of a green belt 'instead of permitting the already too widely-extended boundaries of the metropolis to be surrounded by deserts of ruinous and destructive speculations'.

His principal improvements included a palace in Pall Mall with a frontage of 1,000 feet. Carlton House was to be the eastern pavilion connected to a new centre by quadrants and duplicated to the west on the site of the old Ordnance Office. Influenced by the general wish to commemorate the recent victories he proposed a naval and a military monument. The naval monument was to be on the south bank. Four Corinthian columns 100 feet high holding statues of Admirals Howe, Duncan, St. Vincent, and Nelson were to flank a fluted 'Paestum column' with a colossal Britannia on top. Nelson's column as eventually built is a meagre reflection of this grandiose proposal. The military monument was to take the form of 'a cannon raised vertically' on a plinth 100 feet square crowded with trophies of arms. An antique tripod bearing a statue of the Duke of Wellington was to crown this phallic monstrosity.

Various street improvements were also included in the programme. The chief of these was the formation of a crescent at Charing Cross where Trafalgar Square is now. A crescent would have been far more satisfactory than a square on such a site.

None of these ideas was adopted but Lewis was responsible for one small development in London at 12–17 Suffolk Street off Pall Mall. The scheme included a new house for his own occupation. He moved there in 1827 from Albany.

In 1820 Lewis took six months' leave from the Office of Works to study architecture and collect works of art in Italy. The death of his father had left him a comparatively rich man. He inherited some of the Ford brewing fortune as well as his father's interest in the Birmingham and Liverpool Junction Canal and a percentage of the proceeds of the Penrhyn slate quarry. He was thus able to buy pictures like an eighteenth-century grand tourist, including works attributed to Canaletto, Guardi, Domenichino, Guido, Veronese, Pannini, and Marco Ricci.

86. Willey Park, Shropshire. Designed by Lewis Wyatt, 1812–13.

87. Willey Park, Shropshire, Staircase.

He visited Venice, Florence, Bologna, and Rome. In Venice he bought pictures from Count Savary and in Bologna from the collection of Count Mareschachi and the Palazzo Salina. In Rome he acquired marbles and bronzes including a small model of Trajan's column by Pietro Belli. He also bought a set of neo-classical cameos by Giovanni Dies, some of them after reliefs by Canova and Thorwaldsen, as well as sulphur casts of antique medals by Visconti.

Lewis arrived in Rome in time to witness the magnificent liturgical ceremonies of Pentecost. On Whit Sunday he attended the chapel at the Quirinal Palace where he heard Kenrick preach on the Holy Spirit in the presence of Pope Pius VII. While in Rome Lewis met and became a friend of the neo-classical architect, Angiolo Uggeri. Uggeri came originally from Milan but spent most of his life in Rome measuring and making reconstructions of antique ruins and writing books on architecture. His published works include *Ancient Edifices of Rome and its Environs* (1828) and *Dichiarazione dello Scopo* (1822). His *Ornamenti greci antichi ed inediti* which came out in 1820 was dedicated to Lewis Wyatt. (Lewis had four copies of it in his own library.)[45]

In January 1825 Lewis revisited Paris, this time to supervise repairs to the English Embassy, the Hôtel de Charost in the rue du Faubourg St. Honoré. After consultations with a French architect, Bonneville, and a surveyor, Beauvillain, he recommended extensive repairs to the main buildings, the rebuilding of the Ballroom and Dining-Room, and the erection of a new chapel. In March he wrote, 'I shall be extremely desirous of knowing how far my further services may be required in order that I may arrange my private business accordingly.' The Government did not, however, adopt his scheme and repairs limited to £7,000 were entrusted to a French architect instead.[46]

Either on this visit or on a previous one Lewis bought plaster models of the Antiquities of Athens and the Temple of Vesta at Tivoli, from 'the celebrated Monsieur Fouquet'. He also acquired French books on art and architecture such as Le Pautre's *Oeuvres d'architecture*, Durand's *Receuil des édifices de tout genre anciens et modernes*, and Percier and Fontaine's *Receuil des décoration intérieures*. He added these to an already well-stocked library which included books inherited from his father, a large collection of topographical prints and drawings, and most of the standard architectural works from Desgodetz to Piranesi.[47]

Unlike Jeffry, Lewis was a scholar and connoisseur. His architectural knowledge was unusually wide and well informed, as is made clear by his library. He owned books on 'modern' Italian, German, and French architecture

[45] Christie's, *Catalogue of the library of Lewis Wyatt*, sold 1 June 1853.
[46] V & A, 88.JJ.2, Ambassador's House, Paris, Letter Book.
[47] Christie's, *Catalogue*.

as well as the more usual works on 'antique' architecture and English Gothic. He had, of course, studied French and Italian buildings at first hand. Perhaps more unusual was his interest in English architecture of the Wren period. Even before Lewis became clerk of works at Hampton Court with responsibility for maintaining the forlorn baroque palace, he had developed an admiration for the Wren style and the craftsmanship of the period. He owned a volume of Tijou's designs for the ironwork at Hampton Court. At Lyme Park and Hackwood he devised successful pastiches of late seventeenth-century decoration.

His knowledge of Gothic architecture was as advanced as any of his contemporaries. St. Mary's Church at Stockport, which he rebuilt between 1813 and 1817 in a sumptuous Perpendicular manner, is a serious and substantial work. Much of the detail is archaeologically accurate including the pinnacles and pierced battlements of the tower and the convincing tierceron vault of the nave (executed in plaster).

Lewis was also among the earliest to employ the revived Jacobean and Tudor styles. He used them at least twenty years before they became widely popular in the hands of Salvin and Blore. Such Cheshire houses as Cranage and Eaton-by-Congleton, both built in 1829, are proto-Victorian in their asymmetry, varied outline, and use of diapered Tudor brickwork. Lewis first experimented with the style when he remodelled a genuine sixteenth-century house, Winstanley Hall near Wigan. But as early as 1816 he had recommended rebuilding St. James's Palace in the 'old English style'. His final 'old English' work, Sherborne House in Gloucestershire, rebuilt between 1829 and 1834, is so convincing that it is difficult to tell how much of the exterior is original sixteenth-century work and how much is due to Lewis Wyatt.

He took great pains to mitigate the almost mechanical perfection of early nineteenth-century masonry in order to make it appear more genuine. He wrote about his masons: 'my only fear is that in the ostentation of their superiority they may do it too well for the old work to which it can not be too nearly assimilated in material, workmanship and labour.'[48]

His eclectic historicist approach is well illustrated at Hawkstone Park in Shropshire where he recommended rebuilding the house on a better site in 1826. The new house was to be in many respects a replica of the old. 'The plan of a new House and offices shall be so form'd as to bring in every part of the old house worth preserving. That the Saloon and Chapel shall be the same size and form and everything transferred or copied from one to the other, that casts be taken of all the plaster mouldings or ornaments of good taste and character, that the chimneypieces and other finishings be selected and appropriated. . . .

---

[48] L. Wyatt, *Prospectus . . . for Various Improvements in the Metropolis* (1816); Gloucester R.O., Sherborne MS. D678, Family 322 (1829–1937), Lewis Wyatt to Lord Sherborne, 9 Jan. 1829.

88. Tatton Park, Cheshire, Landing. Designed by Lewis Wyatt, *c.* 1807. An ingenious spatial composition.

89. Rode Hall, Cheshire, door-case. Designed by Lewis Wyatt, 1816–19. A characteristic experiment in primitive classicism.

90. Cuerden Hall, Lancashire. Designed by Lewis Wyatt, 1816–19. An attempt to create a picturesque classical ensemble.

91. Hackwood Park, Hampshire, South front. Added by Lewis Wyatt, *c.* 1820.

'The new one may be contrived to bring in everything worth preserving of the old.'[49]

In the event Sir Rowland Hill kept the original house and Lewis Wyatt restored and extended it between 1832 and 1834. In the exterior he kept to the original early eighteenth-century style. His interiors, however, range from splendid Louis-Quatorze in the Drawing-Room to his personal neo-classical style in the Library and Dining-Room with strong colours, rich materials, and an archaeological accuracy in the adaptation of antique sources. Bronze candelabra in the Dining-Room, for instance, were derived from one discovered at Herculaneum.[50]

Rich neo-classical decoration was his favourite. His designs are close to the French Empire style and were consciously influenced by it. He admired the work of Percier and Fontaine and had three of their books in his library. He is their closest English equivalent. Among English contemporaries perhaps Tatham is the nearest parallel. Lewis's best Empire interiors are the halls at Tatton and Willey and the Dining-Rooms at Hackwood and Rode. Particularly distinctive features of these rooms are the black marble chimney-pieces with bronze mounts of a type not found in the work of other English architects of the period.

His love of the French Empire style antedates his first visit to Paris. It was probably stimulated originally by the interiors of Carlton House. The Entrance-Hall there is certainly the principal source for that at Tatton. The arrangement of griffins and urns above the columns was identical.

Architecturally the most important aspect of his interiors is the handling of space. The extension of Samuel Wyatt's Staircase-Hall at Tatton, for instance, is brilliant. The domed lower part has a central oculus open to the floor above where it is surrounded by arches and a series of galleried landings. This creates an effect of infinite recession akin to the reflections in a looking-glass. The progression of spaces at Willey is even more impressive and on a grander scale. The oval Entrance-Hall leads to the vast central atrium and through a screen of columns to the oval Staircase-Hall where two sweeping flights of steps are connected to the upper galleries by a flying bridge. This design alone establishes Lewis Wyatt 'as one of the most ingenious creators of processional spaces in England'.[51]

His external neo-classical architecture is important for two unusual qualities, his interest in the 'primitive' and his attempt to create picturesque classical compositions. Perhaps the best example of his interest in primitive architecture is the Octagon Lodge designed for Heaton Hall in 1806. It is

---

[49] Salop R.O., Hill MSS., Lewis Wyatt, Hawkestone Memorandum, 25 Jan. 1826.
[50] Ibid., Correspondence between Lewis Wyatt and Sir Rowland Hill 1832–4.
[51] BoE, *Shropshire* (1958), 320.

encircled by eight baseless Tuscan columns, each of which is a sandstone monolith. The dentils of the cornice are enlarged and so widely placed that they have the appearance of beam ends supporting the overhanging eaves. The aedicule framing the door consists of simple square monoliths without capitals. The whole building is a perfect demonstration of the rationalist precepts of the abbé Laugier. In its bold austerity it is only equalled in English neo-classical architecture by such works as Tatham's mausoleum at Trentham. Another experiment in primitive simplicity is a doorway at Rode Hall flanked by the same square half-columns. At Rode the primitivist intent is emphasized by the total absence of an entablature.

Lewis Wyatt's concern to exploit the potentialities of picturesque classicism is clear in the chimneys added to Heaton Hall in 1806. They form open square colonnades on the dramatic model of Vanbrugh's at King's Weston. His most complete experiment of this type is Cuerden Hall in Lancashire. There he attempted to create a composition comparable to Vanbrugh or the Elizabethan 'prodigy houses'. At each corner of the main block he placed square towers which continue above the parapet of the flat roof as chimney-stacks. In the centre the staircase-hall is lit by a clerestory which rises above the mass of the main block as a turreted tower on the pattern of such Elizabethan houses as Gawthorpe Hall. All the detail is curiously attenuated and the total effect is far from beautiful. This does not, however, detract from the originality of the concept. Cuerden is the first nineteenth-century classical house with a belvedere tower. It antedates the sixth Duke of Devonshire's at Chatsworth which in turn preceded Barry's at Trentham. The theme only became popular in the mid-century following its adoption by Prince Albert at Osborne. Cuerden is therefore a monument of the greatest historical importance in the history of Picturesque classicism.

Lewis Wyatt's architectural practice was efficiently organized. His London office was run by a clerk, Mr. Weston, who did all the day-to-day work. On site Lewis provided his own clerk of works to supervise the process of building. All the specialist decorative work was done by the same London craftsmen: Francis Bernasconi for stucco, John Mackell for ironwork, and Joseph Alcott or Joseph Browne for scagliola. Drawings were posted from London as required.

Despite this care his architectural career was damaged as a result of the incompetence of the clerk of works at Sherborne House. Sherborne was reconstructed for Lord Sherborne between 1829 and 1834 at a cost of over £40,000. The work proved disastrously defective and the blame fell on Lewis. The real culprit, however, was the clerk of works, a carpenter called Needham, whose supervision was culpably negligent.

The defects came to light slowly. After the house was finished Lewis, blithely unaware that anything was wrong, sent in his bill for fees, expenses,

VI   Willey Park, Shropshire, Great Hall *facing p.*154

and commission. Lord Sherborne's agent, George Newmarch, refused to pay until various defects in the new work had been investigated and remedied. Lewis did not believe it was a serious matter and replied stiffly: 'After the letter which I received from you . . . I must for the present beg to decline any further communication with you on this subject.' George Newmarch suggested that independent arbitrators should be appointed to investigate the trouble. Lewis still was not convinced anything was wrong and wrote: 'I must beg to be distinctly understood that I do not consider myself in any degree liable – or a party to the present extraordinary proceeding.'

He asked Lord Sherborne for confirmation. The reply made clear that the new house was indeed defective. A combination of poor ventilation and unseasoned timber had caused an outbreak of dry rot in the new floors. The leadwork on the roof had been executed 'with so little judgement' that it was leaking already.

This information greatly upset Lewis. He was concerned that the news would damage his professional reputation. He agreed to submit to the judgement of independent arbitrators. Thomas Allason was appointed to represent Lord Sherborne and Joseph Kay to represent Lewis Wyatt. Sir Robert Smirke agreed to act as umpire. As a result it was decided that the defective work should be replaced at Lewis Wyatt's expense and that various extra precautions to prevent damp and rot should be paid for by Lord Sherborne. The repairs were completed in 1836 costing Lewis Wyatt £996. 6s. 4d.

No sooner was this settled than more serious defects came to light. Investigation of a smoking chimney showed that the construction, of loose rubble, was so poor that the whole chimney needed to be rebuilt. Then the cornice in the Drawing-Room collapsed. All the ceilings in the vast new state rooms needed to be supported by iron girders. Lord Sherborne found it difficult to express his feelings when, after spending £40,000 on 'improving' his house, the new work started to fall down about his ears. He was forced to move temporarily to another house. As his agent put it: 'A considerable period of his Lordship's life has been occupied in witnessing scenes and enduring indescribable inconveniences – arising solely from want of skill and the ordinary attention and care of the architect.' Salvin was called in to supervise the remedial works.[52]

The Sherborne House scandal not only coincided with the termination of his employment with the Office of Works, after thirty-three years' service. It came at a moment of great personal tragedy. His young wife died in childbirth. The baby, his only child, was lost too. But that was not all Lewis's sudden

[52] Gloucester R.O., Sherborne MS.D678, Family 322.

misfortune. In 1835 his competition design for rebuilding the Houses of Parliament was rejected by the committee.

Lewis decided to give up architecture. It had become increasingly unrewarding to him. The concatenation of disasters between 1832 and 1835 made him feel that it was not worth the trouble. So at the age of fifty-eight he left London and retired to the country. He bought a small property, Cliff Cottage at Puck Pool near Ryde in the Isle of Wight. There he spent his last years planting trees, improving his grounds, arranging his collections, enjoying the company of relations and neighbours, and going to church. He was a 'sound and unvarying member of the Church of England' and contributed largely to the erection of St. John's Church in Ryde. As he grew older religion became a greater consolation to him and in his will he left substantial bequests to various missionary societies and other religious bodies.[53]

Lewis Wyatt died in February 1853 at the age of seventy-six. He was buried at St. Helen's Church in Ryde. A large stone sarcophagus was erected to his memory in the graveyard. Most of his books and pictures were sold at Christie's on 1 June 1853 for £686 8*s*. 0*d*. Lord Forester bought a drawing of the Saloon at Willey and Lewis's nephew, Benjamin Wyatt Greenfield, bought some books and paintings. The bulk of his estate was left to his brother James Wyatt of Penrhyn, his cousin William Maddox Wyatt, and Benjamin Wyatt Greenfield. His architectural drawings, including those for the improvement of London, the national monuments, and public buildings, were also left to Benjamin Wyatt Greenfield. Where are they now?[54]

Lewis Wyatt's career illustrates the fragility of personal success and happiness more dramatically than any other of the Wyatts. Yet the years of retirement among the beechwoods of his little park and in the leather-scented quiet of his library cannot have been sad. As a person he remains a mystery. No private letters or relics, not even a portrait, survive to help us penetrate his aloofness. Only Cliff Cottage has managed to escape demolition and is now the staff quarters of Warner's Holiday Camp.

[53] *Gent's Mag.* (1853), i. 670; PRO, Prof 11/2169, Lewis Wyatt's Will.
[54] Ibid.; Christie's, *Catalogue*, 1853.

CHAPTER VI

Carvers, Sculptors, and Painters

The Wyatts are known chiefly as a dynasty of architects but they were also carvers, sculptors, and painters of merit. Edward Wyatt I, who first displayed the family's sculptural talent, was among the most accomplished woodcarvers who have worked in England. His carving is comparable with that of Grinling Gibbons, to whom some of it has been wrongly attributed. A closer comparison is with Jacques Verbeckt, carver to Louis XV at Versailles. Edward's style and technique were consciously French and he enjoyed a similar monopoly of carving and gilding in the royal palaces under George III and the Prince Regent to Verbeckt's in France.

He was born in 1757, the great-grandson of John Wyatt I of Thickbroom. He began his career by making picture-frames at 360 Oxford Street. His shop was next to the Pantheon and he may have got the lease of the premises through his cousin James Wyatt. As well as picture-frames he made pier glasses, girandoles, and furniture.

The important date in his career is 1798 when he was appointed carver and gilder to the Office of Works. As a result he became the leading purveyor of carved and gilded decoration in England. he owed the appointment to the influence of James Wyatt, the Surveyor-General.[1] From 1800 to 1812 he was engaged on carving and gilding at various royal palaces, especially Windsor Castle and Carlton House. At Windsor, as part of James Wyatt's refurbishment of the old State Apartments, he extended and rearranged the Grinling Gibbons carvings as well as producing Gothic work for the new Grand Staircase and repairing cabinet-work and picture-frames. He was again responsible for carving and gilding at Windsor under Wyatville from 1824 onwards but no attempt was made then to preserve the seventeenth-century appearance of the rooms.[2]

His contribution to the redecoration of Carlton House for the Prince Regent was his greatest achievement. Between 1783 and 1796 Henry Holland had created an architectural ensemble at Carlton House pronounced by Horace Walpole to be 'the most perfect in Europe'. In 1802 Holland withdrew from royal patronage and over the next twenty years his masterpiece was overlaid

[1] *King's Works*, 58.
[2] Gunnis, 446; PRO, Works 5/109; Works 5/98.

by the 'eclectic finery' of James Wyatt, Thomas Hopper, John Nash, and Walsh Porter, thus perfectly reflecting the development of taste in Europe from the comparatively austere perfection of the early neo-classical style to the lushly opulent decoration of the French Empire and English Regency.[3]

Edward Wyatt was closely involved in the redecoration, which entailed the total remodelling of the ground-floor rooms as well as the further adornment of the state rooms. He designed some of the decoration himself. In the Scagliola Room, which was converted into a drawing-room in 1804 under James Wyatt's direction, Edward designed ten stucco ceiling panels in a French neo-classical style depicting the Elements, Seasons, and Virtues. In the Throne Room he designed and executed four overdoors representing the Orders of the Garter, the Bath, St. Patrick, and St. Andrew in the form of swags made out of their insignia.[4]

In 1811 he transformed the Blue Velvet Rooms, providing elaborate pier glass frames as well as 'richly carving and gilding in burnish'd gold twenty four emblemmatical door panels'. These doors can be seen in Pyne's *Royal Residences*. Following the demolition of Carlton House in 1826 they were salvaged and rehung in the private apartments at Windsor Castle. Without doubt they are among the most magnificent in England.[5]

Edward Wyatt did a great deal of other work for the Office of Works, including stone gateposts with lions' heads and flowers for St. James's Park, now incorporated in the forecourt screen of Buckingham Palace. In 1818 he was employed by Soane to restore the roof of Westminster Hall. Forty loads of well-seasoned timber from broken-up ships were used and today it is impossible to tell between his work and the original.[6]

He also worked for private architects. In 1817 he did all the Gothic woodwork, pews, pulpit, and reading-desk, in David Laing's new city church of St. Dunstan-in-the-East (now destroyed). But above all he worked for his architect cousins. From 1801 to 1813 at Belvoir Castle under James Wyatt he designed and carved the capitals of the Gothic columns with foliage and animals. They are closely based on medieval prototypes.[7]

He was employed by Jeffry Wyatville at Chesterfield House and Ashridge. His work at the latter included the magnificent stalls in the chapel which, with their pinnacled canopies, are among the earliest examples of serious Gothic revival woodcarving. He worked for Lewis, too, particularly at Hackwood where he provided new carvings in the Grinling Gibbons style to supplement those already in the house. The four great swags of the Seasons in the

[3] D. Stroud, *Henry Holland* (1966), 61–85.
[4] Coll. Mrs. V. U. Tunnicliffe, Edward Wyatt II's Sketch-book; Roy. Arch. 25233.
[5] Roy. Arch. 25340.
[6] Colvin, 736; Gunnis, 446; PRO Works 4/24.
[7] Edward Wyatt II's Sketch-book.

92. London, Carlton House. Designs by Edward Wyatt for ceiling panels in the Scagliola Room.

93. London, Carlton House. Carved and gilded doors by Edward Wyatt from the Blue Velvet Room, now at Windsor Castle.

Entrance-Hall have often been mistakenly attributed to Gibbons but the original accounts prove that Edward Wyatt produced them in 1815.[8]

The technical perfection of Edward Wyatt's work contradicts the frequently repeated assertion that standards of craftsmanship declined in the early nineteenth century. His work was based on careful study. His notebook contains sketches of scythes and rakes, old carvings, and furniture. His principal source of inspiration was seventeenth- and eighteenth-century French woodcarving. He may have visited France, but it is more likely that his knowledge came from engravings. His sketch-book includes pencil drawings of the trophies in the Salle de Guerre at Versailles, details of rococo frames (including one inscribed 'le bas du portrait de Pierre Corneille fameux auteur Française'), together with some trophies 'sketch'd from a perspective view of the interior of a foreign church'.

He could read and write in French, so his education was more than that of a self-taught craftsman. His library contained books on history as well as standard ingredients such as the complete works of Shakespeare.[9] The detail of much of his work, particularly the accuracy of his Gothic carving, reinforces the impression of a studious approach. His portrait by Lawrence shows him looking more a gentleman than a tradesman.

He had social ambitions which were made possible by the financial success of his career. In the 1820s he gave up business in London and bought a small country estate at Merton in Surrey. He also bought a property at Weybridge for William Maddox Wyatt, his eldest son. Thus he was able to achieve the typically English dream of life as a landed gentleman with a country house of his own. When he died in 1833 he left his house and farm to his wife, while to each of his five children he left £11,000.[10] He married twice, first, Ann George, a widow, and second, in 1810, Anne Maddox by whom he had four sons and a daughter. Of the four sons, Edward II carried on his father's business and carved and gilded the cornices at Buckingham Palace. Henry John, as has already been seen, became an architect. William Maddox, after service as a midshipman and lieutenant in the navy during the Napoleonic War, became a clerk in the Office of Works (on the recommendation of Lewis Wyatt). Richard James, the fourth son, achieved international fame as a sculptor.

Richard James Wyatt was born over the shop in Oxford Street on 3 May 1795. While still young he worked for his father and early decided to be a sculptor. He was apprenticed at the age of fourteen to J. C. F. Rossi. In 1812 he entered the Royal Academy Schools and three years later won the Silver Medal for the best model from life. Rossi gave him a good practical grounding in his

[8] Guildhall MS. 3070A, Chesterfield House Account Book; Gunnis, 446; Hants R.O., Bolton MSS., Box 11, M49/371–379.
[9] Some of his books are mentioned in his will.
[10] Coll. Mrs. V. U. Tunnicliffe, Edward Wyatt II's Will.

94. Hackwood Park, Hampshire. Carvings of the seasons in the Entrance-Hall. By Edward Wyatt, 1815, in the manner of Grinling Gibbons.

95. Edward Wyatt, by
James Godby after Sir
Thomas Lawrence.

96. R.J.Wyatt. Attributed
to S.Pearce.

art. While with him Richard carved some marble chimney-pieces and simple memorial tablets, the stock-in-trade of the eighteenth- and early nineteenth-century English sculptor. The memorials included that to Mrs. Hughes in Esher Church and one in St. John's Wood Chapel. In 1819 he exhibited a model of his monument to Lady Ann Hudson for Bessingby Church in Yorkshire at the Royal Academy. In the same year he provided a chimney-piece for the drawing-room at Hackwood Park with a frieze representing the four seasons and flanking figures 'emblematical of Music and Drawing'.[11]

His ambition, however, was to make life-size allegorical and mythological groups and figures. In 1818 he exhibited his first attempt, a *Judgment of Paris*, at the Royal Academy. He determined to go to Rome to complete his training under Antonio Canova. Sir Thomas Lawrence, who admired Richard's work, is reputed to have introduced him to Canova when the famous neo-classical sculptor visited England. Canova promised Richard his protection and permission to work in his studio should he go to Italy.[12]

Richard left England in 1820, stopping first at Paris where he spent some time in the studio of the distinguished sculptor, Baron François-Joseph Bosio. Bosio's best-known work is the equestrian statue of Louis XIV in the place des Victoires but he was also the master of beautifully finished marble figures. There are a number of them in the Hermitage in Leningrad and they foreshadow those which Richard himself was to produce. Bosio was an accomplished marble-worker and the surface of his statues is as smooth as satin. It was probably from him, rather than Rossi or Canova, that Richard learnt the technique of finishing marble so as to give it a warm soft effect.[13]

Richard arrived in Rome early in 1821 armed with letters of introduction to Canova from both Sir Thomas Lawrence and, in a typical vein, from Sir Jeffry Wyatville: 'my cousin, a young sculptor, desirous by study and exertion of simulating the excellence exemplied by the works of the Marchesi'.[14] Canova gave him a place in his studio. There Richard met another young expatriate sculptor, John Gibson, who had already been in Italy for four years. They became lifelong friends.

On Canova's death a year later Gibson and Wyatt transferred to Thorwaldsen's studio for a short time before setting up on their own. They took studios opposite each other in the Via della Fontanella Barberini. Gibson described Wyatt at this time as 'remarkably modest, retiring and very shy, an excellent judge of art'. Gibson was five years older than Wyatt and acted as his protector. The two of them formed part of a larger community of English sculptors resident in Rome, including Joseph Gott, William Theed II, and George

[11] *AJ* (1859), 249; *ILN*, 17 Aug. 1850; Hants R.O., Bolton MSS., Box 11, M49/371–9.
[12] Gunnis, 448.
[13] Ex info Mr. Timothy Stevens.
[14] Bassano del Grappa, Biblioteca Civica, Canova MS. 1772, Wyatville to Canova, 5 Feb. 1821.

Rennie. They knew one another and spent much time in each other's company.[15]

Life in Rome was idyllic. The city was at its most beautiful in the last years of papal rule before the Savoyard conquest and subsequent disfigurement. Gibson thanked God for every morning that he opened his eyes in Rome. Gibson and Wyatt always had breakfast in the Caffe Greco at 86 via Condotti. Founded in 1760 (and still retaining an unchanged nineteenth-century atmosphere) the Caffe Greco was the haunt of the foreign musicians, artists, and writers who flocked to the city – Byron, Liszt, and Stendhal were frequent visitors.

Sometimes Gibson and Wyatt made their way there separately, Wyatt arriving first. Sometimes they met outside their studios and walked together along the Via Quattro Fontane towards Trinita dei Monti and the obelisk silhouetted against the sky. At the top of the Spanish Steps they paused to admire the skyline before descending past the fountain of the Barcaccia (not then full of orange-peel and coca-cola tins) to the via Condotti. At the Caffe Greco they read the newspapers and chatted before going for a walk on the Pincio and then returning to their studios for the day's work.[16]

Richard was very industrious. His only major interest was his sculpture. He lived a retired life and never married. He often worked till midnight. Later when he became famous he was helped by assistants but in the early days he worked entirely on his own. As ideas came into his head he made preliminary clay models but shut them away for six months before translating them into plaster. He first made a clay model, then a small plaster model, then a life-size plaster model with scale-marks to guide the marble-carver. Even at the end of his career when he was very popular and busy, often making three or four replicas of his statues, he finished all his work himself, and this distinguishes him from many of his contemporaries who, as Stendhal acidly noted, left all the marble-carving to assistants. It was with reference to the typical sculptor's programme that Thorwaldsen declared 'clay to be the life of art, plaster its death, and marble its resurrection'.[17]

Immediately after setting up on his own, Richard was lucky to get an important order. In 1822 the Duke of Devonshire, accompanied by Wyatville, visited Rome and ordered a marble version of the plaster *Musidora* in Richard's studio. The Duke wrote in his diary: 'At Wyatt, an English sculptor, I ordered a nymph, he calls it Musidora, which has great merit . . .' The price was 250 louis. On completion in August 1824 it was dispatched to Chatsworth. Musidora is a character from Thompson's *Seasons* and in his adoption of a

[15] Rosemary Martin, 'Life and Work of R.J. Wyatt' (unpub. MA thesis, Leeds Univ.) I am most grateful to Mrs. Warburton for allowing me to make use of her research.
[16] *AU* (1839), 23; Lady Eastlake (ed.), *Life of John Gibson RA* (1870), 131.
[17] A. Hare, *Story of My Life*, v (1900), 166.

subject from modern poetry rather than classical mythology Richard showed some originality. Stylistically, however, the statue was derived ultimately from Canova's *Venus*, but transferred into a sitting posture as if on a rock in the middle of a stream. The Duke was very pleased and later wrote, 'Wyatt's Musidora gave the promise, since fulfilled by him, of becoming a first-rate sculptor.'[18]

Following the completion of *Musidora*, Richard was neglected for a number of years and received no further orders or commissions until about 1829 when a visitor to Rome saw various statues in his studio for English clients.[19] In that year he had an accident. Turner wrote to Charles Eastlake, who was then also resident in Rome, 'I lament to hear that your friend Wyatt has broken his thigh.' He fell from his horse while out riding. The bone did not mend properly and he was lame for the rest of his life.[20]

Once Richard gained recognition he rapidly became one of the most popular and sought-after sculptors of the age. From 1830 onwards he was loaded with commissions from distinguished English and foreign patrons. He catered exclusively for aristocratic taste. In 1831 he started to exhibit again at the Royal Academy and from then on he exhibited every year until his death. He never became a member of the Academy, though he was proposed by his distinguished friend (Sir) Charles Eastlake (later the great director of the National Gallery). The proposal was overruled by Sir Francis Chantrey on the formality that Richard was not resident in England. As this had been waived in Gibson's case Chantrey's opposition can have arisen only from jealousy. Chantrey is known to have made bitter comments about the success of the English sculptors in Rome. This hostility was mutual. Richard thought that Chantrey had no taste and that he could not carve drapery properly, though he admitted that the best portrait busts were very 'clever'. He had a poor opinion generally of his contemporary English sculptors. He thought the Peninsular School monuments in St. Paul's Cathedral 'miserable' and those of Westmacott particularly bad.[21]

In the decade between 1830 and 1840 Richard's art came to maturity. Though he carved some fine monuments and busts it was a virtuoso carver of life-size marble figures and groups, particularly single female figures, that he became best known. His statue of a *Nymph going to the Bath* for the Duke of Leuchtenburg, exhibited at the Royal Academy in 1831, was the first of a series of similar popular works. He produced three different versions of it – *Going to the Bath*, *At the Bath*, and *Coming out of the Bath* – as well as many replicas.

---

[18] Chatsworth, Diary of the 6th Duke of Devonshire (MS.), 21 Dec. 1822; Sculpture Account Book 1822–24; Duke of Devonshire, *Handbook*, 98.
[19] *Literary Gazette* (1829), 476. [20] Rosemary Martin, 25.
[21] RA Library, G1/1/364, R.J. Wyatt to J. Gibson, 9 Aug. 1841.

In the early works the influence of Canova is clear. The beautiful group of *Flora and Zephyr*, exhibited at the Royal Academy in 1834, one version of which is now at Nostell Priory, is based on Canova's *Cupid and Psyche* of 1797. Richard later reproduced the *Flora* as a single statue for Sir Arthur Brooke and exhibited it at the Royal Academy in 1841.

Two other groups produced at about the same time were much praised. The *Ino and the Infant Bacchus* of 1829 for Sir Robert Peel became one of his most popular pieces and was reproduced on several occasions. *The Shepherd Boy protecting his Sister* shown at the Academy in 1836 was a unique experiment with a more dramatic subject. The boy heroically intercepts a thunder-bolt to save the life of his sister. This contrasts with the calm character of most of his work. The group was also bought by Sir Robert Peel as a pendant for a Thorwaldsen in his library.

According to Lady Anne Murray, who saw it in his studio, the plaster model for this group was coloured.[22] This was several years before Gibson's first notorious experiments in tinting sculpture and is a sign of an experimental approach not evident in most of Wyatt's finished work. Obviously he was not satisfied with the result for he never extended the experiment to a marble statue and Gibson later recorded that Wyatt was against colouring.

As well as the influence of Canova, that of Thorwaldsen is apparent in some of Richard's sculpture. Thorwaldsen had plaster models of all his works in his studio in Rome where Richard saw them before they were taken to Copenhagen. In the early 1830s Richard made a number of statues of children, including a group of the two sons of Beilby Thompson and individual statues of the son and daughter of Sir Michael Shaw Stewart. These were obviously inspired by Thorwaldsen's statue of Lady Georgina Elizabeth Russell as a baby, now at Woburn.

Richard's extremely fine memorial tablets with figures in relief are also derived from Thorwaldsen. The best is that to Ellen Legh at Winwick Church in Lancashire. Its source is probably Thorwaldsen's monument to Philip Bethman-Hollweg at Frankfurt-on-Main. The Bethman-Hollweg relief has three figures – the deceased, his brother arriving too late, and a mourning angel. In the Legh monument the action is reversed. An angel is leading Mrs. Legh away, while her sorrowing husband is left behind with their baby. The Legh monument is a masterpiece with its perfect composition and austerely understated emotion.

Richard's success and popularity, which had been increasing all through the 1830s, reached a climax in the 1840s. In 1841 he revisited England for the first and last time. His feelings on this occasion were mixed. He expressed them in a

---

[22] Lady Anne Murray, *Journal of a Tour in Italy* (5 vols., privately printed 1838) (ex info Mr. Brinsley Ford).

97. *Flora and Zephyr*, by R.J.Wyatt, 1834.

98. *Apollo as a Shepherd Boy*, R.J. Wyatt, 1841.
Detail.

99. *Nymph Going to the Bath*, by R.J. Wyatt, 1831.
Detail.

100. *Penelope with the Bow of Ulysses*, by
R.J. Wyatt, 1841.

letter to Gibson: 'though I cannot help feeling much flattered for the kindness and attention that has been shown me during my stay still I shall not be sorry to get away from the hurry and bustle of this immense city.'[23]

He was noticed with special favour by Prince Albert who commissioned a statue of Penelope for the entrance to the Queen's apartments at Windsor Castle. This mark of royal approval was the ultimate recognition of his status as the most accomplished English sculptor of the time. *Penelope* was the first of five works for Queen Victoria.

His other statues for the Queen included a *Glycera* as a pendant to Tenerani's *Flora* at Osborne, two versions of the *Nymph of Diana returning from the Chase*, and a replica of the *Diana taking a Thorn from a Greyhound's Foot*, originally commissioned by the King of Naples for Capodimonte. The combination of a figure and a dog or some other animal such as a dead kid or a leveret was another of his interests. While they were closely based on antique originals, such as the *Artemis* in the Vatican Gallery, they are also a sign of Victorian interest in the depiction of animals in art. They parallel Joseph Gott's doggy sculptures and Landseer's paintings.

Praise for Wyatt's work continued to be enthusiastic. Writing in 1848 of the *Infant Bacchus* exhibited at the Royal Academy, the *Athenaeum* stated: 'Perhaps there is not a single work in this Exhibition of sculpture deserving higher terms of praise than Mr. Wyatt's "Infant Bacchus". As seen from every point of view the modelling is superb. With head upturned to eye the cluster of grapes which his right hand lifts . . . the attitude and action are full of life and appropriate expression.' Wyatt himself wrote of this work: 'the marble . . . is most beautiful being of that warm tint which is so favourable for sculpture. It has been much admired by the many visitors to my studio.'[24]

The year 1848 was one of revolutions throughout Europe. There was a major political upheaval in Rome which culminated in Garibaldi's triumphal entry into the city and an outburst of Italian Nationalist feeling. Though Richard knew Tenerani and some other Italian sculptors there was no close contact between the English and Italian artistic communities in Rome. The Italians resented the greater success of the English. This jealousy broke out into the open in 1848 when the English naturally refused to serve in the National Guard against Austria. They were forced to contribute 20 crowns each to the army instead. Richard was asked to leave his studio in the Via della Fontanella. Though he took a new one in the Via dei Incurabile he never moved there. The proposed eviction upset him greatly and preyed on his mind.[25]

This series of unpleasant episodes culminated in the French bombardment of

[23] RA Library, G1/1/364, R.J.Wyatt to J.Gibson, 9 Aug. 1841.
[24] BRL, Galton 390, R.J.Wyatt to J.H.Galton, 15 Feb. 1848.
[25] Rosemary Martin, 49.

the city, one shot of which still remains where it fell on a shattered marble step in the Gallery of the Palazzo Colonna. Against Gibson's advice Wyatt did not flee with him to Lucca but remained in Rome to safeguard his sculpture. He also protected Gibson's statue of Queen Victoria by building a roof of strong boards over it. Three days later he was woken at three in the morning by the sound of guns firing, shells hissing overhead, and tiles being smashed on the surrounding houses. He dressed hurriedly and went down to his studio. As he entered the room a grenade crashed through the window and burst into nine pieces only four feet from him. One splinter grazed his shoulder while another knocked the lamp out of his hand. He narrowly missed being killed and the shock affected him permanently. Some of his plaster casts were destroyed and others damaged.

When Gibson told the Queen she exlaimed 'Poor Wyatt' and ordered another statue as recompense.[26]

The last two years of his life were clouded by unhappiness. He died prematurely on 27 May 1850 after a short illness. A neglected cold attacked his throat and he began to suffocate in the night. There was nobody to help him and when his maid came in the morning she found him lying on the floor 'speechless and gasping his last'. His arms and legs were bruised and bleeding from having knocked himself about in his agony. He was buried in the English Cemetery and his funeral was attended by nearly fifty artists and friends. Gibson carved his tombstone with a medallion portrait and a resounding epitaph: 'His works were universally admired for their purity of taste, grace and truth of nature. The productions of his genius adorn the Royal Palaces of England, St. Petersburg and Naples as well as the residences of the nobility and gentry of his own country.'[27]

Richard left no will but he is computed to have executed works in his lifetime worth at least £20,000. The Liverpool sculptor Benjamin Spence took over his new studio in the Via dei Incurabile and finished the remaining work. The handful of statues left in the old studio were sold at Christie's on 22 June 1861. His personal possessions including watch-chain, portraits, and Royal Academy Silver Medal passed to his niece with those descendant they remain. In 1851 two of his statues were shown at the Great Exhibition, the *Glycera* from the Royal Collection (sometimes misnamed *Flora*) and the *Infant Bacchus*. He was posthumously awarded the Silver Medal for Sculpture.[28]

Today, like his father, he is almost forgotten and many of his works have been lost. He was, however, the most accomplished English sculptor of the second quarter of the nineteenth century. In quality of finish his work exceeds

[26] RA Library, G1/1/365, R.J.Wyatt to J.Gibson, 3 July 1849.
[27] *AJ* (1850), 249; *Gent's Mag.* (1850), ii, 99.
[28] T.Matthews, *John Gibson* (1911), 134; Christie's, *Catalogue*, 1861.

101. *Ino and the Infant Bacchus,* by
R.J. Wyatt, 1829.

102. *Diana taking a Thorn from a
Greyhound's Foot,* by R.J. Wyatt, 1849.

that of his more famous contemporary, John Gibson. Dr. Waagen was impressed by the 'soft delicate execution' of his statues.[29] The general run of neo-classical sculpture seems cold and harsh by comparison. His compositions are masterly. The *Diana taking a Thorn from a Greyhound's Foot*, for instance, is skilfully composed so that all the main lines of direction meet at the point where the huntress holds the dog's foot.

His carving shows a sensitive concern for contrasts in texture and finish. In the *Apollo as a Shepherd Boy* the different surfaces – flesh, hair, the sheepskin cloak, and bark of the tree-trunk – are beautifully contrasted. This concern for texture never declines to virtuosity for its own sake. It is not carried to excess. Restraint and balance are the key to all his sculpture. He avoids obvious emotion and sentimentality. In the *Diana taking a Thorn from a Greyhound's Foot* critics in 1850 considered the lack of overt sympathy in the huntress' attitude to be a fault.[30] The absence of excessive sentimentality, however, is one of the strengths of his work. More than any of his contemporaries he remained true to the austerity of neo-classicism. Nobody could say of his work, as it has been said of most of that shown at the Great Exhibition, that it was 'mawkishly sentimental' or 'frankly carnal, if not deliberately titillating, being representations of desirable young females ripe for ravishment'.[31]

The lack of development in his art is astonishing. Though he experimented with colour and dramatic naturalism in his model of the *Shepherd Boy protecting his Sister* he rejected both and, unlike Gibson, kept to the standards of Canova, Bosio, and Thorwaldsen till the end of his life. Thus many of the works produced in the 1840s were identical to those of ten years earlier. The *Flora* made for Sir Arthur Brooke in 1841 was a replica of that in the *Flora and Zephyr* of 1834. The *Infant Bacchus*, so greatly admired at the Academy in 1848, was nearly identical to that in the group of *Ino and the Infant Bacchus* of 1829. Nor can the figures with animals he produced in the 1840s be seen as a development towards greater naturalism for his first, *Nymph of Diana returning from the Chase*, was modelled for Sir Matthew Ridley in 1829 and he began work on the *Diana taking a Thorn from a Greyhound's Foot* as early as 1834. When he died he had in his studio a bust of Paris from his first group of 1818.

He was content to represent ideal beauty in his nymphs. The vocabulary of forms is the same throughout, only the gestures alter slightly. His statues all have the same introspective and chaste calm of expression. Their 'props', such as the cup in *Ino and the Infant Bacchus* or the amphora in *Nymph coming from the Bath*, are neo-Greek without being pedantically archeological.

---

[29] G. F. Waagen, *Treasures of Art in Great Britain* (3 vols., 1854).
[30] *AJ* (1849), 176.
[31] P. Beaver, *The Crystal Palace* (1970), 59, 61.

John Gibson wrote that Wyatt had 'acquired the purest style and his statues were highly finished. Female figures were his forte and he was clever in composition and the harmony of lines. No sculptor in England has produced female statues to be compared to those by Wyatt.' An obituarist added that he 'surpassed all living artists in representing the pure and delicate beauty of the female form'.[32]

While statues formed the major portion of his work and his funerary monuments are distinguished he also produced a number of good portrait busts. They are notable for their realism. For example, Lady Murray considered his bust of Lord Selsey to be 'strikingly like'.[33] That of the Marquess of Anglesey is one of the best and shows the sitter with stern features and heroic look worthy of a Roman senator or general.

He was a sculptor of great sensitivity. His neo-classical taste, well founded on a study of the antique, though softened by an interest in poetic and narrative subjects, did not melt into sentimental naturalism or melodrama. His work is a total contrast to the other great Wyatt sculptor, his flamboyant cousin Matthew Cotes.

Matthew Cotes Wyatt, the third son of James, was the most controversial and most criticized of early nineteenth-century sculptors. Much of the criticism was undeserved and was motivated by jealousy. At some stage nearly all his major works provoked controversy or lawsuit. Nevertheless, he produced a handful of sculptural designs which are unequalled in English art for their breathtakingly dramatic character.

Born in 1777, he had a happy youth idling away the summers at Hanworth. His indulgent father allowed him to nurture his sensitivity between leaving school and marriage free from the sordid necessity of earning his living. His diary for 1798, when he was twenty, is full of sentimental descriptions and ecstacies which strike the reader as almost girlish: the sobs and tears when his older brothers left for India, the delight when 'the little children came to the windows with their garlands' on May Day, and the melodramatic descriptions of what, one feels, must have been slight illnesses: 'when I rose I was so unwell that I almost fainted. I trembled all over, my eyes grew dim, my strength failed me, and the cold sweat started from my paled countenance'. (He was reading Beckford's novel *Vathek* at the time which explains the literary style.)

There are affected descriptions of wild animals, hares hopping across the lawn or birds flitting from tree to tree. 'Just before dinner I called into the garden, as I was strolling in the green-house I perceived a little robin with a worm in his mouth. I watched him hop about for some time. At length I saw the little darling fly to a wicker cage where there was a young blackbird. I was

---

[32] Eastlake (ed.), 130; *Gent's Mag.* (1850), ii. 99.
[33] Lady Anne Murray.

delighted to see the little innocent hover over it and greatly surprised to see them recognise each other with many echoed calls. At length she deposited her treasure to the great satisfaction of her young black friend whose mouth was open wide enough to have received the head at least of its tender nurse.'

It is not surprising that this susceptible youth was always falling in love. First there was 'Kitty', the daughter of Sir Thomas Frankland, with whom he spent a lot of time romping round Kensington Gardens. On 5 May 1798 he wrote: 'I went again to Kitty and again attacked the miniature . . . I made her look in my pocket where she saw the little tame squirrel which I bought yesterday. I had a great deal of fun. About two we went to Kensington Gardens where we sat cosy on a roler. This was mad and very funny.'

Then there was Lizie, for whom he felt a passion which caused him great misery. 'While she was in my sight I wished her to be in my possession. When I was from her I thought of nothing else. One night whilst her lovely form glided gently over my troubled brain my fancy addressed her in the following manner:

> O Lizie ever dear
> To tell my want I fear,
> Tis what you alone can give
> And tis but for you I sigh,
> Tis for you alone I wish to live
> And but for you I die.[34]

Finally, on 29 December 1801 he married an attractive older woman, Maria McClellan, widow of Edward McClellan (a sea captain in the East India trade). Apparently he married without telling his father. Farington tells us all we need to know about her. She was 'the natural daughter of some-one, a very pretty woman with a fortune of one or two thousand pounds'.[35]

This dowry was the basis of wealth which he swelled by his successful career as a sculptor and lucky speculation in the development of the Bishop of London's estate in Paddington where he also built his own house. The architects involved with him in this speculative building venture were his eccentric sons Matthew, George, and Henry (see p. 199). By the time of his death in 1862 he had amassed a fortune of £80,000.[36]

Matthew Cotes did not start as a sculptor. After leaving Eton he thought of becoming an architect. When his brothers Benjamin Dean and Charles Burton went to India he toyed for a time with the idea of becoming an underwriter in Calcutta. Neither ambition came to anything. The search for a career caused him much troubled thought. 'My mind is, and has been for some time in an

[34] Coll. Mr. Geoffrey Budenberg, M.C.Wyatt's Diary, 1798.
[35] Farington, 21 Dec. 1803.
[36] Somerset House, M.C.Wyatt's Will, 1862.

unsettled state respecting my future pursuits in life. I have been disturbed day and night by my thoughts on this subject.'[37]

When he was twenty he discovered a talent for painting miniatures. In 1798 he did portraits of himself, of James, of Charles Burton, of 'Kitty' Frankland and her dog Amy. Benjamin Dean tried to dissuade him: 'You say you have lately discovered a happy power of taking likenesses, I think it is a circumstance which may presumably afford you a deal of amusement, but I would never recommend you to adopt that line in preference to architecture, the former is of all professions one of the most precarious and uncertain, whilst the latter with the many great advantages with which you could begin your career could not fail of procuring you . . . a handsome income.'[38]

James Wyatt, however, encouraged him to persevere. James was convinced that his son had exceptional talents. In February 1800 he showed some of the miniatures to Farington who thought them promising. James said that 'that appearing to be his Son's inclination he should not discourage it'. So Matthew was enrolled in the Royal Academy Schools to study drawing and painting; his career as a professional artist had begun.[39]

He exhibited his first painting at the Academy in the same year – a study for a head of Cerberus. From then until 1814 he exhibited paintings regularly, mainly portraits but also religious subjects, including an altar-piece in the form of a Descent from the Cross, and some mythological pieces. He was proposed for associate membership in 1812 but was not elected and never became a member of the Royal Academy.

Through the influence of his father he soon received larger commissions for painting. The earliest was a ceiling at the Concert Room in Hanover Square in 1803. The following year he was paid by the Office of Works for decoration at Carlton House, including twelve allegorical panels in the Dining-Room.[40]

In 1805 he began painting ceilings in the remodelled State Apartments at Windsor Castle. This occupied him for the best part of the next seven years. His appointment at Windsor was seen as a flagrant act of nepotism. Sir Francis Bourgeois was incensed that, for this important work, worth about £4,000, James had chosen his own son 'a young inexperienced artist . . . to the exclusion of artists of known ability'. Bourgeois and Farington both considered Matthew Cotes totally inadequate for the occasion. Beechey, on the other hand, thought 'his ceilings at Windsor . . . would do honour to any artist'.[41] As Wyatville destroyed the lot it is not possible for us to judge.

Matthew Cotes restored Verrio's work in St. George's Hall and painted new

[37] M. C. Wyatt's Diary.
[38] RIBAD, Wyatt MSS., Benjamin Dean to Matthew Cotes, 28 Sept. 1798.
[39] Farington, 3 Feb. 1800.
[40] BL, Egerton MS. 3515; PRO, Works 5/94.
[41] Farington, 21 July 1810; 9 Nov. 1812.

103. Monument to Ellen Legh, Winwick, Lancashire, by R.J. Wyatt, 1831.

104. Bust of the Marquess of Anglesey, by R.J. Wyatt, 1835.

ceilings in the Great Guard Chamber, King's State Dressing-Room, and Queen's State Dressing-Room. He also designed a 'rich ceiling' for the Blenheim Tower but it was never executed. All the work at Windsor was halted when the King's health finally broke down.

Of twenty-eight full-length portraits of the Sovereign and Knights of the Garter for the Tomb House of St. George's Chapel, (restored by James Wyatt) only twenty-one were finished and they have been destroyed. Another historical portrait was one of Edward III for Fonthill which Beckford considered to be 'a beautiful harmony of colours'.[42]

In 1811 he made drawings for decorating the Dining-Room designed by his father in Liverpool Town Hall. The death of James Wyatt in 1813 brought this work to a halt and also ended his employment by the Office of Works. This threw doubt on his future as a professional artist. In 1815 George Dance II told Farington that Matthew Cotes had 'lately applied to him requesting to be recommended by him as a *House Painter*'.[43] From this time he devoted himself almost exclusively to sculpture and it is as a sculptor, not a portrait-painter or decorative painter, that he became famous.

Thanks to powerful patrons, including the Duke and Duchess of Rutland and Sir Frederick Trench, he received a number of highly important public commissions. His switch to sculpture from painting is a sign of an almost Renaissance versatility. His first venture was the design of a statue of Lord Nelson to be erected in Liverpool. Like most of his decorative painting, this opportunity was a by-product of his father's architectural work, in this case the remodelling of Liverpool Town Hall and the laying-out of Exchange Flags.

Though it is difficult for the modern visitor to believe, as he surveys the combined results of well-intentioned 'planning' and less well-intentioned German bombing, Liverpool was once a great neo-classical city comparable to Munich or Helsinki. In the late eighteenth and early nineteenth centuries it produced a scholar and an architectural family of international renown – William Roscoe, historian of the Medici, and the Fosters, architects and surveyors to the Corporation successively until the retirement of John Foster Junior in 1835. Roscoe and the Fosters were determined to embellish the city with magnificent buildings and monuments. Roscoe saw Liverpool as a modern Florence and its bankers and merchants as latter-day Medici. He tried to stimulate patronage of the arts after the example of his Italian Renaissance predecessors. He was the inspiration behind many of the schemes for improving the city.

The enthusiasm of John Foster Senior and John Foster Junior for large new buildings was less disinterested. Their family firm had a monopoly of the

---

[42] Roy.Arch., Add. 17; Farington, 21 July 1810; 2 Nov. 1812; Boyd Alexander, *Life at Fonthill*, 91.
[43] Farington, 3 July 1815.

Corporation's building work. As far as they were concerned the more money spent on lavish building the better. John Foster Junior trained as an architect under James Wyatt and between 1809 and 1813 he accompanied C.R. Cockerell, Baron Haller von Hallerstein (architect to King Ludwig I of Bavaria), Baron Stackelberg of Esthonia, and Herr Linckh of Württemburg on the archaeological expedition that discovered the Greek temples at Aegina and Phigaleia. He was therefore well qualified to design in the most scholarly and progressive style of the day and his buildings surpassed those in London by contemporaries such as Smirke and Wilkins.[44]

John Foster Senior and Roscoe decided that Liverpool should erect a monument to Lord Nelson. Within six weeks of Trafalgar a subscription had been opened and a committee set up with Roscoe as chairman. Designs were sought from different sculptors. With his father's support and encouragement Matthew Cotes himself submitted a model for the monument. John Foster Senior was associated with James Wyatt and therefore went out of his way to extol the virtues of Matthew Cotes's design. On 5 January 1807 Foster Senior wrote to him: 'I cannot abstain from congratulating you upon the success of your *sublime* composition'. In March he reported that William Roscoe had seen and admired the model. As a result the committee's approval was a foregone conclusion. It ordered the model to be carried into execution and authorized the spending of £8,000 on the project.[45]

It is one thing for an 'inexperienced artist' to design a large bronze monument and another to cast it. Matthew Cotes had had no training as a sculptor and was incapable of doing the work himself. He asked various sculptors of 'established merit' for help. John Bacon, who was approached first, refused on the grounds that he could not do it for £8,000. Liverpool was on the verge of changing its mind and commissioning someone else. Matthew Cotes was in despair at the possibility that his name would not after all be 'handed down to posterity with one of the greatest and in one of the principal cities of the first country in the world'.

Fortunately at that moment Richard Westmacott, a friend and protégé of the Wyatts, agreed not only to cast the statue in bronze but to give Matthew Cotes 8 per cent of the £8,000. James Wyatt designed the steps and paving surrounding the monument.

Westmacott executed Matthew's idea brilliantly and the sculptural quality of the monument is due to him. Its imaginative design with crouching prisoners chained to the pedestal shows where Matthew's talent lay.

The Nelson monument was successfully completed in October 1813. Matthew Cotes tactfully told his audience at the unveiling that 'the town of

---

[44] Colvin, 211–13; D. Watkin, *C.R. Cockerell* (1975).
[45] BL, Egerton MS. 3515.

Liverpool is so renowned for virtue, liberality and the encouragement of the fine arts that it may be considered to have given new birth not only to the name but to the life of Lorenzo de Medici'. He was intensely proud of his first work in a new medium. He wrote to Foster: 'This is my darling child and I am anxious that it should appear perfect to the world'. He asked specifically that there should be an inscription stating that he had designed it. He also made a limited number of small plaster copies suitable for libraries and entrance-halls in private houses.[46]

He set out to teach himself modelling and carving. Not much is known about this but presumably he practised in the studios of friends such as Westmacott. He is also known to have visited wrestling matches to study from life and, as he knew Lord Elgin, probably had the chance to study the Parthenon marbles before they were grudgingly acquired for the nation.[47]

In addition to the Nelson monument in Liverpool he was responsible for one other piece of sculpture before 1813; a bronze bust of George III for the Board Room at the Treasury. It was exhibited at the Royal Academy in 1811. He was paid £157 for the piece, which is now in the British Embassy in Lisbon.[48]

Before 1820 he received only one commission for a church monument; that at Newry, Co. Down in memory of the Rt. Hon. Isaac Corry who died in 1813.[49] Following the Battle of Waterloo, however, he hoped to achieve something more ambitious. He designed a huge monument to the recent victories, but like Lewis Wyatt's designs this came to nothing.

The idea of erecting a national *Tropheum* to honour the achievements of British Arms seems to have originated with the Royal Academy. The Government invited the leading artists of the country to submit designs and the suggestion provoked a series of extravagant proposals for crowning such vantage-points as Greenwich Hill with immense and inappropriate structures.

Matthew Cotes proposed his scheme in association with Philip Wyatt. It was for a colossal stepped pyramid 360 feet high. Its twenty-two tiers, adorned with bronze reliefs, were each to commemorate a year of the war. A domed rotunda on the top was to contain a statue of 'our revered monarch George III'. The Duke of York allowed the Wyatt brothers to exhibit their model to the public in his house in Pall Mall. The site chosen for the monument was the King's Mews at Charing Cross. The impact on St. Martin-in-the-Fields would have been devastating but, as one glances up Whitehall towards the elegant incoherence of Wilkin's National Gallery, it is with a twinge of regret for the ornate Tower of Babel which should rear terraces loaded with bronze sculpture

[46] Ibid.; M.C.Wyatt, *Prospectus of a model to Lord Nelson* (1808).
[47] Farington, 1810 (n.d.). Farington met M.C.Wyatt at a wrestling match with a party of artists in Lord Elgin's company.
[48] V & A, Wyatt MS. 86.22.15.
[49] H. Potterton, *Irish Church Monuments* (Ulster Architectural Heritage Society, 1975), 88.

to the heavens in its place.[50]

In a letter accompanying their designs the Wyatts expressed the spirit behind the venture: 'It is not only fit but politic that a nation like this which has obtained such glory from deeds of arms should at the close of so great and brilliant a contest turn its mind to the fine arts.' Though nothing came of the *Tropheum*, the nation did turn its mind to the arts, and particularly to sculpture, in the years following Waterloo.[51]

In switching from painting to sculpture Matthew Cotes made the right decision for, as Benjamin Haydon grumbled in his *Autobiography*, 'In no country has sculpture been so favoured, fed and pampered as in this country . . . If you shower thousands on sculpture and fatten her to idleness with one hand, scatter hundreds into the lap of painting also . . . No; year after year, and day after day, monuments and money are voted in ceaseless round, without discrimination and without thought'. Haydon's hard luck was Matthew Cotes's success. He was employed on a series of important public monuments, beginning with the memorial to Princess Charlotte in St. George's Chapel, Windsor.[52]

Princess Charlotte, the popular heir to the throne and only daughter of George IV, died in childbirth in 1817, a year after her marriage to the man of her determined choice, Prince Leopold of Saxe-Coburg (the future King of the Belgians). Her humour, courage, and discretion distinguished her from her immediate family and appealed to the popular imagination. The suicide of her doctor, confirming the rumour that the case had been mishandled, deepened the sense of tragedy. Her premature death was widely mourned:

> in the dust
> the fair haired daughter of the isles is laid
> The love of millions. How we did entrust
> Futurity to her.[53]

So widespread was the feeling of bereavement that it was possible to pay for her tomb with subscriptions limited to one shilling only.

As well as his old supporters, Sir Frederick Trench, the Duchess of Rutland, and the Duke of York, Matthew Cotes also had access to the ear of George IV through Sir William Knighton (the King's doctor, Keeper of the Privy Purse, and general power behind the throne). He made a model of his proposal which was admired by many artists and connoisseurs, including Sir George Beaumont. Matthew Cotes got the job.[54]

[50] Roy. Library, 12168, M.C. and P.W.Wyatt to the Marquess of Anglesey, 5 Nov. 1815, and drawings.
[51] Ibid.
[52] A. Huxley (ed.), *Autobiography of B.R.Haydon* (1926), 148.
[53] Byron, *Childe Harold*, iv, 169.
[54] Farington, 23 Apr. 1820; BL, Egerton MS. 3515, Sir William Knighton to Matthew Cotes Wyatt, 14 Mar. 1820; 4 Mar. 1824.

105. Unexecuted design for
National Monument at
Charing Cross, by Matthew
Cotes and Philip Wyatt,
1815.

106. Princess Charlotte
Memorial, St. George's
Chapel, Windsor, by
Matthew Cotes Wyatt,
1820–4.

The result is 'the most complete statement of one ideal of early nineteenth century funerary sculpture', a union of the baroque and neo-classical. The whiteness, the chasteness, and the motionless faces are neo-classical but the total effect is baroque in exactly the way that Bernini or a Central European sculptor would have treated the Assumption or the death of a saint.[55]

The corpse of the Princess lies on a marble slab covered with a shroud from under which only the fingers of one hand protrude with macabre effect. She is attended by four life-size mourning figures, entirely veiled. All this is sombre and heavily charged with emotion. Above, by contrast, is a scene of shattering theatricality. The Princess bursts from the tomb and soars heavenwards, her arm upraised in a dramatic gesture and a breast uncovered. She is accompanied by angels, one of them holding her stillborn baby. Originally the whole snow-white, life-size spectacle was enacted in a blaze of golden light from coloured glass in a side window but this has been removed in a fit of misdirected 'good taste'.

This *tour de force* had few immediate precursors in English funerary art. Flaxman in 1784 at Gloucester Cathedral had shown Mrs. Sarah Morley and her child borne heavenwards in the company of angels but that was little more than a tablet in deep relief. Princess Charlotte's memorial is life-size and the figures are fully rounded. Matthew Cotes's source of inspiration was probably not sculpture but painting, namely Arthur William Devis's *Apotheosis of Princess Charlotte* in Esher Church.

The monument was rapturously received on its completion in 1824. Matthew Cotes repeated the treatment in the tomb of the Duchess of Rutland at Belvoir. There the effect is even more spectacular as the apotheosis of the Duchess is the *point de vue* of the specially built mausoleum and the original coloured lighting survives in all its glory.

Princess Charlotte's memorial made Matthew Cotes Wyatt's reputation. He was asked by Lord Liverpool to do the national monument to George III. He first designed a large triumphal trophy showing the King in a chariot, with Victory and Fame, riding down Faction in the form of a writhing dragon. The design was based on Roman medals and gems. There was not enough money and the design was criticized by, among others, his cousin George Wyatt I under the pseudonym 'Sussexiensis' in the *Morning Post*.[56]

A design for a simpler equestrian statue was adopted instead. It was subject to endless delays and was not finished until 1836, sixteen years after the death of George III. The original site in Waterloo Place had to be abandoned because it meant that the Duke of York on top of his column would be turning his back

[55] *BoE, Berkshire* (1966), 40, 278; *BoE, Leicestershire and Rutland* (1960), 65.
[56] BL, *Reasons of a subscriber for opposing Mr. Wyatt's plan for a monumental trophy to the late King George III* (1822) by 'Sussexiensis'.

107. George III, Pall Mall, by Matthew Cotes Wyatt, 1822–36.

108. Fifth Duchess of Rutland, Belvoir Castle, Leicestershire, by Matthew Cotes Wyatt.

on his royal father. An alternative site was chosen in Cockspur Street. A banker in one of the adjoining buildings objected and took out an affidavit in the Vice-Chancellor's Court to stop the statue. It took two months 'of tedious and expensive litigation' to get this reversed by the Lord Chancellor. Then the mould for the hind-quarters of the horse was sabotaged and part of the statue had to be recast. When the statue was finally unveiled on 3 August 1836 the ceremony was disturbed by an unruly mob.[57]

The statue was not greatly admired. *The Times* referred to it as a 'burlesque effigy'. The King's pigtail in particular excited the mirth of Matthew's enemies and Cockspur Street was informally renamed 'Pigtail Place'. In September 'some wretch' daubed the pedestal of the statue. Disappointed and jealous rivals were resentful that there had not been an open competition.[58] The hostility provoked by this continued to grow and reached a crescendo of fury over Matthew's last great public commission, the statue of the Duke of Wellington.

With the exception of his work for the Duke of Rutland and the Princess Charlotte memorial every one of his statues was the victim of dramatic vicissitudes. The group of St. George and the Dragon commissioned by George III for Windsor Castle was never completed and was left unfinished in the sculptor's studio on the King's death.

A similar fate befell his ambitious statue of Lord Dudley's Newfoundland dog, Bashaw. Lord Dudley died before it was finished and his executors, who included the Bishop of Exeter, refused to honour the agreement and pay for it. The cost was 5,000 guineas and it is possible to see why the trustees did not wish to pay such a large sum for a disdainful marble dog trampling on a 'writhing bronze boa constrictor with popping ruby eyes'. But as they refused to see it they cannot have been motivated by a readily understandable desire to protect the house of Dudley and Ward from so monstrous an heirloom.

The statue took three years to complete and the dog sat for his portrait over fifty times. Lord Dudley was thrilled by the model: 'There you stand Bash in propria persona!', he exclaimed delightedly. *Bashaw* was intended for Dudley House in Park Lane and was carried out regardless of cost in coloured marbles and precious stones. Matthew wanted it to be the most elaborate depiction of a quadruped 'ever produced by ancient or modern art'.

Bashaw was the *piece de resistance* of an exhibition of his own work held at home in 1834. The 'select critics' who came were riveted by the amazing spectacle: 'The variegated coat of the animal even to the minutest marks is closely copied in white, black and grey marble . . . The eyes are composed of gems (the Persian topaz and sardonyx), the pupils of black lava; and but that

---

[57] BL, Egerton MS. 3515; H. M. Cundall, 'A Mysterious Bronze Group', *Burlington Mag.* xx. (Feb. 1912), 289–90.
[58] Ibid.

109. Bashaw, by Matthew Cotes
Wyatt, 1831.

110. Belvoir Castle,
Leicestershire, marble
pedestal with marble cloth,
by Matthew Cotes Wyatt.

the form is motionless, it might at a very slightest distance be taken for life.'[59]

Matthew Cotes was so bitter about his shabby treatment by Lord Dudley's executors that he wrote in his will that his executors could dispose of the statue to an art-loving nobleman for any sum they thought fit, except to descendants of Lord Dudley. From them they must exact the original price of 5,000 guineas. If the statue was not sold to an aristocratic connoisseur he hoped it would find a home in the British Museum or some similar national repository. He would be pleased to know that it now stands in the Victoria and Albert Museum midway between Wyatville's designs for Windsor and the furniture from the Great Exhibition to which Sir (Matthew) Digby Wyatt was Secretary.[60]

The hostile criticism which was slowly building up finally burst out when Matthew Cotes was appointed sculptor of the Duke of Wellington's statue. He owed this largely to the influence of the Duke of Rutland who was chairman of the committee of subscribers. The Duke thought Matthew Cotes one of the greatest English sculptors of all time. As well as employing him for the monument to the Duchess in the mausoleum he commissioned a life-size statue and a bust of the Duchess, the chimney-piece in the Regent's Gallery, and a pedestal with a *trompe-l'œil* marble cloth for the Dining-Room at Belvoir. Matthew also completed Hoppner's portrait of the Duchess for him.[61]

The Wellington statute was 'for centuries to commemorate the bravery of the British Hero; the skill of the British Artist and the gratitude of the British Nation'. The Duke of Rutland had no difficulty in getting his committee to accept Matthew Cotes as 'in every respect eminently qualified to be entrusted with the proposed equestrian statue'. Other old friends among the members included the Marquess of Londonderry and, of course, Sir Frederick Trench. Queen Victoria gave her consent in 1839 and all seemed to be going swimmingly, but then the disastrous decision was made to place the statue on top of the unfinished arch at Hyde Park Corner. Decimus Burton, the architect, was not consulted – a tactless omission.

An opponent placed a wooden silhouette on the arch to show how ridiculous it would look. There was a howl of public protest led by Decimus Burton who thought, rightly, that the statue would ruin the appearance of his arch.

No definite decision was reached for the moment. Matthew continued steadfastly with his work, leaving the committee to worry about its eventual destination. He built a new studio 30 feet high, lit by 300 square feet of glazing, adjoining his house at Dudley Grove. Wellington sat to him on various occasions but, Copenhagen now being dead, another horse called Rosemary had to do duty instead.[62]

[59] *Court Journal*, Mar. 1834; John Harris, 'The Story of the Marble Dog', *C.Life*, 21 Nov. 1957.
[60] Somerset House, Matthew Cotes Wyatt's Will.
[61] Eller, *History of Belvoir Castle*, 207.
[62] BL, Egerton MS. 3515.

Matthew decided to show the Duke in formal robes. 'There is one good reason why I discarded the dress of the present day, which is that of the taylor [who] alters it monthly. The Dress of the Lord Lieutenant may endure with little alteration for centuries, the Dress of the Garter much longer . . .' Bronze Cannon captured at Waterloo were supplied by Woolwich arsenal for the work.[63]

All was ready by 1846. A carriage with iron wheels 10 feet in diameter was specially built to take the statue to Hyde Park Corner. Despite gloomy forecasts of collapsed roads and sewers the only casualty on the way was one bent lamppost. Wellington was winched into position on the arch without pomp, for, as the Duke of Rutland pointed out, this would make it less ridiculous if the statue was ordered down again.

When the scaffolding was removed the statue was greeted with derision on all sides. No work of art erected in London has excited more ridicule, not even some of the purchases by the Tate Gallery. The Institute of British Architects protested. Questions were asked in Parliament. Every newspaper denounced it. Even the sculptor himself was not entirely happy. He suggested that it might look better at the new Wellington College in Berkshire.

The expected blow fell on 1 October 1846 – 'Lord Morpeth presents his compliments to Mr. Wyatt and begs to acquaint him that it has been irrevocably decided by Her Majesty and the Government that the Equestrian statue should be removed from the arch'. At this moment the one person who had remained silently aloof throughout the controversy, Wellington himself, let it be known that he wanted the statue to remain. If it were taken down it could be construed as a deliberate snub to himself. He threatened to resign his appointment as Commander-in-Chief and his commission. Faced with this awful ultimatum from the hero of Waterloo the 'grateful government' had no option but to leave the statue where it was. It was finally removed in 1882. The army claimed it and it was re-erected at Aldershot. It looks well there, with the Duke's roman nose and cocked hat riding high above the trees. The statue was unfairly criticized. It was a 'fine, forthright effort' in the wrong place.[64]

There is a postscript to the story. In 1865 the second Duke of Wellington bought the unfinished St. George and the Dragon for the garden at Apsley House so that he could admire the denigrated sculptor's work from the back windows as well as the front windows of his house! His courage in the arts matched his father's on the battlefield.[65]

Contemporary views of Matthew Cotes's work ranged from wild enthusiasm to total derision. He occupies a unique place in English sculpture, midway

---

[63] Ibid.; V & A, Wyatt MS. 86.00.15.
[64] BL, Egerton MS. 3515.
[65] It is now at Stratfield Saye.

between the neo-classical chastity of Flaxman and the naturalistic sculpture of the Great Exhibition. Such details as the yellow marble cushion, into which Bashaw's paws sink so luxuriously, or the *trompe-l'œil* marble cloth at Belvoir, are reminiscent of Bernini's cushions in the Cornaro Chapel or Borromini's marble drapery in the Spada Chapel at S. Girolamo. Indeed his work is closer in spirit to seventeenth-century Rome than to early nineteenth-century England.

His designs were dramatic and full-blooded but not all the life to be found in the models (which so captivated prospective clients) was carried through to the finished work. Whatever the merits of the preliminary models *Bashaw* as executed is to modern eyes just 'a piece of monstrously misapplied virtuosity of touching hideousness'. That the same could be said of some of the works produced by Roman baroque artists does not negate this criticism.

His masterpiece, the apotheosis of the Duchess of Rutland at Belvoir, seen in the setting designed for it – shimmering in the gently diffused purple and green light – creates an overwhelming impression. Like Nash's Regent's Park Terraces, however, the first stunning impact does not stand up to close inspection. Much of the work is not properly modelled. The faces, in particular, are too flat.

In fact, he executed very little, if any, of his own sculpture. The Nelson statue was cast by Richard Westmacott. The *trompe-l'œil* table at Belvoir was carved by another sculptor. Matthew Cotes's second son James II is known to have executed most of the later work. He was specially trained as a sculptor early in life to help his father. As early as 1826, when James II was only eighteen, he was paid £500 for three years' work on the statue of the Duchess of Rutland in the Elizabethan Saloon at Belvoir and the monument in the mausoleum. In 1849 he claimed; 'I have been professionally engaged with my father for a period of more than 29 years upon works of very considerable importance – the Princess Charlotte monument, works at Belvoir Castle, the statue of George III, the colossal statue of Wellington (40 tons in weight) and works for George III [and] the late Lord Dudley.'[66]

The reputation of Matthew Cotes Wyatt should rest, therefore, on his ability as a theatrical designer of the first rank rather than as a sculptor in the usual sense of the word.

James II, as well as executing many of his father's sculptural designs between 1820 and 1862, also worked independently as a sculptor. He was particularly interested in equestrian subjects. He designed the moulds for casting the Wellington statue and made small bronzed plaster copies for distribution to the subscribers. His sketches include many of horses and

---

[66] RIBAD, Wyatt MSS., James Wyatt II to M.C. Wyatt, 11 Apr. 1840; V & A, Wyatt MS. 86.00.15, James Wyatt II to M.C. Wyatt, 1826; BL, Egerton MS. 3515, James Wyatt II to Alfred Padley, 28 Jan. 1849.

harness and he made several models for equestrian statues. Two were exhibited at the Royal Academy – *Mazeppa* in 1843 and an *Arab and his Steed* in 1844. He also exhibited a statue of Richard Coeur de Lion in Westminster Hall in 1844. In 1846 he completed equestrian statues of Queen Victoria and Prince Albert which were shown at the Great Exhibition in 1851. *The Times* thought the Prince's horse 'admirably modelled' and 'nearer to life than any which quite recent art has produced'. It was later bought by the owner of the Coliseum.[67]

In 1843 he won the competition for the pediment of the Commercial Bank of Scotland in George Street, Edinburgh. James II took great pains over it and was proud of the result. Numerous drawings survive. The allegorical group of female figures and putti playing with assorted anchors, packages, and railway engine wheels was intended to represent Goods, Navigation, Plenty, Commerce, the Nation, Enterprise, Service, Genius, and the Railways. In both concept and style it is clearly Victorian with its undiscriminating mixture of classical and realistic symbolism. There is something uncomfortable, if not absurd, about Grecian figures driving railway engines. James did not carve the pediment himself. It was executed by a Scottish pupil of Thorwaldsen, Alexander Handyside Ritchie.[68]

James II was less lucky with his monumental schemes than his father. In 1848 he submitted a design for a life-size bronze statue of Lord George Bentinck for the market-place at Mansfield in Nottinghamshire. It was not adopted, though he made a marble bust of Bentinck. The same fate befell his proposed statue of the Duke of Rutland at Leicester. The committee chose an incompetent Welsh sculptor, Edward Davis, to do the statue instead. Davis's statue was frightful. The *Literary Gazette* wrote: 'would that this gentleman had the power of doing something better'. *The Builder* thought the statue made the Duke 'appear positively intoxicated'. This must have been some consolation to James.[69]

James II also made abortive designs for funerary monuments, including two vast concoctions on the model of the Princess Charlotte Memorial. One was to commemorate William Venables, murdered in the Indian Mutiny, and the other the mother of David Dyce-Sombre, an Anglo-Indian convert to Rome who ended his days in a lunatic asylum.[70]

The most attractive of his works is a private piece, a marble statue of his young daughter Lila asleep. It was exhibited at the Royal Academy in 1838. She lies on a marble cushion reminiscent of Bashaw's with her hands under her cheek. The source is Chantrey's popular memorial to the Robinson children

[67] *Literary Gazette* (1844), 367; Gunnis, 446; V & A, 92.D.59., James Wyatt II's Sketch-book.
[68] V & A, 92.D.59; RIBAD, Wyatt MSS.; Bl, Egerton MS. 3515.
[69] V & A, Wyatt MS. 86.00.15; Gunnis, 122, 446.
[70] V & A, 92.D.59; RIBAD, James Wyatt II, design for Dyce Sombre Memorial.

111. *Mercury tying a Sandal*. Chalk
drawing by James Wyatt II.

112. *Lila Asleep*, by James Wyatt II.

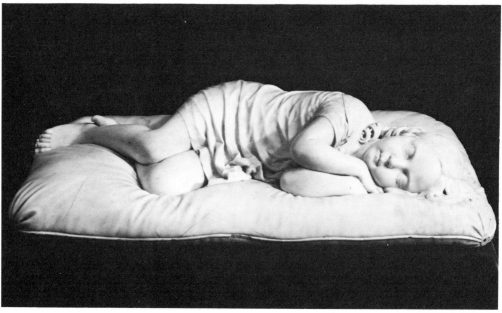

in Lichfield Cathedral which started the fashion for sleeping marble babes. Lila is charmingly carved with curly hair and long eyelashes. Only the folds of her dress are a little too artificially contrived.

James II was a talented artist. In the Victoria and Albert Museum and at the RIBA Drawings Collection are preserved folios of his studies and drawings. They include a series of competent academic nudes in red chalk. According to family tradition he was distinctly lazy. Though he executed a few beautiful pieces of sculpture he could not be bothered to take it up professionally. He also painted but was too fussy about his colours. One day somebody jocularly criticized one of his works in oil and as a result he never put brush to canvas again.[71]

When his father died in 1862 he inherited a substantial share in the family fortune. From that moment he gave up sculpture and embarked on a life of gentlemanly leisure. He married twice; first a widow, Mrs. Read, and second, when he was eighty, Miss Florence King. By his second marriage he had a daughter, the late Miss Emily Wyatt of Tunbridge Wells who died in 1954 – the great-granddaughter of George III's Surveyor-General.[72]

Like the family sculptors the Wyatt painters also have been undeservedly neglected. Writing about the pupils of Lawrence in the *Burlington Magazine* in 1936, Sir Charles Holmes stated: 'If our great English portrait-painters were not as unfashionable with our native critics as they are admired and respected elsewhere one might by this time have begun to know something about them.'[73] Henry Wyatt was Lawrence's most important pupil but as little is known about him today as in 1936 despite the great strides made in English art history in the intervening forty years.

Henry was born at Thickbroom in 1794. His father died when he was three and he was brought up by an aunt and uncle, Maria and Francis Eginton. Francis Eginton was a protégé of Matthew Boulton and in 1781 had pioneered the revival of stained glass making in England. he provided windows for James Wyatt at Fonthill, St. George's Chapel, Salisbury and Lichfield Cathedrals, and for Samuel Wyatt at Temple Mills in Berkshire and St. Paul's Church, Birmingham.

Eginton's artistic interests affected the young Henry Wyatt and he early decided to be a painter. In 1811 he left Staffordshire for London to study at the Royal Academy Schools. Four years later he entered Sir Thomas Lawrence's studio. At first he was unpaid but he did so well that after a year he was offered a salary of £300 to stay on as Lawrence's principal assistant.[74]

He began his independent career in 1817 when he left London to become

[71] Coll. Capt. John Wyatt, T.H.Wyatt II's Family Notes.
[72] Ibid.
[73] Sir Charles Holmes, 'The Heirs of Lawrence 1825–35', *Burlington Mag.*, lxix (Nov. 1936), 195.
[74] *Gent's Mag.* (1840), 555–6.

a portrait-painter in Birmingham. He exhibited for the first time at the Royal Academy in the same year – a portrait of a Wyatt cousin, probably 'Cement Charles'. Altogether between 1817 and 1838 he exhibited eighty pictures in London of which thirty-five were shown at the Royal Academy. From Birmingham he moved to Liverpool for a year and then on to Manchester.[75]

In Manchester he lived at 91 Oldham Street with William Nicolson, a cabinet-maker, and worked with a family of engravers and booksellers, John and William Ford. He drew a series of historical portraits of local commanders in the Civil War for them to engrave. He also painted his own self-portrait while there.[76]

In September 1825 he returned to London where he lived for nine years. At the end of 1834 increasingly troublesome asthma forced him to move to Leamington where his health improved, but on a visit to Manchester in 1837, to paint the portrait of some friends, he had a stroke which paralysed his left side and ended his artistic career. He died two years later and was buried at Prestwich in February 1840.[77]

Henry Wyatt was greatly admired by contemporaries. He specialized in portraits and fancy pictures both of which earned him popularity. He also painted landscapes in oil and water-colour but only exhibited six of them. His sketch-books contain drawings of landscapes, buildings, animals, and wild flowers, 'all drawn with care and ability'. His interest in landscapes may have been mainly a private hobby. He exhibited his portraits at the Royal Academy and his fancy pictures at the British Institution. He also exhibited at the Liverpool Academy.

As a portrait-painter Henry Wyatt continued Lawrence's style for ten years after the great man's death until his own career was prematurely cut short by failing health. The shortness of his active life is one of the reasons why his achievement has been overlooked. But in the 1830s he was the best portrait-painter in the country. He was more accomplished than his closest rival, the president of the Royal Academy, Sir Martin Archer Shee.

In his early works Henry remained true to Lawrence, combining a dashing brilliance of brushwork with a 'gravity of tone and temper which stand out sharply from the prettiness and tinsel all about him'.[78] Later he moved away from this vigorous style with its free handling of paint towards a careful manner using a more liquid technique. In the later portraits he handles oil-paint as if it were water-colour and the dashing elegant poses of the earlier portraits give way to a stiffer though still informal character, closer to early

---

[75] Ibid.
[76] Ex info. Mr. Arnold Hyde.
[77] *Gent's Mag.* (1840), 555–6.
[78] Holmes, 201.

113. Self-portrait, by Henry Wyatt, 1824.

114. Admiral Sir C. Cunningham, by Henry Wyatt.

115. Abraham Wildey
Roberts, M.P. for Maidstone,
by Henry Wyatt, 1832.

116. The children of
J.F.Fraser, by Henry Wyatt,
1834.

nineteenth-century French portrait-painting.

His portraits vary greatly from groups of children, as charming as Archer Shee's, to grand portraits of generals and admirals glittering with medals or sensitive studies of women, many of which have been wishfully attributed to Lawrence. His best works date from between 1830 and 1836 when he was at the height of his powers and before his health began to decline. Unlike Archer Shee, who was only good at painting women and children, Henry was equally good with all sitters. Some of his women verge on the sentimental but many of the men's portraits are surprisingly frank. That of Edward Jenner painted in 1828 is an almost shocking revelation of the sitter's coarse and stubby features and is much more realistic than Lawrence's, Northcote's, and John Raphael Smith's portraits of Jenner.

His most common format for single figures was the three-quarter length. He specialized in small three-quarter-length portraits about 2 feet high. Most of his paintings are on this unusual scale.

Contemporaries admired his fancy pictures at least as much as his portraits. To modern taste *Naughty Pet* and *Juliet*, the two great favourites, are rebarbatively sentimental. Juliet is too obviously a thinly disguised young lady of 1832. Such pictures cause the same embarrassment in the spectator as bad acting. There is no doubt that Henry took them very seriously and made an extensive study of old masters in order to render his detail and costume accurately. He was particularly influenced by Rubens and Van Dyke. In 1828 he exhibited a *Study in Van Dyke Dress* at the British Institution and in 1834 a fancy portrait of Mrs. MacDougall under the title *Le Chapeau noir*. It is strikingly similar to Rubens's *Le Chapeau de paille* now in the National Gallery but then in the collection of Sir Robert Peel.

The best of his fancy pictures are portraits of men such as *The Corsair* dated 1833 and showing the hero of Byron's poem in a dramatic pose against a stormy sky with 'fire in his glance and wildness in his breast'. As late as 1907 Henry's portrait of a Falconer (exhibited at the British Institution in 1834) was considered an admirable work, 'a picture which in spirit and accomplishment is of the highest degree of excellence and only falls short of the work of the supreme masters of portraiture from the lack of [the] gravity with which they invest their sitters'.[79]

His straightforward academic nudes such as *Nymphs Bathing* or the *Mars and Venus* are also good of their kind. The *Mars and Venus* is now in the modern art section of the Pitti Palace in Florence and was formerly attributed to Etty. The treatment of the flesh shows the influence of Rubens. It is a creditable handling of the traditional Grand Manner and 'reveals the hand of a good academic painter'.

[79] *Burlington Mag.* (1907), caption to illustration, no page ref

117. *Le Chapeau noir*, by Henry Wyatt, 1834.

118. *Naughty Pet*, by Henry Wyatt.

Henry Wyatt was an artist who could perform well in many styles and moods. Just as his cousin James Wyatt's architectural achievement has been undervalued because of the ease with which he designed in all styles, so Henry Wyatt has not been taken seriously as a painter because he was capable of producing sentimental females reminiscent of Greuze, stylish portraits often mistaken for Lawrence, charming groups of children like those of Archer Shee, and fleshy academic nudes similar to Etty. By the standards of English painting (which are not as high as those of English architecture or sculpture) this was a dazzling performance. Redgrave's judgement in 1874 is on the whole just and accurate. He was a 'clever painter, his colour good and his subjects pleasingly treated'.[80]

Henry's brother Thomas Wyatt was also a portrait-painter but was not as talented or successful. He too studied at the Royal Academy Schools and accompanied his brother to London, Birmingham, Liverpool, and Manchester. He eventually settled in Manchester but while at Birmingham he played an active role in local artistic affairs. He was Secretary of the Midlands Art Society and founded his own academy of art in the city. He explained its purpose in a letter to Matthew Boulton:

Permit me for a moment to intrude upon your notice a subject intimately connected with the Arts and Manufactures of Birmingham – the utility of a knowledge of Drawing must be obvious to every one. Hitherto persons desirous of obtaining that knowledge in this town have laboured under a serious disadvantage from the want of a proper academy which should enable them to prosecute their studies beyond the mere rudiments of the Art obtained by drawing from small incorrect models from the antique and copying drawings and prints . . .

To obviate this I have been induced to establish an Academy in which will be found every requisite to obtain a correctness of Taste and elegance of Design – I have been careful to make selections from the finest remains of ancient sculpture among which will be found the Fighting Gladiator, the Discobolon, The Ilyssus from the Elgin Collection, the celebrated Torso Belvedere, commonly called Michael Angelo's Torso (from that great man's having formed his style upon it) the Venus di Medici etc. etc. together with a variety of Busts and extremities of the finest description.[81]

From 1840 to 1853 he lived in Princess Street, Manchester. From there he married the daughter of George Hadfield of Failsworth Lodge, a manufacturer. In the same years he exhibited annually at the Royal Manchester Institution. Most of his works were portraits – in 1846, for instance, he exhibited fourteen. But, like his brother, he also did some fancy pieces, including *The Mask*, *The Bouquet*, and *Reconnoitring*, the titles of which are self-explanatory. He also worked in water-colour. His view of Doncaster Parish Church is in the possession of a member of the Wyatt family. In 1854 Thomas retired to his

---

[80] S. Redgrave, *Dictionary of Arts* (1874), 468–9.
[81] BRL, Tew MSS., Thomas Wyatt to Matthew Boulton, 24 Jan. 1820.

native Staffordshire and spent his last four years at Lichfield. He was no longer able to paint but was supported by his family. He died on 7 July 1859.[83]

His brother-in-law Henry Hadfield (1809–87) was a drawing-master and a prolific artist. Thomas's son Francis Wyatt studied under him and in 1851 exhibited a portrait of Henry Hadfield at the Royal Manchester Institution but no other works by him are recorded, so it is not known for how long he continued the artistic traditions of this branch of the Wyatt family.[84]

---

[83] Redgrave, 469.
[84] Ex info. Mr. Arnold Hyde.

CHAPTER VII

Eminent and other Victorians

The years of political reaction, English victory over France, extravagant royal and aristocratic patronage, loosely termed 'the Regency', passed. The pioneering industrial and agricultural development in which the Wyatts had been so closely involved came to fruition. The reforms of the 1830s and the accession of a new queen introduced another world but one in which the Wyatts still played a prominent part. It was a world of the moneyed middle classes, optimism, religious revival, and large-scale urban development. All this is reflected in the work of the Victorian Wyatt architects.

Three of Matthew Cotes Wyatt's sons were architects and builders – Sir Matthew, George, and Henry. They worked mainly in London and co-operated with their father in the development of Tyburnia. Matthew Cotes put up some of the capital while the actual work of designing and building was in the hands of his sons. The eldest, Matthew, was the most active and successful of them. His earliest venture, however, was not in Paddington but on the Grosvenor Estate in Pimlico. Between 1838 and 1840, with a partner John Howell, he built Victoria Square to his own design. He was influenced by the style of Nash's West Strand Improvements, and Victoria Square has similar corner bows and domes.[1]

This speculation was successful and with the proceeds he took leases of several plots of land on the Bishop of London's Paddington Estate. He borrowed money from the London Assurance Corporation and built Stanhope Terrace, Westbourne and Bathurst Streets, Howley Place and Porteus Road, Hyde Park Crescent and Hyde Park Square, all in the same stuccoed Italianate style. Next to Thomas Cubitt, Matthew Wyatt was the largest developer in the Paddington area.[2] In 1847 he moved into one of his own houses, 5 Hyde Park Square, and dropped the title of architect. At that time his name disappeared from the lists of architects in the directories. He also acquired a country house, the Castle at Ryde in the Isle of Wight.[3]

He began a second career as a courtier and gentleman of independent means. On 7 May 1845 he was appointed standard-bearer of the Corps of Gentlemen-

---

[1] Grosvenor Office, GBM vol. ii, fo. 355, Matthew Wyatt's plan for Victoria Square.
[2] Millbank, Church Commissioners MSS.; H. Hobhouse, *Thomas Cubitt* (1971), 339; ex info Mr. Frank Kelsall.
[3] Coll. Capt. John Wyatt, T. H. Wyatt II's Family Notes.

119. London, Victoria Square, Pimlico. Designed by Sir Matthew Wyatt, 1838–40.

120. *An Irish Fair*. Water-colour by Matthew Wyatt II.

at-Arms and in 1848 was knighted. He married twice; first, Emma Feswick, and second, Mary Anne Pywell. He had no children by either marriage but left three illegitimate children.[4]

George Wyatt, the second son, co-operated with Matthew in Tyburnia. He too made a fortune out of London building but over-speculated and went bankrupt. He is reputed to have designed Princes Square and Leinster Square in Paddington and Palace Gardens in Kensington. His brother Henry also worked in the North Kensington area and designed Lansdowne Crescent as well as six Gothic villas in Aubrey Road.[5]

More important were Henry's buildings in Scarborough and the North Riding of Yorkshire. He was occupied in Scarborough from 1837 to 1863 designing the Spa Saloon (demolished), houses on the cliff, St. Nicholas House (now the old Town Hall), and a hotel. The Spa Saloon was castellated but the other buildings were Italianate. His country work in Yorkshire included additions to Aldby Park and the restoration of Buttercrambe Church for H. B. Darley, alterations to Wykeham Abbey, and a new Italianate house at Newby Wiske for William Rutson.[6]

Henry lived to be very old but only exhibited twice at the Royal Academy – a mausoleum at Tempico in 1844 and a Gothic church in 1849. His marriage was particularly unsuccessful – he left his wife on the same day that he married her.[7]

Far more distinguished were the two brothers, Thomas Henry Wyatt I and Sir Matthew Digby Wyatt. Thomas Henry was notable not so much for the quality of his architecture as for its quantity. He was one of the most prolific of all English architects. In the nineteenth century only Sir Gilbert Scott's office produced more buildings. Digby Wyatt (as he was called by the family), though some of his designs are very fine, was pre-eminently a committee -man, lecturer, water-colourist, editor, and writer. He contributed more to the literature of art than any other member of his profession.

Their father, Matthew Wyatt II (1773–1831), was the eldest son of Thomas Wyatt, agent to the Earl of Uxbridge in Staffordshire. Thomas had later moved to Rowdeford House near Devizes in Wiltshire. Matthew was a barrister and a magistrate in England and Ireland with a talent for drawing. His sketch of an Irish fair is reminiscent of Rowlandson. He was also agent to the Marquess of Downshire and Viscount Dillon. He married Anne, daughter of Brigadier-General George Hillier of Devizes, in 1806. In Ireland he lived at Lough-Glin House, Co. Roscommon. On his retirement to Rowde in 1818 he was presented

[4] Ibid.
[5] *LS*, xxxvii (1973), 93, 239.
[6] *Theakston's Scarborough Guide* (2nd edn., 1841, 34; *Scarborough Gazette*, 24 Sept. 1863; North Yorkshire R.O., Darley MSS., ZDA (M) 30–37, 58–70; ZDA 89. (Ex info Mr. H. M. Colvin).
[7] Coll Capt. John Wyatt, T. H. Wyatt II's Family Notes.

with a tribute of respect from his fellows on the Bench, a curious social document, which survives in the possession of a descendant:

By the Grand Jury of the County of Roscommon, Spring Assizes 1818. The following resolutions were unanimously agreed to: Resolved – That we have heard with sincere regret, of the intended departure of Matthew Wyatt Esq. from this country.

That his character, principles, and conduct (with which an intimate experience of many years has made us fully aquainted) eminently entitle him to every mark of our esteem, respect and regard; and that we offer this public testimony of the high opinion we entertain of him, deeply impressed with the regret which this event is calculated to inspire.

That in the various and important duties which his situation in this country has called upon him to fulfil, we have firmly found him, as a Magistrate, a Juror, and a Country Gentleman, enlightened, upright and humane; a zealous supporter of the Laws and a liberal Protector of the Poor!

That entertaining these sentiments, we feel it to be justly due to Mr. Wyatt, to take this opportunity of expressing them accompanied with our most sincere good wishes for his future prosperity and happiness.[8]

Matthew Wyatt II had two younger brothers: Major-General Edgar Wyatt, who became superintendent of the East India Company's stud in Bengal, and Arthur Wyatt, agent to the Duke of Beaufort at Badminton and in Wales. After his retirement (he was succeeded by his son Osmund who kept up the Wyatt connection at Badminton until 1911), Arthur lived at Troy House in Monmouthshire. He occupied himself there by improving the grounds of Troy and Raglan Castle. 'In this he evinced much of the taste of his distinguished relative Sir Jeffry Wyatville . . . many unrivalled scenes on this classic ground and landscapes of enchanting beauty, formerly sealed up and inaccessible now laid open and displayed, are evidences and remain lasting memorials [to him]'.[9]

Troy, which belonged to the Duke of Beaufort, was a late seventeenth-century house. It was then wonderfully undisturbed, full of old furniture and relics, redolent of faded grandeur. Lord Torrington, when he visited Troy in 1781, happily occupied himself 'rummaging in odd places' and discovered an ancient suit of armour, 'John of Gaunt's . . . very probably'. The five great rooms on the *piano nobile* retained their original decoration with panelled walls and the gilt Somerset portcullis all over the ceilings. An older room at the back had elaborate sixteenth-century plasterwork and the rich panelling and chimney-piece now in the Duchess of Beaufort's Sitting-Room at Badminton.

Digby and Thomas Henry spent their summers with Uncle Arthur at Troy. They loved Monmouthshire and the romantic old house stimulated their interest in architecture. They went on jaunts to Raglan and Tintern to sketch the ruins. These enjoyable holidays had an important influence on their lives.

[8] Coll. Mrs. Janet Don.
[9] Obituary in *Monmouth Merlin* (1833).

121. Sir (Matthew) Digby Wyatt, by Ossani.

They both married from Troy. Thomas Henry followed family tradition and married his cousin Arabella Montagu Wyatt. She was Arthur's second daughter. In this generation of the family no fewer than eight Wyatts married their cousins. Digby, however, married Mary Nicholl, the daughter of a Monmouthshire family. The Nicholls lived at Yns Hafod in Usk and Mary's name remains scratched with a diamond ring on the pane of a bedroom window there.

Thomas Henry was intended for a mercantile career and spent some time in Malta 'to learn the beauties of cottons, coffees and calicoes'. He soon lost interest and switched to architecture. He entered the office of Philip Charles Hardwick and is reputed to have helped with the drawings for the Goldsmiths' Hall, the warehouses at St. Katharine's Docks, and Euston Station. In 1832, the year of the Great Reform Bill, he began independent architectural practice. Almost immediately he was appointed District Surveyor for Hackney, a post he held until 1861.

He was lucky in both the timing of his career and his family connections. It was the period of great development in the South Wales valleys. Large numbers of new churches, gaols, assize courts, markets, schools, and other public buildings were needed to meet the needs of the growing populations. Thomas Henry got most of these commissions as a result of his Welsh connections. With the recommendation of the Beauforts he was able to start a country house practice which grew to be one of the biggest in the country. So greatly had he prospered by 1838 that he needed a partner to share the work-load. He chose David Brandon. Their partnership lasted thirteen years. Afterwards Thomas Henry worked on his own almost to the end of his career when he was joined by his eldest son.

In his forty-eight years of practice he designed over four hundred buildings. Many of them were, at least partly, the work of assistants and pupils. When he received the RIBA Gold Medal in 1873 he paid tribute to his helpers: 'No-one can know as well as I do how much I am indebted to others for what there is of interest in those works – I mean to faithful and attached assistants, who have been long with me.' The drawings made for the Hendre in Monmouthshire in 1870 were by his clerk, Henry Pope. The Adelphi Theatre in 1857 was largely the work of Stephen Salter, a pupil, and the interior decoration was designed by Digby Wyatt. The two brothers co-operated on a number of buildings, including the first competition design for Knightsbridge Barracks and the Woolwich Garrison Chapel.

Digby had followed his brother into architecture and trained in his office. Though not as prolific, he is the more interesting of the two. He was among the most modern-minded designers of mid-Victorian England and a member of the enterprising circle which revolved around the Prince Consort. It included Sir Henry Cole and Owen Jones and was sometimes nicknamed the 'South

Kensington Group'. Owen Jones was his closest friend. Digby called him 'my brother in art' and dedicated *An Architect's Notebook in Spain* to him. Other close friends included Edward Lear, William Dyce, and Lord Leighton.

Though both brothers were indefatigable they differed greatly in character, practice, and the organization of their work. Digby did not have a large office and did most of his drawings himself. He was Slade Professor of Art at Cambridge at the time when Ruskin was at Oxford. He designed interior decoration, stained glass, tiles, carpets, metalwork, book illustrations, and cast-iron public lavatories. His architecture was only a small portion of his total achievement.

He was born at Rowde on 28 July 1820 and attended Mr. Bigg's school in Devizes before entering Thomas Henry's office at the age of sixteen. Within a year he won a prize from the Architectural Society for the best essay on Grecian Doric – the first indication of his talent as a writer on art. In 1837 he enrolled in the Royal Academy Schools before deciding to complete his education by travelling abroad. He earned money for his grand tour by doing etching and lithography in his spare time. He also designed a school and parsonage in Monmouthshire, two small houses at King's Town near Dublin, and a factory in Bermondsey.[10]

By 1844 he had saved enough money to set off on his travels. He spent two years on the Continent, making nearly 1,000 drawings in ink and water-colour of 'the principal monuments of architecture and decoration in France, Italy, Sicily and Germany'. The most elaborate were a series of 'specimens of the geometrical mosaics of the middle ages' which were published in facsimile in 1848. The idea of collecting designs of mosaic was John Blashfield's. He introduced Digby to Herbert Minton. This was the beginning of a productive relationship, for it led on the one hand to improved standards of tile-design at Mintons and on the other Digby was asked to advise directly on the floor-tiles for Osborne.[11]

The *Specimens* was the first of a series of publications on the applied arts. A lecture on mosaics at the Royal Society of Arts brought him to the notice of an important group of members who were interested in improving the design of English manufactures. He absorbed their enthusiasm and read further papers to the Society on 'Enamel and Enamelling', 'Metalwork', and 'Services rendered to Ceramic Art by Herbert Minton'. He also started to write regularly for the press.

In 1849 he went to Birmingham on behalf of the *Journal of Design* to study the Exhibition of Manufactures held at Bingley House. On his return he was dispatched to Paris with Henry Cole by the Society of Arts to report on the Exposition there.

---

[10] Coll. Capt. John Wyatt, M.D.Wyatt, 'My Memoir for Mr.C.Knight's English Cyclopedia', 1857 (MS.).
[11] Ibid.; *The Architect* (26 May 1877), 331.

122. The National Gallery. Unexecuted design by Sir (Matthew) Digby Wyatt for rebuilding, 1866.

123. Paddington Station. Sir (Matthew) Digby Wyatt designed the cast-iron decoration, 1850–5. The engineer was I.K.Brunel. From *The Railway Station* by W.P.Frith.

Sir Henry Cole was a leading figure in the Society of Arts, versatile and boundlessly enthusiastic. He reorganized the Public Record Office; fought for the standard railway gauge; published the first Christmas card; helped Rowland Hill reform the Post Office and printed the first stamped envelope to a design by Mulready. He coined the term 'art-manufactures' and was on the organizing committee of the small exhibitions of art-manufactures held by the Society of Arts in 1847, 1848, and 1849. It was his idea to hold a larger exhibition in 1851 on the pattern of those which had taken place in Paris every five years since the beginning of the century. The idea was taken up by the President of the Society, Prince Albert.

Henry Cole and Digby Wyatt were joined in Paris by Francis Fuller and John Scott Russell. Cole and Fuller returned early to England to start raising money, leaving Digby to complete the report. It was well received by the Prime Minister, Sir Robert Peel, and the whole press. As a result Digby was appointed Special Commissioner and Secretary to the Royal Commission responsible for organizing the Great Exhibition.

Cole had originally wanted to hold the exhibition in the courtyard of Somerset House. This was not big enough and Hyde Park was chosen instead. A competition was opened for designs for the exhibition building. As everybody now knows, all the schemes submitted were unsuitable and the day was saved by Paxton's miraculous blotting-paper sketch for a huge glasshouse on the lines of the Lily House at Chatsworth.

The basic design was Paxton's and the work was executed by Fox Henderson and Co., with Digby acting as superintendent architect. In his own words, 'I was employed to superintend the works, make all the contracts with Fox Henderson & Co., regulate the accounts etc. Upwards of £50,000s worth of work was directed by me as sole architect.'[12] Owen Jones designed the Saracenic cresting on the roof and the internal colour scheme. He was not, as is sometimes stated, the executant architect of the Crystal Palace.

As well as being Secretary and executant architect of the exhibition building, Digby was responsible for arranging the exhibits. One parcel arrived from France addressed to 'Sir Vyatt and Sir Fox Enderson Esquire, Grate Exposition, Park of Hide at London. Glace. Softly to be posed upright.' He even designed the share certificate of the Crystal Palace Company. As much as anybody he was responsible for the success of the venture.[13]

The Crystal Palace was only completed with a great deal of opposition and hostility. There was an outpouring of xenophobic feeling in the correspondence columns of *The Times*. It was feared that foreigners and other vagabonds, attracted to London by the exhibition, would spread disease and immorality.

[12] 'My Memoir'.
[13] Beaver, *The Crystal Palace*, 35. One of Digby Wyatt's share certificates is in the Mellon Collection.

The most voluble opponent of the exhibition was Colonel Sibthorp, the ultra-Tory M.P. for Lincoln. He thought that the trees would have to be felled on the exhibition site. 'Are the elms to be sacrificed for one of the greatest frauds, greatest humbugs, greatest absurdities ever known?', he thundered. In fact they were saved by adding the high arched transepts to the design.

Despite all criticism and foreboding the great enterprise was completed within nine months and the building was a triumph. Even *The Times* was won over and restricted itself to grumbling about the lack of 'conveniences for foreigners, who are not particular when certain calls of nature press where they stop to relieve themselves'. It also worried that the salute fired on the Queen's arrival to open the exhibition would 'shiver the glass roof of the Palace and thousands of ladies will be cut into mincemeat'.[14] Both fears were unfounded.

The Crystal Palace was opened on the first of May, a bright clear day, with a ceremony of motley grandezza. A choir of six hundred voices sang the national anthem and the 'Hallelujah Chorus' followed by fanfares of trumpets, organ voluntaries, and prayers. The commissioners had reason to feel satisfied with their achievement. Digby received a private gold medal 'with a gratifying letter commending my services' from Prince Albert and a bonus of £1,000 on top of his salary.[15]

He wrote a 'popular account of the construction of the building' and a 'more elaborate one' for the Institution of Civil Engineers which earned him the Telford Medal. He also produced a two-volume catalogue of the exhibits, *The Industrial Arts of the XIXth Century*, with 160 lurid chromolithographs which involved 'no mean amount of labour'. This was more a work of editing than authorship. Most of the plates were done by others and so was the writing. His pupil William Burges, for instance, contributed fourteen articles. At the same time Digby produced another volume of art-manufactures, *Metal Work and its Artistic Design* with fifty plates.

When the Great Exhibition was over the Crystal Palace was re-erected at Sydenham. Once again Digby was involved with Paxton and Owen Jones in the construction. This disqualified them from having a major direct role in the South Kensington Museum which was now the main concern of the Prince's circle. Sydenham was thought by the purists to be showmanship rather than culture. Nevertheless, Digby maintained his connection with Henry Cole. His *Specimens* was a major influence on the abstract pattern-making in the decoration at South Kensington. He advised Cole where in Italy to find suitable models for the mosaic floors of the museum. This work was executed by convicts, hence its nickname – 'opus criminale'. He also lectured at the Museum and advised on purchases. The great Dutch seventeenth-century

[14] Beaver, 37.   [15] 'My Memoir'.

VII The Great Exhibition, 1851. From *Waiting for the Queen* by Dickinson *facing p.208*

screen from Hertogenbosch which now dominates the Sculpture Courts was bought with his advice. Conversely, the design of the elevations of the Museum affected his own style, as can be seen at Addenbrooke's Hospital in Cambridge.[16]

At Sydenham he was principally involved in the design of the Courts of Architecture which were to demonstrate the art and architecture of 'the great civilisations'. He and Owen Jones spent a considerable time on the Continent ordering plaster casts of the best sculpture for the courts, backed by credit of £20,000. Digby himself designed the Pompeian, Byzantine, English Gothic, and the Italian Renaissance Courts.

Just before the Crystal Palace was due to be opened there was a slight embarrassment. A letter was written by thirteen 'eminent persons' asking for fig-leaves to be added to the plaster statues: 'We demand but a small thing . . . the removal of the parts which in life ought to be concealed, although we are also desirous that the usual leaf be adopted.' The directors of the Crystal Palace capitulated. The offending statues were castrated and fig-leaves were 'riveted on to the emasculated loins of the heroes of old'. This done, the Sydenham Crystal Palace was opened to the public on 3 June 1854. Of course Digby wrote the guidebook.[17]

There were two postscripts to his connection with the Crystal Palace and South Kensington. The first was his appointment as collaborating architect with Brunel at Paddington Station to design all the decorative ironwork in 1852. Brunel's instructions to Digby were that the ornament should be unrelated to any style of the past and be suited to the material – cast iron. This enabled him to put into practice some of the ideas expressed in his lectures and writings. His designs are vaguely Moorish and the decoration is well integrated with the structure. The climax is formed by the oriels of platform one, lighting the station-masters's office and Queen Victoria's waiting-room. The bold decoration is 'expressive of the most advanced taste of the 1850s' and is probably his best-known work.[18]

The second postscript was his involvement in the design of the Albert Memorial and the Albert Hall following the death of Prince Albert in 1862. He was one of seven architects invited to submit designs for the monument and produced three alternative proposals – a seated figure of gilded bronze, a classical temple, and an Italian Gothic 'cross' or shrine. The drawings do not survive. Scott won the competition. The same seven architects produced designs for a hall as part of the memorial scheme. Digby proposed a top-lit circular building in either a classical or Gothic style. His designs were not

---

[16] *LS*, xxxviii (1975), 77, 78, 87; *V & A Year Book* (1969).
[17] *The Times*, 8 May 1854; 'My Memoir'.
[18] H. R. Hitchcock, *Early Victorian Architecture in England* (1954), i. 562.

executed but it was claimed in an anonymous letter to the *Building News* in 1874 that his scheme was the prototype of the hall as built.[19]

Digby, though now an influential member of his profession and an acknowledged expert on Italian art and industrial design, was still a young man. In 1853 he was thirty-three and in that year he married Mary Nicholl, the daughter of a Welsh landowner. The Nicholls were almost a caricature of a hypocritical Victorian family. Her brother, the Revd. Iltyd Nicholl, was at the time of the wedding fighting for the inheritance of a distant cousin, Rachel Morgan, an heiress who died intestate in 1854 leaving an estate at Pantry Goitry worth £80,000. The Revd. Iltyd immediately took possession of the dead woman's house. The following year a collier, Jacob Morgan, appeared, claiming to be the rightful heir. This led to a lawsuit and bizarre trial at Monmouth Assizes in 1857. There was an endless succession of eccentric witnesses and perjurors. All the complications of Welsh family life were displayed to an astonished world. Incest was one of the more straightforward involvements. Many of the Welsh peasants called as witnesses could not speak English and interpreters were necessary. In the end Morgan's claim was dismissed and the Revd. Iltyd Nicholl was confirmed as the rightful heir.

Digby attended the trial for the fun of it and occupied himself sketching caricatures of the witnesses – deaf old women with ear-trumpets and wizened Welsh peasants with only one tooth. Drawing caricatures was one of his hobbies. His notebooks are full of them. A sketch of a fat woman bathing in the sea is called *Brighton Nereid* and a pair of hideous, frumpish German women gossiping to each other in a hotel dining-room is called *Table d'hôte, Munich*.[20]

As soon as the inheritance was secure Iltyd Nicholl sold Pantry Goitry and used the money to rebuild the unassuming eighteenth-century manor-house, the Ham, on his own estate in the Vale of Glamorgan. Digby Wyatt designed it in the Elizabethan style. The resulting asymetrical rock-faced pile with tall chimneys and bay-windows was very impressive. But it was not enough to protect the family from scandal. Iltyd's younger brother William Henry Nicholl had a long liaison with one of the housemaids and finally married her, to the horror of his elder brother. The family had the last word, however, for when William died in 1874, they wrote on his tomb: 'I have blotted out as a thick cloud thy transgressions and as a cloud thy sins return unto me for I have redeemed thee', thus recording his lapse from grace for posterity. Mary Wyatt preferred her younger brother to her stuffier relations and left most of her personal possessions to his child when she died.[21]

The crowning success of Digby's career was his appointment as Surveyor to the East India Company in 1855. This followed the Paris Exhibition of that

[19] *LS*, xxxviii (1975), 178, 184.   [20] Coll. Dr. Paine.
[21] Somerset House, Lady (Mary) Wyatt's Will, Mar. 1894.

year where he and Sir Forbes Royle had arranged the Company's stand. With the Duke of Hamilton he was among the jurors of the exhibition and reported to the British Government on the furniture and decoration. For this he was created a *chevalier de la Légion d'honneur* by the French.[22]

He designed important buildings for the Company both in England and India, including their museum in Leadenhall Street, barracks at Warley, and the general post office and telegraph office in Calcutta. With J. M. Rendel, the engineer, he designed a number of bridges, including the ones over the Rivers Soane, Kent, and Hullohur.[23]

When, following the Mutiny, the East India Company was abolished and the Council of India set up in its place, Digby became Architect to the Council. As part of the reorganization the old India Office in Leadenhall Street was sold and a site for a new office allocated next to the Foreign Office at the seat of government in Whitehall. This was an unexpected threat to Sir Gilbert Scott, Architect to the Foreign Office. Digby's tact and sense of fair play, however, prevented the situation from becoming difficult. Ten years later Scott wrote to him; 'I entered into an agreement with you at a time when, as I imagined, my position was strong and when shortly afterwards and during a lengthened period it unexpectedly became very much the reverse, you adhered with all possible truthfulness to the arrangements made under different conditions. Nor have you throughout flinched from or evinced any but the most friendly feeling of equal and loyal co-operation.'[24]

The two architects co-operated very closely. For the sake of unity it was agreed that Scott should design the exterior in harmony with its neighbours. Nevertheless, the over-all composition of the park-front of the Foreign and India Offices owes much to Digby. Scott generously admitted in his *Reflections* that he had 'adopted an idea as to its grouping and outline suggested by a sketch of Mr. Wyatt'. It was brilliant and the resulting picturesque composition helps to lead the eye step by step inwards to Horse Guards Parade. It contributes greatly to the whole west side of Whitehall from St. James's Park, which is undoubtedly the most picturesque assemblage of government buildings in the world.

The close co-operation between the two architects over the exterior is emphasized by the words with which Digby submitted the drawings: 'Mr. Scott and I as your architects . . .' They were paid jointly 5 per cent on all contracts. The interior of the India Office was, however, entirely Digby's. The sumptuous courtyard is his masterpiece and is closely based on Italian Renaissance sources. The three tiers of arcades recall the cloisters of the Certosa at Pavia.

[22] *Men of the Time, A Biography of Living Characters* (1862) (ex info Mr. E.S. Blake).
[23] Drawings for the Soane Bridge are in the India Office Library.
[24] Scott correspondence, quoted in Lavinia Handley-Read, 'The India Office', *C.Life*, 9 July 1970.

124. India Office Courtyard. Designed by Sir (Matthew) Digby Wyatt, 1868. From a photograph showing the preparations for the Durbar of Edward VII.

125. Ashridge, Hertfordshire, Billard Room. Designed by Sir (Matthew) Digby Wyatt, 1860.

The red and blue 'Della Robbia' majolica friezes were made by Mintons and are a good example of 'art-manufactures'. Polished granite columns contribute to the splendid polychrome effect. The total ensemble is a 'Renaissance fantasy unequalled in this country'. It is the supreme example of the South Kensington style. 'Wyatt's high Victorian Italian expresses the splendour and also the gravity of the national responsibilities towards the Indian subjects who were to be received there.'[25]

His appointment as Architect to the Council of India brought Digby a knighthood. Other honours followed quickly in the 1860s – the Officers' Cross of the San Maurizio and Lazzaro Order from the King of Italy, Honorary M.A. and the Slade Professorship of Fine Art at Cambridge. He was made an honorary member of the Arundel Society, Honorary Secretary, Vice-President, and Gold Medallist of the Royal Institute of British Architects, a Fellow of the Society of Antiquaries, and President of the Graphic Society.[26]

Books and lectures continued to flow from his pen. In 1869 he made a tour of Spain to sketch old buildings. These were engraved and published as *An Architect's Notebook in Spain*.[27] By the time of his death he had created, as editor, writer, and illustrator, a whole library on the fine and applied arts.

His architectural practice also continued to expand. In the 1860s he designed a series of town and country houses which would have occupied any lesser man full time. They range from the colossal Gothic Possingworth Manor in Sussex which cost £60,000 to the Tudor restoration of Compton Wynyates and the Italian Renaissance interior of Ashridge. (He was the fifth Wyatt to work there in succession to James, Benjamin Dean, Edward II, and Jeffry Wyatville.)

By the end of the decade his health was seriously affected by overwork and he contemplated retiring to the Italian Riviera. His friend, Edward Lear, encouraged him. Lear and he shared many of the same interests. Both were talented water-colourists and they had the same sense of humour. Over forty letters from Lear to Sir Digby and Lady Wyatt survive. They are all jocular with puns, deliberate mis-spellings, and caricatures sketched in the margin. They start in 1863 and one of the earliest is a refusal to come to dinner because he was already booked –

> (1)
> O Digby my dear
> It is perfectly clear
> That my mind will be horribly vext
> If you happen to write
> By ill luck to invite
>   Me to dinner on Saturday next

[25] Ibid.
[26] *Br.*, 2 June 1877, Digby Wyatt's obituary.
[27] The original ink drawings are in the Print Room of the V & A.

(2)
For this I should sigh at
That Mrs J.Wyatt
  Already has booked me, o dear!
So I could not send answer
To You – I'm your man Sir! –
– Your loving fat friend
                              Edward Lear

A letter dated '22 toothoktober 1866' contains a 'P.Eth: I had had a thaddak-thident and have broken off my front teeth, so that I shall never thpeak plain again. Thith comest of biting crutht.'

Lear and Digby each wanted to buy land to build a villa somewhere near the Mediterranean. Lear reported suitable sites. In 1868 he suggested Corsica: 'Corsiker is a Niland in the sea and Napoleon Buonapart, Genl. Paoli, Pozze de Bozo Abbaticca and others were all beborn there – it perjuices pine trees and cream cheese, fish and lots of asparagus: most of the people were black and if they have trowsers always keep their hands in their pockets.'

In the end Lear chose San Remo and built himself a villa with a beautiful prospect over the sea. Before long a vast hotel rose in front, blotting out the view. This depressed Lear so much that he thought for a time of emigrating to New Zealand. Lear's sad experience decided Digby not to settle on the Riviera after all. He chose the south coast of Wales instead.[28]

Lady Wyatt was offered one of the Nicholl houses, Dimlands Castle in Glamorganshire. It was accepted and the Wyatts moved there. The view of the sea through the pine-trees on a fine day was not too different from the Mediterranean. The name 'castle' was typical Nicholl pretension. The house was not much bigger than a vicarage but had been done up with battlements and given a toy-fort entrance-lodge in 1844.

The change of air came too late to save Digby's health. Judging from the labour involved in the move it was probably responsible for finishing him off. He planned every detail with manic precision. He made coloured plans to scale of the rooms in Tavistock Place and of Dimlands. They showed where every table, chair, carpet, rug, and window-blind was and where it was to go in the new house. His water-colours of Italy were hung in the drawing-room along-side the chairs he had designed for himself with M.W. carved on their backs and the oak clock with 'M. DIGBY WYATT' on its face instead of numerals.[29]

He died on 21 May 1877 and was buried alongside the Nicholl family in Usk churchyard. His tomb of pink granite with cast-iron railings was designed by Thomas Henry Wyatt. He died as the most distinguished member of the family, loaded with honours from home and abroad; so much so that Lear had

---

[28] The Lear–Wyatt letters are in the collection of Dr. B.W.Paine, Worcestershire.
[29] Glamorgan R.O., D/DC E/52, Lady Wyatt's Will.

126. Detail of cast-iron urinal in Star Yard, off Chancery Lane, London. Designed by Sir (Matthew) Digby Wyatt.

127. West Ham, Rothschild Mausoleum. Designed by Sir (Matthew) Digby Wyatt, 1866.

128. London, Alford House, Kensington. Design exhibited
at the Royal Academy by Sir (Matthew)
Digby Wyatt, 1871. Demolished.

129. *Interior of a Foreign Church.*
Water-colour by Sir (Matthew) Digby Wyatt.

written to Lady Wyatt: 'I entreat you also to prevent the Khedive of Egypt from making Digby a Pasha, which he may take it into his head to do, but Digby Pasha and Lady Wyatt would never sound well and would always appear as if you were not a respectable couple.'

His reputation as an architect has always been overshadowed by his writings, organizational and committee work, and general crusade to improve design. It is his architecture, however, which is the most interesting today. His classical buildings were among the best of the mid-nineteenth century. Despite the triumph of the Goths in church-building and in a number of competitions for public buildings it can be argued that the mainstream of Victorian secular architecture was classical. Digby fills the gap between the early Victorians such as Barry and the late nineteenth-century Queen Anne and free classical revivals.

Though he designed in a variety of styles – Moorish in the smoking-room as 12 Kensington Palace Gardens, Indian in the Soane Bridge, and Elizabethan in some of his country houses – he was never a serious Goth. He thought classical architecture, particularly that of the Italian Renaissance, to be the best. All his greatest works are in this style – the India Office, the Rothschild Mausoleum, the Gloriette in the gardens at Castle Ashby, and the interiors of Ashridge. The Saloon at Ashridge with its marble door-cases, chimney-pieces, and 'Wilton' ceiling would be at home in a Roman palace.

The South Kensington Group believed in Italian classicism and Digby was their most talented architect. In his Slade lectures at Cambridge he emphasized that study of the Five Orders was of real practical use in training the eye to appreciate relations of scale and design. He advocated the grafting of the 'objective practice of Pugin and the Medievalists to the excellent subjective system transmitted to us from the Classical Ages'. This foreshadows the free classical architecture of the late nineteenth century. His obituarist wrote: 'He certainly seemed to have anticipated the present run upon Queen Anne architecture or something cognate'.[30] Alford House in Kensington of 1872, apart from its French pavilion roofs, is very Queen Anne and points the way to the future.

Of his non-architectural work the most attractive is sketching in watercolours and ink. His drawings of Spain are as good as Richard Ford's; they are much better than the engravings after them. On the other hand, his writings have lost much of their relevance. A great many of his books consist of plates with short descriptive texts and nothing more. His more serious work and lectures, with their constant theme that 'form should be coincident with structural fitness', were of great relevance in their day but now seem platitudes. They have none of the fire, literary genius, and sheer eccentricity

[30] *Br.*, 2 June 1877.

which has ensured the survival of Ruskin's writings. Nobody would read Digby Wyatt now except out of curiosity.

Thomas Henry Wyatt I also rose to the top of the architectural profession. He was highly efficient. His well-organized office was able to cope with his large practice and to turn out appropriate designs for every occasion. Thus despite his numerous private commissions he was able to play an active part in public affairs. He succeeded to many official architectural appointments. He was Honorary Architect to the Institution of Civil Engineers (of which he was on the council), the Athenaeum Club (of which he was a member), the Middlesex Hospital, and the Governesses' Benevolent Institution. In his time he was considered an expert on hospital design and he was responsible for two large hospitals in Malta as well as many in England. He was also Consulting Architect to the Commissioners of Lunacy, the Incorporated Church Building Society, and the Dioceses of Salisbury and Llandaff.

His career was that of the quintessential Victorian professional man, playing his part in the internal politics of the profession, sitting on all the committees, and rising to its highest posts and honours where he presided with 'tact, energy and courtesy'. He was president of the Architects' Benevolent Society, Vice-President of the Architectural Society, and finally in 1870 he was elected President of the successor to these two bodies, the Royal Institute of British Architects. In 1873 he received the Gold Medal and from 1879 until a few months before his death was its Honorary Secretary in succession to C. R. Cockerell.[31]

Thomas Henry possessed all the gentlemanly virtues. His manners were unfailingly perfect. 'He was conciliatory and politic; always modest and a gentleman.' But he was so dull! In contrast to jolly Digby he had little sense of humour and never said a really funny thing in his life. Even his obituarist remarked that he was not 'a brilliant wit'.[32]

Though neither a great architect nor a lively personality, he was eminently successful. He worked for all the 'best men' of his time. The secret of his success was his ability to win the confidence and co-operation of his clients. He could rough out a sketch with an astonishing facility. His early training as a business man meant that he could write letters to his clients which they 'could read with interest and understand without difficulty'. His greatest asset was his social standing. Of the architects of his day he was considered to be socially pre-eminent. In a world in which Benjamin Ferrey advised his architectural pupils always to travel first-class on the train and Sir Gilbert Scott felt it necessary to tell us that he was distantly connected with some 'very good families', such a consideration was more important than can be imagined today.

[31] *Br.*, 14 Aug. 1880, T.H. Wyatt's obituary.   [32] Ibid.

130. Thomas Henry Wyatt. Pencil drawing by George Richmond.

131. Arabella Montagu Wyatt, wife of Thomas Henry Wyatt, by George Landseer, 1856.

He adopted and made permanent the myth that the family was descended from Sir Thomas Wyatt. As well as his London house at 77 Great Russell Street he inherited Weston Corbett House in Hampshire from his godfather, George Green. It was a late seventeenth-century red-brick manor-house with a hipped roof, set in a garden of clipped yews. It remained in the Wyatt family until 1929.[33] This small estate made him lord of the manor of Weston Patrick. He brought to his role of country squire the earnestness which governed all his behaviour. He dutifully rebuilt the parish church at Weston Patrick to his own design and largely at his own expense. His combined role of country gentleman and eminent professional was reflected in his dress. In photographs he usually wears the same curious compromise between town and country – pepper-and-salt trousers combined with a hairy tweed jacket and waistcoat.

Though not a great architect nor an artist of any originality, most of his work is competent and scholarly. His later buildings have coarse mechanical detail but they were more or less mass produced by his office. He had a wide knowledge of architecture. He spent his holidays travelling round England, photographing and sketching. In the spring of 1837 he made a long tour through Belgium, Germany, France, Italy, and Sicily. His sketches made on the trip survive. They include the Roman ruins at Nîmes, the Greek temples at Paestum, the great Renaissance and baroque palaces in Naples, Rome, Florence, and Dresden, as well as the Gothic cathedrals of northern France and Germany and such picturesque northern cities as Bruges, Louvain, Nuremberg, Regensburg, and Freiberg.[34]

His earliest buildings are undoubtedly the most attractive visually. They include Llantarnam Abbey designed in 1834 with onion cupolas and filigree Gothic gateways; St. Paul's Church in Newport of 1835 with elongated arches, pinnacles, a spire, and a pretty octagonal entrance-porch; also the noble classical Assize Court at Devizes built in 1835. All these are in the late Regency tradition of his cousins Sir Jeffry Wyatville and Lewis Wyatt.

The 1840s were a boom period when his practice expanded rapidly, following the partnership with David Brandon. His best building was, however, entirely his own work. It is the Parish Church of SS. Mary and Nicholas at Wilton, paid for by Sidney Herbert (Lord Herbert of Lea) and his mother, Catherine, Countess of Pembroke (daughter of Count Worontzov-Dashkow, the lord of Alupka). It was the most ambitious Anglican church undertaken for a hundred years and the first of a great series of churches built on their estates by conscientious Victorian landowners. The explanation for such ambitious offerings to God is carved in letters a foot high on the western tribune at

---

[33] Ex Info Mr. Felix Bedford. The kitchen from this house is now at Sulgrave Manor in Northamptonshire.
[34] Mellon Coll., T.H. Wyatt Album 1837.

132. Devizes Assize Court. Designed by Thomas Henry Wyatt, 1835.

133. Wilton, Church of S.S. Mary and Nicholas. Designed by Thomas Henry Wyatt, 1840–5.

Wilton: 'All things come of thee and of thine own have we given thee'. The cost was £20,000.

The style adopted was Italian Romanesque or Lombardic. This choice was undoubtedly Sidney Herbert's. He was one of a group, which included Samuel Rogers, John Ruskin, and the twenty-fifth Earl of Crawford and Balcarres, all of whom greatly admired the earlier periods of Italian art. In 1848 they founded the Arundel Society to diffuse knowledge of the early Italian Schools in the hope that 'greater familiarity with the severe and the purer styles of earlier art would divert the public taste from works that were meretricious or puerile and elevate the tone of the national school'.[35] The use of the Lombard style on a large scale at Wilton had the same aim. The exterior, particularly the west front, was based on the Churches of S. Maria and S. Pietro at Toscanello. With typical Victorian confidence Wilton was considered to be an improvement on its eleventh- and twelfth-century predecessors 'in consequence of the greater indentation of the canopied porch and the elaborate details surrounding it'. The interior was inspired by the early basilicas in Rome, particularly S. Clemente. The basilican plan was well suited to advanced Anglican worship. The splendour of the proportions is supplemented by specially acquired works of art which make the church a museum. The old stained glass includes some of the finest in England. The pulpit incorporates cosmati work from a thirteenth-century shrine in St. Mary Major's, Rome, bought at the Strawberry Hill sale in 1842. Some of the marble columns were brought from the Temple of Venus at Portovenere in the Gulf of Spezzia.[36]

The church was consecrated by Bishop Denison of Salisbury on 9 October 1845. It is unlikely that he wholly approved of such High-Church magnificence, for he had already forbidden the erection of an altar in the church as contrary to rubrics.

Wilton Parish Church was the first sign of the dramatic revival in English church-building which began in the 1840s. Though at first a variety of styles were adopted, including Lombardic, Greek, and Norman, gradually Gothic became the only acceptable church style. The Camden Society, for instance, criticized Wilton Church for being un-English. The upsurge in church-building was a sign of the revival of the Church of England and coincided with the revolution in its doctrine and liturgy associated with the Tractarian Movement. By 1850 the Gothic revival in its most serious form was well under way. It was a distinctively English architectural phenomenon and between 1850 and 1870 the new churches built in England were of consistently high quality and originality. Thomas Henry Wyatt was not among the greatest of the

[35] Quoted in John Steegman, *Victorian Taste* (1970), 73.
[36] Rev. Canon Olivier, *Wilton Church* (1881). The copy in the Wilton Muniment Room has a pencil note next to the list of sources saying 'This from Mr. Wyatt'.

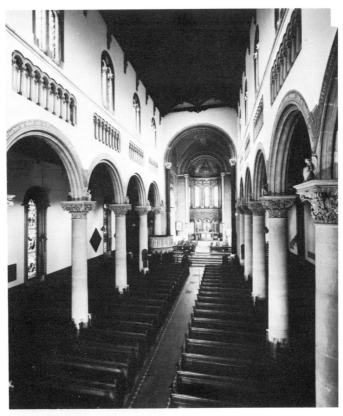

134. Wilton, Church of S.S. Mary and Nicholas, the interior.

135. Savernake, Church of St. Katherine. Design by Thomas Henry Wyatt, 1860.

136. Bemerton, Church of St. John.
Designed by Thomas Henry Wyatt,
1866.

137. Fonthill Gifford, Church of
Holy Trinity. Designed by Thomas
Henry Wyatt, 1866.

Gothic revival architects, but he cannot be overlooked because of the sheer number of churches with which he was involved. As Eastlake observed, his work is interesting because he lived through all the phases of the Victorian Gothic revival and kept to the middle of the road all the way. His churches are a microcosm of English church-building between 1830 and 1880. From the Regency Gothic of St. Paul's, Newport, through the 'simple but picturesque' Welsh churches of his middle period to the series of great Wiltshire estate churches of the 1860s and 1870s – Savernake, Hindon, Fonthill Gifford, Semley, and Bemerton.

Eastlake rightly praised Savernake for the 'ingenious and effective treatment of the interior'. At Hindon he admired the square spire for its originality. At Bemerton he thought the tall square tower with a conical stair turret 'particularly successful' in its proportions and fenestration. But the best of them is Fonthill Gifford. The stone vaulted chancel is impressive and the build-up of the east end from the polygonal apse through the stair turret to the asymmetrical spire is spectacular.[37]

These churches are his most interesting buildings but he was also a prolific designer of houses and public buildings. The latter have been unfortunate. The best three have been demolished: the Assize Courts in Cambridge, the New Exchange in Liverpool, and the Knightsbridge Barracks. All three were in the rich mixed classical style which, with a few well-known exceptions, was the preferred style for mid-Victorian public buildings. The Liverpool Exchange was the finest and was generally considered to be his secular masterpiece. The Knightsbridge Barracks were less interesting, but some people think they were preferable to their successor.

The confidence expressed in such buildings is summed up in the description of the Cambridge Assize Courts in the *Illustrated London News*. 'The style selected is Palladian and the façade somewhat novel and decidedly effective. It reminds the spectator of Palladio's Loggia at the Basilica, Vicenza. It is not, however, a servile imitation of its Italian predecessor; there are many variations and these certainly are in favour of the English Building. The sameness and poverty of the original are avoided by compressing the details, a richness being thus gained which tells favourably for the general effect.'[38]

The style of his town houses varied from Italianate in Kensington Palace Gardens to Frenchy *nouveau riche* in the Park Lane mansion of Sir Dudley Coutts Marjoribanks (a name strongly redolent of money). Some of the country houses were Gothic but most adhered to 'the late Tudor type of architecture'. This was the favourite style of Victorian landowners. Generally speaking in the 1850s and 1860s Italianate or French was preferred for town houses and

---

[37] *Eastlake's Gothic Revival*, 301.
[38] *ILN*, 1 Apr. 1843.

Tudor or Jacobean for country houses.

Thomas Henry's country houses are of little interest to any but the social historian. The style is seen at its limited best at Orchardleigh Park (Somerset) and at its worst in The Hendre (Monmouthshire). Mark Girouard has dismissed the lot as looking as if they were designed when the architect was thinking of something else. Probably neither client nor architect would have made great architectural claims for them. They were meant to be convenient houses and no more. The aesthetic interests of the hard core of Victorian landowners, unlike their eighteenth-century predecessors and some of their twentieth-century descendants, were limited. They considered too refined a sensibility for art and architecture to be 'bad form', if not positively unmanly.

It is all summed up in a contemporary description of Orchardleigh:

The architect of the present Orchardleigh House was Mr. Thomas H. Wyatt of 77 Great Russell Street, London; and in designing the building he endeavoured to graft some of the picturesque outlines of the French Château upon the general form and details of an 'Old English' house, giving a more varied 'sky-line' than the latter usually had. The design of the proprietor and the object of the designer was to make a cheerful and purely comfortable residence, rather than a highly ornamental and pretentious building ... The mansion took rather more than two years to build, and all the materials employed were fire-proof (on Messrs. Fox and Barrett's system); wrought iron girders and joints and concrete instead of the usual timber construction; a precedent which it would be wise to follow in such works, and which cannot be too widely praised.[39]

A description of Thomas Henry Wyatt's presidential address at the Royal Institute of British Architects in 1871 can be applied equally to the man and his architecture: 'absolutely devoid of all affectation and all pretentiousness – without a word that glittered – full of simple sound sagacity and everyday information – rhetoric, except an occasional very dry and harmless gest for the sake of a moment's relief, quite forsaken for the plain language of business'.[40]

In his later years, as his health declined, he was helped by his eldest son, Matthew Wyatt III. Before entering his father's office Matthew III had studied architecture at Paris in the atelier of Monsieur André, a member of the Institut de France. Among other things, Matthew III helped his father with the church at Weston Patrick, the restoration of the great Hall at Winchester Castle, and with several hospitals. After Thomas Henry's death in 1880 Matthew III carried on the practice with Walter L. Spiers who had long worked in Thomas Henry's office. He succeeded his father as Architect to the Middlesex Hospital but was dismissed four years later for 'something which happened on the previous Tuesday'.[41]

---

[39] *Cuzner's Handbook of Froome Selwood* (Froome, c. 1865). I am grateful to Mr. Robert Adams for drawing my attention to this description.
[40] *The Architect* (12 Nov. 1870), 267.
[41] Middlesex Hospital Mins. 1880–85.

138. Liverpool Exchange. Design by
Thomas Henry Wyatt, 1863.
Demolished.

139. Orchardleigh Park, Somerset.
Designed by Thomas Henry Wyatt,
1855–8.

In 1884 he restored St. Bueno's Church in Flintshire after which 'it was difficult even for regular members of the congregation to conceive that the old building with its box pews in which they had worshipped was capable of being so thoroughly transformed'.[42] A house designed by Messrs. Wyatt and Spiers was illustrated in *The Builder* on 16 October 1886. It is the Corner House at Weston Patrick where his granddaughter, Mrs. Janet Don, lived until 1976. It is an example of the newly fashionable Queen Anne style. But there was to be no Wyatt representative of the last great phase of Victorian architecture, the Domestic revival. Matthew III retired from practice five years after his father's death and drank himself to death in his early fifties.

He left all his possessions to his son, Matthew Montagu Wyatt, in a will with such peculiar provisions as to suggest that he was more than slightly deranged. He expressed the wish that his son should be educated at Winchester but Westminster or Charterhouse would do as second best. He was to be given such allowance until he 'shall attain 25 as shall enable him to receive a liberal education and thereafter to ride to hounds and take part in such manly sports (not being horse racing) as shall be consistent with his position'.

He left his house to his wife Augusta for life on the condition that she would not entertain his brother Thomas Henry II or her own brother George Hodge for more than 'three consecutive days or more than six days in any one calendar month'. Matthew Montagu went to Charterhouse, never rode to hounds, and George Hodge stayed at Weston Patrick for months on end.

The cause of the quarrel between Matthew III and Thomas Henry II is not known but Matthew III was 'difficult'. His drinking cut him off from his family and contemporaries. In his will he left nothing to his nephews and nieces because, 'considering the intense avarice of the father,' he thought they would be taken care of independently. He added that it was 'the wicked falsehoods' of their mother that had so 'completely estranged' him from them.[43]

The curtain falls sadly on a cantankerous middle-aged man, prematurely retired, drinking heavily in a Hampshire village. With the death of Matthew III in 1892 the long line of eighteenth- and nineteenth-century Wyatt architects finally comes to an end.

---

[42] Quoted in Brett and E. Beazley, *North Wales, A Shell Guide* (1971), 133.
[43] Somerset House, Matthew Wyatt III's Will, 1892.

140. Florence Railway Station. Designed by Thomas Henry Wyatt, 1847. Water-colour by Sir (Matthew) Digby Wyatt. Demolished.

Conclusion

The Significance of the Wyatts

Much of the importance of the Wyatts is due to their cumulative effect as a dynasty. Though they produced individually great architects it is their total contribution to English architecture, sculpture, and the decorative arts over a long period which makes them so interesting. Much of this interest is due to their being both typical of their times and influential in directing the trend of those times.

The emergence of the Wyatts in the eighteenth century is bound up with the progress of the agricultural and industrial revolutions. At first they were closely involved in the development of the Midlands. The new canals were crucial to the expansion of their building business, enabling them to import necessary materials and to sell timber from the hitherto unexploited Stafford-shire woodlands to other parts of the country when there was a shortage of foreign timber.

Some members of the family were employed as surveyors of the new canals and roads and also to draw up enclosure maps. Others were agents on great estates. Obviously the ability to measure and draw which was necessary for such surveying was an excellent introduction to architecture, the practice of which employed almost identical skills. It is hardly surprising, therefore, that a generation of Wyatt land-surveyors should have been followed by a genera-tion of Wyatt architects.

Many Wyatts were inventors in their own right. After James Watt, John Wyatt II was the most prolific inventor of the period. Several other Wyatts took out patents for new materials and techniques.

They were on intimate terms with some of the leading figures of the Industrial Revolution. Probably through William Wyatt I who was land-agent to Mary Robinson, the rich first wife of Matthew Boulton, the Wyatts came to know Boulton well. Boulton often stayed with them at Burton, Weeford, and in London. They were closely involved in the development of his Soho property. John Wyatt II, 'the Inventor', and two of his sons, John III and Charles I, were employed by Boulton. The New Factory and house there were designed by William Wyatt II, built by Benjamin Wyatt & Sons, and later altered by both James and Samuel Wyatt.

William Wyatt II was the first man in England to manufacture screws by machine in a factory. John III founded and published the *Repertory of Arts* which contained descriptions of recent inventions and industrial processes. Samuel Wyatt, in association with Boulton and Watt, built the first steam-powered flour mill in England, the unfortunately short-lived Albion Mill at Blackfriars.

Just as Joseph Wright of Derby exploited the artistic potential of the Industrial Revolution, so the buildings of James and Samuel Wyatt, with their wide use of newly patented materials, are its highest architectural expression. The combination of a refined neo-classical style and novel constructional techniques and materials makes their buildings the exact architectural equivalent of Wedgwood's pottery and Boulton's metalware.

From James Wyatt's success at the Pantheon in 1772 to Thomas Henry Wyatt I's death in 1880 it is possible to write a comprehensive history of English architecture drawing only on Wyatt examples, for the Wyatts were equally prominent in the parallel fields of neo-classicism and the Gothic revival. Neo-classicism can be traced from James's and Samuel's brilliant adaptation of the Adam style, the lavish Greco-Roman of the Regency period, particularly the work of Benjamin Dean, Lewis, and Jeffry Wyatville, through the South Kensington Italianate of Sir Matthew Digby Wyatt, to the Queen Anne revival of the 1870s.

Likewise the history of the Gothic revival can be followed from James Wyatt's early rococo work through his use of increasingly asymmetrical composition and archaeologically correct detail to Jeffry Wyatville's heavy-handed seriousness at Windsor and the heyday of the Victorian Gothic movement in Thomas Henry's innumerable churches with their yards of pitch-pine woodwork and encaustic tiling.

Passing fashions are also represented, such as Etruscan in James Wyatt's interiors, Benjamin Dean's London works in the Louis-Quatorze style of the 1820s and 1830s, and the Lombardic of the 1840s in Thomas Henry's Wilton Church.

The story of the Wyatt family is not, however, purely an architectural matter. Their lives reflect the wider perspectives of national history in the period of Britain's greatest affluence and power – the crystallization of the Indian Empire in the late eighteenth century, the military and naval victories over Napoleonic France in the early nineteenth century, and the dramatic religious revival of the mid-nineteenth century, were all given concrete form by their buildings.

The great flowering of the arts in England in the years after Waterloo, a time when the Wyatts were playing their most prominent role as architects, painters, and sculptors, was financed by the expansion of agriculture, industry, trade, and banking which was taking place contemporaneously.

Lastly, the vast prosperity and self-confidence of Victorian England, exemplified in the Great Exhibition of 1851, are mirrored in the careers and buildings of Sir (Matthew) Digby Wyatt and Thomas Henry Wyatt. After their deaths the architectural genius finally dried up, though the Wyatts have continued to produce talented individuals down to the present, including such diverse characters as R. G. S. Wyatt, the great cricketer, and Woodrow Wyatt, the writer and former Labour M.P. They, however, are another story!

CATALOGUE OF WORKS

1 Benjamin Dean Wyatt

2 Henry Wyatt

3 James Wyatt

4 Lewis William Wyatt

5 Matthew Cotes Wyatt

6 Sir (Matthew) Digby Wyatt

7 Philip William Wyatt

8 Richard James Wyatt

9 Samuel Wyatt

10 Thomas Henry Wyatt I

11 Sir Jeffry Wyatville

The arrangement is as follows:

Place (followed by (*A*) if altered or (*D*) if destroyed and the style if relevant), work, **patron, date, source in square brackets.** Patrons are referred to by the title they held at the time of their death. Where a building is followed by *Attributed* it means that documentary evidence or a reliable contemporary source is not known but that a combination of stylistic and circumstantial evidence makes it reasonable to ascribe the building to a particular Wyatt. A catalogue entry in parentheses means that the attribution is doubtful. Because of lack of space it has not been possible to give a detailed description of each item in the Catalogue, but for the more important Wyatts this information can be found in:

Frances Fergusson, 'James Wyatt' (unpub. Ph.D. thesis, Harvard, 1972).

John Martin Robinson, 'Samuel Wyatt' (unpub. D.Phil. thesis, Oxford, 1973).

Derek Linstrum, *Sir Jeffry Wyatville* (Oxford, 1972).

Counties are given as before local government reorganization in 1972 as it is thought that this will be more convenient for the users of the standard architectural histories.

1 Benjamin Dean Wyatt

(1775–1850)

Ashridge, Herts. Completed staircase, etc. for seventh Earl of Bridgewater, 1813–14. [RIBAD; Metropolitan]

Belvoir Castle, Leics. Picture Gallery and State Dining-Room (neo-classical) and Mausoleum (Norman) with Philip and M.C.Wyatt for fifth Duke of Rutland, *c*.1816–30. [Belvoir MSS., Correspondence; I.Eller, *Belvoir Castle* (1841), 349–53]

Charlecote, War. Unexecuted design for remodelling the house for George Hammond Lucy, 1825. Rejected on grounds of expense. [Drawings at the House]

Clumber, Notts. (*D*). Alterations for fourth Duke of Newcastle, *c*.1814. [RIBAD]

Devizes, Wilts., Market Cross. For first Viscount Sidmouth, 1814. Gothic, possibly based on a design by James Wyatt. [J.Waylen, *Chronicles of Devizes* (1839), 316]

Elvaston Hall, Derby. Unexecuted design for Earl of Harrington, 1812. [Exhib. RA 1812]

London, Apsley House, Piccadilly. Dining-Room, 1819; neo-classical. Remodelling and addition of portico and Waterloo Gallery, 1828–30. Louis-Quatorze interior. [Stratfield Saye MSS., Correspondence]

London, 6 Carlton House Terrace. (*A*). For Marquess of Tavistock, 1831. Louis-Quatorze interior. [APSD]

London, Crockford's Club, St. James's Street. (*A*) (now Jamaican High Commission). With Philip Wyatt, 1827. Louis-Quatorze interior. [J.Elmes, *Metropolitan Improvements* (1831), 140–1]

London, Drury Lane, Theatre Royal. 1811–12. Neo-classical. [RIBAD; B.D.Wyatt, *Observations on the Design of the Theatre Royal, Drury Lane* (1813)]

London, Duke of York's Column, Waterloo Place. Granite Tuscan column 123′ 6″ high. Cost £25,000. 1831–4. [Stratfield Saye MSS., Correspondence; *Architectural Mag.* (1834), 192–201; Royal Library Windsor, 1892–6, Unexecuted design of 1827 in form of a Corinthian Temple using columns from Carlton House]

London, Londonderry House, Park Lane. (*D*). Remodelled for third Marquess of Londonderry with Philip Wyatt, 1825–8. Louis-Quatorze interiors. [Durham R.O., Londonderry MSS., Accounts]

London, Oriental Club, 18 Hanover Square. (*D*). With Philip Wyatt, 1827–8. Neo-classical. [John Weale, *New Survey of London*, i (1853), 304–5]

London, Spring Gardens. (*D*). Proposed alterations to house for Lord Dover, 1831. [PRO, MPE 839; ex info Mr. H.M.Colvin]

London, Westminster Abbey. Continued restoration of Henry VII Chapel, 1813–22. Restoration of rose window of S. transept, 1814. Rearrangement of choir and new High Altar, 1822–3. [Abbey MSS., Building Accounts]

London, Westminster School. Rebuilt exterior of the Old School in stock brick, 1814. [L.E.Tanner, *Westminster School, Its Buildings & Associations* (1923), 35]

London, York House, St. James's (afterwards Stafford, now Lancaster House). With Philip Wyatt for Duke of York, 1827–37. [Royal Library Windsor, Drawings] For first and second Dukes of Sutherland, 1827–33. Louis-Quatorze interior. [Staffs. R.O., Trentham MSS.]

Maresfield Park, Sussex. Remodelling, including new library, for Sir John Shelley, 1816. Jacobean. [Frank Sabin Gallery 1976, Signed Drawing; R. Edgcumbe (ed.), *Diary of Frances, Lady Shelly*, ii (1913), 67]

Stratfield Saye, Hants. Alterations, including porch and conservatory, for first Duke of Wellington, 1838–40. [Stratfield Saye MSS., Correspondence]

Waterloo Palace. Unexecuted designs for first Duke of Wellington, 1814–18. [RIBAD]

Westport, Co. Mayo, Ireland. Unexecuted design for a theatre, 1812. [Westport House, Drawings]

Westport House, Co. Mayo, Ireland. Unexecuted design for a new house. Library wing, 1819 (*D*). For second Marquess of Sligo. [Westport House, Drawings]

2 Henry Wyatt

(1794–1840)

Portraits

(Unless otherwise stated pictures are in oil)

1817	*C.Wyatt.* Probably Charles Wyatt the cement manufacturer. [Exhib. RA 1817]
1819	*A Portrait.* [Exhib. RA 1819] *Portrait of a Gentleman.* [Exhib. RA 1819]
c.1820	*Sir Jeffry Wyatville and Family.* [Coll. Revd. G.Newenham, Buxton]
1820	*Thomas Harrison.* [Chester Castle]
1822	*Portrait of an Artist.* [Exhib. Liverpool Academy 1822] *Mrs. Abram.* [Exhib. Liverpool Academy 1822] *Revd. Thomas Raffles.* [Exhib. Liverpool Academy 1822]
c.1822	*Thoas Harrison with Propylaeum of Chester Castle.* Engraved by M.Gauci.
1823	*Humphrey Chetham.* Engraved by C.Pye. *William Lockett.* Pencil. [Thomas Agnew & Son Ltd., *Agnews 1816–1967* (1967), 7] *Richard Bannister, Lord Baltimore, George Rigbie.*
1824	*Col. Dukinfield, Capt. Kay.* [Pencil drawing for engraving in John Ford, *Portraits and Views* (Manchester, 1823–4)] *T.Molineux.* Engraved by R.Roffe. *Vittore Zanetti.* Pencil. [Thomas Agnew & Son Ltd., *Agnews 1816–1967* (1967), 2] *Self-Portrait.* Sold at Dorotheum, Vienna, 1948. [photo Courtauld]

1826   Six Children round a Piano. [Photo Courtauld]
          John Hatchard. [Exhib. RA 1826]
          Miss Lavinia Betts. [Exhib. RA 1826]
          Revd. Josiah Pratt. [Exhib. RA 1826]

1827   Hyla Betts. [Exhib. RA 1827]
          Mrs. Macdougal. [Exhib. RA 1827]

1828   William Magee, Archbishop of Dublin. [Exhib. RA 1828]
          John Thornton. [Exhib. RA 1828]
          Don Manuel de la Torre. [Exhib. RA 1828]
          Dr. Edward Jenner. [Wellcome Foundation, London; photo Courtauld]
          Unidentified Man. [Cheltenham Art Gallery]
          Unidentified Woman. [Cheltenham Art Galley]

1829   Lieutenant Birdwood, Madras Engineers. [Exhib. RA 1829]
          Mrs. Carlisle. [Exhib. RA 1829]
          Group of Ladies. [Exhib. RA 1829]

1830   John Tilleard. [Exhib. RA 1830]
          Edward Eyre. [Exhib. RA 1830]
          Mrs. G. Hunt and Child. [Exhib. RA 1830]

1831   Sir George Farrant. [Exhib. RA 1831]

1832   Abraham Wildey Roberts (?), M.P. for Maidstone. [Author's Coll., London]

1834   Sir George Farrant. [Exhib. RA 1834]
          Children of J.Farquhar Fraser. [Exhib. RA 1834; photo Courtauld]

1836   Mrs. W. Lee. [Exhib. RA 1836]
          Sir Mark Isambard Brunel. [Exhib. RA 1836]
          R. Brunel. [Exhib. RA 1836]

1838   Revd. Thomas Thistlethwaite. [Published in Thomas Agnew, *Repository of Arts* (Manchester, 1838)]
          Five Girls of the Ward Hunt Family. [photo Courtauld]

1839   Revd. W.Field.[Exhib. RA 1839]

Undated Portraits

Mrs. Carpenter. Oval. [Sir Charles Holmes, 'The Heirs of Lawrence 1825–35', *Burlington Mag.* lxix (Nov. 1936); photo Caurtauld] private coll., U.S.A.

De M.Chesney. [Coll. Professor J.Bronner, Bournemouth]

Sir C. Cunningham. [National Maritime Museum; photo Courtauld]

Sir Thomas Fellowes. [National Maritime Museum]

Mrs. Greatorex. [Sir Charles Holmes, 'The Heirs of Lawrence 1825–35', *Burlington Mag.* lxix (Nov. 1936); photo Courtauld]

Miss O'Neill. [Private coll., U.S.A.; photo Courtauld]

Alfred, Lord Tennyson. [Photo NPG]

Duke of York. [Apsley House]

Portrait of a Gentleman. [North Carolina Museum of Art; photo Courtauld]

Portrait of a Lady. [Sir Charles Holmes, 'The Heirs of Lawrence 1825–35', *Burlington Mag.* lxix (Nov. 1936); formerly Joel Coll., Maiden Erlegh]

Portrait of a Lady in Black Veil. [Sir Charles Holmes, 'The Heirs of Lawrence 1925–35', *Burlington Mag.* lxix (Nov. 1936); Axelsson Johnson Coll., Stockholm; photo Courtauld]

Lady in a Red Dress. [Photo NPG]

Three Portraits of Unidentified Ladies. [Ehrlich Gallery, New York, 1933; photos Courtauld]

Portrait of a Girl. Sold Christie's 18 Feb. 1972, Lot 212.

Fancy Pictures

1822   *An Old Fruit Woman*. [Exhib. Liverpool Academy 1822, British Institution 1826]

1826   *Head of Gamalial*. [Exhib. RA 1826; the 'head of an old jew' exhibited at the British Institution in 1826 is probably the same]
Mars and Venus. [Exhib. British Institution 1827] Bought by Birmingham Institution for Promotion of Fine Arts. [Now in the Modern Art Section of Pitti Palace, Florence]

1827   *Devotion*. [Exhib. Brit. Inst. 1827]
St. John. [Exhib. Brit. Inst. 1827]
Lilias. [Exhib. Brit. Inst. 1827]
Prometheus. [Exhib. Brit. Inst. 1827]
Recumbent Nymph. [Exhib. Brit. Inst. 1827]

1828   *A Study in Van Dyke Dress*. [Exhib. Brit. Inst. 1828]

1829   *A Magdalen*. [Exhib. Brit. Inst. 1829]

1830   *The Favourite*. [Exhib. Brit. Inst. 1830]

1832   *Archimedes*. [Exhib. RA 1832] Bought by Sir Matthew White Ridley, Bt.
Juliet. [Exhib. RA 1832] Bought by Birmingham Society of Arts. [Now in City Art Gallery]
Girl with Spaniel. [Exhib. Brit. Inst. 1843] Bought by William Wells. [Photo Courtauld]
Lady with Fan. [Exhib. Brit. Inst. 1843] Bought by William Wells.

1833   *Curiosity*. [Exhib. RA 1832, Brit. Inst. 1833]
The Solicitor. [Exhib. Brit. Inst. 1833]
Bacchante and Child. [Exhib. RA 1833]
The Corsair. [Exhib. Brit. Inst. 1833, Royal Manchester Inst. 1834, V & A

Byron Exhibition 1974; private coll., London]

1834   *Le Chapeau Noir*. [Exhib. Brit. Inst. 1834] Bought by William Wells. [Photo Courtauld] Engraved by W. H. Simmons.
The Love Lock. [Exhib. Brit. Inst. 1834, Royal Manchester Inst. 1834]
Gentle Reader. [Exhib. RA 1834, Royal Manchester Inst. 1834, Brit. Inst. 1835] Engraved by T. A. Dean
Ranglers. [Exhib. Brit. Inst. 1834]
The Reverie. [Exhib. Brit. Inst. 1834, Royal Manchester Institution 1834]

1835   *Come away to the Masquerade*. [Exhib. Brit. Inst. 1835, Royal Manchester Inst. 1838]
A Magdalen. [Exhib. Brit. Inst. 1835; presumably different from that exhibited in 1829]
The Falconer. [Exhib. Brit. Inst. 1835; illus. in *Burlington Mag.* xi (June 1907), 170]
Vigilance. [Exhib. RA 1835] Bought by Robert Vernon. [Now in Tate Gallery]
Meditation. [Exhib. RA 1835, Brit. Inst. 1836, Royal Manchester Institution 1838] There were two versions of this picture of differing sizes, 1'2" × 2' and 5' 8" × 4' 10".

1836   *The Palmister*. [Exhib. RA 1836, Royal Manchester Inst. 1836]
'Shall I'. [Exhib. Brit. Inst. 1836, Royal Manchester Inst. 1836]
Agnes Ellen. Pencil. Engraved by H. Robinson.

1838   *Nymphs Bathing*. [Exhib. Royal Manchester Inst. 1838] Bought by H. A. J. Monro.
The Coquette. [Exhib. Royal Mancester Inst. 1838]

Undated Fancy Pictures

The Fair Sleeper. [S.Redgrave, *Dict. of Artists* (1874), 468–9] Engraved by G.A.Periam.

The Philosopher. Bought by Robert Vernon. Destroyed in Tate Flood 1928. [*Gent's Mag.* (1840), 556]

The Astronomer. [S.Redgrave, *Dict. of Artists* (1874), 428–9] Engraved by R.Bell.

The Proferred Kiss. Engraved by G.J.Doo. Bought by G.J.Doo. [*Gent's Mag.* (1840), 556]

The Romance. Bought by Sir Jeffry Wyatville. [*Gent's Mag.* (1840), 556]

Clara Mowbray. Bought by Sir D.Mackworth, Bt. [*Gent's Mag.* (1840), 556]

The Fair Forester. Engraved by G.J.Doo. Bought by Farquhar Fraser. [*Gent's Mag.* (1840), 556]

Naughty Pet. [Birmingham City Art Gallery]

The Ornithologist. Bought by Joseph Walker. [*Gent's Mag.* (1840), 556]

The Gipsy. Bought by John Jease. [*Gent's Mag.* (1840), 556]

The Dark-Eyed Brunette. Bought by Sir Philip Sidney, Bt. [*Gent's Mag.* (1840), 556]

Diligence. Bought by Robert Vernon [*Gent's Mag.* (1840), 566]

Landscapes

1822   *Birkenhead Priory, Cheshire.* [Exhib. Liverpool Academy 1822]
            'Landscape'. [Exhib. Liverpool Academy 1822]

1823   *Radcliffe Hall and Tower.* [Pencil drawing for engraving in John Ford,

Portraits, Old Halls, Antiquities etc. Illustrative of Lancs & Cheshire (Manchester, 1824)]

1836   *Warwick Castle.* [Exhib. Brit. Inst. 1836] Bought by C.Roberts.

1837   *Whitnash Smithy, Leamington.* [Exhib. Brit. Inst. 1837]

1838   *Kenilworth Castle.* [Exhib. Royal Manchester Inst. 1838]
            Hampstead Heath. [Exhib. Royal Manchester Inst. 1838]

Undated   *Sandown Bay, Isle of Wight.* Water-Colour. [V & A, Print Room, W.D. 59]

Sketches

Henry Wyatt's sketches, mainly pencil studies but some ink and wash, were sold at Christie's on 22 November 1977 and were bought by Adrew Wyld. They comprise 252 drawings chiefly measuring $8'' \times 4''$ from his dismembered sketchbooks. Some are dated and signed with his initials and some are on watermarked paper. They cover the period from 1811 to 1833, but the majority are of between 1813 and 1820. They include two designs for decorating bellows with cherubs and leaves, five studies of cherubs with nautical instruments after Richard Westmacott's monument to Lord Collingwood (1813–17) in St. Paul's Cathedral, and a landscape with four children inscribed 'H.W. N.1814 after Gainsborough'. There are 76 landscapes, mainly views in Staffordshire, Derbyshire, Kent, Devon, Dorset, Monmouthshire, and Warwickshire; 18 portrait studies of men; 42 portrait studies of women, many of them seated reading; as well as studies of wild flowers, wildlife, shipping, and objects.

3 James Wyatt

(1746–1813)

Abbeyleix, Co. Leix, Ireland. (*A*). For second Lord Knapton, 1773–6. [Drawings in Metropolitan Museum and National Library of Ireland, LR 72884]

Acton Park, Denbighshire. Alterations for Sir Foster Cunliffe, 1786–7. [Neale, 2nd Ser. v (1829); Fanny Burney, *Memoirs of Dr. Burney*, iii (1832), 247]

Aldwark Hall, W.R. Yorks. (*D*). For Francis Foljambe, 1773–5. [Drawings in Metropolitan Museum and the Pierpont Morgan Library]

Allestree Hall, Derby. For Bache Thornhill, 1795. [Derbyshire County Museum, Drawings; ex info Mr. H.M.Colvin]

Almwch, Anglesey, Church. Designed *c.* 1790. Executed 1800. [Ex info Mr. H.M.Colvin]

Alton Towers, Staffs. (*Attributed*). Began remodelling for fifteenth Earl of Shrewsbury, 1811–13. Gothic. [Staffs. R.O., Building Accounts, no architect is mentioned until 1817, though work began in 1811]

Ammerdown House, Somerset. For T.S.Joliffe, 1788. [Accounts at the house]

Ardbraccan House, Co. Meath, Ireland. Unexecuted design for central block for Bishop of Meath, 1776. [J.N.Brewer, *Beauties of Ireland*, ii (1826), 189]

Ashridge, Herts. For seventh Earl of Bridgewater, 1808–13. Gothic. [RIBAD]

Aston Hall, Salop. For Revd. J.R.Lloyd, 1789–93. [Drawings sold 1969, photos in *NMR*]

Badby, Northants, School. For the Dowager Lady Knightley, *c.* 1812. Gothic. [G.Baker, *History of Northants*, i (1822), 257]

Badger Hall, Salop. (*D* but the Pigeon House survives). Remodelled for Isaac Hawkins Browne, 1779–83. [RIBAD]

Beaudesert, Staffs. (*D*). Interior remodelled for first Earl of Uxbridge. Executed by Ben. Wyatt & Sons, 1771–2. Great Hall Gothic. [S.L., 1.54, Drawing; Staffs. R.O., D603F, 148, 1642, Accounts; Harewood, Joseph Rose Sketch-book]

Belmont House, Clehonger, Herefordshire. (*A*). For John Matthews, 1788–90. [John Britton (ed.), *Beauties of England & Wales*, vi (1805), 586]

Belton House, Lincs. Alterations, including drawing-room and boudoir, for first Lord Brownlow, 1776–8. [Drawings at the house]

Belvoir Castle, Leics. For fifth Duke of Rutland, 1801–13. Castellated Gothic. NE and NW sides remodelled by Revd. Sir John Thoroton after fire, 1816. Wyatt's SE and SW fronts survive. [Drawings at castle; I.Eller, *Belvoir* (1841)]

Bicton Lodge, Devon. Completed for first Lord Rolle, *c.* 1800. [*The Copper-Plate Mag.* v, Pl. ccx (1800); ex info Mr.H.M.Colvin]

Bidborough, Kent, Rectory (now called 'Wyatts'). *c.* 1790. [E.Hasted, *History of Kent* (2nd edn., 1797–1801), v, 275 says 'after a design of Mr. Wyatt's']

Birmingham, Hen & Chickens Hotel, New Street. 1798 (*D*). [*Aris's Birmingham Gazette*, 26 Mar. 1798]

Bishop Auckland Castle, Co. Durham. Remodelled for Bishop Shute Barrington, 1794–6. Gothic. [Drawings at the castle]

Bishop Auckland, Co. Durham, St. Anne's Chapel. Designed 1797. Erected by W. Atkinson, 1800. [Drawing at Newcastle Univ. Library]

Blagdon, Northumb. Lodges, stables, and interior decoration for Sir Matthew White Ridley, 1778–91. [Drawings at the House]

Bowden House, Wilts. For B.Dickinson, 1796. [G.Richardson, *New Vitruvius Britannicus*, i (1802), 1–2; Exhib. RA 1796]

Bristol, Tyndall's Park Crescent. Designed and begun 1793, never completed. [W.Ison, *Georgian Buildings of Bristol* (1952), 26–7]

Broadway Tower, Worcs. For sixth Earl of Coventry, 1794. 'Saxon'. [Croome Estate Office, Drawings]

Brocklesby Park, Lincs. Mausoleum for first Lord Yarborough, 1787–94. [Building Accounts at the house; Exhib. RA 1795] The kennels and Holgate Monument are also attributed to James Wyatt.

Broke Hall, Nacton, Suffolk. For Philip Broke, *c.* 1795. Castellated. [E. Suffolk R.O., HA93/722/159 and 240, Drawings]

Broome Park, Kent. (*A*). Saloon for Sir Henry Oxenden, 1778. [W. Angus, *Seats* (1789), xviii]

Bryanston House, Dorset. (*D* but Gate-Lodge and offices survive). For H.W.B.Portman, 1778. [W.Watts, *Seats* (1786), Pl. lxxxiii]

Bulbridge House, Wilts. Remodelled for Lt.-Gen. Philip Goldsworthy, 1794. [Wilton, Drawings]

Bulstrode Park, Bucks. (D). West wing for third Duke of Portland, 1806–9. Gothic. [J.Harris, 'Bulstrode', *AR*, Nov. 1958]

Burton Constable, E.R. Yorks. Drawing-room 1775–6, Lodge 1785–6, for William Constable. [Drawings and Accounts at the house]

Burton-on-Trent, Staffs., St. Modwen's. (A). Organ-case, 1770. [RIBAD]

Burton-on-Trent, Staffs., Town Hall. (D). For first Earl of Uxbridge, 1770–3. Executed by Benj. Wyatt & Sons. [Staffs. R.O., Paget MS. D603/F148, Building Accounts]

Cambridge, Downing College. Unexecuted design, 1804. [RIBAD]

Cambridge, King's College. Unexecuted design for completing court, 1795–6. [Drawings at College; Exhib. RA 1796, 1797]

Canwell Hall, Staffs. (D). Remodelled and extended for Sir Robert Lawley, *c.* 1795. [Nigel Forbes-Adam, Skipwith Hall, Yorkshire, Drawings; S.Shaw, *History of Staffs.* ii (1801), 22]

Carisbrooke Castle, Isle of Wight. Remodelled Governor's Lodgings for General Orde, *c.* 1794. [Coll. Mrs. Gell, William Porden's Journal (MS.), 13 July 1794, 26–8; ex info Mr. Peter Bezodis]

Cassiobury Park, Herts. (D). Gothic extension for fifth Earl of Essex, 1801–3. [RIBAD; Neale, ii (1819); J.Britton, *Cassiobury Park* (1837)]

Castle Coole, Co. Fermanagh, Ireland. For first Earl of Belmore, 1790–7. [Drawings at the house; Metropolitan Museum; Belfast, City Art Gallery; G.Richardson, *New Vitruvius Britannicus*, ii (1808), 65–70]

Chelsea Farm, Middx. (*Later Cremorne House*). For Viscount Cremorne, *c.* 1790. [F.Faulkener, *Chelsea*, i (1829), 65]

Cheltenham, Glos., St. Mary's. Memorial to Katherine A'Court †1776. Executed by R.Westmacott. [C.B.Andrews (ed.), *The Torrington Diaries*, i (1934), 123]

Chetney Hill, Kent, Lazaretto. 1800–6 (D). [*King's Works*, 448–51]

Chevening, Kent. (A). Refronted and third storey added for third Earl Stanhope, 1786–96. [Accounts at the house]

Chicksands Priory, Beds. Alterations for Sir George Osborn, 1813. Gothic. [Neale, 2nd Serv. v (1829)]

Chiswick House, Middx. (Wings D). Interior of wings, built by John White, and bridge in the gardens for fifth Duke of Devonshire, 1788. [Metropolitan Museum, Drawing for a ceiling; Chatsworth, Accounts]

Cobham, Kent. Mausoleum for fourth Earl of Darnley, *c.* 1783–4. Ruined. [Soane Museum, Drawings; Exhib. RA 1783] Executed by George Dance II. [*The World*, 15 July 1788, 30 July 1789; *Morning Chronicle*, 23 Apr. 1783; ex info Mr. J.Greenacombe]

Cobham Hall, Kent. Alterations, including decoration of Gilt Hall, stables, Gothic dairy for fourth Earl of Darnley, 1789–1810. [Drawings formerly at Cambridge Univ. School of Architecture; Kent R.O., Darnley MSS., Accounts]

Copped Hall, Essex. (D). Internal remodelling for John Conyers, 1775–7. [Essex R.O., D/DWE 38 and 39, Drawings; Metropolitan Museum, Drawings]

Corsham, Court, Wilts. Unexecuted designs for alterations for Paul Cobb Methuen, 1796. [Drawings and Correspondence at the house]

Coventry, War., St. Michael's. Repaired steeple, 1794. Work supervised by Joseph Potter. [J.Sharpe, *Illustrations of the History of St. Michael's Church, Coventry* (1818), 48–9]

Cranbourne Lodge, Windsor, Berks. (D). For George III, 1804–8. [*King's Works*, 394–5]

Croome Court, Worcs. Panorama Temple, Gothic ruin, Doric Lodge, etc. for sixth Earl of Coventry, 1794–1801. [Croome Estate Office, Drawings]

Curraghmore, Co. Waterford, Ireland. Interiors, including drawing-room, staircase, and library, for first Marquess of Waterford, *c.* 1778–80. [Metropolitan Museum, Drawings; *C.Life*, 14 and 21 Feb. 1913]

Dartrey, Co. Monaghan. Mausoleum for first Viscount Cremorne, 1770. Ruined. [National Library of Ireland, Unsigned Drawing]

Derby, Ordnance Depot. 1804–5 (D). [R.Simpson, *Collection of Fragments Illustrative of the History of Derby*, i (1826), 530; ex info Mr. H.M.Colvin]

Devizes, Wilts., Market Cross. Unexecuted design, 1803. [Gloucester R.O., D157 E411. Mr. Salmon to T.G.Estcourt, 15 Mar. 1803, saying that James Wyatt had made a sketch of the proposed market cross 'which will be approved by everybody']

Dodington, Glos., St. Mary's. 1799–1805. [Gloucester R.O., Drawings]

Dodington Park, Glos. For Christopher Codrington, 1798–1813. [RIBAD; Gloucester R.O., Drawings; Exhib. RA 1798]

Downhill, Co. Londonderry, Ireland. For Bishop of Derry, *c*. 1776–9. Executed with alterations by Michael Shanahan. [*C.Life*, 8 and 15 July 1971]

Dublin, Leinster House. Decorated picture gallery for second Duke of Leinster. Before 1794. [C.P.Curran, *Dublin Decorative Plasterwork* (1967), 85]

Durham Castle. Attributed. Restored gatehouse for Bishop Shute Barrington, 1791. Gothic.

Durham Cathedral. Restored for Bishop Shute Barrington, 1795–1805. Unexecuted designs for adding a spire and a Gothic organ. [Drawings in Cathedral Library and Manchester Univ. School of Architecture]

East Grinstead, Sussex, St. Swithun's. 1789. Gothic. [W.H.Wills, *History of E. Grinstead* (1906), 66–7]

Elvaston Hall, Derby. For third Earl of Harrington. Designs executed after Wyatt's death by R.Walker, *c*. 1815–19. [Neale, vi (1823)]

Erddig Park, Denbighshire. Alterations for Simon Yorke, 1773–4. [Drawings and Correspondence at the house]

Escot House, Devon. (*D*). Alterations for Sir John Kennaway, *c*. 1795. [J. Britton, *Beauties of England and Wales*, iv (1803), 301]

Exeter, Devon, Sessions House. Revised design for façade by Messrs. Stowey & Jones, 1773. [Devon R.O., A5/166/22; ex info Mr. H.M.Colvin]

Fawley Court, Bucks. Interior decoration and temple for Sambrook Freeman, 1771. [E.J.Climenson (ed.), *Passages from the Diary of Mrs. Lybbe Powis* (1899), 145–8]

Fonthill Abbey, Wilts. (D except fragments). For William Beckford, 1796–1812. [Mellon Coll., Drawings; RIBAD; J.Rutter, *Delineations of Fonthill and its Abbey* (1823); Exhib. RA 1797 and 1799]

Fonthill Splendens, Wilts. (*D*). Chimney-piece in ante-room, ceiling in Egyptian Hall, Fishing Seat by the lake for William Beckford, n.d. [John Britton (ed.), *Beauties of England and Wales*, i (1801), 208–19]

Fornham Hall, Suffolk. (*D*). For Sir Charles Kent, *c*.

1785. [V & A, 92.D.59; Metropolitan Museum, Drawings]

Frogmore House, Berks. For Queen Charlotte, 1792–5. [*King's Works*, 326]

Gaddesden Place, Herts. (*A*). For Thomas Halsey, 1768–74. [Metropolitan Museum, Drawings; J.E.Cursans, *History of Hertfordshire*, iii (1879), 121]

Gidea Hall, Essex. Bridge and Bath House for Richard Benyon. Before 1780. (Bridge survives.) [Harrison & Co., *Picturesque Views of Seats* (1788)]

Goodwood House, Sussex. Enlarged the house, kennels, and Dower House at Molecombe for third Duke of Richmond, 1787. [Metropolitan Museum, Drawings; W.H.Mason, *Goodwood* (1839), 168]

Great Milton House, Oxon. Enlarged for Sir John Skynner, 1788. [Thomas Ellis, *Some Account of Great Milton* (Oxford, 1819), 18]

Great Yarmouth, Norfolk, Naval Arsenal. 1806. [J. Chambers, *Norfolk Tour*, i (1829), 276]

Gresford Lodge, Denbighshire. (*D*). For John Parry, *c*. 1790. [J. Aiken, *Discription of Country Round Manchester* (1795), 401; S.Lewis, *Topographical Dictionary*, ii (1844), 363 attributes the house mistakenly to Wyatville]

Gunton Hall, Norfolk. Additions for first Lord Suffield. Executed by Samuel and William Wyatt, 1775. [Neale, iii (1820)]

Hafod, Cards, Eglwys Newydd. For Thomas Johnes, 1803. Gothic. [S.R.Meyrick, *Hist. & Antiquities of the County of Cardigan* (1810), 347]

Hagley Hall, Staffs. (*D*). Additions, including an octagonal drawing-room, for Assheton Curzon. Executed by Benj. Wyat & Sons, 1771. [Metropolitan Museum, Drawing; Ceiling Exhib. RA 1771]

Hale, Hants, St. Mary's. Monument to Joseph May †1796. [Signed by Wyatt as architect and R.Westmacott as sculptor]

Hams Hall, War. (*D*). Interior for Mr. Adderley, 1770s. [Metropolitan Museum, Drawing for library]

Hanworth, Middx., St. George's. (*D*). Designed 1808. Executed 1815–16 by B.D.Wyatt. [G.L.C. R.O., DRO 18/B3/1, Trustees Mins.]

Hanworth Farm, Middx. (*D*). For himself, *c*. 1790. [Anthony Dale, *James Wyatt* (1956), 216]

Hanworth Park, Middx. (*D*). Stables for the Duke of

St. Albans, 1790s. [Anthony Dale, *James Wyatt* (1956), 216]

Hartham Park, Wilts. For Lady James, 1790–5. [J. Britton, *Beauties of Wiltshire*, iii (1925), 184]

Hartwell House, Bucks. Completed bridge designed by Henry Keene (*D*). Unexecuted design for offices for Sir William Lee, 1780. [Bodl. Top. Gen. b55, Drawing; W. H. Smyth, *Addenda to the Aedes Hastwellianae* (1864), 21]

Havering, Essex, St. John the Evangelist. Monument to Sir John Smith Burges †1803. [E. W. Brayley and J. Britton, *Beauties of England & Wales*, v (1803), 476]

Heaton Hall, Lancs. For first Earl of Wilton, 1772. [Drawings at Heaton on loan from the Earl of Wilton; Metropolitan Museum; National Library of Ireland, Wyatt Album; Exhib. RA 1772]

Henham Hall, Suffolk. (*D*). For first Earl of Stradbroke, 1793–7. [Drawings at Henham; Neale, iii (1820)]

Hereford Cathedral. (*A*). Restoration following collapse of W. tower, 1786–96. [Cathedral library, Chapter Mins; J. Britton, *History of the Cathedral Church of Hereford* (1831)]

Heveningham Hall, Suffolk. Interior, orangery, and lodges for Sir Gerard Vanneck, *c.* 1780–4. [Drawings at the house; Metropolitan Museum, Drawings; F. Shober, *Beauties of England & Wales*, xiv (1813), 360]

Heytesbury House, Wilts. Attributed. Additions for William P. A. A'Court, 1782. [Anthony Dale, *James Wyatt* (1956), 217; James designed the monument to Katherine A'Court in Cheltenham]

Hinton St. George, Somerset. Additions for fourth Earl Poulett, *c.* 1800–5. [Neale, 2nd Series. iv (1828)]

Hothfield Place, Kent. (*D*). For eighth Earl of Thanet, 1776–80. [V & A, Design for ceiling]

Hurstbourne Park, Hants. (*D*). For second Earl of Portsmouth, *c.* 1780–5. Executed by John Meadows. [Harrison & Co., *Views of Seats* (1787)]

Itchenor House, Sussex. Attributed. For third Duke of Richmond, 1787. [James Wyatt also worked at Goodwood for the Duke]

Kelmarsh Hall, Northants. Interior decoration *c.* 1778 and Gate Lodges (executed 1965–6) for William Hanbury. [Metropolitan, Design for ceiling;

Northampton Public Library, Design for lodges]

Kew Palace, Surrey. (*D*). For George III, 1801–11. Castellated Gothic. [V & A, A189, Drawings; *King's Works*, 356–8]

Lasborough Park, Glos. For Edmund Estcourt, 1794 (a small version of Slane). [Drawings at the house]

Lee Priory, Kent. (*D*). For Thomas Barrett, *c.* 1785–90. Gothic. [V & A, 93.D.59, Drawings; Exhib. RA 1785]

Lewisham, Kent. Armoury Mills. (*D*). For the Department of Ordnance, 1806.

[*XVth, Report of the Commissioners of Military Enquiry* (1811), 355].

Leyden, 19 Rapenberg. For Johannes Meerman, 1778. [Metropolitan, Drawing for ceiling]

Lichfield Cathedral, Staffs. Restored, 1787–93. Executed by Joseph Potter. Monument to David Garrick †1779. [S. L., Staffs. Views, 102, 104, 105, Drawings; J. Britton, *History of Cathedral Church of Lichfield* (1820); F. Culvert and W. West, *Picturesque Views of Staffs* (1830), 3]

Little Aston Hall, Staffs. (*D*). Additions for William Tennant, *c.* 1790. [S. Shaw, *History of Staffs*, ii (1801), 52]

Liverpool, Castle Street. (*D*). Elevation of W. side after road-widening, 1786 [J. A. Picton, *Memorials of Liverpool*, ii (1873), 15]

Liverpool Exchange (now Town Hall). Enlarged 1787–92. Restored interior after fire damage, *c.* 1795–1811. Added dome, 1802. Executed by John Foster. [BL, Egerton MS. 3515, Correspondence; J. A. Picton, *Liverpool Municipal Records 1700–1835* (1866), 265–72]

Liverpool, New Exchange. (*D*). With John Foster, 1803–9. Steps of Nelson Statue. [BL, Egerton MS. 3515, Correspondence; J. A. Picton, *Architectural History of Liverpool* (1858), 11]

London, Apsley House. (*A*). Repairs and redecoration costing £20,000 for first Marquess Wellesley, 1807. [Stratfield Saye MSS., Correspondence]

London, Aubrey House, Notting Hill. Drawing-room for Lady Mary Coke, 1774 (*D*). [*Letters & Journals of Lady Mary Coke*, iv (1891), 398, 399, 438, 439, 466]

London, Belgravia. Attributed. Unexecuted plan for layout of Grosvenor Estate. Before 1813. [Grosvenor Office, Plan inscribed 'Mr. Wyatt's plan.]

London, Buckingham House. Principal staircase for George III, *c.* 1800 (*D*). [*King's Works*, 261]

London, Carlton House. (*D*). Repairs and redecoration for Prince of Wales, 1804 and 1805. Library and strong-room, 1812–13. [*King's Works*, 312, 313, 315]

London, 9 Conduit Street. For Robert Vyner, 1779. Executed by Samuel Wyatt. [B. Higgins, *Calcareous Cement* (1780), 214–15]

London, Devonshire House. (*D*). Repairs and redecoration for fifth Duke of Devonshire, 1776, 1783, 1791. (The Crystal Staircase was not by James Wyatt but by Decimus Burton in 1843; ex info Mr. H. M. Colvin.) [Chatsworth MSS., Drawings and Household Accounts]

London, Downshire House, 20 Hanover Square. (*D*). Interior decoration for first Marquess of Downshire, *c.* 1789. [Metropolitan, Drawing for ceiling]

London, 1 Foley Place (formerly 69 Queen Anne St. East). For himself, *c.* 1780–3 (*D*). [A. E. Richardson and C. L. Gill, *London Houses 1660–1720* (1911), Pl. lxxii]

London, 16 Grosvenor Square. (*D*). Alterations for William Drake. Executed by Samuel Wyatt, *c.* 1773–5. New staircase, 1798. [Bucks. R.O., Drake MSS., D/Dr 5/69, 71; 12/61, Accounts]

London, 41 Grosvenor Square (*D*). For Peter Delmé, 1778–9. Executed by Samuel Wyatt. [Metropolitan Museum, Drawings; B. Higgins, *Calcaeous Cement* (1780), 214–15]

London, Hanover Square Concert-Room. (*D*). 1804–5. The ceiling was painted by M. C. Wyatt. [BL, Egerton MSS. 3515, Correspondence]

London, Kentish Town Episcopal Chapel. (*A*). 1784–5. [Hampstead Public Library, Heal Coll. A5, 31, 32 and 37, Drawings]

London, Lincoln's Inn Chapel. Restoration, 1795–6. [*The Black Books of Lincoln's Inn* (1795–6), iv, 53, 55, 56, 58–60, 65]

London, Middlesex Hospital. Minor repairs and alterations, 1791–2. [Hospital MSS., Mins. 1791–1813]

London, Montagu House, Portman Square. (*D*). Addition of nurseries, 1793. [Dale, 213]

London, Northumberland House. Unexecuted design for south apartments for second Duke of Northumberland, 1790. [Syon MSS., Class B. Div. xv 2e, Drawing]

London, The Pantheon, Oxford Street. (*D*). 1769–72. Converted it into theatre for Italian Opera, 1790–1. [*LS* xxxi (1963), Ch. xiii]

London, 11–15 Portman Square. (*D*). Built as personal speculation perhaps with Samuel Wyatt, 1773–84. [A. J. Bolton, *Works of R. & J. Adam*, ii (1922), 81, 91; S.L., M96, Letter from Samuel to James Wyatt about bricks for 11 Portman Square]

London, 22 St. James's Place. (*D*). For Samuel Rogers, 1802–3. [*LS* xxx (1960), 536–8]

London, The Tower. New buildings. (*D*). For the Department of the Ordnance, 1791–6. [*XVth Report of the Commissioners of Military Enquiry* (1811), 355]

London, Week's Museum, Tichborne Street. (*D*). For Sir Henry Tichborne, *c.* 1795. [*LS* xxxi (1963), 54–5]

London, Westminster Abbey. Arrangements for Handel Festival, 1784. Crossing vault, 1803 (*D*). Restored Henry VII Chapel, 1809–13. [*Gent's Mag.* i (1784), 391–2; S.L., M96, Correspondence]

London, Westminster Palace. (*D*). Alterations to House of Commons; new House of Lords, Speaker's House, etc., 1800–8. [*King's Works*, 517–19, 526, 532–4]

London, Whitehall, Banqueting House. Staircase at N. end, 1809. [PRO, Works 6/24, 1809; *King's Works*, 545–7]

London, Whitehall, Dorset House. (*D*). Alterations, 1808–13. [PRO, Works 1808–15, *passim*; *King's Works*, 550–1]

London, Whitehall, Richmond House. (*D*). Staircase and two rooms for third Duke of Richmond, 1782. [T. W. Hilles and P. D. Daghlian (eds.), *H. Walpole, Anecdotes of Painting*, v (1939), 161]

London, White's Club. St. James's (Attributed). 1787–8. [*LS* XXX (1060), 452–3]

Longford Castle, Wilts. Project for enlarging the house from a triangle to a hexagon for second Earl of Radnor, 1796. Partly executed by G. D. A. Alexander, 1802–17. [Model and Drawings at Longford]

Manchester, St. Peter. 1788–1794 (*D*). [Joseph Aston, *Picture of Manchester* (1804); *Br.* xviii (1860), 575]

Marchwiel, Denbighshire, Church. Steeple for Philip York of Erdigg, 1789. [Ex Info Mr. Gervase Jackson-Stops]

Milton Abbas, Dorset, Abbey Church. Restoration for

first Lord Milton, 1781–91. [RIBAD; *RCHM, Dorset*, iii (2) (1970), 184–9]

Milton Abbas, Dorset, St. James's. (Attributed). **For first Lord Milton, 1786. [Built as village church when the abbey became a private chapel. The date makes it more likely to have been designed by James Wyatt than by 'Capability' Brown or Sir William Chambers]**

Milton Abbey, Dorset. Interior for first Lord Milton, 1775–6. [RIBAD]

Mongewell, Oxon., St. John the Baptist. (Attributed). Remodelled for Shute Barrington, Bishop of Durham, 1791. Gothic. Ruin.

Mount Kennedy, Co. Wicklow, Ireland. For first Lord Rossmore. Designed 1772. Executed *c.* 1782 by T. Cooley. [National Library of Ireland, LR 72884, Drawings]

Mount Stewart, Co. Down, Ireland. Alterations for first Marquess of Londonderry, *c.* 1783. [Belfast PRO, Drawings]

New Hall, Bodenham, Wilts. (D). Enlarged for J. T. Batt, 1792. [J. Britton, *Beauties of Wilts*, i (1801), 114]

New Park, Devizes, Wilts. (D) (now Roundway Park). For James Sutton, 1777–83. [Gloucester R.O., D1571, F614, and F656, Correspondence and payments to James Wyatt from James Sutton; Exhib. RA 1784]

Newark Park, Glos. Remodelled for Lewis Clutterbuck, 1790. Gothic. [J. and H. S. Storer, *Delineations of the County of Gloucester* (1824)]

Norris Castle, Isle of Wight. For Lord Henry Seymour, 1799. Castellated. Also Bailiff's Farm. [John Britton (ed.), *Beauties of England & Wales*, vi (1805), 391]

Norton Priory, Ches. (D). Remodelled for Sir Richard Brooke before 1780. (Garden temple remains.) [B. Burke, *Visitation of Seats & Arms*, ii (1853), 171–2]

Nuthall Temple, Notts. (D). Interior decoration for Sir Charles Sedley, Bt. Before 1778. [Metropolitan, Drawings]

Ottershaw Park, Surrey. Entrance-lodge and dairy for Edward Boehm, *c.* 1800. [G. F. Prosser, *Illustrations of the County of Surrey* (1828)]

Oxford, Balliol College. Altered hall and gave library a plaster vault, 1792–4. [Drawings at College]

Oxford, Bodleian Library. Fitted up the Auctarium, 1878 (*A*). [Mins. of the Curators of the Bodleian Library (MS.), 1786–87]

Oxford, Brasenose College. Library, 1779–80. [*Brasenose Quartercentenary Monographs*, iii (1909), 34–5]

Oxford, Christ Church. Canterbury Quadrangle, 1773–83. Staircase to hall, 1805 (Gothic). Restoration of SE corner of Tom Quadrangle after fire, 1809. [Christ Church MSS., XXXIII. a1 and b3 n, Accounts; Exhib. RA 1780]

Oxford, Corpus Christi College. Unexecuted design for alterations, *c.* 1805. [Bodl. MS. Top Oxon. C.2, fo. 155, Drawings]

Oxford, Holywell Music Room. Rearranged interior, 1780. [Bloxam (ed.), *Magdalen College Register*, ii (1857), 222]

Oxford, Magdalen College. Reroofed chapel and inserted plaster vault, 1790–5. Unexecuted design for enlarging quadrangle, 1791. [Drawings at College and RIBAD; design for quadrangle Exhib. RA 1795]

Oxford, Merton College. Remodelled hall, 1790–2. Gothic. (*D*). [Merton College Register (MS.), 1731–1822]

Oxford, New College. Upper Library, 1778. Hall roof, 1786. Chapel roof, reredos, stalls, and organ-case, 1789–94 (*D*). Monument to John Oglander in chapel †1794. [Signed by Wyatt as architect and R. Westmacott as sculptor; New College MSS., Building Accounts; Bodl. MS. Top Oxon. 9. 29, fos. 65–7, Wyatt's specification for chapel; *VCH Oxon.* iii. 147–9]

Oxford, Oriel College. Library, 1788–9. [Drawings at College]

Oxford, Physic Garden. Conversion of greenhouse into library and residence for Professor of Botany, 1789. [Bodl. MS. Sherard 5, fos. 39–44, 51–60, Correspondence]

Oxford, Radcliffe Observatory. 1776–94. [*C.Life*, 10 May 1930; Exhib. RA 1780]

Oxford, Worcester College. Hall, *c.* 1784 (restored to Wyatt's design in 1964 at Mr. Woodrow Wyatt's expense). Chapel, *c.* 1790 (*A*). [Drawings at College]

Pennsylvania Castle, Portland, Dorset. **For John Penn, 1800. Castellated. [Dorset Arch. Soc. Trans. xxxvii (1916), 248–51]**

Peper Harow, Surrey. Conservatory for fourth Viscount Midleton, 1797 (*D*). [Ampthill, Richardson Coll., Drawing dated 1795]

Petworth, Sussex, County Bridewell. (*D*) 1785–8. [J. Dalloway, *Western Division of Sussex*, ed. Cartwright, ii (i) (1832), vii–x]

Pishiobury Park, Herts. Remodelled for Jeremiah Milles, 1782–4. Gothic. [Neale, ii (1819)]

Plas Newydd, Anglesey. For first Earl of Uxbridge, 1795–7. Completed by Joseph Potter. [RIBAD]

Powderham Castle, Devon. Alterations, including Music-Room, for third Viscount Courtenay, 1794–6. [Building Accounts at castle]

Purley House, Berks. For the executors of Anthony Storer, *c*. 1800. [D. and S. Lysons, *Magna Britannia*, i (1806), 325]

Ragley Hall, War. Extensive alterations and stables for first Marquess of Hertford, 1779–97. [Warwick R.O., Hertford MSS., Cr114A/194, 202, 203, 220/17–20, 195, 196, 197, Accounts; BL Egerton MS. 3515, Correspondence]

Ripon, W.R. Yorks., Town Hall. 1798–9. [Anon., *History of Ripon* (1801), 58]

Roehampton Grove, Surrey. (*A*). For Sir Joshua Vanneck, 1777. [Neale, 2nd Ser. iii (1826)]

Romford, Essex, Workhouse. (*D*). 1786. [Essex R.O., D/DO75]

St. Kea, Cornwall, Church. (*D*). 1802. Gothic. [*A Complete Parochial Hist. of Cornwall*, ii (Truro, 1868), 318; ex info. Mr. H. M. Colvin]

Salisbury, Wilts., Cathedral. Restoration, 1787–92. [W. Dodsworth, *Guide to the Cathedral Church of Salisbury with a particular account of the late Great Improvements made therein under the direction of James Wyatt Esq.* (1792); Exhib. RA 1787]

Sandhurst, Berks., Royal Military Academy. Designed elevation, 1801; executed by John Sanders, after Wyatt was dismissed, in 1807–12. [Farrington, 3 Feb. 1811, 4 Feb. 1812; A. Aspinall (ed.), *Later Correspondence of George III*, iii (Cambridge, 1967), 600; ex info Mrs. Frances Fergusson]

Sandleford Priory, Berks. For Mrs. Elizabeth Montagu, 1780–9. Gothic. [D. Lysons, *Magna Britannia*, i (1806), 353]

Shardeloes, Bucks. External alterations, interior decoration including library, for William Drake, 1773–81. Executed by Samuel Wyatt. Garden pavilion, 1785–6. [Bucks. R.O., Drake MSS., D/DR 5/43, 61, 69a, Accounts]

Sheffield Park, Sussex. For first Earl of Sheffield, *c*. 1776–7. Alterations, *c*. 1780–90. Gothic. [E. Sussex R.O., Holroyd MSS., 5440/55, 58, 63]

Shoebury Castle, Essex. Unexecuted design for Sir John Smith Burges, 1797. Castellated. [RIBAD]

Shrewsbury, The Armoury. 1806. [S. Lewis, *Topographical Dictionary*, iv (1831), 71]

Shrivenham, Berks., St. Andrew's. Monument to second Viscount Barrington †1793. [Signed by Wyatt as architect and R. Westmacott as sculptor]

Slane Castle, Co. Meath, Ireland. For second Lord Conyngham, 1785–6. Castellated. [Drawings at the castle dated 1775 and Metropolitan]

Soho House, Handsworth, Staffs. Remodelled for Matthew Boulton, 1796–8. Completed by Samuel Wyatt after James was dismissed. [BRL, Tew MSS., Correspondence]

Sophia Lodge, Clewer, Berks. Remodelled for William Dawson, n.d. Gothic. [R. Ackermann, *Repository of Arts*, 3rd Ser., ii (1823), 249–59]

Stansted House, Sussex. (*A*). with Joseph Bonomi for Richard Barwell, 1786–91. [J. Dallaway, *Western Division of Sussex*, ii (1815), 159]

Stoke Park, Bucks. Completed for John Penn, 1793. Monument to Thomas Gray, 1799. Memorial Column to Sir Edward Coke, 1800. [BM, Add MS. 32450, E–H, Drawings; J. Penn, *An Historical & Descriptive Account of Stoke Park* (1813), 61–2]

Stoke Poges, Bucks., Parsonage. For John Penn, 1802–4. Gothic. [J. Penn, *An Historical & Descriptive Account of Stoke Park* (1813), 68]

Strawberry Hill, Middx. Built offices to a design by James Essex for Horace Walpole, 1790. [W. D. Lewis, 'Genesis of Strawberry Hill', *Metropolitan Museum Studies*, v (i) (1934), 82]

Streatham, Surrey. House for Dowager Countess of Coventry, 1810 (*D*). [Croome Estate Office, Coventry MSS.]

Sudbourne Hall, Suffolk. (*D*). For first Marquess of Hertford, *c*. 1784. [F. Shoberl, *Beauties of England & Wales*, xiv (1813), 326]

Sufton, Herefordshire. For James Hereford, *c*. 1787. [W. H. Cooke, *Hist. & Antiquities of Herefordshire*, iii (1882), 72 says 'Wyatt']

Sunninghill Park, Berks. Alterations for G.H.Crutchley, *c.* 1805. [Neale, iii (1820)]

Swinton Park, W.R. Yorks. Drawing-room for William Danby, *c.* 1793–4. [Neale, 2nd Ser. iv (1828)]

Syon House, Middx. Unexecuted design for stucco decoration in loggia, 1772; stables, 1789–90; iron bridge, 1790; for first and second Dukes of Northumberland. [Drawings and Accounts at Syon and Alnwick]

Thirkleby Park, N.R. Yorks. **For Sir Thomas Frankland,** *c.* **1785–7.** *(D).* **Samuel Wyatt was not involved in this house in any way.** [Metropolitan, Drawing for ceiling; Leeds Archaeological Library, Payne-Gallwey Coll., Sir Thomas Frankland's Notebook; Neale, v (1818)]

Trentham Hall, Staffs. *(D).* Unidentified work. For first Marquess of Stafford. Before 1797. [A. Dobson (ed.), *Diary & Letters of Madame D'Arblay*, v (1905), 338]

Weeford, Staffs., St. Mary. Executed by Benjamin Wyatt of Sutton Coldfield, 1803–4. [Nigel Forbes-Adam, Drawings; S.L., M96, Correspondence]

West Dean Park, Sussex. *(D).* For first Lord Selsey, *c.* 1804–8. Gothic [Neale, iv (1821)]

Westport, Co. Mayo, Ireland. Drawing-room 1781 and greenhouse 1796 for first Marquess of Sligo. [Drawings at house]

Wetherby Grange, W.R. Yorks. *(D).* *(Attributed).* For Beilby Thompson, *c.* 1784. [Attribution based on style, on Beilby Thompson's connection with the Lawleys of Canwell, and Leeds City Library, Lane Fox Deeds CXVIII, 18, John Carr to Beilby Thompson, 'the alterations you have made to the great Mr. Wyatt's plans'; ex info Mr. H.M.Colvin]

The White Lodge, Richmond Park, Surrey. Altera-

tions for first Viscount Sidmouth, 1801–6 [*King's Works*, 355]

Wilton House, Wilts. Alterations for eleventh Earl of Pembroke, 1801–11. [Drawings and Correspondence at the house]

Wilton, Wilts., S.S. Nicholas and Mary. Monument to tenth Earl of Pembroke †1794. [Signed by Wyatt as architect and R.Westmacott as sculptor]

Wimbledon, Surrey. **Refaced unidentified house for Mr. Bond Hopkins, 1779.** [B.Higgins, *Calcareous Cement* (1780), 215–16]

Windsor Castle, Berks. Remodelled royal apartments and the Tombhouse for George III, 1800–13. Castellated Gothic. *(D).* [*King's Works*, 375–9]

Winnington Hall, Ches. *(Attributed).* New wing and lodges for first Lord Penrhyn, *c.* 1775. [Stylistic evidence makes this work more likely to be by James Wyatt than Samuel]

Woodchester Park, Glos. *(D).* Possible alterations for Lord Ducie, 1776. [Leeds City Library, Ramsden MS. 2c, Lord Ducie to William Weddell, 6 Nov. 1776, saying that 'Mr. Wyatt expected'; ex info Mr. P.Bezodis]

Woolwich, Royal Military Academy. *c.* 1800–6. Castellated. [D. Lysons, *Environs of London*, i (2) (1811), 586]

Woolwich, Royal Military Barracks. 1802–8. [*APSD*]

Worstead Hall, Norfolk. For Sir Berney Brograve, *c.* 1791–7. [Neale, ii (1819)]

Wycombe Abbey, Bucks. For first Lord Carrington, *c.* 1803–4. Gothic. [D. and S.Lysons, *Magna Britannia* (1806), 676]

Wynnstay, Denbighshire. *(D).* Alterations for Sir Watkin Williams Wynne, *c.* 1785–9. Column in park, *c.* 1790. [*C.Life*, 30 Mar. 1972 and 6 Apr. 1972]

4 Lewis William Wyatt

(1777–1853)

Astley Hall, Lancs. (Attributed). East Wing for Robert Townley-Parker, 1825. Tudor, rendered. (Lewis Wyatt designed Cuerdon for Robert Townley-Parker.)

Basingstoke, Hants, Town Hall. 1833. [S. Lewis, *Topographical Dictionary of England*, i (1848), 169; ex info Mr. H. M. Colvin]

Bibury Court, Glos. Minor alterations for second Lord Sherborne, 1830. [Gloucester R.O., D678 Family 322]

Bolton Hall, N.R. Yorks. Added wings and other alterations for second Lord Bolton, 1816–24. [Bolton Hall, Drawings; ex info. Mr. H. M. Colvin]

Cambridge, Downing College. Unexecuted design, 1805. Neo-classical. [Downing, drawings]

Chester, Foregate Street, Lloyd's Bank. *c.* 1815. [J. Broster, *A Walk Round the Walls and City of Chester* (1821) says by 'Wyatt']

Cranage Hall, Ches. For Lawrence Armistead, 1828–9. Tudor, brick. [Ormerod, iii, 129]

Cuerden Hall, Lancs. New main block, lodges, and stables for Robert Townley-Parker. 1816–19. Romantic classical, brick. [RIBAD; E. Twycross, *Mansions of England and Wales*, i (1847), 42]

Dungeness, Kent, Lighthouse. Repaired after extensive damage by lightning for first Earl of Leicester (T. W. Coke), 1822. The light-keeper was saying his prayers at the time and was thus 'providentially saved from the explosion of the electric fluid'. [Holkham Hall, Norfolk, Correspondence; Exhib. RA 1822]

Duxbury Hall, Lancs. (Attributed). (D). For Miles Standish, 1828. Neo-classical. (Traditionally by 'Wyatt'. Geography and stylistic evidence suggests Lewis)

East Stoke Hall, Notts. New Main block added to sixteenth-century house for Sir Robert Bromley, 1823–9. Neo-classical, stone-faced. [Exhib. RA 1812]

Eaton-by-Congleton Hall, Ches. (D). For G. C. Antrobus, 1829–31. Jacobean exterior, brick, plain classical interior. [Manchester School of Architecture, Drawings]

Elstree, Herts., St. Nicholas's. (D). Enlarged the church, 1824. [Ex info Mr. H. M. Colvin]

Flintham Hall, Notts. (D). Library, offices, and conservatory for Thomas Hildyard, 1824–9. Neo-classical. [Flintham, Drawings and Correspondence]

Hackwood Park, Hants. South front, interior, stables, dairy, lodges, farmhouse, and hot-houses for second Lord Bolton, 1807–25. Neo-classical and Wrenaissance. [Hants R.O., Building Accounts; Exhibt. RA 1810]

Hampton Court, Middx., House for Principal Stud Groom. For Office of Works, 1832–3. [PRO, Works 1/20, 73, 81; 1/21, 41, 19/68, Drawings]

Hampton Court, Middx., Water Gallery. Restored after flood damage for Office of Works, 1829. [*King's Works*, 333]

Hawkstone Park, Salop. Alterations, including heightening quadrants, library, staircase, drawing-room, kitchen, conservatory, for Sir Rowland Hill, 1832–4. Neo-classical and Louis-Quatorze. [Salop R.O., Sketches and Correspondence]

Heaton Hall, Lancs. Lodges, orangery, and alterations to house, including chimney-stacks, library, and N. front, for first Earl of Wilton, 1806–24. Neo-classical. [Heaton, Drawings on loan from Earl of Wilton; *Gent's Mag*. i (1853), 670]

London, Houses of Parliament. Unexecuted design. Submission for competition in various historical styles, 1835. [*Parliamentary Papers* (1836), 66, XXXVI]

London, 53 (Lower) Grosvenor Street. Alterations for second Lord Sherborne, 1831. [Gloucester R.O., D678 Family 322]

London, Middlesex Hospital. Minor alterations and repairs, 1823–9. [Middlesex Hospital MSS., Mins. 1818–29]

London, Roll's House. Unexecuted design for a dining-room for Office of Works, 1827. [PRO, Works 12/67/2, fo. 929, Drawing]

London, St. George's Hospital, Hyde Park Corner. Unexecuted design, 1827. [Exhib. RA 1827]

London, 7 St. James's Square. (D). Lengthened first-floor windows and added a balcony for Wilbraham Egerton, *c.* 1807. [Tatton Park, Drawings]

London, 12–17 Suffolk Street. *c.* 1822–3. Neo-classical, stucco. [*LS* xx (1940), 93]

London, Unexecuted Designs. 1816. Naval Monument, military Monument, Palace for Duke of Wellington, Palace for King, Crescent at Charing Cross,

Burlington Subscription Rooms, etc. [L.Wyatt, *Prospectus of a Design for Various Improvements in the Metropolis* (1816)]

Lyme Park, Ches. Alterations including new Wrenaissance dining-room, for Thomas Legh, 1814–22. [Lyme Park, Drawings; Exhib. RA 1816]

Manchester, Lancs., Royal Institution. Unexecuted competition design, 1824. [H.R.Hitchcock, *Early Victorian Architecture in Britain* (1954), 38]

Mount Shannon, Co. Limerick, Ireland. For second Earl of Clare, 1809. Ruin. [Drawing in possession of Constantine FitzGibbon; *Irish Georgian Society Quarterly Bulletin*, xix (1976), 14–19]

Oulton Park, Ches. (D). Interior alterations, stables, and lodge for Sir John Grey-Egerton, 1816–26. Neo-classical. [E.Twycross, *Mansions of England and Wales*, iv (1850), 106; Ormerod, ii, 219]

Paris, British Embassy. Unexecuted schemes for new dining-room, ballroom, and chapel. Sixteen drawings submitted 1825. [V & A, 86.JJ.2, Correspondence]

Patshull House, Staffs. Alterations for Sir George Pigott, executed by Benjamin Wyatt of Sutton Coldfield, 1803–5. [SL, M96]

Radcliffe Chapel, Lancs. (Attributed). (D). For Countess Grosvenor, 1818–19. [*Gent's Mag.* i (1818), 633 says 'Mr. Wyatt']

Rode Hall, Ches. New dining-room and stuccoed exterior for Randle Wilbraham, 1810–12. Neoclassical. [Rode, Building Accounts]

Rostherne, Ches. School and cottage for Wilbraham Egerton, 1815 and 1826. [Tatton, Drawings]

St. Asaph Cathedral, Flints. (D). Ceiled nave and aisle with stucco, *c.* 1822. [D.R.Thomas, *History of the Diocese of St. Asaph* (1870), 207]

Sherborne, Glos., St. Mary Magdalene. He made drawings for additions to the spire and a new family chapel, 1833. In the event the church was rebuilt to the design of another architect *c.* 1850. [Gloucester R.O., D678 Family 322]

Sherborne House, Glos. Rebuilt in Jacobean style for second Lord Sherborne. Drawing-room Louis-Quatorze, dining-room 'William Kent'. Orangery and lodges, 1829–34. [Gloucester R.O., D678 Family 322, Correspondence]

Stockport, Ches., St. Mary's. Rebuilt except for chancel, 1813–17. Perp. [Soane Museum, XLVII 10, 1–11, Drawings]

Tatton Park, Ches. Completed house, orangery, lodges for Wilbraham Egerton, 1807–21. Neoclassical. [Tatton, Drawings; Exhib. at RA 1811, 1812]

Wemyss Castle, Fife. Gothic gate for William Wemyss, 1808. [Exhib. RA 1808]

Wigginton Lodge, Staffs. For Sir Charles Clarke. Executed by Benjamin Wyatt of Sutton Coldfield, 1804. [S.L., M96]

Willey Park, Salop. For first Lord Forester, 1812–13. Neo-classical. [U.S.A. Columbia Univ. Avery Architectural Library, Drawing. Salop R.O., Drawings]

Winslade, Hants, St. Mary's. (A). For second Lord Bolton, 1816–17. [Hants R.O., A/XB/5/3]

Winstanley Hall, Lancs. Alterations to Elizabethan house for Meyrick Bankes, 1818–19. [Lancs. R.O., Drawings]

Wonham House, Surrey. (D). For first Viscount Templetown, *c.* 1805–10. [R.Ackermann, *Views of Country Seats*, ii (1830), 48; Exhib. RA 1810]

Unidentified. Hunting-box for Lord Dorchester, 1826. [Flintham Hall, Drawing]

5 Matthew Cotes Wyatt

(1777–1862)

Paintings

1798   *Miniatures of Charles Burton, James and Philip Wyatt, Kitty Frankland, her Dog Amy, Charles Palmer and a Self-Portrait.* [Coll. G.Budenberg, M.C.Wyatt's Diary (MS.)]

1800   *Three Miniatures.* [Farington, 3 Feb. 1800]
Study for Head of Cerberus. [Exhib. RA 1800]

1801   *A Royal Tyger.* [Exhib. RA 1801]

1803   *Portrait of Revd. Mr. Wright.* [Exhib. RA 1803]
Nymph Attiring. [Exhib. RA 1803]
Concert Room Hanover Square, Ceiling Paintings. [BL, Egerton MS. 3515]

1804   *A Witch.* [Exhib. RA 1804]
Portrait of a Naval Officer. [Exhib. RA 1804]
Portrait of a Little Girl. [Exhib. RA 1804]
Portrait of Mr. G.Plowden. [Exhib. RA 1804]
Carlton House, Four Painted Panels, a Transparent Window, and Decorative 'Bronzes' in the Entrance-Hall and Octagon. [PRO, Works 5/94]

c. 1805–11   *Windsor Castle, State Room Ceilings, Portraits of Knights of the Garter.* [RIBAD; Wyatt MSS.; PRO, Works, Accounts 1805–1811; Farington, 1 June 1810; 9 Nov. 1812]

1806   *Portrait of a Lady.* [Exhib. RA 1806]
Portrait of Tipoo Sahib. [Exhib. RA 1806]

1808   *Portrait of a Lady, Portrait of James Wyatt, Portrait of a Lady.* [Exhib. RA 1808]

1809   *Portrait of a Gentleman, Infant Bacchus, Portrait of a Lady.* [Exhib. RA 1809]

1810   *Portrait of Revd. Sir C.Anderson Bart.* [Exhib. RA 1810]
Portrait of Edward III for William Beckford at Fonthill. [Boyd Alexander, *Life at Fonthill* (1957), 91]

1811   *Liverpool Town Hall* Painted panels for the Dining-Room. [BL Egerton MS. 3515]

1812   *Portrait of Mr. de Lucke.* [Exhib. RA 1812]
Portrait of Dr. Lind. [Exhib. RA 1812]

1813   *Descent from the Cross.* [Exhib. RA 1813]

1814   *Portrait of Master J.Taylor.* [Exhib. RA 1814]
Portrait of a Child. [Exhib. RA 1814]
Portrait of a Lady. [Exhib. RA 1814]
Portrait of a Gentleman. [Exhib. RA 1814]
A Wood Nymph. [Exhib. at British Institution 1814]
Venus and Adonis. [Exhib. British Institution 1814]
Susannah and the Elders. [Exhib. British Institution 1814]

1815   *St. Sebastian.* [Exhib. British Institution 1814]

1816   *Decorative Work at the Royal Mint.* [PRO, Works 5/112]

1821   *10 St. James's Square. Decorative Work for Lord Blessington.* With Philip Wyatt. [BL, Egerton MS. 3515]

1824–5   *Belvoir Castle.* Designed the decorations and painted the ceiling of the Elizabeth Saloon. Completed Hoppner's portrait of fifth Duchess of Rutland for fifth Duke of Rutland. [Belvoir MS. 2.20.5, Correspondence; I.Eller, *Belvoir Castle* (1841)]

c.1828   *Kilruddery, Co. Wicklow.* Designed
            Louis-Quatorze decoration in
            Drawing-Room for tenth Earl of
            Meath. [Drawings at the house; ex
            info Mr. John Cornforth]

Sculpture

1807–   *Nelson Monument, Liverpool.* Executed
            by Richard Westmacott. Also small
            bronzed plaster models. [BL, Egerton
            MS. 3515, M.C.Wyatt, Prospectus of
            a Model to Lord Nelson (1808);
            Exhib. British Institution 1808]

1810   *Bust of George III.* For Board Room at
            the Treasury. Bronze. Now in British
            Embassy in Lisbon. [V & A,
            86.22.15, Account 1810; Exhib. RA
            1811]

1811   *Seal depicting Commerce.* For Corpora-
            tion of Liverpool. [V & A, 86.22.15,
            M.C.Wyatt to John Foster, 25 May
            1811]

c.1813   *Monument to Rt. Hon. Isaac Corry.*
            †1813. Newry, Co. Down. [H.Potter-
            ton, *Irish Church Monuments* (Ulster
            Architectural Heritage Society,
            1975)]

1815   *Waterloo Monument.* Unexecuted
            design with Philip Wyatt in form of a
            terraced pyramid 360 ft High. [Royal
            Library, Windsor, Correspondence
            and Drawing]

1820–4   *Princess Charlotte Memorial*, St.
            George's Chapel, Windsor. [BL,
            Egerton MS. 3515, Correspondence]

1821   *Small Equestrian Statue of Marquess of
            Anglesey in Ivory.* [Exhib. British
            Institution, 1821]

1822   *Bust of Princess Charlotte.* Now at
            Brighton Pavilion. [Exhib. British
            Institution, 1822]

1822–36   *George III Monument.* Unexecuted
            design in form of a quadriga. Eques-
            trian bronze statue erected in Cock-
            spur Street. ['Sussexiensis' *Reasons
            for Opposing Mr. Wyatt's Plan for a
            Monumental Trophy* (1822); BL,
            Egerton MS. 3515; V & A, 86.00.15;
            Burlington Mag. xx (1912), 289–90]

1823   *Monument to Charlotte Piggot.* †1823.
            St. Mary and Holy Cross, Quainton,
            Bucks. [Signed]

c.1826–34 *Belvoir Castle.* For fifth Duke of Rut-
            land. Marble *trompe-l'œil* pedestal in
            dining-room. Chimney-piece in
            Regent's Gallery. Bust and statue of
            fifth Duchess of Rutland (replica of
            bust at Castle Howard). Monument
            to fifth Duchess of Rutland in the
            Mausoleum. [Belvoir MSS., Corres-
            pondence; BL, Egerton MS. 3515;
            I. Eller, *Belvoir Castle* (1841)]

1829   *Buckingham Palace, Two Chimney-
            pieces in the Armoury.* Cost £1,050.
            [*King's Works*, vi, 299]

1831   *Model of Statue of Duke of York.* Unex-
            ecuted competition design for Duke
            of York's Column. [Stratfield Saye
            MSS., Correspondence]
            Bashaw. For Earl of Dudley. Now in
            the Victoria & Albert Museum.
            [RIBAD; Wyatt MSS.; John Harris,
            'The Story of the Marble Dog', *C.Life*,
            21 Nov. 1957; Exhib. Great Exhibi-
            tion 1851]

1838–46   *Wellington Statue.* Now at Aldershot.
            [V & A, 86.00.15, Correspondence;
            John Physick, 'Banishment of the
            Bronze Duke', *C.Life*, 27 Oct. 1966;
            King's Works, 494]

1844   *St. George and the Dragon.* Horse and
            dragon without St. George cast in
            1844. Originally commissioned by
            George III. Now at Stratfield Saye.
            [Gunnis, 447; Exhib. at Great Exhib-
            ition]

6 Sir (Matthew) Digby Wyatt

(1820–1877)

(*Br. = Br.*, Obituary, 2 June 1877)

Aldingham Hall, Lancs. For Revd. John Stonard. 1846–50. Gothic with a tower. [*Churches, Castle and Halls of North Lancashire* (pub. E. J. Milner, 1880), 105; ex info Sir Nikolaus Pevsner]

Ashridge, Herts. Remodelled interiors and the Fernery for second Earl Brownlow, 1860. [RIBAD; Exhib. RA 1859]

Azores, Mansion. [*Br.*]

Bramridge House, Hants. For Sir Thomas Fairbairn, 1869–76. [*BN*, 25 May 1877; Exhib. RA 1869]

Brentwood, Essex, St. Thomas. (*D*). 1857–8. [*Br.*, 30 Jan. 1858]

Bristol, Temple Meads Station. Engine-shed, offices, and refreshment rooms. 1865–78. Gothic. [BR Western Region, drawings]

Calcutta, India, Post Office. 1857. [*Br.*, 30 Jan. 1858; Exhib. RA 1857]

Cambridge, Addenbrooke's Hospital. 1863. South Kensington style. [Exhib. RA 1865]

Cambridge, Clare College. (*A*). Remodelled interior of hall in sumptuous Caroline style, 1870. [Exhib. RA 1871, 1873]

Cambridge, Fitzwilliam Museum. Unexecuted design for completing the Staircase Hall, 1870. [Drawings and Correspondence at the Museum]

Cambridge, Pitt Club, Jesus Lane. Attributed. *c.* 1865. (He owned it and built it.)

Castle Ashby, Northants. Water-tower and garden buildings for third Marquess of Northampton, 1867–8. [*Br.*, 18 Jan. 1868; 1 June 1867; Exhib. RA 1867]

Chatham, Kent, Brompton Barracks. Royal Engineers' Crimean War Memorial Arch. 1861. [*Br.*]

Chichester Cathedral, Sussex. William Huskisson Memorial Window, 1851. Cartoon by Clayton. Glass made by Gibbs. [Mellon Coll., Drawing; Coll. Capt. John Wyatt, Autobiographical note by M. D. Wyatt]

Coed-y-Pane, Monmouthshire, Church. n.d. [Exhib. RA 1860]

Compton Wynyates, War. Restoration, including new

E. front and staircase, for third Marquess of Northampton, 1867. [Metropolitan Museum, New York, Signed Drawing; Exhib. RA 1861, 1864]

Coolhurst, Sussex. New house, n.d. [*Br.*]

Crystal Palace, Sydenham, Courts of Architecture. (*D*). With Paxton and Owen Jones, 1852–4. Queen's Screen, Court of Christian Monuments, Pompeian House, Byzantine, Medieval, Renaissance, and Italian Courts. [V & A, Box 85, Drawings; Exhib. RA 1853–6]

Dublin, 24 and 25 Grafton Street. Office building in style of 'ancient Irish architecture' for William Longfield, 1862. [*Br.*, 17 May 1862; Exhib. RA 1862]

Ealing, Middx., Lunatic Asylum. n.d. [N. Pevsner, *Matthew Digby Wyatt* (Cambridge, 1950), 36]

Englefield Green, Surrey, Royal Indian Engineering College. Added S. wing and chapel, 1870–1. [*Br.*; Exhib. RA 1872]

The Ham, Glamorgan. (*D*). For Revd. Iltyd Nicholl, 1859–63. Tudorbethan. [*BN*, 7 May 1869; Exhib. RA 1865]

India, Hullopur, Kent, and Soane Bridges. With J. M. Rendel, *c.* 1855. [India Office Library, Drawings; Coll. Capt. John Wyatt, MS. note]

Inveraray Castle, Argyll. Glass *porte-cochère* for eighth Duke of Argyll, 1848. [Inverary MSS., Drawings]

Isfield Place, Sussex. Restoration for Henry King, *c.* 1877. [*Br.*, 2 June 1877; Exhib. RA 1869]

Kingstown, nr. Dublin, Ireland. Two small houses, 1840. To earn money for his Continental grand tour. [Coll. Capt. John Wyatt, MS. note]

Little Warley, Essex, East India Co. Barracks. Chapel in early Christian style, 1857–62. [*BN*, 24 Apr. 1863]

Loch Ryan, Dromond, Ireland. Estate office for Earl of Leitrim, *c.* 1871. [Exhib. RA 1871]

London, Adelphi Theatre. (*D*). Designed interior decoration, 1848. *See also* T. H. Wyatt. [Coll. Capt. John Wyatt, MS. note]

London, Albert Memorial. Three unexecuted alternative designs, 1863; also unexecuted design for Albert Hall. [*LS* xxxviii (1975), 178]

London, Belvedere Road. (*D*). Indian Government stores for East India Co., 1861–4. [*Br.*; Exhib. RA 1863]

London, Bermondsey. 'Manufacturers shed', 1840. [Coll. Capt. John Wyatt, MS. note]

London, Burlington Fine Arts Club. [*Br.*]

London, Ennismore Gardens. Alford House for Lady Marion Alford, 1871. [New York, Cooper Hewitt Museum, Drawing; *Br.*]

London, Garrick Street. **Debenham Store & Co., designed by Arthur Allom as an Italian palazzo. (Matthew) Digby Wyatt was consultant, 1860**

London, Gracechurch Street. (*D*). Shops and offices for Lloyds, 1877. [*Br.*]

London, Kensal Green Cemetery. Granite monument to J. M. Rendel, 1862. [Exhib. RA 1862]

London, 12 Kensington Palace Gardens. Florentine Library and Moorish Smoking-Room for Alexander Collie, 1864. [*LS* xxxvii (1973), 168; Exhib. RA 1866]

London, Knightsbridge Barracks. Unexecuted competition design with T. H. Wyatt, *c*. 1855. [Coll. Capt. John Wyatt, MS. note; *Br.*, 2 June 1877]

London, Leadenhall Street. (*D*). East India Co. Museum, 1857–8. [*ILN*, 6 Mar. 1858; Exhib. RA 1858]

London, National Gallery. Unexecuted design for rebuilding, 1866. [RIBAD; Exhib. RA 1867]

London, Oak Lodge, Kensington. Unexecuted design 187–. [RIBAD; *LS* xxxvii (1973), 125]

London, 314 Oxford Street. Shop and offices for Purdey and Cowlan, *c*. 1864. [Exhib. RA 1864]

London, Paddington Station. Architectural decoration with I. K. Brunel and Owen Jones, 1850–5. [B.R. Western Region, Drawings; Coll. Capt. John Wyatt, MS. note]

London, Piccadilly, Northampton House. (*D*). Garden, conservatory, and saloon for third Marquess of Northampton, *c*. 1857. [*BN*, 25 May 1857]

London, Royal Albert Hall. Unexecuted design for a circular hall, 1862–6. [*LS* xxxviii (1975), 178]

London, St. James's Park. (*D*). Decoration on suspension bridge designed by J. M. Rendel, 1857. [*Br.*, 27 June 1857]

London, Whitehall, India Office. For Council of India, 1868. Italian Renaissance. [*Br.*, 26 Oct. 1867; Exhib. RA 1868]

Newells, nr. Horsham, Sussex. For Charles Scrase Dickins, 1869. [Exhib. RA 1869]

North Marston, Bucks., St. Mary's. **Restored in memory of J. C. Neild for Queen Victoria, 1853. Perp. [RIBAD;** *ILN*, **29 Sept. 1855; Exhib. RA 1856]**

Oakley, Hants. Cottages for Mrs. Chamberlayne, *c*. 1872. [Exhib. RA 1872]

Old Lands, nr. Uckfield, Sussex. For A. Nesbitt, 1869. Tudor. [RIBAD; *Br.* 1869; Exhib. RA 1874]

Prince Edward Island. 'Varied work', n.d. [N. Pevsner, *Matthew Digby Wyatt* (Cambridge, 1950) 36]

Possingworth Manor, Sussex. For Sir Louis Huth, 1866–8. Cost £60,000. Varied and asymmetrical Gothic. [*Br.*, 26 Sept. 1868; Exhib. RA 1868]

Rangoon, Burma. Iron church with 900 Sittings, n.d. [*Br.*, 30 Jan. 1858]

Rowde, Wilts., St. Matthew's. Font, 1850. [*VCH*, Wilts. vii (1953), 221]

Stoke Park, Bucks. Alterations and conservatory for Lord Taunton, *c*. 1850. [Coll. Capt. John Wyatt, MS. note]

Stratford-upon-Avon, War. Unexpected design for Shakespeare Memorial, *c*. 1865. [Exhib. RA 1865]

Uckfield, Sussex. Unidentified house, not Old Lands, *c*. 1870. [Exhib. RA 1870]

Upper Norwood, Surrey, The Mount. For J. G. Tollemache Sinclair, 1862. [*Br.*, 17 May 1862; Exhib. RA 1862]

Usk, Monmouthshire. Nicholl family graves, n.d. Polished granite with iron railings. [Ex info Mr. W. Robins]

West Ham, Essex, Rothschild Mausoleum. For Baroness Eveline de Rothschild, 1866. Domed rotunda in sumptuous classical style. [*Br.*]

Wolverhampton, Staffs., St. John's. Furnishings, 1869. [*Br.* (1869), 841]

Woolwich, Kent, Garrison Church of St. George. With Thomas Henry Wyatt, 1862–3. [*Br.*, 17 May 1762; *ILN*, 21 Feb. 1863]

Unidentified

School and Parsonage in Monmouthshire. 1840. [Coll. Capt. John Wyatt, MS. note]

Monument to a Friend. 1869. [Exhib. RA 1869]

Designs for Objects, Furniture, etc.

Grand Trunk Railway Co., Presentation Medal for good conduct to Richard Trevithick, 1858 [Mellon Coll.]. Chairs with M.D.W. Monogram and clock with 'M.Digby Wyatt' on the dial for his own house [Lady Wyatt's Will]. Designs for roofing tiles for Maw & Co. [V & A, Print Room c117]. Designs for carpets for Templeton [*Br.*]. Designs for wall-papers for Messrs. Woollham [*Br.*], for Hurrell James & Co. [N.Pevsner, *Matthew Digby Wyatt* (Cambridge, 1950), 36.]. Design for candelabrum, 1857 [RIBAD]. Cast-iron public conveniences [*Transactions of the RIBA* (1879–80), 187; ex info Mr. Andrew Saint, one exists in Star Yard off Chancery Lane]

Calligraphy and Book Design

Cardiff Church Sonnets 1841 [Mellon Coll.]. Crystal Palace Co. Share Certificates [Mellon Coll.]. Messrs. Lloyd Bros. & Co., Sale Invitation [Mellon Coll.]. City Corporation, Invitation to Guildhall Banquet [Mellon Coll.]. Various programme covers [Mellon Coll.]. Frontispiece to *Proceedings of the Institution of Civil Engineers* (1850) [Mellon Coll.]. Frontispiece in Renaissance style to Carlo Bossoli, *The War in Italy* (1859) [ex info Mr. Roger Ellis]. Designs for *Metal Work & Its Artistic Design* (1852) [RIBAD].

7 Philip William Wyatt
(d. 1835)

Bishop Wearmouth, Co. Durham, St. Thomas's. (D). 1827–9. Gothic. [W.Fordyce, *History of Durham*, ii (1855), 322)]

Conishead Priory, Lancs. For Colonel T.R.Gale Braddyll, 1821–9. Gothic. [Durham R.O., Londonderry MSS., Correspondence; R. Wallis, *Lancashire Illustrated* (1829), 96]

Great Yarmouth, Norfolk, St. Nicholas's. Restoration. 1813. [BRL Tew MSS., M.Yatman to M.Boulton, 25 Apr. 1814]

London, Berkeley Square. Unexecuted design for large house for E.H.Ball Hughes on N. side, *c.* 1819. [Boyd Alexander, *Life at Fonthill* (1956), 296]

London, Drury Lane, Theatre Royal. Unexecuted design, 1811. [BL, Egerton MS. 3515, Correspondence]

London, 10 St. James's Square. With M.C.Wyatt. Internal decoration for Lord Blessington, 1821. [BL, Egerton MS. 3515, Correspondence]

London, Thames Quay, etc. Unexecuted designs for metropolitan improvements for Sir Frederick Trench, 1824. [V & A, 51.G.9 and 51.a.58]

London, 40 Upper Brook Street. Internal alterations for E.H.Ball Hughes, 1819. [Boyd Alexander, *Life at Fonthill* (1956), 296]

London, Waterloo Monument. With M.C.Wyatt. Unexecuted design, 1815. [Royal Library, Windsor, Drawings and Correspondence]

Red Hall, Haughton-le-Skerne, Co. Durham. For Captain Robert Colling, 1830. Tudor. [B. Burke, *Visitation of Seats & Arms*, i (1852), 116; ex info Mr. H.M.Colvin]

Seaham Hall, Co. Durham. Alterations and lodges for third Marquess of Londonderry, 1828. [V & A, Print Room, DD21, Sketch for Lodges; Durham R.O., Londonderry MSS., Accounts]

Weymouth, Dorset, Holy Trinity. 1834–6. Gothic. [*RCHM Dorset*, ii, 2 (1970), 334]

Wynyard Park, Co. Durham. For third Marquess of Londonderry, 1822–30, Neo-classical. [Durham R.O., Londonderry MSS., Drawings and Building Accounts]

8 Richard James Wyatt

(1795–1850)

Before 1815 Monument to Mrs. Hughes, Esher Church. [*ILN*, 17 Aug. 1850]

Before 1815 Monument, St. John's Wood Chapel. [*ILN*, 17 Aug. 1850]

1815   Best Model From Life. [RA Silver Medal]

1818   Judgment of Paris. [Exhib. RA 1818]

1819   Chimney-piece and Coat of Arms for Hackwood Park, Hants. For second Lord Bolton. [Hants R.O., Bolton MSS., Box 11, M49/371–9]
Monument to Lady Ann Hudson, Bessingby Church, E.R. Yorks. [Exhib. RA 1819]

1820   Monument to Richard Thompson, Escrick Church, E.R. Yorks. Attributed.

1822   Musidora. For sixth Duke of Devonshire. [Chatsworth, 6th Duke's Diary (MS.) and Sculpture Account, Chatsworth]

1829   Nymph of Diana returning from the Chase with Leveret and Greyhound. For Sir Matthew Ridley. Cost £140. Completed in 1834. [Northumberland R.O., Ridley MS. ZRI, 33/5, Receipt, Correspondence, and Notes]
Monument to Lady Barrington. [Lady Anne Murray, *Journal of a tour in Italy* (5 vols. privately printed, 1838)]
Monument to Charlotte Buller, Poltimore Church, Devon. [Exhib. RA 1831]
Ino and the Infant Bacchus. For Sir Robert Peel (now in the Fitzwilliam Museum, Cambridge). Replicas for G.Cornwall Legh (now in Chester), Marquess of Abercorn, Miss Webb, J. Neeld, and Sir Arthur Brooke (formerly at Colebrooke, Co. Fermanagh).

1831   Monument to Ellen Legh, Winwick Church, Lancs.
Nymph going to the Bath. For the Duke of Leuchtenberg. Replicas made for Earl de Grey (Wrest Park), H.N.Sandbach, R.Openshaw [*AU* (1846), 17; (1848), 50; *AJ* (1848), 268; Exhib. RA 1831]

1831   Two Sons of Sir Paul Beilby Thompson (created Lord Wenlock 1839). [Exhib. RA 1832; Coll. Nigel Forbes-Adam]

c.1831   Bust of Lady Beilby Thompson. [Exhib. RA 1832; Coll. Nigel Forbes-Adam]

1832   Monument to Cook Family, Merton Church, Surrey. [Signed and dated]

1833   Statue of an Infant Son; Statue of an Infant Daughter of Sir Michael Shaw Stewart. [Exhib. RA 1833]

1834   Flora and Zephyr. For Lord Wenlock. Cost £400. Replicas for Lord Otho FitzGerald and one also at Nostell Priory. [Exhib. RA 1834; *AU* (1846), 17]

1835   Nymph of Diana with Leveret. For Queen Victoria. [Exhib. RA 1835; Buckingham Palace]
Bust of Mr. Barber Beaumont. [Exhib. RA 1835]
Bust of Mrs. Barber Beaumont. [Private coll. Yorkshire]
Bust of Lady Sydney. [Exhib. RA 1835]
Monumental alto relievo. [Exhib. RA 1835]
Bust of Marquess of Anglesey. [Exhib. RA 1835; Formerly at Hinchingbrooke Castle]
Bust of Lord Selsey. [Lady Anne Murray, *Journal*]

1836   Nymph at the Bath. Replicas for H.J.Hope, Lord Townshend, and one sold at Christie's in 1861 to Holloway. [Exhib. RA 1836]
Bust of Sir John Bayley. [Exhib. RA 1836]
Shepherd Boy protecting his Sister from the Storm. [*AJ* (1854), 352; *Gent's Mag.* (1850), 99]

1838   *Monument to Elizabeth Bayley, Meopham Church, Kent.* [Signed and dated]

Bust of Lady Wilhelmina Stanhope. [Exhib. RA 1838]

Bust of 4th Earl Stanhope. Both at Chevening.

1839   *Hebe.* For Earl de Grey (Wrest Park). [*Athenaeum* (1839), 418; Exhib. RA 1839]

1841   *Apollo as a Shepherd Boy.* For Sir Arthur Brooke (formerly at Colebrooke, Co. Fermanagh). Replica for Duke of Sutherland (Trentham). [*AU* (1846), 17, 298; Exhib. RA 1841]

Penelope with the Bow of Ulysses. For Queen Victoria. [*AU* (1841), 185; (1843), 44, 309] Windsor Castle.

Hunter with his Dog. [Count Hawks Le Grice, *Walks through the Studios of the Sculptors at Rome* (1841), 91]

Nymph coming out of a Bath. For Mr. Wild. Replicas for Mr. Foot, Lord Canning (1847), Sir Arthur Brooke, and at Sudeley House (Liverpool) and the Camelia House (Chiswick). [*AU* (1846), 17; Exhib. RA 1841]

Flora. For Sir Arthur Brooke. A replica of that in the *Flora and Zephyr.* [Count Hawks Le Grice, *Walks through the Studios of the Sculptors at Rome* (1841), 91; formerly at Colebrooke, Co. Fermanagh]

1844   *Bacchante crowned with Flowers.* [*Gent's Mag.* ii (1844), 71; *Athenaeum* (1844), 527]

Bacchante with a Cup. [*Gent's Mag.* ii (1844), 71; *Athenaeum* (1844), 527]

Glycera. For Queen Victoria (on loan to Wrest Park). Replica for Duke of Westminster (Eaton). [*AU* (1848), 50; *AJ* (1850), 249 Exhib. Great Exhibition 1851]

1848   *The Infant Bacchus.* For J. Howard Galton (Hadzor House, Droitwich). [Exhib. RA 1848; Great Exhibition 1851]

The Nymph Eucharis and Cupid. [*AU* (1848), 50; *Athenaeum* (1848), 536; Exhib. RA 1848; formerly at Dorchester House]

Huntress of Diana with Leveret and Greyhound. For Queen Victoria. Possibly a replica of that for Sir Matthew Ridley of 1829. [Exhib. RA 1850]

1849   *Diana taking a Thorn from a Greyhound's Foot.* For the King of Naples (Capodimonte). Replicas for Queen Victoria (Buckingham Palace), Lord Charles Townshend, and at Temple Newsam. Wyatt began work on this subject in 1834. [Northumberland R.O., Ridley MSS., R. J. Wyatt to Sir M. W. Ridley, 25 June 1834]

1850   *Youth mourning a Dead Kid.* [*AJ* (1851), 95; (1854), 352]

Undated   *Bust of George Lushington* (Raby Castle), *Busts of Paris, Penelope, Nymphs preparing and at the Bath* (sold at Christie's, 1861), *Busts of Sir Thomas and Lady Cullum* (Public Library, Bury St. Edmunds)

9 Samuel Wyatt

(1737–1807)

Amersham, Bucks., St. Mary's. (*A*). Restoration for William Drake, 1776–85. [Bucks. R.O., Drake MSS., D/DR/12·60, 61, 65, 5/65, Accounts and Correspondence]

Ashtead Park, Surrey. Built the house to Bonomi's design for Richard Howard (originally Bagot), 1790. [F.E.Paget, *Some Records of the Ashtead Estate* (1873)]

Bangor Cathedral, Caern. Library and registry in shell of Chapter House; organ-loft in Cathedral, 1776–86 (*D*). Gothic. [National Library of Wales, B/DC/V/3. Chapter Acts and Accounts 1747–91. The architect is called 'Mr. Wyatt' but the proximity of Baron Hill and Penrhyn makes it most likely to have been Samuel]

Baron Hill, Anglesey. (*D*). For seventh Viscount Bulkeley, 1776–9. [Bodl. MS. Top Anglesey A.2., Drawings; Bangor Univ. Library, Baron Hill MSS. 5050–8, Accounts]

Belmont Park, Kent. For first Lord Harris, 1787–92. [Drawings at the house]

Berechurch Hall, Essex. (*D*). Additions for Sir Robert Smythe, *c*. 1772. [A folio of accounts for Berechurch is included in L.F.Abbott, portrait of Samuel Wyatt in the Baker Furniture Museum, Michigan, U.S.A.]

Birmingham, Livery Street. (*D*). Warehouse for Matthew Boulton, 1787–8. [BRL; Tew MSS., Correspondence]

Birmingham, St. Paul's. East window, 1785. [*AR* (June 1947), 227]

Birmingham, Theatre Royal, New Street. (*D*). New façade, *c*. 1777–82. [BM, King's Maps XLII 82.1, Drawing; BRL, 5047 Lee 387, List of the proprietors for building a Playhouse in New Street (MS.)]

Blithfield Hall, Staffs. Alterations for first Lord Bagot, 1769–70. [Drawings at the house; Staffs. R.O., Bagot MS. D1721/2/215, Accounts]

Bostock Hall, Ches. (*A*). for Edward Tomkinson 1775. [E. Twycross, *Mansions of England and Wales*, iv (1850), says 'Wyatt' but the Tomkinson connection suggests Samuel – see Dorfold Hall]

Buckenham House, Norfolk. (*D*). Alterations for ninth Lord Petre, 1803. [Essex R.O., Petre MS. D/DP

A177, Account between Lord Petre and the late Sam Wyatt, Sept. 1807]

Colworth House, Beds. Unexecuted design for boathouse for William Lee Antonie, 1778. [Coll. Mr. H.M.Colvin, Drawing]

Coton House, War. For Abraham Grimes, *c*. 1784. [BRL, Tew MSS., S. Wyatt to M. Boulton, Feb. 1784 refers to a house for Mr. Grimes. Stylistically there can be no doubt that Samuel designed Coton]

Culford Hall, Suffolk. (*A*). For first Marquess Cornwallis, 1790–6. [Morton Arboretum Library, U.S.A., H.Repton Red Book for Culford, *c*. 1792]

Delamere Lodge, Ches. (*D*). For George Wilbraham, 1784. [Cheshire R.O., Transcript of the Wilbraham family diary (MS.), says 'Wyatt' but stylistically there can be no doubt that it was by Samuel]

Deptford, Kent. (*D*). Alterations to almshouses for Trinity House, 1792–1803. [Trinity House MSS., Minutes 1797, 1801, 1803; Cash Book 1792]

Deptford, Kent, Victualling Yard. (*D*). Timber barn, 1782. [PRO., ADM 111/89]

Digswell House, Herts. For Hon. Edward Spencer Cowper, 1806. [Herts. R.O., D/EPT240SB. Unexecuted designs. Panshanger Box 49, incomplete accounts]

Doddington Hall, Ches. New house, offices, stables, lodges, hot-houses, and Demesne Farm for Revd. Sir Thomas Broughton, 1776–1800. [three drawings at the house; Cheshire R.O., Delves Broughton MS. DDB/Q/3, Drawings; G.Richardson, *New Vitruvius Britannicus*, i (1802)]

Dorfold Hall, Ches. Attributed. Library for James Tomkinson, 1771. [Stylistic attribution supported by a piece of paper among the Wyatt drawings at Tatton inscribed 'Henry Tomkinson Esq., Dorfold Hall']

Dropmore, Bucks. For Lord Grenville, 1792–4. [Cornwall R.O., Fortescue MS. DDF 259, Accounts 1794–1802]

Dungeness, Kent, Lighthouse. (*A*). For first Earl of Leicester ('Coke of Norfolk'), 1791. [T.H., Drawing; Holkham MSS., Accounts 1787–94]

Egginton Hall, Derby. (*D*). Additions for Sir Edward Every, *c*. 1780–3. [Egginton, Coll. Sir John Every, Accounts 1753–83]

Flamborough Head, E.R. Yorks., Lighthouse. For Trinity House Corporation, 1806. [T.H. MSS., Minutes 1805–6]

Foulness, Norfolk, Lighthouse. (*D*). Reconstruction of interior to provide accommodation for the light-keeper, 1793. [T.H. MSS., Minutes 1792–3]

Gravesend, Kent. Scheme for the first tunnel under the Thames from Gravesend to Tilbury, 1799–1803. Never finished. [R.P. Cruden, *History of Gravesend* (1843), 456–65]

Hackwood Park, Hants. For first Lord Bolton, 1806–7. Completed by Lewis Wyatt. [Hants R.O., Bolton MSS., 11 M49/365–92, Accounts]

Heathfield House, Staffs. (*D*). For James Watt, 1787–90. [BRL, Box MIII and Box 36, Drawings and Correspondence]

Heaton House, Lancs. Attributed. Stables, alterations to house including Music Room. For first Earl of Wilton, 1777–83. [Stylistic attribution supported by a letter from Samuel Wyatt to Matthew Boulton in 1783 implying that he was working at the house then]

Herstmonceux Place, Sussex. For Hare Naylor, 1777. [J. Dallaway, *Discourses upon Architecture* (1833)]

Holkham, Norfolk. Estate buildings for first Earl of Leicester ('Coke of Norfolk'), *c.* 1780–1807, namely, in the park: kitchen garden and vinery, 1780–6; restoration of St. Withburga, 1784–5 (*D*); Church Lodge, 1784–7; Rose Cottages, 1785–7 (*A*); North Lodge Cottages, *c.* 1785 (*D*); Cow House, 1786–7 (*D*); New Inn, 1786–8; unexecuted design for boat-house, 1789; West Lodge, *c.* 1790; Great Barn, *c.* 1790; Wells Barn, *c.* 1790 (*D*); Skoyles Barn, *c.* 1790 (*D*); Longlands Farm, 1792–8 (*A*); Longlands Village, consisting of 14 cottages in semicircular layout, 1794–5 (*D*); East Lodge, 1799–1801; Octagon Cottage, 1801–2; Branthill Lodge, 1805–6 (*A*); 10 cottages in Holkham Village, 1805–6 (*D*); alterations to stables, 1806–7 (*D*). Elsewhere on the estate: Kempstone Lodge, 1788–93; South Creake, Leicester Square Farm, 1791–3; Castle Acre, Wicken Farm, 1784–97 (*A*), Lodge Farm, 1797–1800 (*A*); Warham, Northgate Farm, 1795–9, St. Mary's Rectory, 1801–3; Wighton Hall Farm, 1803–6; Burnham, Crabhall Farm, 1803–7. [Holkham MSS., Audit Books 1780–1806; Household Accounts 1780–1814]

Hooton Hall, Ches. For Sir William Stanley, 1778—8 (*D* but the lodges at Childer Thornton survive). [W. Watts, *Seats* (1799), 23]

Hurts Hall, Suffolk. (*D*). For Charles Long, 1803. [H. Davy, *Views of Seats in Suffolk* (1827)]

Ightham Court Lodge, Kent. Restoration for Col. Richard James, 1801–7. [Kent R.O., USS/E9 and E11, Accounts, etc.]

Kedleston, Derby. Pedestal for statue of lion on south lawn, 1766. Rectory, 1771. (moved from the park then but the old façade rebuilt). [Kedleston MSS., Correspondence and Accounts]

Kinmel Park, Denbighshire. (*D*). For Revd. Edward Hughes, 1790–1802. [Bangor Univ. Library, Kinmel MSS., Drawings and Accounts]

Lambeth, Surrey, St. Mary's. (*D*). **Restoration,** 1786–7. [G.L.R.O., DW/OP/1787/2, **Drawings**]

Little Grove, East Barnet, Herts. (*D*). Stuccoed the exterior for Hon. Justice Willes, 1799. [Bryan Higgins, *Calcareous Cement* (1780), 214–15]

Livermere Park, Suffolk. (*D*). *Attributed.* Remodelled for Nathaniel Lee Acton, 1795–6. [West Suffolk R.O., Acc. 2285, Wage Book of the De Carles, 1790–1811 records mason's work by them but does not give the architect. A chimney-piece, now at Shrubland Park, is identical to ones at Shugborough and Trinity House]

London, 2 Adam Street, Adelphi. (*D*). Lengthened first-floor windows for Thomas Williams, *c.* 1790. [*See* Temple House]

London, Albion Mill. (*D*). 1784–6. Abortive plans for rebuilding 1791, 1795, and 1802. [BRL, Boulton & Watt Coll., Steam-Boat Box, Drawings; PRO, MR99, MPD128, MR98, MPD124, Drawings; BRL, Tew MSS., Correspondence]

London, 63 Berwick Street. (*D*). Alterations for himself, n.d. [*LS* xxxi (1963), 233; xxxii (1963)]

London Bridge. Unexecuted design for cast iron bridge, 1800. [*Parliamentary Papers, Reports of the House of Commons 1792–1802*, XIV, 28 July 1800, 543–6]

London, Chelsea Hospital. New drains, alterations in Governor's Lodging, unexecuted plan for accommodation for 300 pensioners, 1798–1805. [PRO, AO3 622–8, Accounts; Minutes at the Hospital]

London, 4 Cleveland Row. (*A*). For Lord Grenville, 1794–6. [Cornwall R.O., Fortescue MSS., Accounts and Correspondence]

London, 53 Davies Street (now Grosvenor Office). Alterations for Assheton Curzon, 1778. [Bryan

Higgins, *Calcareous Cement* (1780), 214–5]

London, 10 Grosvenor Square. (*D*). Alterations for Dowager Lady Petre, 1801–3. [Essex R.O., Petre MS. D/DP A177, Accounts]

London, 45 Grosvenor Square. (*D*). Reconstructed for ninth Lord Petre, 1801–6. [Essex R.O., Petre MS. D/DP A177, Accounts]

London, 20 Hanover Square. Attributed. Reconstructed for Mrs. Elizabeth Coke, *c.* 1785. [Stylistic attribution plus the fact that Mrs. Coke was Coke of Norfolk's mother]

London, Isle of Dogs. Unexecuted design for new London Docks without warehouses, 1795. [PRO, maps MPD40 and MPD60, Drawings; *Parliamentary Papers, Reports of the House of Commons 1795–6*, 47, 155–163]

London, Manchester Square. Well 110 feet deep for an unidentified gentleman, 1786. [BRL, Tew MSS., S. Wyatt to M. Boulton, 1 Sept. 1788]

London, Mile End, Trinity Almshouses. New quadrangle, 1806 (*D*). [T.H. MSS., Accounts and Minutes]

London, 29 Old Burlington Street. Attributed. Alterations including porch for Sir John Call, *c.* 1785 (*D*). [*LS* xxxi and xxxii (1963); Sir John Call was one of the Albion Mill proprietors]

London, 13 Park Street (originally 113 Park Street). (*D*). Internal alterations for first Lord Harrowby, 1774–6. [Sandon Hall MSS. 334 and 337, Accounts]

London, 3 St. James's Square. Alterations for the third Earl of Hardwicke, 1806. [Correspondence sold at Sotheby's, 6 June 1966; ex info Mr. H. M. Colvin]

London, Lichfield House, 15 St. James's Square. Alterations for first Viscount Anson, 1791–4. [Staffs. R.O., Anson MS. D615/E(H) 59, Accounts]

London, Spring Gardens. (*D*). Unidentified work. [A folio of accounts for Spring Gardens is shown in L. F. Abbott in the Baker Furniture Museum, Michigan, U.S.A.]

London, Trinity House. For Trinity House Corporation, 1792–7. [T.H. MSS., Drawings, Minutes, and Samuel Wyatt's Cash Book, Exhib. RA 1794]

London, Trinity Square. (*A*). Laid out oval centre, 1797. [T.H. MSS., Drawings and Minutes, 2 June 1796]

London, 6 Upper Brook Street. (*D*). Reconstruction for William Weddell, 1787. [Cumberland R.O.,

Pennington-Ramsden MSS., Drawing for ceiling of Mrs. Weddell's dressing-room signed 'S.W.'; Leeds City Library, Ramsden MS. 36, Correspondence from Revd. W. Palgrave and Revd. John Wheler to William Weddell]

London, 36 Upper Brook Street. Alterations for Sir Edward Littleton, *c.* 1781–4. [Staffs. R.O., D260/M-E/116–9]

London, Westminster Hall. Temporary rearrangement for trial of Warren Hastings, 1787–8. [PRO, Works 5/77]

Longships, Cornwall, Lighthouse. For Trinity House Corporation, 1792–5. [T.H. MSS., Minutes]

Lutterworth, Leics., Rectory. For Hon. and Revd. Henry Ryder, 1803. [Lincs. R.O., MGA 39, Drawings and Accounts]

Marble Hill House, Surrey. Alterations, 1781–3. [Norfolk R.O., Hobart MS. 21089, Correspondence]

Marlow, Bucks., Market House (now The Crown Inn). For Thomas Williams, 1806–7. [J. Langley, *Hundreds of Desborough* (1797)]

Marston House, Somerset. Added wings for seventh Earl of Cork and Orrery, 1776. [A folio of accounts for Marston appears in S. Wyatt's portrait by L. F. Abbott; *Proceedings of the Somerset Arch. Soc.* 118 (1974)]

Movable Hospitals for H.M. Distant Possessions. Prefabricated wooden buildings 83 ft long by 20 ft wide. [BRL Tew MSS., S. Wyatt to M. Boulton, 10 and 26 Dec. 1787 and 12 Apr. 1788; *The World*, 12 Apr. 1788]

Needles, Isle of Wight, Lighthouse. Stuccoed for Trinity House Corporation, 1806. [T.H. MSS., Byminutes, 13 Mar. 1806]

Panshanger, Herts. (*D*). Enlarged for fifth Earl Cowper, 1806–7. Gothic. The work was completed after Wyatt's death by Thomas Atkinson. [Herts. R.O., Cowper MSS., Panshanger Box 49, Accounts]

Penrhyn Castle, Caern. Reconstructed castle, stables, entrance-lodge, estate cottages, and Lime Grove for first Lord Penrhyn, 1782 onwards (*D*). [Penrhyn, Coll. Lady Janet Douglas Pennant, Drawings]

Portland, Dorset, Low Lighthouse. Repairs for Trinity House Corporation, 1792. [T.H. MSS., Minutes 6 Sept. 1792, Cash Book 8 Dec. 1792]

Portsmouth, Hants., Royal Dockyard, Commissioner's House (now Admiralty House). For the Navy Board and Commissioner Martin, 1784–5. [Greenwich Maritime Museum Library, Letters and Accounts]

Portsmouth, Hants., Victualling Yard. Timber storehouses, 1782 *(D)*. [PRO, ADM 111/87 and 89]

Ramsgate Harbour, Kent. (D). Lighthouse, 1794–5; Harbour-Master's House, stores, gateway, lodges, 'piazzas', 1794–7; Pier House, 1800–2; unexecuted designs for storehouses, workshops, and dry dock, 1806. For the Trustees of Ramsgate Harbour. [Ramsgate Public Library, Local History Coll., Drawings; PRO, MT 22/32–34, Ramsgate Harbour Mins. 1792–1806]

Rugby School, War. Unexecuted design for new Headmaster's House, 1806. [Nicholas Carlisle, *Endowed Grammar Schools* (1825)]

St. Agnes, Scilly Isles, Lighthouse. Rebuilt top of lighthouse and designed a new lantern for Trinity House Corporation, 1806. [T.H. MSS., By-minutes 1805–6]

St. Asaph, Flints., Episcopal Palace. Attributed. For Revd. Lewis Bagot, 1792. Stylistic combined with the Bagot connection.

Sandon, Staffs., All Saints. Restoration for first Lord Harrowby, 1782–4. Gothic *(A)*. [A.Scrivener, 'Sandon Church', *North Staffs. Field Club Transactions*, 45 (1910–11)]

Sandon Hall, Staffs. Alterations, new offices, Home Farm for first Lord Harrowby, 1777–84 *(D except farm)*. [Sandon Hall MSS., Drawings, Accounts, first Earl's Shorthand notes, Autobiography of first Earl of Harrowby]

Shugborough, Staffs. Reconstructed house, kitchen garden, five lodges, dairy in the Tower of the Winds, White Barn Farm, Park Farm, cottages at Great Haywood for first Viscount Anson, 1790–1806. [Staffs. R.O., Anson MSS., P615/E(H) 1/3, 2/1–8, Accounts 1763–1768 and 1790–1806]

Sledmere House, E.R. Yorks. Unexecuted design, ?1787. Supplied looking-glasses for Sir Christopher Sykes, 1793. [Sir Christopher Sykes designed Sledmere himself but collected drawings from professional architects. In the library are drawings for the house in different hands, one of which dated 1787 but unsigned is attributable to Samuel Wyatt. The house as completed is obviously influenced by Samuel Wyatt's style]

Soho House, Handsworth, Staffs. Completed reconstruction of the house for Matthew Boulton after James Wyatt failed to give satisfaction, 1798. [BRL, Tew MSS., Correspondence]

Somerley Park, Hants. (A). Unexecuted design, 1785. Revised design, also stables, cottages, lodges, and New Farm for Daniel Hobson, 1792–5. [Drawings at the house]

Stafford, Shire Hall. Samuel Wyatt made the plan, his pupil John Harvey designed the elevation, 1793. [Staffs. R.O., Q/SME/5, Sessions Mins. v]

Sundridge Park, Kent. Completed the house begun by Nash and Repton for Claude Scott, 1796. The whole of the interior, the roof, and probably the dome are by Samuel. He also designed the stables. [W. Angus, *Select Views of Seats* (2nd Ser. 1804)]

Tatton Park, Ches. House, offices, stables, for William Egerton, *c.* 1785–90. Unexecuted designs for Samuel Egerton, *c.* 1774. Unexecuted design for Rostherne Lodge, 1781, and for completing the house for William Egerton, 1806. [Drawings at the house]

Temple House, Berks. (D). For Thomas Williams, 1790. [Farington, 5 Sept. 1805; E.J.Climenson (ed.), *Passages from the Diary of Mrs Lybbe Powis* (1899), 288–9]

Temple Mills, Berks. (D). Additions for Thomas Williams, *c.* 1790. [H.M.Colvin, 'Architectural History of Marlow', *Records of Bucks*, xv (1947), 2]

Thorndon Hall, Essex. Completed the interior of Paine's house and designed Hatch Farm, Lion Lodge, and Octagon Lodge for Lord Petre, 1777–1801. (The interior, including Samuel's Great Hall with eighteen scagliola columns, was burnt in 1878. The farm and lodges survive.) [Essex R.O., Petre MSS., D/DP/P146, Drawing for farm; D/DP/A177, Statement of account]

Tixall House, Staffs. (D). Interior of south wing for Hon. Thomas Clifford, *c.* 1780. [T.Clifford, *Topographical and Historical Description of the Parish of Tixall* (1817)]

Wimbledon Park, Surrey. (D). Converted stables into temporary house and new house for steward for second Earl Spencer, 1790. [Althorp MSS., Drawings and Correspondence]

Winnington Hall, Ches. Poultry-house for first Lord Penrhyn, *c.* 1785 *(D)*. [The house at Winnington is attributed by me to James Wyatt on stylistic grounds. The semicircular poultry-house, however, must have been by Samuel Wyatt. He was working at Winnington in 1785; BRL, Letter to Matthew Boulton]

Wrotham Rectory, Kent. For Revd. George Moore, 1801–2. [C. Greenwood, *Epitome of Kent* (1838)]

Unidentified. Addition of pedimented wings to an older house. [Henry E. Huntington Library, U.S.A., Col. Stowe H.H., LSM 1, 2, 3, Drawings]

10 Thomas Henry Wyatt I
(1807–1880)

This list of works is based on that published in Thomas Henry Wyatt's obituary in *The Builder* on 14 August 1880. Where given as a source this is abbreviated to *Br.* without a date. *Br.* with a date refers to some other more detailed article dealing with a specific building. I have amplified the list from *The Builder*, drawing on other sources such as a MS. list of works executed by the Wyatt and Brandon partnership signed by David Brandon, now in the RIBAD. This is shortened to 'RIBA list' where given as a reference; 'G-R' refers to the Goodhart-Rendel Index of Victorian Churches at the NMR and SDROF indicates that there is a Faculty for Works in the Salisbury Diocesan Record Office. Many of the drawings belonging to Mrs. Janet Don were sold at Sotheby's on 18 November 1976.

Abbeyleix, Co. Leix, Ireland. Alterations to house by James Wyatt for third Viscount de Vesci, *c.* 1860. Classical. [*Br.*]

Abbeyleix, Co. Leix, Ireland. Church for third Viscount de Vesci, *c.* 1860. Gothic with spire and apse. [*Br.*]

Acton Turville, Glos. St. Mary's. 1853. [*Br.*]

Alfpuddle, Dorset, St. Lawrence's. Restoration, n.d. [*Br.*]

All Cannings, Wilts., All Saints. Restoration, n.d. [*Br.*]

Alvediston, Wilts., Parsonage. *c.* 1866. [*Br.*]

Alvediston, Wilts., St. Mary's. Rebuilt Church except for tower, 1866. [*Br.*]

Arley Hall, Ches. (A). Large additions to a house built by J. Lathom (1833) and altered by Salvin (1853) for R. E. Egerton-Warburton, 1860. [*Br.*]

Ascot, Berks. Alterations to house for Admiral Greville, n.d. [*Br.*]

Ashampstead, Berks., Parsonage. With David Brandon. Before 1851. Tudor. [RIBA list]

Atherstone, War., St. Mary's. With David Brandon, 1849. The medieval octagonal crossing tower was retained. [RIBA list]

Baden, Switzerland, All Saints English Church. 1866–7 with a spire. [*Br.*, 28 Sept. 1867]

Badminton, Glos., St. Michael's. Monument to sixth Duke of Beaufort, 1837. Classical white marble tablet carved by John Edwards. [Badminton MSS., Correspondence 1837–8]. New Chancel, 1875. Classical. [*Br.*]

Badminton House, Glos. With David Brandon. Offices and new entrance on W. front for sixth Duke of Beaufort, 1838–51. Classical. [*Br.*]

Barcote Manor, Berks. For the Marchioness of Westminster, 1875. Tudor. [*Br.*]

Basildon Park, Berks. With David Brandon. Minor alterations for J. Morrison. Before 1851. [RIBA list]

Basildon, Berks., St. Bartholomew's. With David Brandon. Restoration. Before 1851. [RIBA list]

Basing, Hants., St. Mary's. Drastic restoration, 1874. [*Br.*]

Basingstoke, Hants, Cottage Hospital. n.d. [*Br.*]

Basingstoke, Hants, Mechanics' Institution. 1866. [RIBAD]

Basingstoke, Hants, School. n.d. [*Br.*]

Bemerton, Wilts., St. John's. Memorial Church to George Herbert for twelfth Earl of Pembroke, 1860–1. Stone with a square tower. [RIBAD; *Br.* (20 Apr. 1861), 266]

Berwick Bassett, Wilts., St. Nicholas's. 1857. [SDROF]

Birkenhead, Ches., St. Aidan's Theological College. Unexecuted design with David Brandon, 1850. [Exhib. RA 1850]. Executed design with Henry Cole, 1854–6. Tudor Gothic. Brick, Asymmetrical. [*Br.*]

Bishop's Cannings, Wilts., St. Mary's. Restoration, 1860. [SDROF]

Bishop's Fonthill, Wilts., All Saints. Restoration, 1879. [*Br.*]

Bishopstone, Wilts., St. John the Baptist. Restoration, 1858. [SDROF]

Bodfari, Flints., Church. 1865. [G-R; L. Brett and E. Beazley, *N. Wales, A Shell Guide* (1971), 126]

Bodmin, St. Petroc's (?). Restoration, 1867. [*Br.* says Bodvan Church but there is no such place and it is probably a misprint for Bodmin]

Borough Green, Cambridgeshire, Parsonage. n.d. [*Br.*]

Bower Chalke, Wilts., Holy Trinity. S. aisle and chancel, 1866. Perp. [*Br.*]

Boyton, Wilts., St. Mary's. Restoration, 1860. [*Br.*; SDROF]

Bratton, Wilts., St. James's. Restoration, 1860. [*Br.*; SDROF]

Bray, Berks., St. Michael's. Restoration and new chancel, 1859. [*Br.*]

Brecon, Cemetery. With David Brandon, 1840. [Exhib. RA 1840]

Brecon Market. n.d. [*Br.*]

Brecon, St. Mary's. Restoration, 1838. [Exhib. RA 1838]

Brecon School. n.d. [*Br.*]

Brecon Shire Hall. 1842. Grecian. [*Br.*]

Bredenbury, Herefordshire, St. Andrew's. 1877. [*Br.*] W. Tower.

Bredenbury Court, Herefordshire. For W. H. Barnaby, 1873. Italianate. [*Br.*]

Bretby, Derby., St. Wystan's. 1877. [*Br.*]

Bretby Park, Derby. Minor alterations for Earl of Chesterfield, n.d. [*Br.*]

Broad Chalke, Wilts., Parsonage. n.d. [*Br.*]

Brockenhurst, Hants, School. c. 1869. [*Br.*]

Brockenhurst House, Hants. Unexecuted design for J. Morant, 1869. [RIBAD; Exhib. RA 1869; *Br.*]

Brookthorpe, Glos., Parsonage. With David Brandon, 1846. [RIBA list]

Broughton Gifford, Wilts., Parsonage. 1848. Jacobean. [*Br.*]

Brown Condover, Hants, St. Peter's. 1845. Flint. Perp. Lead spire. [G-R]

Brymbo, Denbighshire, St. Mary's. 1871–2.

Brymbo, Denbighshire, Parsonage. 1871–2. [*Br.*]

Brynford, Flints., St. Michael's. For Viscount Fielding (later eighth Earl of Denbigh), 1851–2. A part-replacement for Pantasaph after Lord Fielding became a Roman Catholic. *See also* Gorsedd, St. Paul's; Pantasaph. [Coll. Mrs. J. Don, Drawing; *Br.*]

Brynford, Flints., School. c. 1851. [*Br.*]

Bryn Glas, Monmouthshire. Alterations for J. Cordes, M.P., before 1850. [*Br.*]

Buckhorn Weston, Dorset, St. John the Baptist. Restoration, 1861. [SDROF]

Buckland Newton, Dorset, Holy Rood. New E. window, 1870. [*Br.*]

Burbage, Wilts., All Saints. Rebuilt church except tower, 1854. Added Stanton Memorial Aisle, 1876. Flint. Perp. [*Br.*; SDROF]

Burbage, Wilts., Parsonage. 1853. [*Br.*]

Burcombe, Wilts., St. John the Baptist. N. aisle, 1859. [SDROF]

Burr Hill, Surrey. Alterations for F. Bircham, n.d. [*Br.*]

Burton Joyce, Notts, St. Helen's. S. aisle, 1878. [*Br.*]

Cadley, Wilts., Christ Church. For Lord Bruce, 1851–3. Dull except for lively W. front. [*Br.*]

Calne, Wilts. With David Brandon. Unexecuted design for a new church, 1840. [Exhib. RA 1840]

Cambridge, Court House. (D). With David Brandon, 1840–3. Italianate. [RIBAD; RCHM Model; *ILN*, 1 Apr. 1843; *Br.*; Exhib. RA 1842]

Capel Manor, Kent. (D). For Frances Austen, 1859–62. Venetian Gothic in cream, brown and green stone. According to Eastlake the owner exerted considerable influence on the design. [RIBAD; *Br.*; Exhibt. RA 1860]

Carclew, Cornwall. (D). Alterations for Col. Tremayne, n.d. [*Br.*]

Cardiff, Glamorgan, Gaol. n.d. [*Br.*]

Carlett Park, Ches. (D). For John Torr, M.P., 1859–60. Brick. [RIBAD; *Br.*; Exhib. RA 1860]

Cascaes, Lisbon, Portugal. For Duke of Palmella, n.d. [*Br.*]

Castle Caereinion, Montgom., St. Garmon's. Restoration of spire, 1863. [*Br.*, 2 May 1863 n.]

Castle Rising Hall, Norfolk. (D). For Hon. Greville Howard, n.d. [*Br.*]

Cefyn Tylla, Monmouthshire. For first Lord Raglan, 1853. Gothic. [Drawings at house; *Br.*]

Cerne Abbas, Dorset, St. Mary's. Restoration, *c.* 1870. [*Br.*]

Chalk, Kent, St. Mary's. Restoration, *c.* 1860. [*Br.*]

Charlton, nr. Hunton, Wilts., All Saints. 1850–1. Brick. EE. [*Br.*, 3 May 1851]

Chepstow, Monmouthshire, Market. Before 1850. [*Br.*]

Chepstow, Monmouthshire, St. Mary's, Supervised completion of restoration, 1839. [Ex info Mr. H. M. Colvin]

Cherkley Yews, Surrey. For A. Dixon, n.d. [*Br.*]

Childe Okeford, Dorset, St. Nicholas's. With David Brandon. Restoration, 1850, 1878–9. [*Br.*; SDROF]

Chilmark, Wilts., St. Margaret's. With David Brandon. Restoration, 1856. [RIBA list; *Br.*; SDROF]

Chitterne, Wilts., All Saints. 1863. Flint. Perp. Large. [*Br.*]

Chittoe, Wilts., St. Mary's. 1845. Dec. [*Br.*]

Cholderton, Wilts., St. Nicholas's. With David Brandon, 1840–50. Flint with polygonal turret and spire. [*Br.*; Exhib. RA 1842]

Cholsey, Berks., St. Mary's. With David Brandon. Restoration. Before 1851. [RIBA list]

Cirencester Abbey, Glos. (D). Alterations for J. M. Masters, n.d. [*Br.*]

Clarendon Park, Wilts. Ballroom and offices for Sir F. Bathurst, n.d. [*Br.*]

Cobham, Kent, St. Mary Magdalene. Restored the chancel, 1865–6. The chancel arch is by Sir G. G. Scott, 1860. [*Br.*]

Cobham, Kent, Parsonage. c. 1874. [*Br.*]

Cobham, Kent, School. 1874. [*Br.*]

Codford St. Mary, Wilts., St. Mary's. (D). With David Brandon. Restoration, 1843. [SDROF]

Codford St. Peter, Wilts., St. Peter's. Restoration, 1864. [*Br.*]

Colchester, Essex, Essex and Colchester Hospital. Additions, n.d. [*Br.*]

Coombe Bissett, Wilts., St. Michael's. Restoration and New W. front, 1845. [*Br.*]

Corfe Castle, Dorset, St. Edward's. 1859–60. [*Br.*; SDROF]

Corwen, Merioneth, Church. n.d. [*Br.*]

Craig-y-nos, Breconshire. With David Brandon for Rhys D. Powell, 1847. [Exhib. RA 1847]

Cranmore Hall, Somerset. For Sir R. H. Paget, *c.* 1866. [*Br.*]

Crewkerne, Somerset. With David Brandon. House for Mr. Hoskins. Before 1851. [RIBA list]

Crickhowell, Breconshire, Town Hall. 1833–4. Italianate. [*Br.*]

Crockerton, Wilts., Holy Trinity. With David Brandon, 1843. Norman. Large. [*Br.*; Exhib. RA 1842]

Croxteth Hall, Lancs. New wing for fourth Earl of Sefton, 1874. [Coll. Mrs. J. Don, Drawing; RIBAD; *Br.*]

Dalton, Lancs., St. Michael's. 1875–76. Tower with saddle-back roof. [*Br.*]

Dawlish, Devon. Unidentified house, n.d. [Coll. Mrs. J. Don, Drawing]

Deene, Northants, St. Peter's. 1868–9. Ornate EE [*Br*, 6 Nov. 1869]

Deene Park, Northants. Ballroom wing and lodge for Earl of Cardigan, c. 1850–63. Interior decoration of Ballroom by Crace. [Northants R.O., Brudenell MSS., Drawings and accounts (ex info Mr. J. Cornforth); Coll. Mrs. J. Don, Drawing for lodge; *Br.*; Exhib. RA 1850]

Derry Hill, Wilts., Christ Church. With David Brandon for third Marquess of Lansdowne, 1839–40. Perp. W. tower with spire. [Bowood MSS.]

Devizes, Wilts., Assize Court. 1835. Grecian. [*Br.*; Exhib. RA 1835]

Devizes, Wilts., Roundway Hospital. With David Brandon, 1851. Italianate. [Coll. Mrs. J. Don, Drawing; RIBA list]

Devizes, Wilts., St. Mary's. Chancel restoration, 1875–6. [*VCH Wilts.* x (1975), 172]

Devizes, Wilts., Wiltshire Barracks, Militia Store. 1856. [*Br.*]

Dewlish, Dorset, All Saints. S. aisle, 1872. [*Br.*]

Didmarton, Glos., St. Michael's. 1871–2. EE. [*Br.* (26 Oct. 1872), 852]

Dilton, Wilts., School. 1844. [*Br.*]
Dilton Marsh, Wilts., Holy Trinity. 1844. Norman [G-R]

Dingestow, Monmouthshire, Church. New tower, 1846. [Ex info Mr. H. M. Colvin]

Ditton, Lancs., St. Michael and All Saints. 1875. [*BN*, 12 Nov. 1875]

Dodington Park, Glos. Unexecuted design for Ball-room for Sir John Codrington, n.d. [Gloucester R.O., Codrington MSS.]

Downing, Flints. With David Brandon. Cottages for Viscount Fielding. Before 1851. [RIBAD]

Downing, Flints. Alterations to house for Viscount Fielding, 1858. [*Br.*; Exhib. RA 1858]

Downton, Wilts., St. Lawrence's. Restoration, 1858. [*Br.*; SDROF]

Dublin, Palmerston House. For Earl of Mayo, n.d. [*Br.*]

Dublin, St. Bartholomew's. 1865. [*Br.* (10 May 1865), 314]

Dunmore, Stirling, Church. n.d. [*Br.*]

Dyrham, Glos., St. Peter's. Restoration. [*Br.*]

East Cranmore, Somerset, St. James's. 1846. Small spire. [*Eccl.* vi (Nov. 1846), 193; *Br.* calls it West Cranmore]

East Harnham, Wilts., All Saints. 1852–4. [Coll. Mrs. J. Don, Drawing; RIBAD.; *Br.*]

East Harnham, Wilts., School. c. 1852. [RIBAD; *Br.*]

East Woodham, Hants, School. With David Brandon, 1849. [*Br.*]

East Woodham, St. Thomas's. With David Brandon, 1849. With spire [Coll. Mrs. J. Don, Drawing; *ILN* 20 Oct. 1849]

Erryrys, Montgom., St. David's. 1864. [*Br.*]

Estcourt House, Glos. (D). Alterations, including new Billiard Room, for Rt. Hon. T. S. Estcourt, *c.* 1864. [*Br.*]

Evancoyd, Radnor. For B. Mynors, *c.* 1870. [*Br.*]

Evancoyd, Radnor, St. Peter's. For B. Mynors, 1870. [*Br.*, 1 Oct. 1870]

Fairholme, Surrey. Alterations for H. Rogers, n.d. [*Br.*]

Fisherton, Wilts., St. Paul's. With David Brandon, 1851–3. With tower. [*Br.*, 1 Mar. 1851; SDROF]

Florence, Italy, Railway Station. (D). With David Brandon, 1847. [RIBAD; *Br.*; Exhib. RA 1847]

Fonthill House, Wilts. (D). With David Brandon for James Morrison, 1847. Italianate. [V & A, Print Room, A174, Drawings; *Br.*; Exhib. RA 1847] Not to be confused with Fonthill Abbey by Burn.

Fonthill Gifford, Wilts., Holy Trinity. For second

Marquess of Westminster, 1866. Large with NE spire. [Coll. Mrs. J.Don, Drawing; *Br.* (23 June 1866), 472; Exhib. RA 1864]

Fovant, Wilts., St., George's. Restoration, 1863. [*Br.*]

Glanogwen, Caernarvonshire, Christ Church. 1855–6. With spire. [*Br.*]

Glyndyfrdwy, Monmouthshire, St. Thomas's. 1859. [G-R]

Glyntaff, Glamorgan, SS. Mary and Luke. 1838–41. With tower. [G-R]

Goring, Oxon., St. Thomas of Canterbury. With David Brandon. Restoration. Before 1851. [RIBA list]

Gorsedd, Flints., St. Paul's. For Viscount Fielding, 1852–3. A part-replacement for Pantasaph after Lord Fielding became a Roman Catholic. *See also* Brynford, Pantasaph. [Coll. Mrs. J.Don, Drawing; *Br.*]

Gorsedd, Flints., School. c. 1852. [*Br.*]

Govilon, Monmouthshire, Church. 1847. [Ex info. Mr. H.M.Colvin]

Goytrey, Monmouthshire, National School. 1872. [Ex info Mr.H.M.Colvin]

Gravely, Breconshire, School. n.d. [*Br.*]

Great Bedwyn, Wilts., St. Mary's. Restoration for second Marquess of Ailesbury, 1853–4. [*Eccl.* xiv (1 Oct. 1853), 380; *Br.* says Little Bedwyn]

Greensted, Sussex, St. Andrew's. With David Brandon. Brick plinth for log walls, 1848. [*Br.*, 10 Mar. 1849]

Harewood Lodge, Berks. Alterations for Revd. N.J.Ridley, n.d. [*Br.*]

The Hendre, Monmouthshire. Extensive additions for J.A.Rolls, M.P., 1870–2. Red brick, Tudor Gothic. [Monmouth R.O., Correspondence and Drawings by Pope, T.H.Wyatt's clerk; Coll. Mrs. J.Don, Drawing; *Br.*]

Hensol Castle, Glamorgan. With David Brandon for Rowland Fothergill, 1848. [RIBA list; Exhib. RA 1848]

High Legh, Ches. (D). Alterations for Col. Legh, n.d. [*Br.*]

Hilperton, Wilts., St. Michael's. 1852. Dec. Undistinguished. [*Br.*, 8 Jan. 1853; SDROF]

Hindon, Wilts., St. John the Baptist. For Dowager Marchioness of Westminster, 1870–71. Reduced and less successful version of Fonthill Gifford. [*Br.*, 26 Mar. 1870; 29 July 1871]

The Hole, Kent. With David Brandon. Before 1851. [RIBA list]

Holt, Dorset, St. James's. Chancel, 1875. [*Br.*]

Homington, Wilts., St. Mary's. Drastic restoration, 1860. [SDROF]

Honor Oak, Kent. Alterations for M.C.Marquardt, n.d. [*Br.*]

Horningsham, Wilts., St. John the Baptist. With David Brandon. Rebuilt the church except W. tower, 1844. Perp. [RIBA list; *Br.*]

Horringer, Suffolk, Parsonage. n.d. [*Br.*]

Horsmonden, Kent, St. Margaret's. Restoration, 1867. [*Br.*]

Houghton, Huntingdonshire, St. Mary's. With David Brandon. Restoration. Before 1851. [RIBA list]

Hull, E.R. Yorks. Seamen's and General Orphan Asylum. (*D*). n.d. [*Br.*]

Humber, Herefordshire, St. Mary's. Restoration, 1876–8. [*Br.*, 23 Dec. 1876]

Iwerne Minster, Dorset, St. Mary's. Restoration, 1870. [*Br.*]

Jedburgh, Roxburghshire, Church. n.d. [Coll. Mrs. J.Don, Drawing; *Br.*]

Jedburgh, Roxburghshire, Parsonage. n.d. [*Br.*]

Kempshott Park, Hants. Alterations for Sir Nelson Rycroft, n.d. [*Br.*]

Kiplin Hall, N.R. Yorks. Alterations, including the wing which destroys the symmetry of the house, 1874. [*Br.*]

Langton, Dorset, All Saints. 1861. Large with trancepts. Flin, [*Br.*]

Languard, Isle of Wight. Alterations for Col. Atherley, n.d. [*Br.*]

Lathom House, Lancs. (D). Alterations, including new dining-room and addition of second storey to centre, for first Earl of Lathom, 1860. Classical. [NMR, Copies of correspondence; *Br.*; Exhib. RA 1860]

Laverstock, Wilts., St. Andrew's. 1858. [Coll. Mrs. J.Don, Drawing; *Br.*, 24 July 1868; SDROF]

Little Bedwyn, Wilts., St. Michael's. Restoration, n.d. [*Br.*]

Little Langford, Wilts., Parsonage. c. 1864. [*Br.*]

Little Langford, Wilts., St. Nicholas's. 1864. *Some old fragments incorporated*. [*Br.*]

Littleton Drew, Wilts., All Saints. 1856. Perp. Old tower incorporated. [RIBAD, dated September 1855]

Liverpool, Lancs., Exchange Flags, Exchange Buildings. (*D*). 1863–7. Italianate. Replaced James Wyatt's. [RIBAD; *Br.* (20 Jan. 1866), 47; Exhib. RA 1864, 1867]

Llandaff, Glamorgan, Cathedral of S.S. Peter and Paul. Restoration 1840–5. [RIBAD, Sketches of medieval details dated 1845; *Br.*]

Llandogo Priory, Monmouthshire. With David Brandon for John Gough, 1838. [*Br.*; Exhib. RA 1838]

Llandyssil, Montgom., St. Tyssil. 1863–5. [Coll. Mrs. J. Don, Drawings; G-R]

Llandyssil, Montgom., School and Teacher's House. c. 1863. [Coll. Mrs. J. Don, Drawing; *Br.*]

Llangattock, Monmouthshire, Church. Restoration for J. A. Rolls, 1875. [*Br.*]

Llangattock Manor, Monmouthshire. Alterations for J. A. Rolls, 1877. [*Br.*; Exhib. RA 1877]

Llangattock Park, Breconshire. Shooting-box for seventh Duke of Beaufort, 1837–8. Tudor. [Badminton MSS., Correspondence; *Br.*; Exhib. RA 1838]

Llantarnam Abbey, Monmouthshire. For R. S. Blewitt, 1834–5. Faced in Bath stone. Tudor. Details derived from Thornbury. [*Br.*; Exhib. RA 1835]

Llanvihangel, Monmouthshire, Church. Restoration, n.d. [*Br.*]

Londesborough, E.R. Yorks., All Saints. Restoration, n.d. [*Br.*]

London, Adelphi Theatre. 'Ably assisted by one of his former pupils Mr. Stephen Salter'. Interior decoration by Matthew Digby Wyatt, 1858. [RIBAD; *Br.*, 25 Dec. 1858; RIBA list]

London, Athenaeum Club. (*A*). Alterations, including subterranean smoking-room, billiard room, and servant's hall, 1865–8. He was Honorary Architect to the Club from 1864 to 1880. [*LS* xxix (1960), 396]

London, 2 Audley Square. House for Lord Arthur Russell, M.P., n.d. [*Br.*]

London, Brompton Hospital for Consumption. Additions, 1879–82. Tudor. Assisted by Matthew Wyatt III. [RIBAD; *Br.*; Exhib. RA 1879]

London, 16 Bruton Street. (*D*). Alterations for fourth Earl of Carnarvon, *c.* 1873. [*Br.*]

London, Devonshire Club. Minor alterations, n.d. [*Br.*]

London, Governesses Benevolent Institution, Kentish Town. With David Brandon, 1848. [*Br.*, 10 June 1848 n.; RIBA list]

London, 39 Hill Street. (*D*). Alterations for second Earl of Durham, n.d. [*Br.*]

London, Holy Trinity, Clarence Way. (*A*). With David Brandon, 1847–50. Kentish rag. Originally tall SW. spire. [RIBAD.; Coll. Mrs. J. Don, Drawing; *Eccl.* xi (Oct. 1850), 197; xvi (Apr. 1855), 111–16; Exhib. RA 1850]

London, Holy Trinity Schools, Clarence Way. (*A*). *c.* 1850. [Coll. Mrs. J. Don, Drawing]

London, Institution of Civil Engineers, George Street, Westminster. (*D*). Alterations with David Brandon. Before 1851. [RIBAD; RIBA list]

London, Kensington Palace Gardens. With David Brandon.
  6, 7. For John Blashfield, 1844–6.
  N. Gate, lodges. For John Blashfield, 1845.
  S. Gate, lodges. Completed after Blashfield's bankruptcy, 1849.
  16. For John Sperling, 1846–9.
  25 and 26. (*D*). For John Blashfield, 1844.
(Kensington and Chelsea Library, Drawing for N. Gate lodges; Exhib. RA 1845; PRO, MPE, 1181; *LS*, xxxvii (1973), 154, 156, 163, 178, 184]

London, King's College Hospital. Unexecuted competition design, 1851. [Ex info Dr. J. M. Crook]

London, Knightsbridge Barracks. (*D*). unexecuted competition design with Matthew Digby Wyatt, *c.* 1855. Executed design 1878–9. [*Br.* (2 Feb. 1878), 112; Exhib. RA 1877]

London, Lansdowne House, Berkeley Square. Alterations, including new gallery adjoining Sculpture Gallery, for third Marquess of Lansdowne, n.d. [*Br.*]

London, Literary Institute, Southwark. With David Brandon. Before 1851. [RIBA list]

London, Mark Lane, Corn Exchange. Unexecuted

competition design with Stephen Salter, jun., 1870. [Ex info Dr. J.M.Crook]

London, Middlesex Hospital. (*D*). With David Brandon. Alterations, including top storey, porch, extensions to wings and conversion of two-seater lavatories to single-seaters, 1842–9. [Hospital MSS., Drawings and Minutes]

London, Osnaburgh Street Cancer Hospital. (*D*). Alterations, n.d. [*Br.*]

London, 77 and 78 Pall Mall. Two houses converted into one and substantially remodelled for Marquess of Ailesbury, 1862. [*Br.*; *LS* xxix (1960), 418]

London, Park Lane, Brook House. (*D*). For Sir Dudley Coutts Marjoribanks, M.P., 1867–70. [Drawing sold at Sotheby's, 23 Mar. 1976; *Br.*, 23 July 1870; Exhib. Paris 1878]

London, Polytechnic Institution. n.d. Unidentified. [*Br.*]

London, 41 Portland Place. Alterations for first Earl of Latham, n.d. [*Br.*]

London, Portman Square, Montagu House. (*D*). Alterations for Hon. W.B.Portman, n.d. [*Br.*]

London, 38 Queen Anne's Gate (formerly 15 Queen Square). (*D*). House for Sir Charles Forster, M.P., n.d. [*Br.*]

London, Royal Exchange. With David Brandon. Unexecuted competition design, 1840. [Exhib. RA 1840]

London, St. Andrew's, Bethnal Green. (*D*). With David Brandon, 1840–1. [*Eccl.* i (Aug..1842), 195–6; Exhib. RA 1842]

London, St. Luke's Hospital. n.d. [*Br.*]

London, St. Mark's, Goodman's Fields, Stepney. (*D*). With David Brandon, 1838–9. [Ex info Dr. J.M.Crook]

London, St. Mary's Hospital. With David Brandon. Alterations and additions. Before 1851. [RIBA list; *Br.*]

London, St. Matthias's, Bethnal Green. (*D*). With David Brandon, 1846–7. Lombardic, cheap, brick. [Coll. Mrs. J.Don, Drawing; *Eccl.* viii (June 1848), 392]

London, Stockwell Fever Hospital. New wing, n.d. [*Br.*]

London, Stockwell Smallpox Hospital. 1869. [*Br.*]

London, 19 Stratford Place. (*D*). Alterations for first Lord Ampthill, n.d. [*Br.*]

London, Tower Hamlets' Cemetery. (*D*). With David Brandon. Dissenters' and Anglican Chapels, 1847–9. [*Eccl.* vii (Mar. 1847), 205; *ILN*, 24 Mar. 1849; Exhib. RA 1847]

London, 1–5 Upper Berkeley Street. (*D*). House for Sir Baldwin Leighton, M.P. Designed 1871–3. [RIBAD.; *Architect* i. v. 1875; *Br.*]

London, Whitehall. Unexecuted design for addition to Banqueting House on site of Gwydir House with Matthew Digby Wyatt, 1844. [RIBAD.; Exhib. RA 1844] Unexecuted designs for Government Offices, 1855. [Ex info Dr. J.M.Crook]

London, 15 Whitehall Place. With David Brandon. Alterations for Sir John Rennie, 1846. [G.L. R.O., MBO Plans, 315–18]

London, 30 Wilton Crescent. Alterations for twelfth Earl of Kinnoull, n.d. [*Br.*]

Long Newton, Glos., Holy Trinity. 1841 and 1870. Old tower retained. [*Br.*]

Lullington, Somerset, All Saints. Restoration, c. 1862. [*Br.*]

Lullington, Somerset, School. For William Duckworth, n.d. [RIBAD.; *Br.*]

Lysways Hall, Staffs. Alterations for Sir Charles Forster, M.P., n.d. [*Br.*]

Lydney Park, Glos. Alterations for Revd. W.Bathurst. Before 1877. [*Br.*]

Lypiatt Park, Glos. New wing for J.E.Dorrington, 1876. [*Br.*]

Malpas Court, Monmouthshire. For Thomas Prothero, 1838. [*Br.*; Exhib. RA 1838]

Malshanger Park, Hants. For Wyndham Portal, n.d. [*Br.*]

Malta, Asylum for the Aged and Infirm. n.d. [Mrs. J.Don, Drawing]

Malta, Hospital for Incurables. n.d. [Mrs. J.Don, drawing; *Br.*]

Malverleys, Berks. For J.Forster, n.d. [*Br.*]

Manchester, Lancs., Town Hall. Unexecuted competition design, 1867–8. [Ex info Dr. J.M.Crook]

March, Cambridgeshire, St. John's. 1872. Rock-faced. [*Br.*]

March, Cambridgeshire, St. Peter's. 1880. [G-R]

Marlborough, Wilts., S.S. Peter and Paul. Remodelled chanel, 1862–3. [*Br.*]

Market Lavington, Wilts. St. Mary. Restoration, 1857. [SDROF]

Martin, Lincs., Holy Trinity. 1876. Polygonal apse and transepts. [G-R]

Melksham, Wilts., St. Michael's. With David Brandon. Restoration, 1845. [*Br.*: SDROF]

Mere, Wilts., St. Michael's. Restoration, c. 1865. [*Br.*; SDROF]

Merthyr Tydfil, Glamorgan, St. David's. With David Brandon, 1846–7. [RIBA list; *Br.*; Exhib. RA 1842]

Merthyr Tydfil, Glamorgan, Market. 1838. [*Br.*; Exhib. RA 1838]

Monkton Deverill, Wilts., St. Alfred the Great. 1845. Old tower retained. [G-R]

Monmouth, Club. n.d. [*Br.*]

Monmouth, Gaol. n.d. [*Br.*]

Morecombelake, Dorset, St. Gabriel's. With David Brandon, 1841. Nave and chancel in one. Bellcote. [G-R]

Moreton-in-Marsh. Glos. Alterations to house for Major Bird, n.d. [*Br.*]

Nannerch, Flints., St. Michael's. 1853. [RIBAD.; *Br.*]

Nantleys, Flints., St. Asaph's. For P.P. Pennant, n.d. [*Br.*]

Nettlebed, Oxon., St. Bartholomew's. Alterations, 1872. [*Br.*]

Newbridge, Monmouthshire, Church. 1836. [Ex info Mr. H. M. Colvin]

Newnham Paddox, War. (D). Alterations, including addition of mansard roofs, for eighth Earl of Denbigh, 1875. [*Br.*]

Newnham Paddox, War., R.C. Chapel of the Sacred Heart. For eighth Earl of Denbigh, 1877–80. [*Br.*; Exhib. RA 1877]

Newport, Monmouthshire, Market. (D). n.d. [*Br.*]

Newport, Monmouthshire, St. Paul's. 1835. [Exhib. RA 1835]

Newport, Monmouthshire, Workhouse. 1837. [Ex info Mr. H. M. Colvin]

Newton Tony, Wilts., St. Andrew's. With David Brandon, 1844. Flint. Dec. SW. spire. [*Br.*; SDROF]

North Bradley, Wilts., St. Nicholas's. 1862. Large. Some old bits retained. [*Br.*]

North Perrott Manor, Somerset. Attributed. For H.W. Hoskyns, 1878. Jacobean. Now called Beaminster Court.

Norwich, Norfolk, Norwich and Norfolk Hospital. Consultant architect to new wing by E. Boardman, 1879. [*BN*, 13 June 1879; *Br.*]

Nunton, Wilts., St. Andrew's. 1854–5. Some old bits retained. [SDROF]

Oakley, Hants, St. Leonard's. 1869. Perp. SW. tower. [Coll. Mrs. J. Don, Drawing; *Br.*]

Oakley Hall, Hants, for W.W. Beach, M.P., n.d. [*Br.*]

Oatlands Park, Surrey. With David Brandon. Converted it into a hotel, 1856. Yellow brick, Italianate with a tower. [RIBA list; *Br.*]

Odiham Priory, Hants. Alterations for Rt. Hon. G. Sclater-Booth, n.d. [*Br.*]

Ogbourne St. George, Wilts., St. George's. Restoration, 1873. [*Br.*]

Old Sodbury, Glos., St. John the Baptist. Restoration, 1858. [*Br.*]

Orchardleigh Park, Somerset. For William Duckworth, 1855–8. Mixed Elizabethan. [*Br.*, 19 Apr. 1855; Exhib. RA 1858]

(*Otterbourne, Hants, St. Matthew's. Attributed.* 1875. [Paul Ferriday Index])

Pantasaph, Flints., St. David's. For Viscount Fielding, 1849. Begun as an Anglican Church but converted into a Catholic one on Lord Fielding's conversion to Roman Catholicism. Interior completed by Pugin. *See also* Brynford; Gorsedd, St. Paul's. [*Br.*]

Pensandane, Cornwall. Alterations for R. F. Bolitho, n.d. [*Br.*]

Pixton, Somerset. Minor alterations for fourth Earl of Carnarvon, n.d. [*Br.*]

Plaitford, Hants, Parsonage. n.d. [*Br.*]

Poland. Mansion for Prince Woronzoff, n.d. [*Br.*]

Pontryffydd, N. Wales. Alterations for Captain Mesham, n.d. [*Br.*]

Pontypool, Monmouthshire, St. James' Chapel. Enlarged, 1854. [Ex info Mr. H. M. Colvin]

Portland Lodge, Dorset. Alterations for H.Vizard, n.d. [*Br.*]

Preshute, Wilts., St. George's. 1854. Old tower retained. [*Br.*; SDROF]

Prestatyn, Flints., Christchurch. 1863. [*Br.*]

Prestatyn, Flints., Parsonage. c. 1863. [*Br.*]

Presteign, Dorset, St. Andrew's. Restoration, 1855. [*Br.*; SDROF]

Raglan, Monmouthshire, Church. Restoration, 1868. [*Br.*]

Ramsfort, Ireland. For Mr. S.Ram, n.d. [*Br.*]

Rhydymwyn, Denbighshire, Parsonage. n.d. [*Br.*]

Ringwood, Hants, Corn Exchange. 1867–8. [*Br.*, 11 July 1868]

Ringwood, Hants, Town Hall. (D). n.d. [*Br.*]

Rood Ashton House, Wilts., West lodge. For Richard Long, *c.* 1847. [*VCH Wilts.* viii (1965), 204]

Rotherwick, Hants, Church. Chancel 1865, N. aisle 1876. [*Br.*]

Salisbury, Wilts., Infirmary. Additions, 1868. [*Br.*]

Salisbury, Wilts., St. Paul's. 1851–3. SW. tower, 'in style of *c.* 1300'. [*VCH Wilts.* vi (1962), 192]

Savernake, Wilts., St. Katherine's. For the Marchioness of Ailesbury, 1860. Transepts and apse. Spire. Flint. thirteenth-century details. [RIBAD; Exhib. RA 1860]

Seaborough Court, Dorset. Attributed. 1877. [*BoE*]

Semley, Wilts., St. Leonard's. For Marchioness of Westminster, 1866. Aisles. High W. tower. [Coll. Mrs. J.Don, Drawing]

Sevenoaks, Kent, Crown Hotel. n.d. [*Br.*]

Shaftesbury, Dorset, St. James's. 1866–7. W. tower. Dec. to Perp. [*Br.*]

Shaw, Wilts., Christ Church. (D). 1836–8. [G-R]

Shelford, Notts, St. Peter's. Restoration, 1874–5. [Coll. Mrs. J.Don, Drawing; *Br.*]

Sherston, Wilts., Holy Cross. Restoration, n.d. [*Br.*]

Shipton Moyne, Glos., Parsonage. c. 1864. [*Br.*]

Shipton Moyne, Glos., St. John the Baptist. Rebuilt the church retaining old bits, 1864–5. EE, SW. tower. Pulpit. Italianate with reliefs by A. Barbetti of Florence. Estcourt Chapel. Railing. Monument to

Eleanor Estcourt †1829. Neo-Greek. Carved by Joseph Edwards. [*Br.*]

Shirburn, Oxon., All Saints. Restoration for sixth Earl of Macclesfield, 1876. [*Br.*; *VCH Oxon.* viii (1964), 196]

Shorne, Kent, S.S. Peter and Paul. Restoration, 1874–5. [*Br.*]

Shrewsbury, Royal Salop Infirmary. Additions, n.d. [*Br.*]

Shrewton, Wilts., St. Mary's. 1855. Perp. Some old bits retained. [Coll. Mrs. J.Don, Drawing; *Br.*; SDROF]

Silchester, Hants., St. Mary's. Restoration, n.d. [*Br.*]

Sopworth, Wilts., St. Mary's. Restoration, 1871. [*Br.*]

South Moreton, Berks., St. John the Baptist. With David Brandon. Restoration. Before 1851. [RIBA list]

South Newton, Wilts., Parsonage. c. 1862. [*Br.*]

South Newton, Wilts., St. Andrew's. 1862. Perp. Tower with pyramid roof. [*Br.*]

Spetisbury, Dorset, St. John the Baptist. 1859. [*Br.*; SDROF]

Stalbridge, Dorset, St. Mary's. 1878. Old bits retained. [*Br.*]

Stansfield Lodge, Kent. Alterations for Mrs. Duncan, n.d. [*Br.*]

Stanton Lacy, Salop, St. Peter's. Restoration, 1847–9. [Kelly, *Directory*]

Star Cross. n.d. Unidentified Italianate house. [Coll. Mrs. J.Don, Drawing]

Stone, Bucks., St. John's Hospital. With David Brandon, 1850–3. Brick. Italianate. [RIBA list]

Stourpaine, Dorset, Holy Trinity. 1858. Old tower kept. [*Br.*; SDROF]

Stourpaine, Dorset, Parsonage. c. 1858. [*Br.*]

Sutton Court, Somerset. Restoration for Sir E.Strachey, 1858. [Drawings at the house; *Br.*]

Sutton Mandeville, Wilts., All Saints. 1862. Old tower kept. [G-R]

Sutton Waldron, Dorset, St. Bartholomew's. Restoration. Before 1847. [*Br.*]

Swainston, Isle of Wight. Alterations for Sir Barrington Simeon, n.d. [*Br.*]

Swanage, Dorset, St. Mary's. Nave, chancel, and S. transept, 1859–60. [*Br.*; SDROF]

Swansea, Glamorgan, Gaol. Additions, n.d. [*Br.*]

Swansea, Glamorgan, School. With David Brandon. Before 1851. [RIBA list]

Sydmonton Court, Hants. Alterations for W. H. Kingsmill, n.d. [*Br.*]

Tanfield, Yorks., Church. Restoration, n.d. [*Br.*]

Tarrant Gunville, Dorset, St. Mary's. 1844–5. Flint. Old tower kept. [*Br.*]

Tarrant Keynston, Dorset, All Saints. N. aisle, 1852–3. [*Br.*; SDROF]

Tetbury, Glos., Cottage Hospital. (*D*). n.d. [*Br.*]

Tilgate, Sussex. (*D*). For G. Ashbourner, n.d. [*Br.*]

Tilshead, Wilts. With David Brandon, 1845. [SDROF]

Tingleton, Dorset, Parsonage. n.d. [*Br.*]

Tixall, Staffs., St. John's. With David Brandon for Hon. J. C. Talbot, 1849. Stone with bellcote, small. [RIBA list]

Tolpuddle, Dorset, Parsonage. c. 1855. [RIBAD]

Tolpuddle, Dorset, St. John the Evangelist. Remodelled chancel, 1855. [RIBAD.; *Br.*; SDROF]

Tormarton, Glos., St. Mary Magdalene. Restoration, including E. window, S. porch, and vestry, 1853–4. [*Br.*]

Trelawne, Cornwall. Additions for Sir J. Trelawney, n.d. [*Br.*]

Trevithin, Monmouthshire, Church. Extensive restoration amounting to almost total rebuilding, 1845. [*Br.*]

Treuddyn, Flints., St. Mary's. 1875. [*Br.*]

Tunbridge Wells, Kent. House for Lady Selina Bidwell, n.d. [*Br.*]

Upavon, Wilts., St. Mary's. Restoration of chancel, 1875. [*Br.*]

Upton Scudamore, Wilts., Parsonage. 1848. [*Br.*]

Usk, Monmouthshire, Assize Court (Sessions House). 1875. [*Br.*]

Usk, Monmouthshire, Church. Restoration, 1844. Also designed Sir Matthew Digby Wyatt's grave in churchyard, *c.* 1877. [*Br.*]

Usk, Monmouthshire Gaol. 1840. [*Br.*]

Usk, Monmouthshire, Town Hall. Consulted about building a new one in 1855 but not executed. [Ex info Mr. H. M. Colvin]

Warminster, Wilts., Christ Church. New chancel, 1871. [*Br.*]

Warminster, Wilts., Lecture-Hall. n.d. [*Br.*]

Warminster, Wilts., Market. For fourth Marquess of Bath, 1855. [*VCH Wilts.* viii (1965), 116; *Br.*]

Warminster, Wilts., School. n.d. [*Br.*]

Wednesfield, Staffs., St. Thomas's. (*D*). With David Brandon. Chancel, 1842–3. [G-R]

Wellesbourne, War., St. Peter's. Attributed. 1873. [Kelly's *Directory* say 'Wyatt']

West Ashton, Wilts., St. John the Evangelist. With David Brandon, 1846. Perp. NW. tower and spire. [Coll. Mrs. J. Don, Drawing]

Westbury, Wilts., All Saints. W. window, etc., 1847. [*Br.* says Whitsbury]

Westbury, Wilts., School. c. 1847. [*Br.*]

West Littleton, Glos., St. James's. 1855. Perp. Some old bits kept. [*BoE*]

West Orchard, Dorset, Church. 1876–7. Small with bellcote. [*Br.*]

Westerdale Hall, N.R. Yorks. 1844. Baronial with stepped gables and tower. [RIBAD]

Weston Patrick, Hants, Parsonage. c. 1868. [*Br.*]

Weston Patrick, Hants, St. Lawrence's. 1868. Flint with a bell turret. His own church built largely at his own expense. The E. window is a memorial to his parents. [Coll. Mrs. J. Don, Model; *Br.*]

Whorlton-in-Cleveland, N.R. Yorks., Holy Cross. 1877. Large with spire. [*Br.*]

Wilsford, Wilts., St. Michael's. 1851. Old tower kept. [*Br.*; SDROF]

Wilton House, Wilts. With David Brandon. Minor alterations for twelfth Earl of Pembroke. Before 1851. [RIBA list]

Wilton, Wilts., S.S. Mary and Nicholas. 1840–5. Lombardic. [RIBAD; *Eccl.* ii (Oct. 1842), 20; vi (Nov. 1846), 169–74; Exhib. RA 1840, 1843]

Wimblington, Cambridgeshire, St. Mary-in-the-Fen. 1872. [RIBAD; *Br.*]

Wimblington, Cambridgeshire, St. Peter's. 1872–4. [RIBAD; *Br.*]

Wimborne Minster, Dorset. Restoration of the Minster, 1855–7. [*Br.*; SDROF; Exhib. RA 1858]

Winchester, Hants, Castle. Restored Great Hall and renewed the roof. Added the Assize Courts, 1873. [RIBAD; Coll. Mrs. J. Don, Drawings dated 1871; *Br.*]

Winterborne Earls, Wilts., St. Michael's. 1867–8. Flint. Perp. to EE. Tower. [*Br.*, 13 July 1867]

Winterborne Houghton, Dorset, St. Andrew's. 1861–2. Flint. Perp. [*Br.*; SDROF]

Winterborne Steepleton, Dorset, Manor. For W. C. Lambert, 1870. Tudor. [Coll. Mrs. J. Don, Drawing; *Br.*]

Winterborne Zelston, Dorset, St. Mary's. 1865–6. Flint. Old tower kept. [*Br.*]

Winterslow, Wilts., All Saints. With David Brandon. Restoration, 1849. [*Br.*; SDROF]

Wishford Magna, Wilts., St. Giles's. 1863–4. Old bits kept. [*Br.*]

Wolverton, Bucks., St. George the Martyr. With David Brandon, 1843–4. Large. EE. Small spire. [RIBA list; *Eccl.* vii (Mar. 1847), 115]

Woodborough, Wilts., St. Mary Magdalen. 1850 and 1861. [*Br.*, 15 Feb. 1862]

Woodford, Wilts., All Saints. 1845. [*Br.*]

Woodsford, Dorset, Parsonage. 1857. [SDROF Mortgage]

Woodsford, Dorset, St. John the Evangelist. 1861–2. EE. Old bits kept. [SDROF]

(*Woolton Hill, Hants, St. Thomas's. Attributed.* 1849. Flint. NE. spire. [G-R]

Woolwich, Garrison Church of St. George's. 1862–3. Built when Sidney Herbert was Secretary of State for War. Assisted by Sir Matthew Digby Wyatt. Lombardic. [*Br.*, 17 May 1862; *ILN*, 21 Feb. 1863]

Woolwich, Royal Military Barracks. Recreation Hall, Theatre, and Mess Rooms, n.d. [*Br.*]

Worminghall, Bucks., S.S. Peter and Paul. Restoration, 1847. [*Br.*]

Worton, Wilts., Christ Church. With David Brandon, 1843. Dec. with ogee capped bellcote. [*Br.*]

Wroughton, Wilts., St. John the Baptist and St. Helen's. Restoration, 1846. [*Br.*]

Wyle, Wilts., St. Mary's. With David Brandon. Partial rebuilding, 1844–6. [*Br.*; SDROF]

Unidentified House in Breconshire. c. 1845. [Coll. Mrs. J. Don, Drawing]

Unidentified Reformatory School in Wilts. [RIBAD]

11 Sir Jeffry Wyatville

(1766–1840)

Abingdon, Berks., Gaol. Built by Daniel Harris to Wyatville's designs, 1805–11. [Linstrum, 258]

Allendale House, Dorset. For William Castleman, 1823. [H. Ashton, *Illustrations of Windsor Castle* (1841)]

Ashridge, Herts. Additions to house, estate buildings, and Bridgewater Column for seventh Earl of Bridgewater, 1803–39. [RIBAD; Mellon Coll., Drawings for lodges; Herts. R.O., AH 2495–2684, Correspondence; Exhib. RA 1816 and 1817]

Badminton, Glos. Alterations, 1809–13. [Mellon Coll., Sketch of E. front; Building Accounts at house; Exhib. RA 1811]

Banner Cross, W.R. Yorks. For Revd. William Bagshawe, 1817–21. Tudor Gothic. [Mellon Coll., Drawings; Sheffield City Library, AP/53/1–5, Drawings; Rylands, Bagshawe MSS., 6/1/342–386, Building Accounts, etc.]

Belton, Lincs, S.S. Peter and Paul. Mortuary Chapel for first Earl Brownlow, 1816. [Exhib. RA 1816]

Belton House, Lincs. Alterations, dairy, orangery, hen-house, and cottages for first Earl Brownlow, 1809–20. [Drawings at house; Mellon Coll., Drawings; Exhib. RA 1811]

Berkhamstead, Herts., St. Peter's. Restoration, *c.* 1820. [*VCH Herts.* 11 (1908), 174]

Bishop's Wood House, Herefordshire. (D). Attributed. For John Partridge, *c.* 1820. Tudor. [RIBAD]

Bladon Castle, Staffs., For Abraham Hoskins, *c.* 1799. Castellated. [Exhib. RA 1799]

Brancepeth Castle, Durham. Attributed. Alterations for Matthew Russell, *c.* 1817. [APSD]

Bretby Hall, Derby. For fifth Earl of Chesterfield, *c.* 1812. Castellated. [S. Glover, *History of the County of Derby*, ii (1833), 157; Exhib. RA 1812 and 1815]

Bretton Hall, W.R. Yorks. For Col. Thomas Richard Beaumont. Also Camelia House and estate buildings. *c.* 1815. [RIBAD; Neale, v (1822); Exhib. RA 1815]

Brixton, Devon. A cottage, 1799. [Exhib. RA 1799]

Brocklesby Park, Lincs. Unexecuted design for a neo-classical palace for first Earl of Yarborough, 1820. [RIBAD; Mellon Coll.; Exhib. RA 1824]

Browsholme Hall, W.R. Yorks. Drawing-Room for Thomas Lister Parker, 1806. [Drawings at house]

Bulstrode Park, Bucks. Unexecuted design for completing the house for eleventh Duke of Somerset, 1812. [RIBAD]

Burley-on-the-Hill. Rutland. Terrace for ninth Earl of Winchelsea, 1801. [D. Stroud, *Humphrey Repton* (1962), 106; Exhib. RA 1801]

Bushy Park, Middx., Ranger's Lodge. Alterations for Queen Adelaide, *c.* 1837. [Linstrum, 232]

Buxton, Derby. Layout of St. Anne's Cliff for sixth Duke of Devonshire, *c.* 181. [Rylands, Bagshawe MS. 6/1/362, J. Wyatt to Murray, 24 Jan. 1818]

Cadland, Hants. (D). Additions for Andrew Robert Drummond, 1836. [Cadland Estate Office, Drawings]

Cambridge, Sidney Sussex College. Additions, 1821. Gothic. [Drawings at College; Exhib. RA 1822, 1833]

Cassiobury Park, Herts. (D). Continued James Wyatt's alterations for fifth Earl of Essex, after 1813. [RIBAD; J. Britton, *Cassiobury Park* (1837)]

Chatsworth, Derby. Vast additions, lodges, and estate buildings for sixth Duke of Devonshire, 1818–41. [Drawings and Building Accounts at the house; Exhib. RA 1821, 1822, 1829]

Chillingham Castle, Northumb. Alterations for fifth Earl of Tankerville, 1824. [Linstrum, 234]

Claverton Manor, Somerset. For John Vivian, *c.* 1820. [G. Vivian, *Some Illustrations of the Architecture of Claverton and the Duke's House, Bradford* (1837)]

Cobham Hall, Kent. Repaired interior of N. wing and designed Gothic entrance for fifth Earl of Darnley, *c.* 1835. [C. Greenwood, *Epitome of County History: Kent* (1838), 215]

Denford Park, Berks. For William Hallett, *c.* 1815. [APSD]

Dinton Park, Wilts. For William Wyndham, 1812–17. [RIBAD]

Doddington Hall, Ches. Unexecuted design for enlarging stables for Sir John Delves Broughton, 1815. [Chester R.O., Broughton MS. DDB/Q3, Drawing]

Drumlanrig Castle, Dumfries. Alterations for fifth Duke of Buccleuch, 1840. [Coll. Mrs. J.Don. Buccleuch to Wyatville, 18 Jan. 1840]

Eastbury House, Surrey. Additions for Revd. Edward Fulham, before 1832. [E.W.Brayley, *Topographical History of Surrey*, v (1841–8), 225]

Endsleigh Cottage, Devon. For sixth Duke of Bedford, 1810. [Woburn Abbey, Drawings]

Frome, Somerset, St. John's. Forecourt screen for eighth Earl of Cork, 1814 (*D*). [W.J.E.Bennett, *History of St. John, Frome* (1866), 46]

Golden Grove, Carmarthenshire. For first Earl of Cawdor, 1826–34. [Carmarthen R.O., Cawdor MSS., 2/85–88; 2/130; Exhib. RA 1829]

Gopsall Hall, Leics. Alterations and lodge for first Earl Howe, 1819. [RIBAD; Exhib. RA 1819]

Greatham Hospital, Durham. For seventh Earl of Bridgewater, 1803. [J.Dugdale, *British Traveller*, ii (1819), 305]

Hastings, Sussex, 14 Marine Parade. Unidentified work for Comte de Vandes, 1824. [Linstrum, 237]

Hengrave Hall, Suffolk. Alterations for John Gage, *c.* 1824. [Coll. Mrs. J.Don, 'Drawings to be made']

Hillfield Lodge, Herts. For Hon. George Villiers, *c.* 1800–5. [RIBAD; BM, Print Room, 198/C15/2/70; 30/171; 32/177; 40/193; 40/194, Drawings; Exhib. RA 1805]

Hinton House, Somerset. Additions for fourth Earl Poulett, 1814. [Exhib. RA 1814]

Hyde Hall, Herts. Remodelling and lodges for second Earl of Roden, 1803. [BM, Print Room, 109/C15/42/197; 42/198; Mellon Coll., Drawing]

Kelmarsh, Northants. Unexecuted design for rectory for Revd. G.Hanbury, 1815. [Northants R.O., BH (K) 206–209]

Kew, Surrey, St. Anne's. Alterations for William IV, 1837–8. [E.W.Brayley, *Topographical History of Surrey* (1841–8), iii. 153]

Kew Gardens, Surrey. King William's Temple, 1836–7. [*King's Works*, 347–8]

Kew Palace, Surrey. Unexecuted design for new wing, 1834. [RIBAD]

Landsberg, Germany. Consulted about design for castle by Duke of Saxe-Meiningen, 1837. [RIBAD]

Langold Park, W.R. Yorks. Unexecuted design for

new house for Henry Galley Knight, 1814. [RIBAD]

Lexham Hall, Norfolk. (*D*). Additions for Col. T.W.Keppel, n.d. [Linstrum, 240]

Lilleshall Hall, Salop. For second Duke of Sutherland, 1824–9. [Mellon Coll., Drawings; Staffs. R.O., Sutherland MS. N/3/10/12B; Exhib. RA 1829]

Little Gaddesden, Herts., S.S. Peter and Paul. Additions for Executors of eighth Earl of Bridgewater, 1819 and 1830. [Linstrum, 240]

Liverpool, Lancs., St. George's. Advised on state of spire with William Porden, 1809. [J.Picton, *Liverpool Municipal Records*, ii (1886), 398]

London, Bedford Lodge, Campden Hill. Alterations for sixth Duke of Bedford, *c.* 1824. [Woburn Abbey, drawings]

London, 1 Cavendish Square. Alterations for first Earl Brownlow, 1925. [Belton, Drawing]

London, Chesterfield House. (*D*). Alterations for fifth Earl of Chesterfield, 1811–13. [Guildhall Library, MS3070A, Accounts; ex info Mr. H.M.Colvin]

London, 5 Grosvenor Square. (*D*). Alterations and repairs for sixth Duke of Beaufort, 1810. [Badminton, Accounts 1809–17]

London, 7 Grosvenor Square. (*D*). Alterations for seventh Earl of Bridgewater, 1816. [Linstrum, 241]

London, 6 Grosvenor Square. (*D*). Minor alterations for second Marquess of Bath, 1809. [Longleat, Accounts]

London, Holdernesse House, 24 Hertford Street (Later Londonderry House). (*D*). Alterations for second Lord Middleton, 1802. [Linstrum, 241]

London, Holly Grove, Highgate. (*D*). Additions for Mrs. Thomas Coutts, 1826. [Coll. Mrs. J.Don, Drawings]

London, Hyde Park. Unexecuted design for Entrance-Gate, 1794. [Exhib. RA 1794]

London, Kensington Palace. Internal alterations, including conversion of kitchen to chapel, 1833, 1835. [*King's Works*, 347–8]

London, 39 Lower Brook Street. Additions and alterations for himself, 1821–3. [Grosvenor Office, Board Mins. and Site Plans]

London, St. James's Palace. Unexecuted design for extensions, 1831–5. [RIBAD]

London, Scott's Bank, 2 Cavendish Square. Extensions for Sir Claude Scott, 1825. [Westminster Bank, Drawing]

Longleat, Wilts. Alterations, stables, conservatory, and estate buildings for second Marquess of Bath, 1800. [Drawings and Accounts at the house; Exhib. RA 1801, 1811, 1815]

Lypiatt Park, Glos. Additions and alterations for Paul Wathen (later Sir Paul Bagot), 1809. [RIBAD; Mellon Coll., Drawing; Exhib. RA 1809]

Marbury, Ches., St. Michael's. (*A*). Rebuilt chancel for seventh Earl of Bridgewater, 1822. [Linstrum, 245]

Marston House, Somerset. For eighth Earl of Cork and Orrery, *c.* 1817. [*Proceedings of Somerset Arch. Soc.* (1974), 118]

Meiningen, Germany. Design for villa for Duke of Saxe-Meiningen, 1835. [RIBAD]

Milton Abbot, Devon. School and Schoolhouse for sixth Duke of Bedford, *c.* 1810. [Woburn Abbey, Drawings]

Nonsuch Park, Surrey. (*A*). For Samuel Farmer, 1802. [RIBAD; Exhib. RA 1802. 1803]

Oakley Park, Suffolk. Unexecuted design for Sir Edward Kerrison. [RIBAD]

Orchardleigh Park, Somerset. Unexecuted design for Sir Thomas Champneys, n.d. [RIBAD]

Quebec, Canada. Unexecuted design for a House of Assembly, 1812. [Exhib. RA 1834]

Raglan Castle, Monmouthshire. Unexecuted design for restoration for sixth Duke of Beaufort, 1820. [H. Durant, *The Somerset Sequence* (1951), 175]

Renishaw Hall, Derby. Unidentified work for Sir George Sitwell, *c.* 1824. [Coll. Mrs. J. Don, 'Drawings to be made']

Roche Court, Hants. Lodge for Sir J. S. W. Gardiner, 1810. [Exhib. RA 1808]

Rood Ashton House, Wilts. (*A*). For Richard Godolphin Long, 1808. [*VCH Wilts.* viii (1965), 203]

Sans Souci, Dorset. Greenhouse for Sir Claude Scott, *c.* 1822 (*D*). [J. Hutchins, *History and Antiquities of the County of Dorset*, iii (1868), 360; Exhib. RA 1822]

Shobdon Court, Herefordshire. (*D*). Alterations for first Lord Bateman, 1835. [Coll. Mrs. J. Don; E. Haycock to Wyatville, 21 Oct. 1835]

Slane, Ireland. Market House, 1800. [Exhib. RA 1800]

Somerhill, Kent. (*A*). Alterations for James Alexander, *c.* 1824. [J. Britton, *Descriptive Sketches of Tunbridge Wells* (1832), 121]

Stackpole Court, Pembrokeshire. (*D*). Remodelled and a bridge built for first Earl of Cawdor, *c.* 1832. [Neale, v. (1822); S. Lewis, *Topographical Dictionary of Wales*, ii (1849), 373]

Stockton House, Wilts. Attributed. Staircase, *c.* 1800. [Traditionally attributed to 'Wyatt', the lantern has Jacobean decoration similar to that at Longleat]

Stubton Hall, Lincs. (*A*). For Sir Robert Heron, M.P. [Exhib. RA 1816]

Tatton Park, Ches. Unexecuted design for completing the house for Wilbraham Egerton, 1807. [Drawings at Tatton]

Teddesley Hall, Staffs. (*D*). Alterations for Hon. George Lyttelton [Linstrum, 249]

Thurland Castle, Lancs. (*A*). Restoration and additions for Richard North, *c.* 1809. [Exhib. RA 1809]

Tissington Hall, Derby. Unexecuted design for additions for Sir Henry Fitzherbert, *c.* 1820. [Drawings at the house; RIBAD]

Tottenham Park, Wilts. Unexecuted design for first Marquess of Ailesbury, 1821. [Coll. Marquess of Ailesbury, Drawings]

Townley Hall, Lancs. Alterations for Peregrine Townley, 1821. [Drawings at the house]

Trebartha Hall, Cornwall. (*D*). Alterations for Francis Hearle Rodd, 1815. [RIBAD]

Trebursey House, Cornwall. For second Earl of St. Germans, *c.* 1820. [Linstrum, 250]

Whiteley Wood Hall, W.R. Yorks. (*D*). Additions for William Silcock, *c.* 1822. [Exhib. RA 1822]

Wilton House, Wilts. Consulted about completion and alterations to Bulbridge House by eleventh Earl of Pembroke, 1826. [Drawings at Wilton]

Wimborne Minster, Dorset, Allendale House. For William Castleman, *c.* 1815. [APSD]

Windsor, Berks., St. John's. Supervised rebuilding by Charles Hollis, 1820. [Linstrum, 252]

Windsor Castle, Berks. Restoration for George IV and William IV, 1824–40. Royal Mews for Queen Victoria, 1839. [Drawings at Windsor; H. Ashton,

Illustrations of Windsor Castle (1841); *King's Works*, 373–94]

Windsor Great Park. Adelaide Lodge, alterations for William IV, 1830; Gardener's Cottage [BM, Print Room, Drawing]; Lodges [Mellon Coll., Drawings]; Cumberland Lodge, addition to stables, 1828; Fishing Pavilion for George IV, 1825 [New York, Cooper-Hewitt Museum, Drawing by Crace]; Fort Belvedere, alterations for George IV, 1827 [*King's Works*, 397]; Royal Lodge, additions for George IV, 1823–30 [*King's Works*, 391–401]; Snow Hill – plinth for statue of George III for George IV, 1829; Virginia Water, rebuilt bridge and erected ruins from Lepcis Magna to form the Temple of Augustus, 1826–9 [*King's Works*, 396–7]

Woburn Abbey, Beds. Alterations to Sculpture Gallery and estate Buildings for sixth Duke of Bedford, 1816, 1836–8. [Drawings at Woburn; Exhib. RA 1818]

Wollaton Hall, Notts. Alterations for sixth Lord Middleton, 1801–23. [Mellon Coll., Drawings; Univ. of Nottingham, Middleton MS. MIP3, Drawings; Exhib. RA 1802, 1824]

Woolley Park, Berks. Alterations for Revd. Philip Wroughton, *c*. 1799. [G. Richardson, *New Vitruvius Britannicus*, ii (1808), Pls. 36–8; Exhib. RA 1799]

Woolley Park, W.R. Yorks. Lodge and design for additions for George Wentworth, 1820. [Univ. of Leeds, Wentworth–Woolley MSS., Drawings]

Wynnstay, Denbighshire. Memorial tower at Nant-y-Belan, 1806. [BM, Print Room, Drawing signed and dated 1806]

Yester House, East Lothian. Keeper's Lodge for eighth Marquess of Tweedale, 1824. [Exhib. RA 1824]

SELECT BIBLIOGRAPHY

Only a selection of the more general sources is given here. MS. Sources and many more individual printed sources can be found in the footnotes and the catalogues.

Ackerman, R., *Microcosm of London* (1808).

Alexander, B., *Life at Fonthill* (1957).

Anon., *John Wyatt, Carpenter and Inventor* (1885).

Ashton, H. (ed.), *Illustrations of Windsor Castle by the late Sir Jeffry Wyatville RA* (1841).

Aspinall, J. (ed.), *Later Correspondence of George III* (Cambridge, 1967).

Bamford, J. and Duke of Wellington (ed.), *Journal of Mrs. Arbuthnot* (1950).

Beaver, P., *The Crystal Palace* (1970).

Blanc, A.A.P.C., *The History of the Painters of all Nations*, ed. M.D.Wyatt (1852).

Bolton, A.J., *The Architecture of R. and J. Adam* (1922).

Britton, J., *Graphic and Literary Illustrations of Fonthill* (1823).

—*Memoir of Sir Jeffry Wyatville* (1834).

—*Cassiobury Park Hertfordshire* (1837).

— and E.W.Brayley, *The Beauties of England and Wales* (1801–15).

Broadbank, G., *History of the Port of London* (1921).

Clark, K., *The Gothic Revival* (1950).

Clifford, T. and I.Hall, *Heaton Hall Bicentenary Exhibition Catalogue* (Manchester, 1972).

Colvin, H.M., *Biographical Dictionary of English Architects 1660–1840* (1954).

Croft Murray, E., *Decorative Painting in England* (1962 and 1970).

Crook, J.M. (ed.), *Eastlake's Gothic Revival* (1970).

Dale, A., *James Wyatt, Architect 1748–1813* (1956).

Devonshire, sixth Duke of, *Handbook of Chatsworth and Hardwick* (privately printed 1845).

Dickinson, H.W., 'Origin and Manufacture of Wood Screws', *Newcomen Society*, xxii (1946).

Doherty, H., *Divorce Report between H.Doherty and P.W.Wyatt* (1811).

Eastlake, Lady (ed.), *The Life of John Gibson RA* (1870).

Eller, I., *History of Belvoir Castle* (1841).

Elmes, J., *Metropolitan Improvements* (1831).

Farington, J., Diary (MS. in Royal Library, Windsor, typescripts in the Ashmolean Museum, Oxford and the British Museum).

Fergusson, F., 'James Wyatt' (Univ. of Harvard Ph.D. thesis 1972).

Fleming, J., *Robert Adam and His Circle in Edinburgh and Rome* (1962).

Girouard, M., *The Victorian Country House* (Oxford, 1971).

Goodhart-Rendel, H.S., *English Architecture since the Regency* (1933).

—Card Index of Victorian Churches at the *NMR*.

Goodison, N., *Ormolu: the Work of Matthew Boulton* (1974).

Gore, J. (ed.), *The Creevey Papers* (1948).

Graves, A., *Royal Academy Exhibitors* (1905).

—*The British Institution* (1908).

Greville, C., *The Greville Memoirs* (1888).

Gunnis, R., *Dictionary of British Sculptors 1660–1851* (1951).

Hague, D. and R.Christie, *Lighthouses* (Llandysul, 1975).

Hare, A., *Walks in Rome* (1923).

Harris, J., *Catalogue of British Drawings in American Collections* (1971).

—*Sir William Chambers* (1970).

Hawks Le Grice, Count, *Walks through the Studios of the sculptors in Rome* (1841).

Higgins, B., *Calcareous Cement* (1780).

Hobhouse, H., *Thomas Cubbit* (1971).

Holmes, Sir C., 'The Heirs of Laurence 1825–35', *Burlington Magazine*, lxix (Nov. 1936).

Hope, W.St.J., *Windsor Castle, an Architectural History* (1913).

Hunt, T.F., *Archittetura campestra* (1827).

Hussey, C., *The Picturesque* (1927).

—*English Country Houses: Mid Georgian* (1955).

—*English Country Houses: Late Georgian* (1958).

Huxley, A. (ed.), *Autobiography of B.R.Haydon* (1926).

Kaufmann, E., *Architecture in the Age of Reason* (New York, 1955).

Linstrum, D., *Sir Jeffry Wyatville* (Oxford 1972).

—*Catalogue of the Drawings Collection of the R.I.B.A.: The Wyatt Family* (1973).

Martin, R.A., 'Life and Work of R.J.Wyatt' (Univ. Of Leeds M.A. thesis 1972).

Matthews, J., *John Gibson* (1911).

Murphy, J.C., *Plans, Elevations, Sections and Views of the Church of Batalha* (1795).

Murray, Lady Anne, *Journal of a Tour in Italy* (privately printed 1838).

Nash, J., *Windsor Castle* (1848).

Neale, J.P., *Views of Seats* (1819–26).

Nicolson, P., *Architectural Dictionary* (1819).

Nilsson, S., *European Architecture in India* (1968).

Papworth, W.A.V.S. (ed.), *Architectural Publication Society Dictionary* (1852–92).

Pevsner, Sir N., *Matthew Digby Wyatt* (Cambridge, 1950).

—*The Buildings of England* (1951–   ).

Picton, J.A., *Architectural History of Liverpool* (1858).

Pitt, W., *Topographical History of Staffordshire* (1817).

Pückler-Muskau, Prince, *Tour in England, Ireland and France in the Years 1828 and 1829* (1832).

Pyne, W.H., *History of the Royal Residences* (1819).

Quennell, P. (ed.), *The Private Letters of Princess Lieven to Prince Metternich* (1937).

Raynes, H.E., *A History of British Insurance* (1964).

Redgrave, S., *Dictionary of Artists* (1874).

Rennie, Sir J., *British and Foreign Harbours* (1854).

Richardson, G., *New Vitruvius Britannicus* (1802, 1808).

Robinson, John Martin, *Samuel Wyatt* (Univ. of Oxford D.Phil. Thesis 1973)

Roll, E., *An Early Experiment in Industrial Organisation* (1930).

Russell Hitchcock, H., *Early Victorian Architecture in Britain* (1954).

Rutter, J., *Delineations of Fonthill and its Abbey* (1823).

Shaw, S., *History of Staffordshire* (1801).

Skempton, A.W., 'Samuel Wyatt and the Albion Mill.', *Architectural History* (1971).

—'Early Members of the Smeatonian Society', *Newcomen Society*, xliv (1971–2).

Smiles, S., *Lives of the Engineers* (1862).

Steegman, J., *Victorian Taste* (1970).

Stevenson, D.A., *The World's Lighthouses before 1820* (1959).

Stroud, D., *The Architecture of Sir John Soane* (1961).

—*Humphrey Repton* (1962).

—*Henry Holland* (1966).

—*George Dance* (1971).

Summerson, J., *John Nash* (1935).

—*Architecture in Britain 1530–1850* (1953).

—'The Classical Country House', *Journal of the Royal Society of Arts* (1959).

Thompson, F., *A History of Chatsworth* (1949).

Thompson, F.M.L., *English Landed Society in the Nineteenth Century* (1969).

Trench, F.W., *Collection of Papers Relating to the Thames Quay* (1827).

Uggeri, A., *Ornamenti Greci Antichi ed Inediti* (Rome, 1820; dedicated to Lewis Wyatt).

Waagen, G.F., *Treasures of Art in Great Britain* (1854).

Watkin, D., *Thomas Hope and the Neo-Classical Ideal* (1968).

—*C.R.Cockerell* (1975).

Weale, J., *New Survey of London* (1853).

Whinney, M., *Sculpture in Britain 1530–1830* (1964).

Wilson, E., *The Middlesex Hospital* (1845).

Woodcroft, B., *Index of Patentees* (1854; **2nd Edn. 1969).**

Wyatt, B.D., *Design for the Theatre Royal, Drury Lane* (1813).

Wyatt, G., *Description for a Theatre* (1812).

—('Sussexiensis'), *Reasons of a Subscriber for opposing Mr. Wyatt's plan for a Monumental Trophy to the Late King George III* (1822).

Wyatt., H., *Address on Protection to Agriculture* (1827).

—*Free Trade in Corn* (1834).

Wyatt, J. (ed.), *Repertory of Arts and Manufactures* (1st Ser. 1794–1802; 2nd Ser. 1802–25).

Wyatt, L., *A Collection of Architectural Designs Rural and Ornamental* (1800).

— *Improvements in the Metropolis* (1816).

Wyatt, M.C., *Model to the Memory of Lord Nelson* (1808).

Wyatt, M.D., 'On the Art of the Mosaic, Ancient & Modern', *Trans. Soc. of Arts* (1847).

—'Mosaics as Applied to Architectural Decoration', *Sess. Papers, RIBA* (1847).

—*Specimens of Geometrical Mosaic of the Middle Ages* (1848).

—*A Report on the Eleventh French Exposition of the Products of Industry* (1849).

—*Further Report made to H.R.H. Prince Albert ... of Preliminary Enquiries into the Willingness of Manufacturers and Others to Support Periodical Exhibitions of the Works of Industry of all Nations* (1849).

—Observations on Polychromatic Decoration in

Italy (MS., RIBA, 1850).

—'The Exhibition under its Commercial Aspects', *Journal of Design and Manufactures*, V (1851).

—'On the Construction of the Building for the Exhibition . . . in 1851', *Proc. Inst. Civ. Engineers*, x (1851) (also in the Official Catalogue of the Exhibition, London, 1851).

—*The Industrial Arts of the Nineteenth Century* (1851–3).

—'An Attempt to Define the Principles which should determine Form in the Decorative Arts', *Lectures on the Results of the Great Exhibition* (1852).

—*Speciments of Ornamental Art Workmanship in Gold, Silver, Iron Brass and Bronze* (1852).

—*Metalwork and its Artistic Design* (1852).

—'Remarks on G. Abbati's Paper on Pompeian Decorations, *Sess. Papers, RIBA* (1853).

—*The Byzantine and Romanesque Courts in the Crystal Palace* (with J.B. Waring) (1854).

—*The Italian Court in the Crystal Palace* (with J.B. Waring) (1854).

—*The Medieval Court in the Crystal Palace* (with J.B. Waring) (1854).

—*The Renaissance Court in the Crystal Palace* (with J.B. Waring) (1854).

—*Views of the Crystal Palace* (1st ser. 1854).

—*An Address delivered in the Crystal Palace at the opening of an Exhibition of Works of Art belonging to the Arundel Society* (1855).

—'Mosaics . . . of Sta Sophia at Constantinope', *Sess. Paper, RIBA* (1865).

—'Observations on Renaissance and Italian Ornameht', in O. Jones, *The Grammar of Ornament* (1856).

—*Paris Universal Exhibition: Report on Furniture and Decorations* (1856).

—*Notices of Sculpture in Ivory* (Arundel Society, 1856).

—'Notices of the late John Britton', *Sess. Papers, RIBA* (1857).

—'The Sacred Grotto of St. Benedict at Subiaco', *Sess. Papers, RIBA* (1857).

—*Specimens of Geometrical Mosaics manufactured by Maw and Co.* (1857)

—'On the Principles of Design applicable to Textile Art', in J.B. Waring, *The Art Treasures of the United Kingdom* (1857–8).

—'Observations on Metallic Art', in J.B. Waring,

The Art Treasures of the United Kingdom (1857–8).

—*Influence Exercised on Ceramic Manufactures by the late Herbert Minton* (1858).

—'Early Habitations of the Irish, and especially the Cramoges or Lake Castles', *Sess. Papers, RIBA* (1858).

—'On the Architectural Career of Sir Charles Barry', *Sess. Papers RIBA* (1859–60).

—*Illuminated Manuscripts as Illustrative of the Arts of Design* (1860).

—*The Art of Illuminating* (with W.R. Tymms) (1860).

—*What Illuminating Was* (1861).

—'On the Present Aspects of the Fine and Decorative Arts in Italy', *Journal Soc. of Arts* (1862).

—'The Loan Collection at South Kensington', *Fine Arts Quart. Rev.*, i and ii (1863).

—'On Pictorial Mosaic as an Architectural Embellishment', *Sess. Papers, RIBA* (1866).

—*A Report to Accompany the Designs for a National Gallery* (1866).

—'The Relations which should exist between Architecture and the Industrial Arts', *Architectural Association* (c. 1867).

—'On the Foreign Artists employed in England during the Sixteenth Century', *Sess. Papers, RIBA* (1868).

—*The History of the Manufacture of Clocks* (1868).

—*Report on the Art of Decoration at the International Exhibition* (Paris, 1867; London, 1868).

—*Introduction and Notes on Examples of Decorative Design, Selected from Drawings of Italian Masters in the Uffizi at Florence* (1869).

—*Fine Art; its History, Theory, Practice* (Slade Lectures at Cambridge) (London and New York, 1870).

—*Report on Miscellaneous Paintings, London International Exhibition, 1871* (1871).

—*An Architect's Notebook in Spain* (1872).

—*On the Most Characteristic Features of the Building of the Vienna Exhibition of 1873* (1874).

—*The Utrecht Psalter; Reports on the Age of the Manuscript* (by Sir M.D. Wyatt and others) (1874).

Wyatt, W. H., *Compendium of the Law of Patents for Inventions* (1826).

Wyatt, Parker & Co., *Artificial Stone Catalogue* (1841–2).

INDEX